Radzyn Memorial Book (Poland)

Translation of *Sefer Radzyn*

Edited by: Yitzchak Zigelman

Originally Published by

**The Radzyn (Podlaski) Immigrants Association in Israel,
Tel Aviv, 1957**

Translators: Nachman Goldwasser, Temy Goldwasser and Yaakov Goldwasser

Published by JewishGen

An Affiliate of the Museum of Jewish Heritage - A Living Memorial to the Holocaust
New York

Radzyn Memorial Book (Poland)
Translation of *Sefer Radzyn*

Copyright © 2016 by JewishGen, Inc.
All rights reserved.
First Printing: September 2016, Elul 5776
Second Printing: March 2019, Adar II 5779

Editors:
Translation Project Coordinator: Yaakov Goldwasser (Gesher Haziv, Israel)
Translators: Nachman Goldwasser, Temmy Goldwasser and Yaakov Goldwasser
(Gesher Haziv, Israel)
Layout: David Kaplan (Miami, FL)
Image Editor: Martha Forsyth (Newton MA)
Cover Design: Nina Schwartz (Alexandria, VA)

Published by JewishGen, Inc.
An Affiliate of the Museum of Jewish Heritage
A Living Memorial to the Holocaust
36 Battery Place, New York, NY 10280

"JewishGen, Inc. is not responsible for inaccuracies or omissions in the
original work and makes no representations regarding the accuracy of this
translation. Digital images of the original book's contents can be seen
online at the New York Public Library Web site."

The mission of the JewishGen organization is to produce a translation of
the original work and we cannot verify the accuracy of statements or alter
facts cited.

Printed in the United States of America by Lightning Source, Inc.

Library of Congress Control Number (LCCN): 2016934387
ISBN: 978-1-939561-43-5 (hard cover: 358 pages, alk. paper)

Front cover image of the old wooden synagogue of Radzyn is based upon a
photograph courtesy of Yad Vashem.

JewishGen and the Yizkor-Books-in-Print Project

This book has been published by the **Yizkor-Books-in-Print Project,** as part of the **Yizkor Book Project** of **JewishGen, Inc**.

JewishGen, Inc. is a non-profit organization founded in 1987 as a resource for Jewish genealogy. Its website [www.jewishgen.org] serves as an international clearinghouse and resource center to assist individuals who are researching the history of their Jewish families and the places where they lived. JewishGen provides databases, facilitates discussion groups, and coordinates projects relating to Jewish genealogy and the history of the Jewish people. In 2003, JewishGen became an affiliate of the **Museum of Jewish Heritage - A Living Memorial to the Holocaust** in New York.

The **JewishGen Yizkor Book Project** was organized to make more widely known the existence of Yizkor (Memorial) Books written by survivors and former residents of various Jewish communities throughout the world. Later, volunteers connected to the different destroyed communities began cooperating to have these books translated from the original language— usually Hebrew or Yiddish—into English, thus enabling a wider audience to have access to the valuable information contained within them. As each chapter of these books was translated, it was posted on the JewishGen website and made available to the general public.

The **Yizkor-Books-in-Print Project** began in 2011 as an initiative to print and publish Yizkor Books that had been fully translated, so that hard copies would be available for purchase by the descendants of these communities and also by scholars, universities, synagogues, libraries, and museums.

These Yizkor books have been produced almost entirely through the volunteer effort of researchers from around the world, assisted by donations from private individuals. The books are printed and sold at near cost, so as to make them as affordable as possible. Our goal is to make this important genre of Jewish literature and history available in English in book form, so that people can have the personal histories of their ancestral towns on their bookshelves for themselves and for their children and grandchildren.

A list of all published translated Yizkor Books in the project with prices and ordering information can be found at:
http://www.jewishgen.org/Yizkor/ybip.html

Lance Ackerfeld, Yizkor Book Project Manager

Joel Alpert, Yizkor-Book-in-Print Project Coordinator

JewishGen
Yizkor Book Project

This book is presented by the
Yizkor Books in Print Project
Project Coordinator: Joel Alpert

Part of the
Yizkor Books Project of JewishGen, Inc.
Project Manager: Lance Ackerfeld

These books have been produced solely through volunteer effort
of individuals from around the world. The books are printed and
sold at near cost, so as to make them as affordable as possible.

Our goal is to make this history and important genre of Jewish
literature available in English in book form so that people can have
the near-personal histories of their ancestral towns on their bookshelves for themselves and for their children and grandchildren.

Any donations to the Yizkor Books Project are appreciated.

Please send donations to:
Yizkor Book Project
JewishGen
36 Battery Place
New York, NY 10280

JewishGen, Inc. is an affiliate of the
Museum of Jewish Heritage
A Living Memorial to the Holocaust

Title Page of Original Yizkor Book

ספר רדזין
יזכור-בוך

כינס וערך

יצחק זינגלמן

המערכת: י. אבי-ערה, ב. בורשטין, מ. גוטמדינר, ל. וינדרבוים,
י. לוסט, א. לור, א. דזילק (מורוגסט), מ. ליכטנשטיין (ניו-יורק)

Translation of the Title Page of Original Yiddish Book

Radzyn Book
Memorial Book

Editor:

Yitzchak Zigelman

Editorial Board: Y. Avi-Ara, B. Borshtein, M. Gotesdiener, L. Vinderboim, Y. Lust, A. Lazar, A. Danilak (Toronto), M. Lichtenshtein

Dedications and Acknowledgements

In appreciation to Henry H. Goldberg, Carol Brown Goldberg and Rita Segerman, for their contributions to the translation and publication of this book. It is dedicated in loving memory to Mr. Goldberg and Ms. Segerman's parents, Frances and Hyman Goldberg (Radzyn resident).

This book is also dedicated in loving memory to Mendel and Celia Goldwasser.

Special thanks to the National Yiddish Book Center in Amherst, Massachusetts and the New York Public Library for supplying the high resolution images used in this book.

Our sincere appreciation to the late Pesach Tunkelshwartz from Tel Aviv, the last President of The Radzyn Podlaski Immigrants Association in Israel, for his invaluable help and permission for the online translation of the Yizkor Book and his efforts regarding the commemoration of the town.

Thanks also to Yaakov Goldwasser who was of great assistance in the production of this book.

Geopolitical Information:

Radzyń Podlaski, Poland: 51°47' N, 22°37' E

Region: Siedlce

Alternate names for the town are: Radzyń Podlaski [Polish], Rodzin [Yiddish], Radzyn' [Russian], Radzyń, Radzin, Kozirynek

	Town	District	Province	Country
Before WWI (c. 1900):	Radzyń	Radzyń	Siedlce	Russian Empire
Between the wars (c. 1930):	Radzyń	Radzyń	Lublin	Poland
After WWII (c. 1950):	Radzyń Podlaski			Poland
Today (c. 2000):	Radzyń Podlaski			Poland

Nearby Jewish Communities:
Czemierniki 7 miles S
Stok 7 miles WNW
Wohyn 7 miles ESE
Kock 13 miles SW
Serokomla 13 miles WSW
Lukow 14 miles NW
Adamow 15 miles WSW
Międzyrzec Podlaski 16 miles NNE
Parczew 16 miles SE
Firlej 17 miles SSW
Jeziorzany 20 miles SW
Lubartow 22 miles S
Ostrow Lubelski 22 miles SSE
Zbuczyn 22 miles NNW
Rossosz 23 miles ENE
Kamionka 23 miles SSW
Michow 23 miles SW
Lomazy 25 miles ENE
Baranow 25 miles SW
Wisznice 26 miles E
Sosnowica 27 miles SE
Biala Podlaska 28 miles NE

Siedlce 30 miles NNW

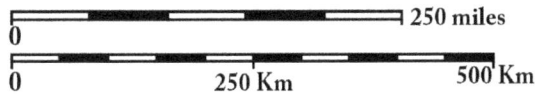

BALTIC SEA   LITHUANIA

RUSSIA   Vilnius ●

POLAND   BELARUS

GERMANY

● Poznan   Warsaw ●   **Radzyn**

● Lodz   ●

● Prague

CZECH REPUBLIC   ● Krakow   UKRAINE

SLOVAKIA

|———————————————| 250 miles
0

|———————————————| Km
0   250 Km   500 Km

POLAND - **Current Borders**

Map of Poland with Radzyn

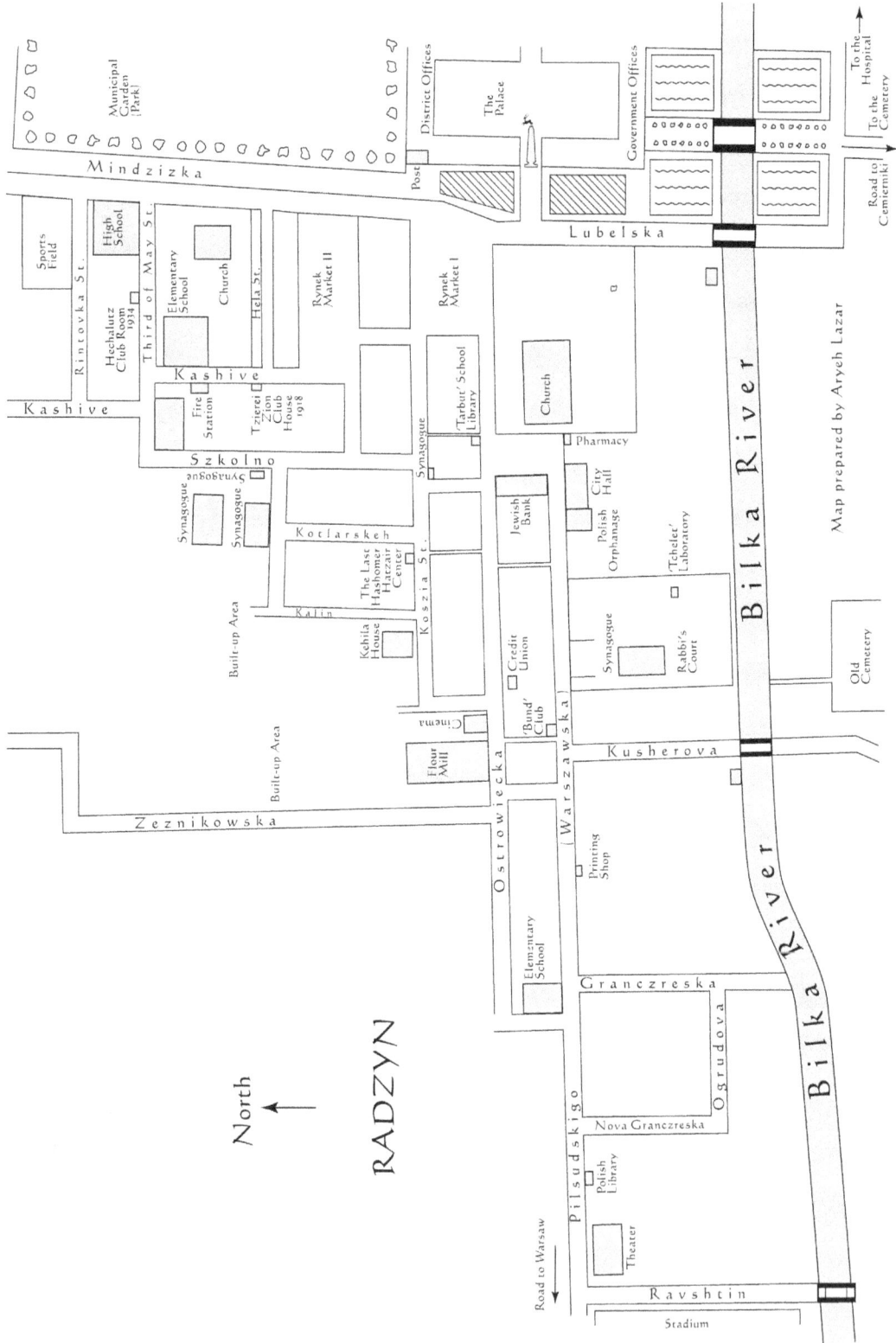

RADZYN

North ←

Map prepared by Aryeh Lazar

Municipal Garden [Park]

Mindzizka

District Offices

The Palace

Post

Government Offices

To the Hospital
To the Cemetery
Road to Cemierniki

Sports Field

High School

Rintovka St.

Third of May St.

Hechalutz Club Room 1934

Elementary School

Church

Hela St.

Rynek Market II

Rynek Market I

Lubelska

Kashive

Kashive

Fire Station

Tzjerei Zion Club House 1918

Szkolno

Synagogue

Tarbut' School Library

Church

Pharmacy

Synagogue

Synagogue

Kotlarskeh

The Last Hashomer Hatzair Center

Koszia St.

Jewish Bank

City Hall

Polish Orphanage

'Tchelet' Laboratory

Bilka River

Built-up Area

Kalin

Kehila House

Credit Union

Synagogue

Rabbi's Court

Old Cemetery

Built-up Area

Cinema

'Bund' Club

Warszawska

Kusherova

Flour Mill

Ostrowiecka

Zeznikowska

Printing Shop

Elementary School

Granczreska

Ogrudova

Bilka River

Pilsudskigo

Nova Granczreska

Road to Warsaw

Polish Library

Theater

Ravshtin

Stadium

Places marked on the map.

Stadium. Built in the years just before the war. Its sports fields and modern swimming pool were for the use of the whole population.

Palace. A very old magnificent building with many statues and ornaments. At one time it was the residence of the local rulers and in later years housed the municipal and district offices.

"Bund". One of the first Jewish political parties in the town, active in many areas of public life. Maintained a club room, library and sports club and for a short time, a school.

Jewish Bank. Founded in 1906. After years of growth, moved into its own building and stayed there until the outbreak of W.W.II.

"Tarbut" (Culture) School. Founded in 1916 under the name "David Fishel's School". For a long time it maintained only a few elementary school classes with a very comprehensive educational curriculum. Many of the finest youth studied there. In 1933 it was incorporated into the "Tarbut" network with seven different classes.

Elementary School. A government school that provided free education for all the children of the town.

Synagogues. Were scattered throughout the town and filled with Jews praying and studying the Torah, the most outstanding of them was the "Great Synagogue".

Gmilat Chesed. (Free Loan Association) Founded in 1912. Helped the needy.

Gymnasia. The Municipal High School that had very few Jewish students because of high tuition and because Saturday classes were mandatory.

Hashomer Hatzair. (The Young Guards) Founded in 1915. Included most of the Zionist youth in the town. In 1935 the first members emigrated to Eretz Yisrael. The majority of the Radzyn immigrants to Israel were from among the members. When the war broke out many of its young members joined the Anti-Nazi Underground.

Hechalutz. Educated toward preparation for and immigration to Palestine. Its' members were scattered on training farms throughout Poland.

The Rabbi's Courtyard. It began with the arrival in Radzyn of "Beth Yaakov" (The House of Jacob) and the discovery of the snail used in manufacturing of the "tchelet" (the blue color used to color the fringes of their prayer shawls) by his son Reb Gershon Chanoch. During the World War II, the last Radzyn Rabbi Reb Shlomoh, who had called for resistance to the Germans and the "Yudenrat", was killed by the Nazis on the eve of Shavuoth 1942.

Library. Founded in 1923 and served all Radzyn readers. When the Communists took over, the local authorities closed it down and its books confiscated and dispersed.

Tziere Tzion Poele Tzion (Young Zionists, Labor Zionists) Among the first Zionist groups in the town. Founded in 1918. Maintained clubhouses and carried on organizational political activities.

A Short History of the Jewish Community of Radyzn

(Radzyn County, Lublin District)

Year	Total Population	Jews
1827	1,966	875
1857	2,472	1,301
1897	5,332	2,853
1921	4,833	2,895

At the beginning of the15th Century, Radzyn was a village owned by the family of the nobleman Pototzki. It was then called Cozi-Rinc. In 1468 it was recognized as a city, and the name was changed to Radzyn. In the 17th Century, it was one of the centers for Protestantism in Poland. In the middle of that century, it was seriously damaged in the Swedish invasion of Poland.

At the beginning of the 18th Century Radzyn was rehabilitated from the damage caused by the Swedes. Its economy and demography were revived, to a great extent by the market days and fairs held there that attracted visitors from the whole region. In the last partition of Poland in 1795, Radzyn became part of Austria, and in 1815 it was included in the Monarchy of Poland that arose under the auspices of Russia.

In the course of the 19th Century, light industries were established in Radzyn, including flourmills, tanneries and breweries.

A few Jewish merchants are mentioned for the first time in the 16th Century. The Jewish community grew slowly during the 17th and 18th, despite both the Swedish War and the invasion by the Cossacks. In records from that time, a few Jews are mentioned as lessees of distilleries. Most of the others were craftsmen. During the Austrian rule and afterwards, during the government of 'Congress Poland', the number of Jews in Radzyn grew steadily, despite the limitations on their residence in the border areas imposed by the Russian authorities in1823-1862. In 1857 they comprised more than half the population remaining at that level until the end of the First World War.

In the middle of the 19th Century, the Jews constituted an important factor in the economy of the city that had developed as a center of trade and crafts for the agricultural periphery. Most of them engaged in petty trade (storekeepers, market stall owners and peddlers) while some were craftsmen (tailors, shoe makers, butchers, etc.) others made their livelihood from collecting customs fees and inn keeping. In Radzyn, as well as in many other places, the market days and the annual fairs were one of the main sources of income for the Jews. Toward the end of the 19th Century, when development of small industry and manufacturing took place in Radzyn, the local Jews founded two metal goods factories, a sawmill and a flourmill.

In the 17th Century, there already was an organized Jewish community in Radzyn which had a leading position among the Jewish communities of the district. It had representatives on the 'Council of the Four Lands' mentioned in the records of the discussions in that council. In 1752 Jews from some of the surrounding villages were incorporated into the Radzyn Jewish Community.

In the 19th Century, Radzyn became famous among the Jews of Poland as a center of Torah learning thanks to Reb Yaakov Leiner the author of 'Beth Yaakov' (The House Of Jacob). He had inherited the leadership of the Izbitzeh Chassidic Dynasty from its founder his father Reb Mordecai Yosef Leiner (d.1854). Reb Yaakov settled in Radzyn in 1867. His son, Gershon Henich Leiner, who replaced his father in 1878 wrote the tractate to the Seder 'Kdoshim' (a division of the Mishnah). He had it set up in print in the format of the traditional tractates of the six books of the Mishnah, thereby calling down on him the wrath of a number of rabbis. He is most famous for having renewed the use of the tchelet (blue dye), for the tzitziot (ritual fringes), which he extracted from the blood of a snail that he found on the shores of the Mediterranean in Italy. Only his Chasidim (followers) and those of Breslav adopted his method. He was also the Town Rabbi. After his death (1891) his son Reb Mordecai Yosef Eliezer Leiner, the author of 'Tiferet Yaakov' (The Glory of Jacob), succeeded him. During the First World War he moved to Warsaw. However his son, Reb Shmuel Shlomo, returned to Radzyn and founded a yeshiva called 'Sod Hayesharim' (The Secret of the Righteous) after the title of one of his father's books. He was the only Chassidic Rabbi who urged his followers to flee into the forests and not to cooperate with the Germans. He perished in the Holocaust.

The existence of a large chassidic center in Radzyn served as an important stimulus for the local economy and for the growth of the Jewish population. The Chassidim who crowded into the Rabbi's court needed lodging and places to eat. The shops and workshops, too, enjoyed a brisk trade. Not only the economy was influenced by the presence of the Chassidim. It affected the character of the Jewish community itself, which maintained its extreme religious orientation. Secular Jewish life developed much later. It was not until the eve of World War I, that a group of Jewish workers formed a credit union that could be seen as a precursor of 'Bundist' (Bund=Jewish Workers Socialist Party) activity. Only then did the core of the Zionist Idea, especially in its 'Mizrachi' (Religious Zionist) interpretation first penetrate to some of the students of the 'Beth Midrash' (study hall) of the Rabbi's followers.

Changes in the political and public life of the Jews of Radzyn came about during World War I. Despite the destruction and hardships, the conquering German authorities removed the strict restrictions on political, labor and similar activities that had been imposed during the Russian regime. 'Mizrachi' and 'Young Mizrachi ' branches were established in Radzyn. In 1917 a branch of the 'Tzeire Zion' (Young Zionists) was established which later formed the basis for the 'Poele Zion ZS' (Zionist Workers) faction. The Zionists established a library that also served as a meeting place for a dramatic group.

The Jews between the two World Wars

In the 20's and 30's the Jewish population of Radzyn remained unchanged. The local Jews continued with their traditional forms of occupational activities but their economic situation became gradually worse. This was due to both the economic crises that struck Poland at that time and the boycott of Jewish crafts, trade and services that the anti-Semites imposed in the late 30's. In addition to all this, a great fire broke out in June of 1929 that consumed many of the Jewish houses and left their tenants homeless.

In an attempt to cope with the situation, the Jews of Radzyn established a number of organizations and institutions of their own. In 1928 they founded the Jewish Merchants Association. At about the same time a Jewish Cooperative bank was established that provided commercial credit, at low interest rates, to Jewish merchants and tradesmen.

The 'Gemilat Chesed' (Free Loan Fund) that had been established during the war increased its capital and credit and in 1928 it had some three hundred members. It granted interest free loans to small businessmen and to the needy. The 'Kehillah' (Official Jewish Community Organization) also helped the most needy from its treasury. The 'Linat Tzedek' (Care for the Sick Association) added to its traditional activities the financing of medical care for the needy.

In the period between the two World Wars a Zionist rabbi, Reb Chaim Fine, served in the community. With the outbreak of the Second World War he fled to Russia but died on the way.

Even though orthodoxy was dominant in Radzyn for many generations, after World War I, very vigorous Zionist activities flourished. In addition to the branch of the 'Mizrachi' (Religious Zionist Party) that had been established during the war, branches of other Zionist parties and youth movements were founded. These included the 'General Zionists' (The 'On the Watch' and 'Time to Build' factions) 'Hitachdut' ('The Union' in 1929) and the 'Poele Zion Smol' (The Left Wing Young Zionist Workers) the 'Revisionists' and the Youth Movements 'Gordonia', 'Betar', 'Hashomer Hatzair' and 'Hechalutz'. In 1930 'Gordonia' established a pioneer training farm in a village near Radzyn.

For the 21st Zionist Congress (1937) some 400 'Shekalim' (A fee that entitled one to vote in the elections for the Zionist Congress) were sold in Radzyn. The 'Labor Bloc' won a majority among Radzyn Zionists.

Despite the growth of Zionism, the orthodox maintained their power. In 1921 a large and active branch of 'Agudath Yisroel '(ultra-orthodox party) was established. The 'Bund' (General Jewish Workers Socialist Party), which had been founded during the war years, became stronger and expanded its activities. Its members founded labor unions and established branches of its youth movement 'Zukunft' (Future) and its children's organization SKIF. A few local Jews were active in the communist underground but concealed this by focusing their activities on the labor unions.

In the elections to the 'Vaad Hakhillah' (Jewish Community Council) in 1924 and 1929 'Agudath Yisroel' got half of the mandates. But in 1931, it lost power while the combined slate of 'Zionim Klalli'im' (General Zionists) 'Mizrachi' and representatives of the craftsmen won a majority.

The vigorous community and political activities of this period were accompanied by similar lively activity in the areas of culture and Jewish education. The various political parties and youth movements sponsored amateur dramatic clubs, and evening classes. Some of them maintained libraries. The sports organization 'Hakoach' had a branch in Radzyn (established in 1923).

Many of the children from the community continued learning in the traditional 'Talmud Torah'. In the beginning of the 20's, a school belonging to the 'Tarbut (Culture) Network' was established. However, it closed a few years later. In 1929 'Agudath Yisroel' erected a 'Beis Yisroel' (House of Israel) Girl's School.

Some Jewish children, usually girls, studied in the local state run schools especially of the 'Shabasovka' type that were closed both on Saturday and Sunday.

The Jews of Radzyn were represented in the City Council almost proportionally. In the elections of 1924 and 1930 they won nine places out of the 18 on the city council. In 1939 they presented a united list ('The Citizens Bloc') but gained only 6 seats.

The virulent anti-Semitism that spread throughout Poland during this period did not fail to hit Radzyn. At the end of 1935 and the beginning of 1936, there were anti-Semitic incidents, which forced the municipality to issue a public condemnation. In 1937 Polish youths ran wild smashing windows of Jewish houses and businesses. Five of the leaders were arrested.

In the Period of the World War II

Only in the middle of October 1939 did the Germans conquer Radzyn, after most of the other towns in the district had already fallen into their hands. Their entrance into Radzyn was held up by the fierce resistance of units of the Polish Army commanded by General Kalbers. The Red Army held Radzyn for some time, but when they retreated eastward to the line agreed upon in the Molotov-Ribbentrop Agreement, many young Jews accompanied them. Before being conquered by the German Army, the city was bombed heavily by the German Air Force causing many deaths and heavy damage.

In the very first days of the conquest SS personal reached Radzyn and the persecution began. One rainy day, the SS broke into the synagogue and the religious school, ripped up the Torah books and threw them into the mud. They grabbed some religious Jews and tore off their beards ordering the Jews to dance and sing obsequiously with the mud covered and torn Torah Scrolls.

On the 3rd of December1939 a number of wagons loaded with Jews who had been driven out of Lubartov, arrived in Radzyn. They told that all the Jews had been evacuated from their town and were only allowed to take very little baggage with them. On hearing the account of the deportees, a number of young people together with a few families decided to cross the Bug River into the territory that was controlled by the Russian Army.

In November 1939 the Germans imposed on David Lichtenstein, the last head of the 'Kehillah', the task of raising a fund of 30,000 zlotys, meanwhile taking ten Jews as hostages. Lichtenstein, who was 70 at the time and among the richest members of the community, paid 10,000 zlotys from his own pocket and managed to raise the remaining sum, and due to him the lives of the hostages were spared.

On their arrival in Radzyn the Germans began to kidnap Jews for slave labor. The gendarmes and the policemen who guarded the laborers would humiliate, torture and beat them at every opportunity.

On December 6th 1939, most of the Jews were driven out of Radzyn to neighboring Slavatitzeh. Only a few were left in Radzyn. On orders from the Germans, Lichtenstein established a Judenrat of nine members most of whom had been Zionist leaders. The Judenrat made Shimon Kleinboim, who had been an official of 'The Joint' in Poland, responsible for matters of welfare and mutual aid including aid to the Jews in the vicinity. (His son, Mosheh Sneh was a well-known Zionist leader in Poland and in Israel and later a leader of the Israel Communist Party). The Judenrat was also responsible for seeing that the Jews appeared for forced labor. Males between the ages of 15 to 60 were obliged to work one day a week on a rotation basis. Most of them did so in maintenance of the soldiers quarters, chopping wood, cleaning the grounds and sweeping the streets. Along with the Judenrat, a Jewish Police force was set up. At the beginning of 1940 all Jewish property was confiscated "for the good of the Reich".

In April of 1940, most of those who had been banished to Slavatitzah were returned to Radzyn. The main streets had already been cleared of Jews, so they were forced to find places to live in the side streets.

Meanwhile additional Jews from Slavatitzah and Miedzyrzec Podlaski (Mezerich) arrived and the number of Jews in Radzyn reached some 2000 souls.

At the end of 1940 the Judenrat was ordered to move all the Jews in Radzyn, both veterans and the newcomers, to three streets in the old Jewish quarter of the town. Up until the fall of 1941 the ghetto was open and its inhabitants were allowed to move freely to other parts of the city.

During that period most of the Jews were employed in agriculture in the vicinity of Radzyn. In July of 1940 some three hundred Jewish males from Radzyn were taken to partially open work camps, where they worked regulating the flow of the Kishnah River. The Germans made the Jewish Police responsible for organizing the draft to the forced labor brigades. The policeman also accompanied the Jews on their way to work and made sure that they did not go through those streets that Jews were forbidden to go into.

On the 1st of January 1941 the Judenrat was ordered to collect up all items made from fur belonging to Jews and turn them in to the Gestapo headquarters. The Judenrat did as it was ordered and collected the furs. However the Germans were not satisfied with the amount that they received. They broke into the Jewish houses, searched them smashing everything in sight, stealing belongings, insulting, beating and torturing the Jews. In addition to the furs, the Judenrat was ordered to give the Germans two kilograms of gold. This time too, they took five Jews hostages whom they shot in order to terrify the Jews.

In May of 1942, there were 2,071 in the Radzyn ghetto. A clandestine youth group, composed of members of the 'Hashomer Hatzair' and other

Zionist organizations was operating in the ghetto. They were very active in various cultural activities but their main purpose was to arrange for Jews to flee to the forests and to set up fighting units. Among those who supported the flight to the forests and active resistance, was the Hassidic Rabbi Shmuel Shlomo Leiner. In June of 1942, the Gestapo learned of this through informers. When the Gestapo came to his house to arrest him he came out wrapped in his prayer shawl and with a prayer on his lips. Accompanied by his weeping followers he was led to square in front of the synagogue and executed there. The poet Yitzchak Katznelson commemorated this event in his poem 'The Song About The Radzyner'.

On the 22nd of September 1942 the Gestapo arrested Jews, marched them out of town and shot them.

In the beginning of October 1942, the commander of the SS ordered all the Jews to gather in the open space between the synagogue and the study hall for a roll call. The members of the Judenrat were ordered to explain to the crowd that this was necessary to disprove the rumor that Jews from other ghettoes had infiltrated and found asylum in Radzyn without registering with the Judenrat. This was an act of deception that was intended to prevent Jews from fleeing. On that day 800 residents of the ghetto were deported to Treblinka. This 'aktzia' was followed by additional 'aktzias'. On the 14th of October a group of German gendarmes, SS members and Gestapo officers came to the Radzyn ghetto accompanied by Polish policemen. The Jewish police were ordered to lead them to possible hiding places. Those Jews who were caught were rounded up and held in an empty lot. By the 16th of the month, some 1000 of these hidden Jews, men, women and children were captured and deported to the ghetto at Miedzyrzec. On the 27th of October they together with Jews from other ghettoes in the vicinity were sent to Treblinka. Some Jews died along the way from overcrowding and thirst. When the train reached Treblinka some 10 to 15 dead were found in each railroad car. Many of the deportees tried to escape by jumping from the train, some of whom died in the attempt, while many others were captured by Poles and handed over to the Germans.

A few escaped successfully and joined the Partisan groups or found shelter with peasants.

After this expulsion Radzyn was declared 'Judenrein' (purged of Jews). The Gestapo employed a small group of Jews from Radzyn in well-guarded labor camps.

The Jewish partisans from Radzyn, who fled to the forests, organized themselves into a number of groups. One group lead by Yitzchak Kleinman hid in two bunkers, fifteen fighters in each bunker which they erected in the forest that extended in the direction of Kotzk. A peasant from one of the nearby villages promised to get them arms in return for a substantial payment. At first he promised them 15 rifles. A group of fighters went far away to get the promised weapons. When they returned to the bunker they did not find any of their comrades among the living. It turned out that some informers turned them over to the Germans, who blew up the bunker and its inhabitants. The Germans captured, tortured, and executed two of those who had returned. The survivors from this group, fifteen young people led by Yitzchak Kleinman, organized partisan activities. In their first action in February 1943, they liquidated two Gestapo officers who were outstandingly cruel. Latter they eliminated a 'Folksdeutsche' (A German living in Poland), an anti-Semitic owner of a dairy in the village of Stare Viyesh, who had denounced to the Gestapo every Jew that he met. They loaded the products of his dairy onto wagons and hauled it to their bunkers in the forest. They continued liquidating informers and ambushed a German vehicle carrying three Nazi officers, killed them and took their weapons and uniforms. Unfortunately, Yitzchak Kleinman took sick with typhus and there was no choice but to hospitalize him in the Miedzyrzec Ghetto where he was killed in his hospital bed by the Germans during one of the last 'aktzias' that took place in that ghetto.

Another partisan group of Radzyners led by Leib and Laizer Pantshak operated in the forests between Radzyn and Vishnitzeh. Together with other Jewish partisan groups from the vicinity, they carried out a number of daring operations. However in the summer of 1944, a short time before the Red Army liberated the area, this group of partisans was liquidated by a group of Polish partisans belonging to the 'Armya Krajowa' (the Polish Underground connected with the Polish Government in Exile in London).

A number of additional Radzyn residents were spread out among different partisan units. Among them was Dinah Rosewald who fought in the forest of Vilna, and Yaakov Pantshak, Moshe Agmon and a number of others.

Table of Contents

Title	Author	Page

The Shtetl, a Jewish Mother

A Memorial to the Town (H *)	Yitzchak Zigelman	2
Holy to God (Poem)	Meir Segal	4
My Shtetl (Poem)	Abba Danielak	5
Radzyn	Mendel Lichtenshtein	8
The Jewish Community in Radzyn (H)	Levy Winderbaum	9
The Song About the Radzyner (Poem)	Yitzchak Katzenelson	11

The Past Generations

My Shtetl Radzyn	Benzion Burshtein	14
The Synagogue and the Beit Midrash; Sabbath in the Shtetl	Abba Danielak	32
What Was	Yaakov Greenblat	40
Radzyn Characters	Mendel Goldwasser	49
Bright Figures	Yisroelke List	51
My Radzyn	Mendel Lichtenshtein	57
Radzyn Portraits	Abba Danielak	57
Moishe Smolaz	Shmuel Daniely	62
Songs From My Home	Meir Segal	64

Radzyner Chasidism

The Rabbi's Court	Abba Danielak	66
The House of Izbitzeh and Radzyn (H)	M. S. Gshuri	79
Yisrael From Kotzk Goes With the Rabbi to Find the Snail (H)	Yisrael Kantor	90
The Rabbi Who Shook Up Poland	Y. Y. Trunk	92
The Rabbi and the Colonel	M. Ben-Shmuel	96
From Those days (H)	M. Ben-Shmuel	98
The Golden Chain	Leib Rochman	99
The Unbroken Blue Chain (H)	Mordechai Tanenbaum	102

Life and Youth

In Your Streets Radzyn (H)	Yitzchak Kenani	104
My Shtetl	Levi Vinderbaum	123
In the Shadow of the Town (H)	Simcha Hochenberg	126
Memories of Radzyn	Abraham Zigelman	130
The Teachers of Small Children – The Whip and Youth	Zanvil Zaltzstein	134

Episodes From the Jewish Workers Movement in Radzyn	Zvi Liberson	136
The Jewish artisans	Zvi Liberson	144
Interest Free Loans (H)	Dov Katzenelenbogen	146
The Founding Gathering of the Poele Zion	Tzipah Rosenfeld	150
The Poele Zion in Radzyn	Shprintzeh Gottesdiner	153
Gottlakes	Abba Danielak	154
Nathan Shvalbeh	Nachman Meisel	158
Lazerkeh Szalasheh and the Radzyn Amateur Artists	Henich Applebaum	160
Hashomer Hatzair in Radzyn (H)	Emmanuel Tor	162
The Amateur Stage of "Hashomer Hatzair" (H)	M. Ben-Shmuel	167
About the Educational Activity in the Hashomer Hatzair Branch in Radzyn (H)	Y. Zeligman	169
About Our Development	Ch. Shlimak	172
From the Melting Pot (H)	David R.	176
The Ascender (Poem)	L. Vinderbaum	179

Destruction and Extinction

The Beginning of the Storm and Extinction (H)	Abba Lichtenshtein	180
The Beginning of the Disaster	Rachel Zaltzshtein Freter	190
The History of the Extinction (H)	Yehoshua Rosencrantz	195
Hellish Experiences in the Radzyn Ghetto	Sarah Bashe Voyazsher	214
Five Years in the Abyss	Sarah Ashman Zaltzshtein	217
In the Struggle For Survival	Liber Farbiash	229
Two Years in a Dark Pit	Sarah Fass	235
The Parting	Sarah Basha Vyaszisher	242
In the Inferno Unknowingly (H)	Chana Burshtin	243
With My Father the Rabbi Chaim Fine in Russia (H)	Sarah Achicam-Fine	245
My Return Home	Ethel Keitelgisser	253
Radzyn After the Destruction	Rachel Zaltzshtein Freter	255
On the Ruins of My Shtetl	Zvi Lieberson	260
Radzyn in 1946 - After the Destruction	Zevel Zaltstein	263
The Jews of Radzyn in the Partisan Groups	Zvi Lieberson	265
Leibel Lev – the Leader of a Partisan Group	Shifrah Lev	269
The Survivors of Radzyn		271
About Moishelach and Shloimelach and a Life that Vanished (Poem)	Aryeh Lozer	283
Yisrael Lichtenstein: His Last Will and Testament (H)	Idah Zigelman	287
Among the Fallen		289

New Roots

Radzyners in Israel (H)	Yitzchak Avi-Arah	291
Asher Rosenfeld (H)	Simcha Reichenberg	297
The Editorial Board for the Book		300

Radzyners in America   Yaakov Greenblatt   301
Radzyners in America   Mendel Lichtenstein   303
Meir Segal   306
Yosef Danilak- Of Blessed Memory (H)   Idah Z – n   307
Yaakov Greenblatt – Of Blessed Memory   308

Yizkor
List of the Missing   310
With the Fallen (H)   323
Map of Radzyn   324

*All articles are in Yiddish, except those marked (H) are in Hebrew

Notes to the Reader:

Within the text the reader will note "{34}" standing ahead of a paragraph. This indicates that the material translated below was on page 34 of the original book. However, when a paragraph was split between two pages in the original book, the marker is placed in this book after the end of the paragraph for ease of reading.

Also please note that all references within the text of the book to page numbers, refer to the page numbers of the original Yizkor Book.

The original book can be seen online at the NY Public Library site:
http://yizkor.nypl.org/index.php?id=1140

A list of this book and all books available in the Yizkor-Book-In-Print Project along with prices is available at:
http://www.jewishgen.org/Yizkor/ybip.html

INDEX of the pages i through xxii

A

Achicam-Fine, xxi
Agmon, xix
Applebaum, xxi
Ashman, xxi
Avi-Ara, vi
Avi-Arah, xxi

B

Ben-Shmuel, xx, xxi
Borshtein, vi
Burshtein, xx
Burshtin, xxi

D

Danielak, xx, xxi
Daniely, xx
Danilak, vi, xxii

F

Farbiash, xxi
Fass, xxi
Fine, xv, xxi
Fishel, xi
Forsyth, ii
Freter, xxi

G

Goldwasser, i, ii, vii, xx
Gotesdiener, vi
Gottesdiner, xxi
Greenblat, xx
Greenblatt, xxii
Gshuri, xx

H

Hochenberg, xx

K

Kalbers, xvi
Kantor, xx
Kaplan, ii
Katzenelenbogen, xxi

Katzenelson, xx
Katznelson, xviii
Keitelgisser, xxi
Kenani, xx
Kleinboim, xvii
Kleinman, xviii, xix

L

Lazar, vi
Leiner, xiii, xviii
Lev, xxi
Liberson, xxi
Lichtenshtein, vi, xx, xxi
Lichtenstein, xvi, xvii, xxi, xxii
Lieberson, xxi
List, xx
Lozer, xxi
Lust, vi

M

Meisel, xxi

P

Pantshak, xix
Pototzki, xii

R

Reb Gershon Chanoch, xi
Reb Shlomoh, xi
Reb Shmuel Shlomo, xiii
Reichenberg, xxi
Rosencrantz, xxi
Rosenfeld, xxi
Rosewald, xix

S

Schwartz, ii
Segal, xx, xxii
Shlimak, xxi
Sneh, xvii

T

Tor, xxi
Trunk, xx

V

Vinderbaum, xx, xxi
Vinderboim, vi
Voyazsher, xxi
Vyaszisher, xxi

W

Winderbaum, xx

Z

Zaltstein, xxi
Zaltzshtein, xxi
Zaltzstein, xx
Zeligman, xxi
Zigelman, i, vi, xx, xxi

The Shtetl,
a Jewish Mother

[Pages 5-6]

A Memorial to our town

Yitzchak Zigelman

Even before the roar of the cannons of World War II died down, while our dead still lay heaped up in Treblinka and Oeswenciam, the desire and the inner necessity arose to remember and record those terrible events we witnessed. They were among the worst in our long history of martyrdom, and in the history of humanity.

At that time a decision was taken that affected our whole being, to erect a monument to our town, a memorial to its Jews and to our relatives in order to fulfill their will and testament.

The testaments were most tangible. Here is a brother's will that reached us when death appeared at our windows: "Disperse and save your souls. Perhaps one of you will be able to reach safety and to relate the 'unbelievable' so that it might be recorded for eternal disgrace."

There was the will of a youthful friend which was uncovered together with the wooden boxes that contained the Ringleblume Archive and was addressed to both the community and the individual.

Wherever we turned we felt the same pairs of eyes, which in the last minutes before their destruction, whether in the murkiness of the gas chambers or under the mounds of earth covering living beings, pleaded and begged: 'Erect a memorial to us.'

So I set to work collecting gleaning thinning and editing. I collected and wrote down testimonies from survivors. When it was necessary, I looked for pictures to fit to what was told to me. The number of events and their details grew. The participants included people who had literary experience as well as others who had difficulty writing down their stories. However, the latter, most of whom had been personally involved in the terrible events, wrote their stories with their blood. They recorded shocking evidence of strangulation and stoning from which could be heard the terrible sounds of their own death throes and those of their relatives.

This book is intended to be a memorial to the glorious town of our birth on which the modern Amalek engraved these terrible events that left us with dates of deaths, strangulation, ashes and graves. Where the suffering and death throes that happened to our brothers in their last moments are revealed. For us it will be a way of performing the final justice to the Jews of our town.

The important thing about this book that resulted is that it is a collective effort in which we found a way to express our ideas each in his own special way.

* * * * *

However this book will not only tell about destruction and extinction. It will also tell about dynamic life that existed both in the far and recent past. It is intended as a memoir of Radzyn. It will tell about generations existing in the distant and recent past; about God-fearing Jews who sought redemption; about Chassidim and Chassidoth; about ideological disputes; about revolutionary movements to which many of our best young men were attracted who had only yesterday occupied the benches of the Bet Hamedrash; about the excitement of redemption, that many of our best young people, tired of the degenerate life in the Diaspora, experienced; and about their wandering to the countries of the world and about their new life in the Homeland.

The chain has not been broken. The remnants of our people are gathering together again; the dry bones have come back to life. New centers have been established, including the greatest and most natural one, Israel, where most of the remnants have found a safe haven. Therefore, it is understandable that the memorial to our town was erected there.

Mass grave of the Radzyn martyrs in the Meseritz ghetto

[Pages 7-8]

Holy to God

Maier Segal (New York)

A sad glow shatters the setting sun
Onto the evening trees.
Small figs weigh heavy close to the ground
And are submerged between Mincha and Maariv.

Soldiers rush through the city
With carts and laden oxen. -
From cooking kettles arises steamy vapor
From coffee, brewed and burnt.
Upon carts clatter knives.
Pikes gleam sharply.
Sad is the setting sun.

Jews, stooping, go for Mincha, go for Maariv.
Soldiers spring from carts. -
Whips pierce, knives bloody in hands
Knives slash through the sun, pale faces turn bloody.
Jews in city homes fall dark
Between Mincha and Maariv – holy to God...

My Shtetl (My Village)
Abba Danielak (Toronto)

Like from a foggy, gray morning
The sun, radiant in gold, peeks out
In my memory, where the years are concealed,
You rise in your many-colored form.

Above narrow, winding streets
Houses stooped with age and gray,
Huddle together under weighty loads
Of moss-covered shingles and straw.

Your three markets of communities arranged by ritual practice
Divided by sovereignty and discord –
Russian split from Polish split from Jewish trade
Living hundreds of years side by side.

I see you in summer's golden beginning:
The sky above arched in pale blue.
Nighttime dreams insistently weave,
Lie discarded in the dewy field.

Bodies fatigued, faces weary –
The day awakens to a new song, to life
Some to the well with bucket to draw water
Some to the synagogue with tallit to give God's Sabbath.

With wheat, wagons and horses,
Laden with peasant goods, they encircle the markets
intelligent foreheads, milked Jews
They set the price, they huddle, they bargain.

Women disheveled, dress and apron stained,
Their skin and faces wrinkled with concern
Their stores wide open with herring and salt
And sugar – the peasant's daily bread.

[illegible], craftsmen
Jew and gentile, for generations, clothing,
Needle and hammer – their lot
And they sing of their woe and joys.

Living poor, struggling, as fate has decreed
For man and women and child and bond.
The morrow threatens, poverty – a tough lot –
Concern for livelihood, clothes, and bread.
                    -.-
A summer evening as if touched by the paint brush,

Glorious heaps of magic tossed, piled
Into the void. In seas of light, a polished prism
The day immerses itself, sinking in shadow.

In hellish fire on the sky's edge
The sun dips, copper red, dips, disappears.
At the nefarious tip of the cross, embers aflame
Ablaze: fright, fear, from medieval times...

Ding-dong, ding-dong, the bell tolls:
Dark shadows, they spread and spread
And by the time the final bell goes silent
Heaven and earth – a black abyss.

From the cemetery, hard against the river, spirits shriek forth
From open graves: frogs croak, crickets chirp
– Foreign forces awaken to life
From gentile streets – hoarse, mean barking.

Families gathered in homes of the DLD
In air thick with sweat and stink,
Mother and father in bed with a pointing infant
They rest on straw, on the sleeping bank.

Dreams weave from hidden worlds,
Of magic and gold, of prince and princess,
No more poverty. Clothes aplenty, fancy soles.
Heaps of mint and full to bursting...
                    -.-
Batei midrash Hasidic prayer halls surround
– Evidence of Jewish endurance and mystery –
There Jews sing out the grief and woe of generations
In study and prayer to lighten their burden.

Little cradles of *Tchelet* valued by Hasids.
Fathers greet each other, guarding for loyalty,
And wisdom and learning and pedigree
Having taken their place with honor, [illegible]

Mordechai Yossef Elazar, the Radzyn Rabbi, son of Gershon Chanoch, possessor of the Tchelet

Radzyn

Mendel Lichtenstein (New York)

On the map of Europe there is a country called Poland which has many cities and towns on it, and under every name there is a dot. Our Radzyn is marked with such a dot.

A very insignificant stream wends its way between the endless fields and the adjacent forests. In the summer it disappears almost completely except for one place where it suddenly expands, becomes visible and flows around the edge of the shtetl of Radzyn. That may be the reason that the 'first Radzyner', a few hundred years ago, found it to be a place suitable for settlement.

Aside from that it was a shtetl like all shtetls. From outside it looked like the stain made by a spider web on some wall. However, internally, Radzyn stood out with specific characteristics. It gave the impression that it is proud, distinguished and aristocratic. That may be the reason why it was always the district capital (Powiat).

We do not know exactly how old Radzyn is. We remember old gray Radzyners who were born in the shtetl and who remembered their childhood...etc. etc. The gray palace in the shtetl tells us a lot about its age. It was built in the Rococo style most likely in the 17th Century. Legend has it that when the architect finished the building his eyes were put out so that he would never be able to build another such beautiful palace. Radzyn boasts of this. Only such a beautiful and romantic town could think up such a legend.

We Jews too had our own romantic legends. The synagogue was built at the edge of the town so that the living would not be frightened when the souls of the departed wander through the fields at night on their way to the synagogue.

We remember the Beis Hamedrash, our community center, where we studied, debated, dreamt, and acquired the knowledge to become citizens of the world. We remember the Rabbi's house, its impressiveness, its festive atmosphere, altogether a miniature Jewish kingdom. We can never forget all the different characters who passed away or were annihilated!

Radzyn, our precious shtetl, you cannot be forgotten. When we do think of you we are proud to have been Radzyners.

———

[Page 12]

The Jewish Kehillah Organization in Radzyn

L. Winderbaum (Tel Aviv)

Up until 1928, ten years after the establishment of Polish state, the Jewish people in Radzyn did not have any legal representation. 'Influential people' were usually appointed by the authorities to manage public affairs, with no democratic control. The first elections to the Jewish Kehillah in the city took place in 1928. According to the new Polish law, the elections were free and proportional, the same as for any elected governmental body. This raised a wave of joy and hope, especially in nationalist circles of the Jewish community.They saw the elections as a basis for creating greater national cultural autonomy and the rebirth of national life. At the head of the election committee stood the Shaul Blumenfeld, of blessed memory, from the Mizrachi organization.

Most of the parties and organizations in the town submitted their lists of candidates:

The General Zionists, the Ultra-Orthodox, the Bund, Poele-Zion, the Artisans,etc. Yisrael Winderbaum, Yehoshua Finkelshtein, Yeshayahu Zilberberg and Haim-Yitzchak Gelerman, Velvel Tenenbaum, Yoel Butman and David Lichtenshtein were elected. The new board started working energetically hoping that it could expand the framework of the existing Kehillah, because it was not possible to take care of all the educational, cultural, national, social and other needs under the previous arrangement. The government however intervened immediately and cancelled all items that were not intended for strictly religious purposes. This action by the government caused great disappointment in the nationalist circles, clipped their wings, and in place of enthusiasm the public became completely indifferent to all Kehillah activities. Again the rich and the influential on one hand, and on the other hand, the Jewish "Hsnatziah" followers (a not very successful or understandable imitation of the governmental 'Hsnatziah' party, which arose among the Polish electorate at that time) took control. Again the Kehillah was emptied of any national and social aspirations and remained, as in the past, an institution that could fulfill only minimal religious needs.

The main sources of income of the Kehillah were from kosher slaughter and "ATAT" – a special tax imposed on the residents by the board of the Kehillah with permission of the authorities. The major part of the budget was from the income from ritual slaughter.

The main expenses were: Support of the Rabbi (Rabbi Haim Fine) the ritual slaughterers and a few other salaried employees; synagogue and cemetery maintenance expenses; plus administrative expenses. From time to time there were special social expenses.

The "Magistrat" (the municipality) collected the Kehillah tax, because the board of the Kehillah was not allowed to collect the tax by itself. This was occasionally the cause of great difficulties. At times the anti-Semitic municipality collectors decided to collect the tax on Friday evenings and caused great anger when they tried to confiscate candlesticks and the board members had to redeem them and return them to their owners, without violating the Sabbath...

The cry of the generations
Painting by Mandel Lichtenstein

[Page 13]

The Song about the Radzyner

Yitzhak Katzenelson

The Germans rush into the Hasidic prayer house –
Shrieking wildly: The Rabbi must come!
The holy Rabbi... Jews, tell us –
We're going to shoot him, just the holy one...
One Jew by way of all: Where is he? Tell us where.
We'll let you live, we'll leave you be...
He's not in Radzyn, the godly man...
He's among you, he's there among you.

He has left Radzyn for Włodawa –
The Jews – a chill runs down their backs:
The rabbi isn't here with us, dear folks.
The rabbi is already dead, has been dead for some time.
He was very old. He's no longer with us...
Bring out the young one, the young one!
The young Rabbi. You'll bring him immediately
And if you don't give him up – we'll shoot you!

There is news: Lublin is being ravaged!
The rabbi raises his hand and shakes his fist.
Lublin, the venerable Jewish holy city –
Lublin – is being destroyed... O, God, save us!

There is news – one's blood goes cold –
What is man doing? He himself knows not what he does...
The rabbi, standing frozen in the corner and listening –
Of Lublin, of what's becoming of the Jews,
Of the Jews, and what is being done to them –
The rabbi, the rabbi, he stands guard...
The rabbi smiles, he still continues to smile.
His smile is bitter, his tears like salt,
They drip and drip – of it he knows not.
It sneaks by onto his brow,
From his brow onto his cheek, from his cheek into his beard –
He stands frozen, stands in his spot
And suddenly – the rabbi shouts out with a cry:
Almighty Lord of the world, I do not stand alone!
The two of us stand together on guard... you also
Look to Lublin, watching from afar...
You also wait hidden as I do here... watching –
And you can do nothing for your people, the same as I!
I do not stand guard here between the walls alone –
You also... and the rabbi shakes his fist.

The Rabbi bursts into tears... o, cry not, conceal!

Conceal your face, the world ought not see it...
The world, o, the world, the outside world – o
It can, God forbid, still be shamed
A tale to bear. God forbid!
From bearing the horror and watching the amusement...
The conscience can begin to torment you – ah
The conscience, of the world – it simply can't keep up...
Germans, they do it, and the world watches –
O, which of them is worse? Do say!
No, don't raise your heavy head to him, no, no!
And it ought not hear, the world ought not hear your cry!
A filthy world ought not be reflected in your tears.
It loves the Nevi'im, it loves sin more.
Its eye grows white, its soul is black.
It sins and embeds itself deep in hearts,
And its thinking is crude, its language vain.
In its heart, seven horrors; in its hand, the *Tanakh*...
O, do not raise your head, o, do not raise it, no!
It should not see you, the world, as you cry.
The world, ah, the world... who thinks of the world,
No one, no sign of it in the tent,
The rabbi's tent, it leaves be for the time being.
No one there at all, only God, may He be blessed.
The rabbi, the rabbi – he bursts out into tears,
Bursts into tears before God, and he is one in all
Whether the world sees it or whether the world sees it not.
He gives the lie to the world, the saintly one, the Jew.
He denies it as it denies his god
Before whom he now cries, before whom he
Rejected the [illegible] his head –
He raises it in despair, and lets it drop
He can't do it, the rabbi, can't watch God's – anguish,
He can't look him in the face,

His face downcast, his heart saddened –
The presiding member to his side, he grew ashamed
The rabbi cries silently, his voice can hardly be heard –
They, the residents of Radzyn, pity him
He cries – and God chokes, hot, hot with his tears –
And the residents of Radzyn let their heads fall heavily.

Rabbi Shlomo'le, the last Rabbi of the Radyn dynasty, second from left

The Past Generations

My Shtetl Radzyn

Ben- Zion (Yonah) Burstein (Ramat Gan)

1. Streets and Buildings

Radzyn, or Radin in Russian, is located on the side road branching off from the wider one that leads from Warsaw to Brisk. It was a small shtetl of approximately nine hundred Jewish families and a few hundred non-Jewish families, most of whom lived on the perimeter surrounding the Jewish streets with an iron band. The town did not have its own railroad station. The nearest one was seven kilometers away and called 'Badlena' in a village of the same name. The old timers' tales had it, that the Russian railroad engineers demanded a bribe for building the station close to Radzyn. Since the Jews could not afford it, the engineers, out of spite, built the station far from the town.

Radzyn was small, not only in population, but also in its outward appearance in which it resembled most Polish small towns. Its streets were small and narrow and mostly unpaved. The small one-story wooden houses were usually covered with shingle roofs. The only street worthy of that name was Ostroweitzka, most of whose houses were made of brick. It also was the street that served as a promenade especially for young loving couples.

The synagogue was very old. Legend had it that it was two or three hundred years old and was built in the style of that period. It had a large anteroom at the entrance in which could still be seen the signs of the chains of the pillory to which those sinners who were waiting to be flogged were tied. For a harsher sentence, every person who passed by on his way to or from prayer would spit in the sinner's face. For the real serious "criminals" the flogging was carried out while they were laid out on the table on which the dead were prepared for burial, so as to remind them that is the place where they belong. Another reason for this custom was that the sinner should be reminded of his death and repent.

The Holy Arc, which was one of the oldest and most beautiful in Poland, was of great historical and artistic value. It covered the whole of the eastern wall and was covered with very beautiful woodcarvings of fruits and birds of great artistic value. Later when more 'enlightened' synagogue wardens and community leaders appeared, they invited an artist to restore the arc. He did it very well and reestablished its value as an historical relic.

There was another group of buildings of great historical significance but they did not belong to the Jewish part of the town. Their imposing size and high towers made them visible from all parts of the town, yet a mythical veil and fog surrounded them. These were the buildings of the castle of the Radzyner Lord Shlubovski. The castle and its owner were enshrouded in a legendary cloak. He did not have any children and did not have an inherited or battlefield bestowed title of count. He was simply called Lord, and was very rich, one of the richest landowners of Congress Poland. He owned many fields, forests, ponds and some villages with many slaves. On top off all that he was lame and had a reputation for being very miserly. Like all landowners, he was surrounded by 'his' Jews who bought his forests, grain, livestock, and profited nicely from it. As the Jews told it, the profits they made from him were always through devious means. Because of his great miserliness, he could never allow anyone to make an honest profit.

The regular visitors to Shlubovski revealed many of the secrets about his origin and his castle. They spoke about his introverted character, about his always being absorbed and detached. His castle too had a detached chamber, which no one was allowed to enter, not even his closest friends from the nobility. All sorts of theories and legends circulated concerning it, among others, that this was a place where devils and the souls of the dead reside. These two conspicuous buildings, the synagogue and castle, each cast a similar fear on me when I was a child.

They used to say that it was forbidden to go through the synagogue at night, because the dead gather there to form a quorum and pray. He that passes through is in danger of being called up to read the Torah, and that is a sure sign that he will die that week. I had that very same feeling when passing by Shlubovski's castle. The reflections of the setting sun on the high tower windows I imagined as being devils and other evil spirits. The only difference was that in the synagogue the souls that hid out there were those of Jews who were looking for their redemption, while the souls in the castle were non-Jews.

2. The Essence of Radzyn

When I look back and search for what was specific and peculiar in my Radzyn, the whole Radzyn world, with all of its lights and shadows, passes before me as in a kaleidoscope. I see the usual morass that we encountered in most of the Jewish towns and villages: all of the religious officials, wardens, sextons, cantors, and other 'honorable' Jews; the different sects of Chassidim (Followers) and their Misnagdim (Opponents), the 'German' Jews wearing silk and satin coats. Then, too, there were the hard working common people with their plain cloth coats and high boots, which they smeared with cod liver oil in honor of the Sabbath. There were also those intense, intelligent youth in the basei midrash (study halls) who lived within the confines of the Halacha (Jewish law) and got their satisfaction from the depths of the Talmud and its casuistry. Then, too, there were the 'golden youths' who laughed at the 'bench warmers' and found their satisfaction in more practical areas. These were very highly cultured young people who bound up their personal fate with that of their people and therefore threw themselves wholeheartedly and with youthful zeal into the struggle for the Zionist-National idea. Then there was the youth for whom the struggle for their own people did not provide enough satisfaction and therefore flung themselves into the struggle for all of mankind by joining the 'Bund' (Jewish Workers Socialist Party). Others blended Zionism and Socialism and created the Poale Zion (Zionist Workers) Movement. Secular cultural activists established evening courses and lending libraries. Religious officials founded Talmud Torah's (Religious Schools), Yeshivas (advanced schools for studying the Talmud) and opposed the secular cultural movement with the excuse that 'the new is forbidden by the Torah'.

There were founders and creators of savings associations and credit unions as well as artisans' associations. There were also synagogue treasurers who together with their wives went around with kerchief in hand to collect money to help a poor bride or on Friday for some soup for a sick woman in childbirth.

Everything it would seem was just as it was in the other shtetls, but yet it was different, very Radzynish! Somehow all these parties and groups did not have in them that extreme sharpness which is so abusive when turned on one's opponents. What was missing was the crippling, uncreative sectarianism that spews poison and creates an unbridgeable chasm between the parties. There was a very humane and often even a friendly relationship between opponents. Could this have been because of their superficiality or conciliatory disposition? No! Each one was ready to jump into the fire for his beliefs, ideas, and truths and not back down in the least bit. Some of them were 'talkers' who later became ideologues for their 'truths' but because of their 'Radzynism' they did not allow themselves to be so stubborn and blind that they could not see the positive side of their opponents. Their healthy instincts whispered to them that even someone who thinks differently could still be good, honest and a good personal friend. Only in Radzyn was it possible for all classes, sects and people with different worldviews to live together harmoniously. Radzyn never experienced the vicious struggle between Chassidim and Misnagdim or between different 'Shtibls' (followers of specific chassidic rabbis). I do not know of any single case where a student was excluded from a shtibl or beis medrash (seminary) because he changed his attire to the 'German' style. The spread of the new ideas about the Jewish renaissance was not linked to antagonism, as was common in many of the other towns and villages. Only in Radzyn was it possible that pious Jews, like my father of blessed memory, and Reb Itshe Meir, Reb Eishes, Reb Simcha Bashes, Reb Simcha Tiles and others, who were very strict with themselves and with their children yet never insulted anyone because of his lack of observance. The opposite was true. They greeted everyone with a broad smile and with a good word. Radzyn never witnessed any of the serious disputes between the rabbis that were an almost natural occurrence in most of the Jewish towns and villages. Only in Radzyn could such an amazing happening take place; only there could a rabbi who was a Misnagid and a Litvak from birth (an outstanding student of the Voloshin Yeshiva), Reb Chaim Fine of blessed memory, (where he studied together with

Bialik) live out his whole life in a shtetl in which the majority were Chassidim. Yet he did not want to move to other larger towns, many of which invited him to become their rabbi. Privately too, you never heard of arson or informers to the authorities as often happened in other towns. It is true that Radzyn had in its time fierce disputes, such as during the time of the Radzyner Rabbi, Reb Gershon Henoch, of blessed memory, the discoverer of the tchelet (the azure coloring used to dye the tzitiot the ritual fringes) and the author of the Tractates on Purification. However, they never became deeply ideological, for or against the tchelet. No, the Radzyner was by nature not a zealot. The opponents of the tchelet quietly tolerated the Rabbi's supporters and vice versa. The reason for this lay in the dispute itself. The crusading nature of the great genius Reb Gershon Henoch, who quarreled with the whole world and had the entire rabbinical and Talmudic world against him did not fit in with Radzyn's calm, cold, stoic population. Maybe that was the reason for the revolt against his followers. His son and successor at the Radzyn 'Court', Rabbi Mordecai Yosef, became 'Radzynized' and became a 'peace seeker' although in political life he was a fighter and therefore won the sympathy and admiration of the town's citizens.

To further my depiction of Radzyn, it is worth quoting what the above-mentioned Rabbi Gershon Henoch said. As is well known Radzyn is located half way between Mezeritch and Kotzk. About this the Rabbi said: "Radzyn is the illegal child of the misalliance between Mezerich and Kotzk." True, Radzyn inherited the depth and incisiveness of the Kotzk mind, with its desire for change and to always be part of the leadership. From Mezeritch it inherited appearance of propriety, cultured poise and composure.

3. The Ascent of the Socialist Movement

When I try to recall the near and dear figures of my childhood years a thick veil shrouds my memory. It is drawn there by the passing of time and mostly because of the unprecedented tragic events of Jewish history brought about by the Nazi snake which magnified by a thousandfold my brief experiences, I therefore rarely succeed in seeing those years clearly. Some of them come out as blurred bits and pieces that I find difficult to fit together into a complete picture. Some of them come out as silhouettes viewed through an opaque glass. Many of the people however, stand before me living and full blooded, so that I imagine us continuing those long interrupted arguments or discussions and their telling me of the agony and suffering in the last experiences of martyrdom.

My earliest memories lead me to a small crowded shtibl (hut) someplace below the beis-medrash street. There I see some tens of children sitting by tables while others sit on the floor. The teacher, Itshele Chaneh's, sits by the table. In one hand he holds the pointer with which he shows the children the letters of the alphabet. In the other hand, he holds a belt with which he rocks the cradle that hangs from a rope in the middle of the room. The words and the tunes alternate: "Nu say already, you dunce, kametz aleph ohh"-he says in an angry voice. A minute later the words change and he sings "Quiet, quiet fall asleep already". His wife, a small thin woman, was almost always in bed either before or after childbirth. The number of the rabbi's children never stayed fixed. Every year a new child was born –and another died. He had his family doctor in the person of Gershon the Feldsher (barber surgeon), a man with a professorial rabbinical face, a long silver-white beard combed and brushed so that every hair lay in its place, with a high white forehead covered with a four-cornered linen skullcap, and a pair of deep blue eyes. This "doctor" was a permanent visitor in my rabbi's house. He had special prescriptions for sick children, some of which have remained in my memory: fried frogs that often caused us children to almost faint from the horrible smell they gave off while frying. I don't remember now if this was for internal or external use, to be eaten or just to be spread on the skin. On the other hand, I remember clearly how the other prescription was used and I will describe it exactly to preserve it for science sake. You take the tail of a herring and bandage it tightly to the sore on the child's foot until the sore absorbs the herring. The result was that every year a new child's grave was added in the Radzyn cemetery.

As I have already mentioned the cheder (religious school for young boys) was located not far from the beis medrash so that the attention of the rabbi was divided, one half on his child with the other half on the other two score children. In this way each student got only a few minutes of attention everyday. We children exploited this situation and were frequent guests in the beis medrash. There we met two opposing camps 'Russians' and 'Japanese', for this was the time of the Russo-Japanese War. The Hebrew newspaper 'Hatzfirah' ('the Siren) passed from hand to hand and served as a map of the battle lines, each side using it to prove that 'their side' was victorious. The leader of the Russian side was Yoske Yehoshua Dovid's, an elderly Jew, a scholar and the author of books, two of which remain in my memory: 'A Glut of Celebrations' and 'Thchelet (Azure) Disqualified' – polemics against 'The Tchelet Fringe' which was written by Radzyner Rabbi. Yoske Yehoshua was a fanatic. His attachment to Russia was so great that he often came to blows when someone dared say that Japan would be the victor. I do not remember the supporters of the Japanese side, but they were from the younger generation permeated with hate for Czarist Russia and they supported the Japanese, according to the saying: The enemies of my enemies are my friends.

When the Russians suffered serious defeats on the Russo-Japanese front, it affected the arguments that went on inside the walls of the beis medrash by strengthening the pro-Japanese faction. In the street and in the shtetl, they provoked a new, previously unknown reaction. First there were whispers that gradually became bolder and open about the organization of a Jewish Socialist Party led by a group of ruffians. Suddenly there appeared right inside the beis medrash or in the courtyard, new unfamiliar faces that entered brazenly and acted as if they were its owners. They looked down with contempt on the 'bench warmers' and their silly concern with what 'the Rabbis said' when they had in their pockets a new gospel, that of Karl Marx which promised freedom for all the oppressed including the very same 'bench warmers'.

The mysterious Radzyn castle

Their infiltration into the beis medrash caused great anxiety to its regular residents who suddenly felt fear of the new people and ideas that surrounded them. This caused them to draw closer one to another so as to create a greater distance between them and the new 'tenants'. However, to tell the truth, it must be noted that some of the beis medrash boys were infected with the new doctrine.

One of those who has remained in my memory is Gedalia –Yudel, the Sexton's son, on whose account Yudel, a learned and God fearing Jew, suffered terribly especially at the hands of Berele- Moshe Golde's who often told him off.

The reason for this estrangement between the two camps was not only their different attitude toward the new doctrine. No! The regular residents such as; Yaakov Moshe and Yehoshua Kupietz, Levi Yudel the Sexton, Zishe Godl's, Hershel Avram the son of Moshe the Ritual Slaughterer, Chaim Yoel Levi, Chaim Kisles, Berl Luria and others were of a very high cultural level and all these 'new theories' were not foreign to them. On the contrary, they devoted to all these Marxist theories with their Babel (Isaac Babel) and Kautzkian (Karl Kautzky, Socialist leader and theoretician) commentaries, that same Talmudic acuteness. But what was foreign to them was the strange 'non Jewish' behavior of the 'new comers'. Not only could they not wield weapons and long knives which the 'newcomers' used, but they could not see others carrying them and sometime using them against their own friends.

The boldness of the 'newcomers' grew from day to day. Sometime they would suddenly invade the beis medrash, between the afternoon and evening service, when the place was full and sit armed by the entrances and exits so that no one of those present could leave. The regular attendants were forced to sit trembling, listening to the hour-long agitation against the Russian Czar and Radzyn bourgeoisie. These frequent 'visits' to the beis medrash finally had their effect and the public avoided attending services because they were afraid of the place being attacked by the Russian police and the Cossacks who began to show interest in the socialist activities.

Like a storm-tossed wave, the revolution began spreading and enveloping larger and newer sections of the population. Almost all the working youth were drawn into this revolutionary activity which was led by the students who had come back to Radzyn from other places of study. The beis medrash and its courtyard became too small to contain this wave and it poured out into the streets. Once a week there was a meeting on the 'bourse'. The 'bourses' were on Kozia and Kotlarska Streets. The young boys and girls would stroll from time to time and shout 'Forward Nikolai'. Quite often as a result of these outbursts, a group of Cossack horsemen would come galloping up and with their shining swords and disperse the demonstration. In a few minutes the 'bourse' was emptied and doors and windows were locked, resulting in some broken widows and wounded people. Of course this did not prevent the people gathering there the following week and shouting the same slogan.

On a hot summer's day in 1907 or 1908 a religious pilgrimage to Czermierniki (about 12 kilometers from Radzyn) took place which was attended by many thousands of peasants and tenants. A group of Radzyn socialist youth, led by Leibel Barver's son, went there to stir up the participants to revolt against their landlords. Their agitation achieved immediate results. On their way back from Czermierniki, the selfsame tenants, to whom they had wanted to bring freedom and joy, met them in the forest. The latter, having been incited by their landlords, killed two of the agitators, among them Leibel Barver's son. It also caused a small pogrom in Czermierniki and agitation for a boycott of the Jews.

4. The Zionist Movement

The campaign of suppression instituted by the Czarist provincial governors (satraps) and led by the 'Black Hundreds' who caused rivers of blood to run in the Russian Revolution, had an effect on the Radzyn socialist movement. The activities, which had begun with great impetus, almost came to a standstill. The small number of true revolutionaries went underground and back to whispering to each other in the beis medrash. In their place, there appeared new faces of a very different age and appearance. Sermonizers, wealthy merchants who did not have the courage to come out openly, replaced the agitators. Instead they preached in narrow circles of rich households, such as that of Akiva Rubinstein and my uncle Yehoshua Lichtenstein, where they were invited to speak to the local intelligentsia. One of these speakers was the well known banker, from Mezerich, S.B. Mintz (the grandfather of the present Polish Finance Minister Hilary Mintz), who would, over a glass of tea, challenge the intelligentsia to place itself at the head of broadened Zionist activity. He asked them not to be satisfied with only buying the shekel, (a fee which entitled one to vote in the elections to the Zionist Congress) or buying shares in the Anglo-Palestine Bank and feeling that thereby they had fulfilled their debt to the Jewish people. He urged them to go down to the people and initiate a great campaign for Jewish National enlightenment.

Not only were these new speakers different from those Bundist speakers, but the tone and content were different. That of the Bundists was filled with venom and malice aimed not only far away toward the Czar and his hirelings, but also against the local Radzyn Jewish 'bourgeoisie' (dealers in bread and herring). They were pictured as blood suckers and parasites of the proletariat and the laboring classes thereby causing a rift and introducing hate in the Jewish community to the point where the expression 'klal Yisroel' (The Jewish Community) became an expression of disgrace. These new speakers came in the name of klal Yisroel, pointing to the Jew hatred of the surrounding population that did not differentiate between rich and poor or between proletarian and bourgeois Jews and calling for ahavat yisroel (Love of Israel).

Today from the perspective of a few decades, it is not clear to me why the speakers who stood firmly with two feet on the soil of Jewish national and religious preaching did not also use the positive side of the Jewish national home in their arguments. They did not mention its own indigenous Jewish culture, the tradition of the use of the Hebrew language which was not possible in the Diaspora, but only concentrated on the negative side of the diaspora, "shlilat ha'Galut".

* * * * *

At that time, Zionist agitation, which was utopian in character, did not and could not have the desired effect on the cold blooded, sober, comfortable class which was involved head and shoulders with the problem of earning a living. (Only a small group were 'infected' by the Zionist 'fantasizers'. Among them, I remember were Yehoshua Lichtenstein, Shimon Kleinboim, Akiva Rubinstein,

Shaul- Henich Rosenwald, Avremeleh Wolf, Yankele Kantor, Avraham Greenberg, Yehuda Blechovitz, Shimon Kupietz, Chanale Adelman, Eli Tennenboim, Nochuniah Ackerman, Alter Blechovitz, Mendel Einbinder, etc.) It did however, have a deciding effect on the organization of the Jewish community, first from the economic side which was accompanied by national-cultural activities. Thanks to this national consciousness with which they were infected by the Zionist fantasizers on one hand, and the increased agitation for an anti-Jewish boycott on the other, an intensive self–defense action was initiated. One of its first expressions was the founding of a credit union at the head of which stood the above mentioned Zionists. The following played an especially important role in this activity: Yehoshua Lichtenstein, Shimon Kleinboim, Shaul- Henich Rosenwald, and Yankele Kantor, who was its director for many years. The credit union had an undeniable and almost immeasurable effect on the economic condition of the petty businessmen and artisans who otherwise would have reached rock bottom as a result of the enhanced boycott agitation that was augmented by the newly founded consumer coops which operated under the slogan of 'Poles! Buy Polish!' This drew the peasants away from the Jewish businesses and artisans. It was only thanks to the help from the Credit Union that these enterprises managed to stay on their feet. As a result the Credit Union also became, in a spiritual sense, the center of Jewish Radzyn. It became the backbone of social life, but even more, it became a holiday in the gray daily life of the small and indigent shtetl. Every Jew put on his finest garments to go to his Credit Union. There he felt himself safer and stronger, not alone but part of the new Judaism. Was that because of the partially revealed new light called Jewish National Emancipation?

* * * * *

The Zionist movement had a great effect on the organization of the social and economic life of the older generation. For us the younger generation, its effect was on the national-cultural level. The first lending library for Jewish literature was opened. Yehoshua Lichtenstein carried out this pioneering work with the help of Gittel Rubinstein, and Esther Lichtenstein. Looking back, I find it hard to understand from where they got the first books. Most likely from Akiva Rubenstein's library which had many thousands of volumes, most of which were in Hebrew. Just as the Credit Union was the meeting place of the members of the older generation, the library was the meeting place of the younger one. Interestingly enough, despite the differences in class and conviction, the youth got along well with each other and saw nothing wrong with this mixture.

5. The Beis Medrash Boys

The only exceptions to the above were we the students from the beis medrash for whom it was dangerous not only to enter the library but even to walk down the street where the library was located. But despite all this, the books from the library somehow found their way to us. Quite often there were heated arguments and differences of opinion about the true meaning of a story by Peretz or of an essay from 'Al Parshat Drachim' (On the Parting of the Ways) by Achad Haam. At that time the Beis Medrash Boys were: Abba and Yoseph Danielak, Yankel Blachavits, Kalman and Chuneh Roisenboim, Yehoshua Toibman, Henich Berman, Laizer Boruch the son of Hersh, Yekutiel Kalinka, Yechiel Katzenelenbogen, Henich and Moshe-Yitchak Gliksberg, Hershel Koppelman, Uziel Weisman, Yona Zigelman, Yechezkel Hauptman, Moshe Appeloig, Mottel Falshspan, and many others.

In addition to the 'genuine' Beis Medrash Boys, there was a group of permanent guests who, to tell the truth, never opened a Gomorra, (Part of the Talmud with comments on the Mishnah) but who were present there as often as the 'genuine' ones. Among the outstanding ones were: Yechezkele Greenblatt the leader of the 'Bund' who felt more at home spending the day among the Beis Medrash Boys than in the his party's headquarters where he spent the evening. Then there was Avremele Zilberberg who was older and was a real 'politician' who could recite all the news that appeared in the newspaper without missing a letter. It was a great pleasure to carry on a political discussion with him.

* * * * *

'All of Israel is responsible for the behavior of every single individual.' This applied even more so to us the Beis Medrash Youth. It was sufficient that one of us was caught committing such a 'cardinal sin' such as going for a walk at night with a girl, for all of us to suffer severely. It took very little for the appellation Beis Medrash Boy to become a synonym for a term of contempt. One such story remains in my memory. One morning, when I arrived at the beis medrash, I saw that the whole place was in the midst of a great commotion. The worshippers were divided up into dozens of small groups from which loud and excited voices could be heard. On drawing closer to such a circle I heard of the terrible transgression which had been committed. A Beth Medrash Boy had been caught strolling with a girl at the edge of the town. Yoel Isaac, the coachman, shouted out, "God helped me that there is no 'Smedrash Boy in my family."

In the gallery of beis medrash personalities it is worth mentioning some from the older generation who had some influence on us: Yaakov –Moshe and Yehoshua Kupietz and Levi Yudel Shamesh's. Despite their age they remained 'Boys' in the beis medrash. They stood out in their religious studies and were very cynical in their general orientation and laughed at everything and everyone, including themselves. They caused us young ones to adopt a critical view on many accepted truths and conventions.

There were two other boys who made a great impression on us but in different directions, in the direction of striving for education and entering the wide world. They were Berl Leib Appeloig, who through self study was accepted in Vevelberg's School in Warsaw and came to Radzyn dressed in the school uniform. He served as an example to us as to how far one can get by one's own efforts. Then there was Shlomo Tzucker who came to the shtetl with credentials from a literary journalistic organization in his pocket and a bundle of poems and novels in his briefcase. After his arrival an 'epidemic' of writers and poets broke out in our shtetl, led by Yosef Danilak.

6. The First World War

Dark heavy clouds covered the clear blue Radzyn skies at the end of the summer days of 1914. Alarming reports about the approach of a worldwide catastrophe began to appear in the newspapers. On the already darkened faces Radzyn Jews there appeared new wrinkles together with a frightened look in their eyes. Suddenly, wailing was heard from the houses where the man of the house or one of the children had received an order to report for military service either in the reserves or 'red cards' (emergency call up to the Polish army). To this day there remains indelibly inscribed in my memory that tragic end of the summer's night when all those eligible for military service gathered in the beis medrash to recite Psalms in public. The beis medrash as well as the women's gallery overflowed. Blond Artshe, who was himself a reservist, served as cantor. The wailing of the men broke the hearts of the women and every few minutes another newly fainted woman was carried out. The spasmodic cries and wails of the women and the quiet crying of the men combined to create a concert of lamentations that deprived me of sleep for many months.

Tragic days began then for all of Radzyn's inhabitants. The first sign of the war was the appearance of refugees. On one cold fall day they started appearing ragged, naked, dirty Jews, some on carts and some on foot. (The trains did not carry civilians.) They were men, women and children that were accused by military intelligence of being possible spies for those great friends of the Jews, the Germans. They were Jews from Pakshevnitze. Naturally these new guests activated the town. Committees were set up to care for the homeless. Most of them were quartered in all three stories of the beis medrash, in the almshouse behind the beis medrash, in the beis medrash itself and also in the women's gallery, in the corridor, in the Rabbi's Beis Hamedrash and in all the Chassidic prayer huts. This was a special pleasure for us, the young people. First it created a sphere of activity for us (this was new for the Radzyn youth) and in addition augmented our numbers especially with members of the female sex. This social-philanthropic activity as well as the growth in the number of young people created the need and the possibility of cultural-social activities for the youth that were often carried out in private homes.

This idyllic situation did not last long. The front lines began to move closer and closer and with them came the terrible tidings. Here the whole Jewish population was driven out in a matter of hours. There the Cossacks' 'enjoyed' themselves at the expense of Jewish women and property. Here a rabbi who prayed on his balcony was declared a spy, who was trying to send signs to the enemy, was court-martialed on the spot and sentenced to be hanged. There the Jewish leaders of the shtetl were taken away to serve as hostages. Radzyn began to sink into darkness and poverty. No one dared to move and with trepidation awaited the unknown future.

The municipal Gymnasium (high school)

7. In the Year 1915

On a dismal fall morning individual groups of German soldiers appeared. The Jewish inhabitants immediately hid in their homes, closed their businesses and nailed shut the shutters. From time to time the sounds of cries for help could be heard from those houses that the military had 'visited'. A larger group of infantrymen, who were to be stationed in the town arrived around noon headed by the town commander. Having gained experience from other towns, the Jewish leaders immediately called a meeting of citizens at the Rabbi's house. On the spot they collected a sizeable sum, from all the well to do citizens, to be given as a 'gift' to the commander, so that he would take the Jews under his protection. This practical approach saved the town from large-scale pogroms and robberies (which were almost daily occurrences in the neighboring shtetls). It did not prevent smaller scale attacks that were more episodic and 'dry', that is, bloodless attacks. To be historically correct it must be added that Radzyn's getting off safely should not be accredited only to these bribes. To them should be added the brave and bold behavior of the ordinary Radzyners, with the Koptshak family (a family of coachmen and porters) in the lead, who did not hide at the appearance of the attackers but ran to oppose them. I remember a case where the Radzyner Koptchakes disarmed an attacker, took his sword and marched him to the town commander.

* * * * *

According to the rule that "bad luck lasts only four weeks" life in the shtetl quickly returned to more or less normalcy. People got used to living without access to the railroad. The only connection to the outer world was via Yentle's 'Line' to Mezerich and Yoel Isaac's to Lukov. People got used to the police imposed curfew that permitted movement in the streets only till seven in the evening. This interfered with social life that usually took place in the evenings. The young people found a way to avoid the eyes of the military patrols by sneaking around through the labyrinth of small back streets. This 'normal' way of life lasted for a few months during the summer of 1915. Then on one clear bright morning there suddenly appeared masses of soldiers from different services. An order was given to free the castle for the Russian General Staff. This was after the great breakthrough of the Central Powers on the Russian Pshemishyl Front. With the appearance of the General Staff the task of 'defending ' Radzyn was taken away from the local commander. A great fear overcame the Jewish population that was well acquainted with the hostile attitude to the Jewish population. Off the head of the General Staff, Nikolai Nicoliawitz, the Czar's uncle, the echoes of the black terror reverberated anew. The shutters were kept shut all day long. Most people stayed in their homes. Only a few ventured out running through the streets and looking to all sides to see if there were any soldiers. Rumors spread that expulsion was imminent. The young people were afraid to get together since any illegal gathering could be considered, by the Russians, as espionage and could end in death. Individual refugees from the small towns in the vicinity began to appear in Radzyn. Most of them were from among the richer and more prominent citizens who were in danger of being taken as hostages. Reb Shmuel Chaim Landau, of blessed memory (the founder and ideologue of the Poele Mizrachi organization, Religious- Zionists Workers) hid out in our house after fleeing from Tzmernick. This situation lasted for about two weeks until one morning it became clear that the whole Russian army had withdrawn quickly. It was our luck that they did not have enough time to close accounts with the internal 'enemies', the Jews. The Jewish population breathed a little more freely. However the actual danger was even greater since we found ourselves in no-man's land, without any protection. There were individual soldiers who stayed behind for the purpose of robbery and murder and could slaughter all the inhabitants. Immediately a secret self defense group, consisting of all those who knew how to use weapons, was formed and took up guard posts all over the town. The arms were purchased from the retreating Russian soldiers.

8. The Austro-German Occupation

"I should only live to see the Messiah the way that I have just seen an Austrian patrol!" shouted the messenger who came in from the street after he had left his hiding place to take a look at what was happening outside. In a few minutes the entire Jewish population was out in the street. There was a look of excitement on all the faces. Some of them where successful in capturing a lingering Cossack and dragging him to the schoolyard, trying him and carrying out the verdict. At about eight in the morning the first soldiers of the Regular Austrian Army appeared. The whole town lined up on the sidewalks on both sides of Ostrovietska Street, down which the troops marched. The local population greeted them with great joy and pelted the triumphant army with flowers. Special joy and pride gripped us when a Jewish officer approached, and speaking to us in pure Yiddish greeted us saying: "Jews! You have been rescued because our Royal Highness Franz Yosef is a friend of the Jews." These words, spoken by a Jewish officer, the likes of which we had never seen in the Russian Army, caused us to shed tears of joy.

* * * * *

The shtetl quickly returned to an almost normal life style. However, because of the proximity of the front, certain military statutes remained in force. The railroad was closed down. Many Jewish officers were billeted in the Jewish homes that increased the feelings of security from pogroms initiated by Poles. Commerce and crafts flourished and with them Jewish social and cultural life.

This 'Garden of Eden' did not last very long and in a short time the Austrians withdrew from Radzyn; their positions were supposed to be taken over by Germans. This created an unstable situation that allowed the Polish Jew- haters to take revenge on the Jews for those 'happy days' during the Austrian occupation.

A citizens committee of Poles and Jews was set up headed by Dr. Shitkovski (one of the few Righteous Gentiles) and a number of other refined Polish citizens. Together they established a citizen's militia, which almost all the Jewish youth joined. The city hall was reorganized, (the Russians had taken the archives with them when they fled) and a new census was carried out. One of the main organizers was Yanush Turkltoib who was its chief secretary for many years until the beginning of Polish independence.

When the Germans settled in the town they found a half-normal city management. They immediately installed one of their military men to be the Town President. It was then, twenty years before Hitler, that we felt the weight of the brutal paw of the German oppressor.

First, the objective circumstances: Because of its geographical location Radzyn found itself on the front line and was considered a military zone. This dictated certain limiting statutes such as a curfew, which at the beginning allowed traffic in the streets only until six in the evening. Entering or leaving the city was only by a special pass that was issued by the county commander. The applicant had to present very important reasons for travelling, making it difficult to obtain such a pass. When it was finally issued it was good only for a limited period of not more than ten days. The movement possibilities in

Radzyn area were as follows: The Bug River marked the boundary between the German and Austrian Occupation Authority. As a result the other side of the Bug River was completely off limits to citizens of Radzyn. The village of Statshek, which is midway on the road between Radzyn and Lukov, was the boundary between the civil and military authority. Passenger traffic only as far as Lukov was semi-legal. There was however, very strict supervision and no items of value, especially foods, were allowed through. This, of course, affected both the economic situation as well as the mood of everyone. A special type of smuggler-merchant came into being who did not bring honor to Jewish merchants and did not raise morale.

In addition to the above mentioned, so-called objective reasons, we Jews had much to complain about for specifically Jewish troubles. The Jews were hard hit by the forced labor. Every few days a large group of German soldiers would go out to round up young Jews for working behind the front lines. They would seal off the streets, conduct a house to house search, dragging out and sending off all those males fit for labor. A certain portion of those sent off disappeared completely. For fear of these sudden ambushes, the young people hid out for weeks in attics and cellars. Some of them would leave town. In addition the German brutes often sought out Jewish bodies old and young, men and women whom they could beat up. I especially remember the terrible picture of a certain German soldier named "Haltz", a tall, heavily built tough nut with sadistic tendencies. When he showed up in the street everyone fled to his hideout. More than one stick was broken over Jewish backs. Naturally, under such circumstances there could be no talk of any social-political Zionist or Socialist matters. The young people passed the time in small groups. We would meet at the Walpes' home or at Yehoshua Lichtenstein's and quite often at the credit union center, which eventually became a central meeting point for the youth.

Despite the very strict censorship imposed by the Germans that did not allow any information from the other side of the front to get through, a few important items did get through. Through them we learned about the formation of the Jewish Legion by Jabotinsky which was fighting on the same side as the British Army and whose aim was to take back Eretz Yisroel from the Turks.

9. The Balfour Declaration and Zionist Activity

The tidings of the Balfour Declaration, in which the British Government recognized the Jewish claim to Palestine as the Jewish National homeland, reached us in November of 1917. It lit up our existence like a brightly-lit meteor on a dark night. As quick as lightning the glad tidings spread throughout the whole town. Jews congratulated and even kissed each other. In the besei medrash the Hallel (Praise) prayer was added to the daily services.

This news had a very unsettling effect on the Jewish population, which became, for the most part, pro Zionist but did not result in any practical

Zionist activity. This for two reasons: firstly, in the time of the German occupation it could be considered treason. Secondly there was no field for practical activities. Immigration was unmentionable and even the collection of funds was impossible since there was no way to transfer the funds. So the love of Zion became purely platonic. However, this period of clear idealistic Zionism which did not lead to any differences of opinion, such as usually result from the translation of ideas into reality, was the golden era for sowing the seeds of the Zionist ideal around which all the Jewish intelligentsia of Radzyn rallied.

As a result of the defeat suffered by the German army at the front and the success of the Russian revolution that caused the abdication of the Czar, the town underwent a change of spirits. The German "heroes" such as Haltz and others holed up in their hiding places so the Jewish youth could move about freely in the streets. In one of the nicest locations a youth association called "Liberation" was founded. The association included nearly all of the youth without reference to class or political point of view. Even we, the former Beis Medrash Boys participated actively in its cultural activities. Its aim was the dissemination among its members of education and culture, uncolored by politics. A few times a week there were readings and discussions, as well as social activities. The lectures and discussions attracted a massive audience of auditors and participants who showed great interest. In the course of these debates two opposite points of view began to crystallize. The majority, which included almost all of the Beis Medrash Boys, was satisfied with emancipating only the Jewish People. The other part, influenced by the Russian Revolution, wished to undertake the emancipation of all mankind. The discussions took on a more bitter format and again created a greater distance between the two sides. The result of this was the formation of and independent Zionist organization called "Tzeire Tzion"(The Young Zionists).

10. Poland Becomes Independent

In November of 1918 the whole population joyfully celebrated the granting of independence to Poland. The streets were inundated in a sea of red and white flags. The windows and balconies were decorated with tapestries and pictures of Pilsudski. But what about the Jews? I don't know how this Polish celebration affected the Jews in other towns. I can only say truthfully that by us in Radzyn there was very little festivity. Looking at it objectively, it would seem that taking into consideration the terrible troubles that were caused by the Nazis' predecessors (the Austro-Germans), that the Jews had now gotten rid of, they should have been happy. However, knowing the mentality and the great 'love" of the Poles for us Jews, we could not have great expectations from their liberation. This caused the great miracle of Polish liberation to awaken in us the desire for our own land and showed us the way of achieving it.

With a total youthful enthusiasm we threw ourselves into Zionist indoctrination. Lectures were held a few times each week at the Tziere Tzion Center and were usually well attended by the youth. There were also some older people among those who visited the center quite frequently, some of whom were later elected to the Central Committee, including Yehuda Blachovitch, Shimon Kupietz, and Shaul Henich Rosenwald. Concurrently with the strengthened Zionist movement, a great movement for the Hebrew language came into being. Evening courses and similar activities took place at the Center. At the secular folk-school that had been founded a few years earlier, there developed almost an entire generation of proud Zionist youth, well rooted in the Hebrew language and culture. Many of them are in Israel today. I often think: Who can know the ways of the Divine Will? What would have happened to many of those who are in Israel today, had it not been for these few Zionist 'fanatics' who founded the Zionist nucleus in Radzyn and thereby created a desire for aliyah (immigration to Palestine)? Had they gone other ways they may have ended up as Hitler's victims.

Jewish School in Radzyn

Standing in the back row: 1) Yitzchak Zigelman. Editor of this "Radzyn Yizkor book"; 2) Hershel Levi, assistant teacher, now in Brazil; 3) Moshe Sneh (Kleinbaum), famous work director in Israel; 4) Yisroel Lichtenstein, teacher and writer, perished in the Warsaw ghetto, hid the ghetto archives in Warsaw together with Miss Ringelblumen. Seated: 5) Yehoshua Freidman; 6) Guta; 7) Anga Turkeltaub; 8) Yakov Blachowitz (all four (5-8) in the second row are teachers in the school).

Yaakov Blachovitch, its director, who devoted all of his energies to it, headed this school. His first assistants were Yehudit Lichtenstein (now Zakalik) Yehoshua Freedman-On, and a newcomer to Radzyn, Leon Rochles.

Radzyn also contributed significantly to the first elections to the legislative Seim (Polish parliament). A council for the elections was set up consisting of all the Zionist groups including the Mizrachi (Religious Zionists). It carried on a lively campaign for the Zionist candidate, the Advocate A. Hartglass. Some of us traveled to the neighboring shtetls to make election speeches. Our efforts were met with success when the Zionist slate got the largest number of votes and Advocate Hartglass, from our group, was elected.

* * * * *

In keeping with the Hertzlian slogan of 'conquering the community', the Tzierei Tzion gave me the task of organizing the Jewish Community on a democratic basis.

At that time, the beginning of Polish national independence, there was still complete chaos in Polish political life in general and in municipal affairs particularly. Jewish community affairs, too, were in a complete state of chaos and anarchy. There was no talk at all of collecting taxes. The only source of income was from the fees levied on kosher slaughter which were in the hands of the slaughterers and who would occasionally 'grant' the rabbi a certain percentage.

We immediately formed an organizational commission, whose function was making preparations for elections for community council and taking over the supervision of ritual slaughter.

[Pages 43-50]

The Synagogue And
The Communal Bais Hamedrash

Abba Danilak (Toronto, Canada)

Far away at the end of the town, near the non-Jewish gardens, stand these two holy places. They stand opposite each other with a vacant lot, called the Synagogue Court, between them. It is used on two important occasions in the lives of the citizens: weddings are performed there as well as eulogies for the recently departed.

They both have high walls but are very different in style and construction. The synagogue has one tall storey with high round windows divided into four-cornered dark panes. It is covered with a roof in the Gothic style of the kind that was built hundreds of years ago and was intended make it look eternal and it was supposed to be the highest wall in the town. However the landowner, that Jew hater, ordered the wall of the church adjoining it to be raised higher, so that the cross would dominate the town.

The entrance to the synagogue was through a dark corridor that was called the 'polish' (Yiddish for antechamber). Deep at the far end stood the table on which the bodies of the deceased were placed and sometimes also the cart used to move them to the cemetery. The Jewish worshipers would go through polish with an inner shiver caused by the presence of these instruments of death. Four steps led down from the polish to the synagogue. The antique interior of the synagogue caught the eye. The ceiling was decorated with all sorts of artistic representations of birds, animals and signs of the zodiac. The holy arc blended with the fine gold leaf of the gilded animals, the many colored fruits and the heavenly figures. The magnificent gold stitching on the curtain on the Holy Ark aroused feelings of wonder and sanctity. Words and sounds other than those of the holy prayers rarely disturbed the holy silence. The places occupied during prayers were called "shtet" (towns) and were passed down from fathers to sons. Despite the fact that many Jews never worshipped in the synagogue the whole town felt that it belonged to all. On the western side, there were small windows covered with curtains that hid the women's balcony, from which groans and crying could occasionally be heard. Under the windows on the left side, there was a small holy arc containing all of the town's invalid Torah scrolls.

Stories about the ghosts of the dead who, at midnight, open the arc and read the scrolls out loud, were handed down from generation to generation and cast gloom on the late night passers by. The synagogue was used only for prayer, and because it was never heated, there were no prayers on frosty mid-winter days. On the dark winter nights the black windows were scary and no one would have dared to visit the synagogue if not for shinning lamps of the

Communal Bais Hamedrash which stood opposite and flooded the synagogue yard with light and warmth.

The Communal Bais Hamedrash was built much later than the synagogue and did not contain any features that would recall antique styles. The white walls were covered with books. The bright lamps illuminated the long tables. The high stove near the door glowed with heat and warmed the frozen hands and faces of porters and butchers who happened there on winter nights. The voice of Torah never ceased here. Young and old bent over heavy, clumsy, Gomorra volumes and other books. They became heated up and twitched with wild movements and broke out into a sad melody, as if through it, they might find the key to the sadness and longings of Jews of all generations. In the evenings crowds of ordinary people occupied the place. At twilight they left the hustle and bustle of this world and, with enthusiasm and feeling, latched onto Mincha and Maariv (afternoon and evening) prayers for spiritual refreshment. On some of the winter evenings the 'ordinary Jews' dominated the Bais Hamedrash. It was customary for itinerant preachers to come to the town. They were representatives of the big Yeshivas in Lithuania who came to collect contributions for the holy institutions. Most of them were Litvaks with sharp tongues, whose preaching was peppered with moralizing and lively with wit and shrewdness; they were the main attraction in town. On those winter evenings ordinary people slammed shut their iron gates and the coachmen would put aside their whips, and would go vigorously to the Bais Hamedrash. The well-to-do shrewd landlords who rarely attended the spectacle wrinkled up their noses and belittled the preacher's teachings. Therefore the ritual slaughterers spread out their arms and took control, not allowing anyone through who did not deposit some coins in bowls that are set up on the table by the glowing oven.

In the Beit Midrash- everyday matters conversation
Painting by Manuel Lichtenstein (New York)

The Bais Hamedrash was packed with people, the noise deafening, and the air thick and smelly. Suddenly there was a knocking on the lectern. Everyone held his breath and stayed glued to his place with all eyes turned to the Holy Ark. The preacher, with a prayer shawl covering his head, moved slowly up the few steps that led to the Holy Arc. He stopped and remained standing for a while looking at the congregation with his penetrating eyes as if trying to decipher what was going on in the minds of these hardworking Jews and what sermon would be most suitable for them. Quickly he sized up his audience and instead of preaching to them about morality and punishment for not being sufficiently observant and keeping Kosher, he chanted the different interpretations of the teachings of 'Our Sages of Blessed Memory', and of the Talmud and fantastic legends. By his great speech-making talent he made the whole weight of the Exile and its burden of troubles and sorrows seem as nothing, just a passing dream. Instead he painted for them a very artistic picture of the ordinary Jew and his reward in the world to come, with the Garden of Eden, the Leviathan and The Wild Ox, and all the other dazzling sights that await him. The audience with open mouths and dreamy eyes, as if in a trance, forgot its poverty and everyday worries. For a moment they were enthralled by the vision of a better, more beautiful world. Under the influence of this delightful description they rubbed their hands in satisfaction while the women in the gallery shed tear after tear often accompanied by groans. To lift their spirits, the clever preacher concluded his sermon with witticisms or a prediction of tomorrow's weather.

The preacher concluded his sermon long ago. The audience left for home in high spirits feeling as if the burden of exile suddenly has become lighter and almost disappeared. Long, long after, these soothing sermons still echoed in the painful hearts of these innocent Jews. They helped to encourage and to strengthen them in their struggle for a livelihood and for a better life in those gray days.

* * * * *

Every morning, at exactly the same time, one meets two Jews hurrying through the streets and alleyways that lead to the Communal Bais Medrash. In front goes a black polished cane with a silver handle that seems to cry out "Make way, the Rabbi is coming." Behind it comes the Rabbi himself. Yudel the Sexton carrying the Rabbi's prayer shawl under his arm accompanies him. They slink along the sides of the houses so as not to meet the gaze of women. The observant Jewesses, on seeing the Rabbi, push the protruding strands of hair under their bonnets and with embarrassment quickly withdraw. The men bow to him and wish him a good day.

He is slightly taller than middle height and has a high forehead with wise penetrating eyes that always show signs of unrest, deep wisdom and understanding. This is the Litvak Rabbi, Chaim Fine. His strange Litvak accent, the only one of its kind in the town, provoked great respect from all the Jews of the town. Even the Chassidim related to him with great respect. They appreciated his scholarship, his morality and worldly knowledge. As befits a Litvak scholar he bore his rabbinical thought with worthiness and tact. In his younger years he already showed signs of becoming a prodigy with a very sharp mind. After finishing the Yeshiva he was immediately lured into becoming the son in law of Reb Zavel the famous educator and rabbinical authority in Warsaw. While the controversy still flared in Radzyn, the local gentry decided, as if to spite the Chassidic Rabbi, to appoint a Litvak to the position of Town Rabbi. Reb Zavel filled the position of Rabbi with his son in law. Twice a year, on Sabbath Tshuvah (the Sabbath between Rosh Hashanah and Yom Kippur) and on Shabbat Hagodol (the Sabbath before Pesach), he delivered his scholarly sermons. He captivated his audience with his cleverness and straightforward approach.

Sabbath in the Shtetl

The arrival of the Sabbath made itself felt in the town on Friday afternoon. The bright young boys, who had just been released from the Cheder (school), made their way home noisily. They shouted with joy and jumped around with pent-up energy like recently released colts. Jews, with felt like-beards and sideburns, appeared in the streets carrying small brooms. They were headed for the steam-bath which was located far away at the end of the town not far

from the non-Jewish gardens. From a distance, one could see the one storey
hut with its high chimney from which poured forth black smoke. The odor of
humid salt water spread in the air and irritated the mouth and nostrils.
Through the open windows one could hardly see the shadows moving around
inside because of the thick gray steam that poured out. However the heated
voices could be heard plainly: "Where is the scoop? Give me the whiskbroom."
Then a suddenly drawn out breath: "A Mechaiyeh!' (What a pleasure!) This
came from the flogged tender red bodies on the highest benches who felt the
pleasure spreading through all of their organs.

Life took on a different degree of sweetness as the Sabbath approached.
The walk back from the baths had a special charm. Red faced, with a twinkle
in their eyes and with soggy beards and sideburns, breathing heavily and
slowly the men marched back ready to greet 'The Sabbath Queen'. With
disheveled hair, and hats askew and wearing greasy aprons, the women
rushed with their clay covered Cholent (Sabbath bean stew) pots, to the
bakery. Suddenly the air was rent by a dull, half hoarse voice, "Jews! Get you
to the synagogue." That was Moshe, the assistant sexton, who stood panting
in the middle of the street. He drew in his breath, raised his head proudly to
the heavens and, acknowledging the importance of his mission, loudly sang
out the final word.

There ensued a wild chase, as if a storm had blown through the town.
Women customers who were caught in the shops by the sound went out
quickly and breathlessly saying as if to themselves, "Goodness, it's Sabbath
already!" and hurried home. The sound of iron shutters and the grating of the
shop doors being slammed shut signaled the end of the week-long hustle and
bustle and the beginning of the Sabbath Peace spreading over the town.
Suddenly, the sound of a wagon followed by that of a horse galloping over the
paved street of the non-Jews was heard. They belonged to a belated wagon
driver pursuing the Sabbath who whipped his wretched horse and disturbed
the oncoming Sabbath. The streets and alleyways were suddenly filled with
Sabbath Jews. Fathers with sons and sons-in-laws were attracted happily to
the Batei Medrash and Shtibles (Small prayer halls) to welcome the Sabbath. A
non-Jew who chanced into the Jewish neighborhood at this hour felt out of
place and disappeared quickly. Jews who saw him shook their heads and
looked at him with pity; even though he was one of God's creatures, he was
incapable of experiencing the pleasures of the Sabbath. Women wearing clean
white bonnets and their Sabbath garments crept out slowly from behind the
houses as if they too wanted to catch a glimpse of the Sabbath Queen who, in
the shadowy twilight, was spreading out her wings over the town, and
obliterating the grim weekday mood. As the shadows deepened and covered
the town in darkness, the glitter of the Sabbath candles shone out more
brightly through the windows. They sparkled like stars along the sides of the
streets adding to the restful Sabbath atmosphere a breath of solemnity and
holiness.

Kozia Street on Saturday

In the silence, the first sounds of ordinary Jews could be heard, rushing home to quench their hunger, on a feast of meat and fish. A little later, proud Chassidim dressed in rustling silk and satin poured forth. With their hands tucked under their belts they walked graciously step by step so as not to walk too quickly. Smart young men with smiling faces and sparks of passion in their eyes walked back and forth dancing and singing to the tune of the Rabbi's melody. The sounds of doors being opened and the grating of bolts could be heard. Jews kissed the Mezuzahs throwing in a 'Happy Sabbath' while not looking at their wives, who, as befits Jewish modesty, blushed and lowered their eyes to the floor. They paced back and forth in the small study rooms while singing out the well-known Shalom Aleichem (A Sabbath hymn) melody. Soon the sounds of dull, half-hoarse, voices were joined by those of young shrieking ones. The thousand year old Jewish sorrow found its expression in these Sabbath melodies. Their reverential tones suddenly changed into songs of joy, hope and belief in the eternity of Israel. The melodies of pain and joy spread out over the whole town reaching the outermost fields and woods and maybe from there reaching directly to The Heavenly Throne.

As soon as the day broke, the wagon drivers and porters, wearing cloth hats and greasy caftans and with prayer shawls under their arms, streamed toward the Tailors Synagogue next to the Community Bais Hamedrash. They quickly joined the babble of the prayers and hurried on in an exalted mood to the tavern to make a Kiddush in honor of the Sabbath. They looked with contempt at the well-to-do and well-rested homeowners who marched majestically to the Sabbath prayers in The Synagogue. Women, dressed for the Sabbath, with shinning earrings and pearls around their necks and thick prayer books under their arms and with bashfull looks, strolled down the side streets so as not to confront strange men. Silently, they made their way to the Women's Balcony. The prayers and hymns from below mingled with the pleading and crying of the women from above, together pushed their way through the windows to rise up to the heavens. The Jews, having conversed with the Almighty through the incomprehensible prayers, felt as if a heavy burden had been removed from their hearts and sang out "A Good Sabbath" before hurrying home. There the fragrant, tasty Cholent (traditional Sabbath stews) awaited them.

Warsaw Street

After the Sabbath nap the courtyard around the palace came to life. This was because the ordinary Jews strolled with their wives for hours under the trees. They strode silently down the side streets, cracked seeds, and enjoyed God's world and the Sabbath rest. Toward evening the Jewish aristocracy appeared at the courtyard. Their conversations were of a higher level. Words and phrases that the ordinary Jews did not understand rang through the air so they left the place respectfully.

The young people had their romantic strolls on the highway that led to the road to Chmerniki. Young boys with passionate gleams in their eyes and young buxom girls, their faces feigning modesty, strolled on separate paths. First they cast sidelong passionate glances at each other covering up their turbulent young blood with dart like biting words. Slowly they drew closer, one hand touched another and, glowing with overflowing emotion, they silently snuggled up one to another, the beating of their hearts replacing the words. Intoxicated by the rays of twilight that radiated between the fields and woods they seemed to be swallowed up by the evening shadows into a very unreal world. The lights that suddenly glittered in the windows of Jewish houses bring them back to reality. The twinkling of the flames reminded them that their mothers have finished reciting "God of Abraham" and the Sabbath Queen has already left the city and the weekday atmosphere has stolen in. The young people go back their separate ways to the town with a gnawing longing for the Sabbath day.

What Was...

Tales from Radzyn

Yaakov Green (New York)

Like most Jewish Shtetls, Radzyn did not have any industry. People earned their livelihood from cultivating fields and gardens. Jews were mostly shoemakers, tailors, old clothes dealers, watchmakers, tinsmiths, hatmakers, draymen and peddlers who went on foot from village to village. It is clear that for young people there was nothing to do. Therefore they went to the big cities such as Warsaw, Lodz, etc. to learn a trade or acquire some other occupation. Girls became servants or worked as seamstresses.

Twice a year, on Passover and Succoth, they would come home all dressed up and would be enviously admired. Not every one of us could have new clothes for the holidays. Only a few tailors like Yoresh, Yudel Moishe Mates (Kolenko) and hatmakers such as Yankel and Ephraim who employed workers and earned a good living could afford new garments. They worked from early morning to late at night and often on Thursday through the night. They started again on Saturday evening right after Havdalah (the ceremony marking the end of the Sabbath).

To learn a trade in Radzyn, one had to work as an unpaid apprentice for three years. After that one received a few Gulden a week. It was no wonder then, that many preferred going to Warsaw where they earned more. Therefore the shtetl did not grow and so there were no new places of employment.

Making a living brought with it throat cutting competition. Many times the Kopchakes (a family of coachmen) fought furiously with other coachmen over passengers. Among the shopkeepers too, there were no lack of informers and denunciations to the authorities as well as other quarrels. I remember that one Leibush Boruch set fire to the grocery store near him owned by his widowed sister-in-law. Her eighteen-year-old son was burned to death. Later this same Leibush Boruch went to America (Detroit) where he tried to pass as some sort of a Rabbi. At that time there were not many Radzyners in Detroit and he would have been able get away with this deception for a long time if it had not been for Itshe-Meir from Sladowitz. He recognized this fellow and revealed everything that Leibush Boruch had done in Radzyn and so had him removed from the pulpit.

———

Sour pickles were a commodity in Radzyn. The vegetable growers bought up the herring barrels, soaked them and packed them with pickles which they shipped to Warsaw and other big cities in Poland. The Radzyn onions too had a good reputation. There were some that weighed half pound or more. These too were shipped all over.

———

The Koptshakes carried passengers as well as freight, sugar, herring kerosene, etc. for the storekeepers. But their main source of income was from the Rebbe, carrying the Chassidim to him for the holidays. This was easier work and generated more income. One day a rumor spread that the Rebbe was moving to Mezeritch. There was uproar in the shtetl and the Koptchakes screamed that blood would flow if the Rebbe left. He did not leave.

The Rebbe's Court was the source of additional income for many Radzyners. When the Chassidim came for the holidays, those that lived near the Rebbe's Court, such as Leibel Toker and others, would convert their homes into hostels. If there was a shortage of pillows they would rent some from poor people living further away paying fifteen kopecks as rental fee. This way the poor people would sleep during the holidays on a 'hard bed' but would earn some added income.

––––––

There were also fishermen such as Moishe Zelig, Chaim Shimon, and Dovidl Gradwitzer. The richer homeowners would buy pike, bream and small fish. The poorer people would have to make do with dace (a fresh water fish) threescore to the pound and so their gefilte fish had a darker color. However they still knew that they were at the Sabbath table and sang "Meat and fish".

The Tsholent (Sabbath stew) was an ancient tradition. The angel would insure its success. It was placed in the baker's oven together with the Sabbath tea. The Kugel (a kind of pudding) of noodles or of rice was delightful. I remember that after the great Friday night fire of 1898, when all houses from Hershel Shachar's house up to the salty well burnt down. There was nothing left to eat after the Saturday morning prayers for those whose houses had burnt. Then someone remembered that the ovens remained unharmed. They took out the Tsholent and there was enough to eat!

––––––

After the Saturday afternoon nap we would go to the Small Bais Medresh (House of Learning) to hear Yoske Shaya Dovid and the black Rochelle's son-in-law, preach about the weekly Torah portion. Then we felt like real Jews. The more erudite met with Reb Simcha Tiles to study a page of the Gomorrah. (Part of the Talmud that comments on the Mishnah) The ordinary craftsmen met on Saturday afternoon at Yudel-Mish- Motel's and amused themselves around a barrel of beer.

––––––

At the beginning of the century, Radzyn too was affected by the appearance of the Bund (Jewish Worker's Party) and other Jewish ¥e shtetl so that even religious Jews allowed their children go abroad rather then have them perish at home, God forbid.

––––––

There almost was a pogrom in Radzyn about that time which was when they were building the railroad to the town. Suddenly one Friday night, a gang of drunken Russians, who were laying the tracks, started to overturn stalls in the market as a prelude for a pogrom. Second hand clothing dealers such as the Fartigs and others went out to meet them with sharpened clothes hangers and drove them out of the town.

It happened quite often that young peasants came into town to pick fights and beat up some Jews. They were met by the Vashners, Mendel and Pinchas, as well as some of the Koptchakes and later the Kelbas and others who saved the shtetl.

———

The story of the great controversy between Reb Moishe-Chaim Feigles and Gershon-Hanoch about the Tcheles (azure) Tzitzes (fringes of the prayer shawl) which the latter had introduced among his Chassidim, was often repeated in Radzyn. In the Community Bais Medrash they ripped off the Tcheles Tzitzes from the prayer shawls of anyone who dared wear them. Yoske Shyeh -Dovids a, scholarly Jew. , printed up a booklet attacking the Tcheles and proving by 'signs and wonders' that after the destruction of the Second Temple when animal sacrifice, Shmitah (fallow year) and the like were abandoned, the Tcheles too was annulled. This caused quite a clamor in the shtetl. When Reb Gershon Henach passed away his son Reb Mordecai Yosef became the Radzyner Rebbe. When the new Rabbi Reb Chaim Fine arrived, both sides made peace living together and joining forces to root out the heretics.

———

There were plenty of those. A 'modern' teacher called Shiyeh showed up in the shtetl. He was from Mezerich (Miedzyrzec) although his wife was from Radzyn. He taught Hebrew by the 'new method' and the boys knew Hebrew after a short time. He also taught them to sing Hebrew songs while he was out walking with them. One time, it was on Lag Ba'omer (a festival), Shiyeh went walking with his boys on the Visnicz Highway while singing Songs of Zion. The Rebbe Reb Mordecai-Yosef passed by and heard them singing Hebrew songs. He went and told the Rabbi who sent his Shamash (caretaker) to find out from which Siddur (prayer book) Shiyeh took the songs which the Rebbe had heard. Don't ask what happened when it turned out that the songs did not come from a Siddur at all but from a 'living language' book with pictures of a table and a chair etc. The Rebbe went to the parents and ordered them to immediately take their children away from Shiyeh the Teacher so as to save the town from the danger of heresy and apostasy.

The poor teacher was forced to leave the shtetl and went to Sedlitz (Siedlce)- where there were more Zionists. Five years later I met him together with another teacher from Radzyn, Henechel Areshtant's brother. They were both teaching Hebrew by the 'new methods'.

Only 'kosher' teachers such as Shloimele Mekeh, Yossel Glantz, Lozer Melamed, Itshe and Mendel Koones and others were left in Radzyn. The 'great wisdom' that they instilled in their pupils can be seen to this day.

There was however no shortage of atheists .By the river in Radzyn there lived a Jew called Yossel Midlarnik (the soap maker) who wanted to make a

Mikveh (ritual bath) with real fresh water without the odors that arose from the communal Mikveh. The Rabbi did not want to certify the kashruth of this 'modern' mikveh. Midlarnick had no choice but to sell the boiler to Pesach Greenblatt from Mezeritch, and Radzyn was saved from heresy and continued on its tried and true way.

Superstition was rampant. For treating patients they went all the way to Kilembrod to the 'sorcerer'. They told a story about Mashke Zelikovs who cut of the hand of a dead child so that with the help of this 'amulet' they could rob someone without being caught. Feival Yisroel Moishe's mother, wanting to bury a stillborn child tripped over another grave, fell, and came home sick. In the "second cholera" (epidemic) the prescribed remedy was to set three kugel pots filled with water in the window and to write the letter 'tof' (the last letter of the Hebrew alphabet) on each one of them.

Wolf's teeth and rabbit's mouths where hung as charms around every child's neck. That this was not very sanitary can be seen from the fact that only one woman did not have a number of children buried in the cemetery. That woman was called Crazy Sarah'le. Mothers would 'sell' her everything in exchange for a remedy for their children and in addition would bring her a roll on Friday. The children were told to call Sarah'le mother to deceive the angel of death.

That the first readers of "Hatzfirah" (the first Hebrew newspaper published in Poland) and other such newspapers had to do so secretly. It is interesting to note that later, Reb Yoske Shiyah Dovid's himself, borrowed these abominations, read them in secret, and returned them. It was also rumored that Avraham Zalman Michel's was caught in the act.

Apparently progress was unstoppable. Shiyeh Mlamed had been forced leave Radzyn because he taught Modern Hebrew and love of Zion. Later Laizer Beinish, who was also from Mezeritch came to the shtetl and began to replant Zionism anew.

[Page 57]

Radzyn Characters

Mendel Goldwasser (Cambridge, U.S.A)

1. Eliyahu-Aaron, The Simchat Torah General

His name was Eliyahu –Aaron but everyone called him Eliorke. When I met him- I was then a child of about six- he was already old, but still tall straight and well built, with a lovely patriarchal beard and grey eyebrows. This tall, handsome, powerful Jew was an institution in Radzyn. Whenever anyone got sick, even in the middle of the night, he was the first one we ran to for help, banging on his door and shouting "Reb Eliorke my child is 'going' (or my husband)". Eliorke would get up immediately and would say good naturedly: "What are you yelling about? I'll come right over and see." Eliyahu-Aaron would come in to the house, feel the patient's forehead ,ask him to stick out his tongue and tell him to take castor oil. Having taken a load off the family's, he would some times recommend that they call the feldsher (barber-surgeon) in the morning and maybe even the doctor himself. However in every case he would drop in every day to observe the patient's and to help as much as possible. If the patient was the family breadwinner he made sure the family was provided for.

Eliyahu-Aaron came into our house every day, because my father, who was paralyzed, lay in bed all the time unable to turn over by himself. Eliyorke spent a few hours every day in our house, picking up my father, washing him, changing his clothes, making him comfortable and laying him down again, all the time reassuring him that he would recover.

But that was not the end of Elyorke's activities. He had an additional responsibility. A regiment of soldiers was stationed in Radzyn (Radzyn was the district center) among them many Jews. It was his responsibility to see to it that they got leave on the holidays and that they have what to eat on those days. He set quotas for the number soldiers each of the homeowners would take. This bothered some of the wealthy people, but they did not dare complain to Eliorke. If after all his efforts there were still some soldiers left without a place to eat, he would say: "Don't worry, you can all come to my house" There was always a sack of potatoes there. The soldiers ate together with Eliyorke, sang songs and even danced.

What did Elyorke live from? From that store which stood in a passageway near the bridge that looked out on the market, the courtyard, the church and Warsaw Street. Where Yudel the sexton would cry out on Friday evening in his high pitched and drawn out voice: "Time to go to the synagogue". Elyorke had long ago turned the store over to his children and lived with his wife in a corner house in which the beds were arranged like the Hebrew letter Daled. It had belonged to Elyorke's family for many generations. To make a living, he went to a market or a fair, bought a calf and earned a few Gulden for the week.

Only on Simchat Torah evening before the Hakafot was this old ruin and the surrounding streets lit up by candles and torches. All the Jewish soldiers were decked out in their finest uniforms, their buttons gleaming. They dressed Elyorke in a general's uniform with a general's hat and they paraded him to the synagogue with candles and torches. The streets echoed with the soldier's chants: "Long live our general Gorki Hu-rr-ah!"

In the synagogue Elyorke prayed in front of the ark and led the Hakafot. It was an unforgettable sight to see the soldiers marching around the platform with Torah scrolls in their arms led by a tall, attractive, patriarchal general who sang out "Thou who helpest the poor, save us," (from the Hakafot of Simchat Torah.)

[Page 58]

2. Yechiel Chana's and Reb Yoel-Yosef

When I was a little boy, Reb Yoel-Yosef was already an old man. He was the greatest scholar in Radzyn. He was a teacher but had only two or three students from whom he made his living. Of course his students came from the wealthiest families. In addition to being a great scholar, he was also very observant, but he was also an idler and very neglectful. Word had it that when Rabbi Gershon- Henich invited him to his home to discuss Torah he had to remind him to blow his nose. On the coldest of Saturday mornings he went to the cold ritual bath and was careful not to commit any of the transgressions connected with immersion. On Rosh Hashanah he blew the Shofar (The Ram's horn blown to signal the beginning of the New Year). Of course before that he went to the ritual bath, he studied the Zohar. Only then he mounted the platform with a serious, mournful expression, wearing a white linen robe and his prayer shawl which covered his head. After the end of the prayer, when they got to read the Psalms, he would take the Shofar in hand and blow into it. But it often happened that he got stuck in the middle and could not finish- 'a devil got into the horn' as they say. In such cases, there was no solution but to turn to Yechiel Chana's.

Yechiel Chana's had inherited from Chana the tavern and restaurant. At that time he was middle aged, very attractive with a small blond trim beard. He was always clean and well dressed when he set the table for his landowner customers. Since he was also a good dancer, all the landowners' wives strove to dance with him. It is obvious that he was not observant, since he could not avoid an occasional squeeze and maybe even a sip of unkosher wine. It was also hard to resist tasting a non-kosher morsel from those tables loaded with delicacies. On Saturday he did not go to the unheated ritual bath and did not have to worry about transgressions.

The second market of the town
Painting by Manuel Lichtenstein (New York)

However when Yoel Yosef got stuck and could not continue sounding the Shofar, he gave the horn over to Yechiel. He wiped the horn with a clean handkerchief, brought it up to his lips and without any special effort managed to produce a hundred notes with one breath.

When they asked Yechiel "How is it that by that virtuous Yoel Yosef the devil gets into the Shofar and by you, who is so light headed, the devil has no influence?". He replied: "I have an agreement with the devil. All year I will obey him. In return, on Rosh Hashanah, the devil will obey me and not get into the Shofar".

[Page 60]

3. Itshke the Pig

I very much enjoyed visiting our neighbor Yankel the Coppersmith. I loved to watch how the heat melted the brass in the crucible and turned it into a liquid that was poured into forms and came out as Sabbath candlesticks, menorahs and machine parts.

A couple of times in the year a Jew from Vohin called 'Itshke the Pig' came to visit Yankel the Coppersmith. He would travel around trading in gold, jewelry, rings watches and the like. He looked like Mattiyahu the Hashmonae, tall, slender, with a grey beard and a very alert look. I remember how he used to tell, with great delight, how he had managed to get money from stingy rich families to be used for buying matzoth for the poor.

The rampart road to the castle

What seemed strange to me was that a person with such an unsympathetic name as 'Itshke the Pig' was always spoken of with such great respect. After some inquires, I came to the following conclusion: The whole story began in 1863, when Itshe was a young man but not called 'The Pig'. The Polish revolt to obtain independence from Russia took place at that time. In Vohin the Poles succeeded immediately because the whole Czarist 'might' consisted of ...one patrolman. But as is usual with the Poles, their first act was to start up with the Jews and their first planned action was to slaughter all the Jews. The only way the Jews could be saved was to get word to Radzyn where there was, in addition to police force, an army regiment. However the Poles posted guards on all the roads leading out from of the city to prevent anyone leaving.

What did Itshe do? When night fell, he wrapped himself in a pig's skin, crawled on all four, grunted like a pig until he reached the other side of the town. He entered Radzyn, and a unit of soldiers and policemen was immediately dispatched to Vohin that arrested the leaders of the progrom. From that time on "The Pig" was added to his name and his whole family became know as the "Pig Family". Every year a special feast took place in Vohin where Itshe sat at the head of the table with his family, with the town notables around him and a special "Pig's Scroll" was read.

Vohin and all the surrounding shtetlach were proud of "Itshke The Pig" and the "Pig Feast".

———

[Pages 62-64]

In the holy memory of my loving parents

Bright Figures

Yisroelke List (Ramat Gan)

1. Chaim Shimon Fisher

In our house we heard a lot about my mother's uncle Chaim Shimon. As a young man right after his marriage to Chana Pesseh, when he came to the Kotzk to visit the Rabbi on the Sabbath or the High Holidays, he was always invited by the Rabbi to sit near him. He was also very good with figures. In a few minutes he could do the most difficult calculation on his fingers and taught almost everyone in the family to do the same. But this is only in passing. The most important thing that I wish to tell you about this Radzyner Jew is what I saw and from which I have been unable to free myself all my life.

He was called Chaim Shimon Fisher because he was a fish merchant in the village of Zabialeh about two kilometers from Radzyn. In the warm summer evenings the non-Jewish inhabitants caught fish in the local stream. Actually, he had another occupation in addition to being a dealer in fish. During the summer he would rent, in these very same villages, one or two small orchards, and in the winter, his wife would sell the fruit to the well-to-do Radzyn householders. What was left over she would sell from her stall in the market-place. Despite these two occupations, Chaim Shimon remained impoverished. He had four grown-up daughters the oldest of whom, Tobeh, they barely managed to marry off. Right after the birth of her first child she caught cold and developed breathing problems. When she had an attack, they would bring oxygen and pump it in to her. Only then would her breathing return to normal. It is therefore no wonder that she should be the apple of her parents' eyes.

One very hot summer's day, when Chaim Shimon went to the village to buy some fish, Tobeh had an attack, and before they could get help she passed away. You can imagine what happened then around Chaim Fisher's house. He was living on Kozia St in an arcade belonging to Mordechai Shochet. (Ritual slaughterer). The street was filled with people crowding around the house from where could be heard heart-rending cries accompanied by the quiet sobbing of the crowd.

While people were standing there they suddenly saw in the distance Chaim Shimon coming with a sack of fish on his shoulder. They began to pull back not wanting to be close enough to see how such a terrible tragedy affected the father. What actually happened was quite different. When Chaim Shimon entered the house, Chana Pesseh saw him and began screaming anew in her hoarse voice: "Chaim Shimon bless you. Look at our disaster! Our Tobah is gone, the light of our life has been extinguished in the middle of a bright day". Despite these heartrending cries, Chaim Shimon did not say a word. He just threw down the sack, went over to the corner where there stood a wooden pail filled with water. He took the copper measuring cup that stood there, poured some water over his hands and in a trembling voice said: "God is the only true judge! God gives and God takes away." Then turning to his wife, who was still screaming he said: "Moron, fool what are you screaming about? To whom are you complaining? Don't you know that there are three partners to the human being, the father, the mother and the Holy Spirit?" Then pointing with his bony trembling fingers at dead body of his daughter, he said: "The third partner came and took away his share. Our shares are still here"

2. Yudel The Shamash (Sexton)

He always sat up front by the lectern in the Bais Hamedrash looking into a book. He was a scholar. He made judgments in many cases so that there was no need to go to the Rabbi. He was quiet and modest, dressed both in summer and winter in a thin loose cloak with a shirt collar that was always turned upside down and unbuttoned and with his hand in the wrong sleeve. That is the way he looked on Thursday when he visited the patrons to collect his weekly salary or when he went to invite them to a hearing before the Rabbi. He never hurried and always walked slowly. However, on Friday evening just before the candle lighting time, he would 'fly' through the shtetl. Every time he stopped, he would straighten up his always-bent back and would yell out: "Jews get you to the synagogue". Then the Jewish shopkeepers knew that the week had come to an end. The clanging of sliding bars and closing locks were heard and the flames of the Sabbath candles began to appear in the windows of the shtetl.

In Yudel Shamash's house there were, in addition to his wife Rishe, four grown sons and three daughters none of who ever worked or earned anything. The only breadwinner in the family was Yudel Shamash. It is therefore no wonder that scarcity and need were permanent guests in the house, especially when there were few weddings or other celebrations from which something could be earned. Occasions when there were such celebrations were a holiday in the house, Rishe would open the door and a loaf of ruddy brown rye bread would protrude from under her scarf. On one such day, Rishe quarreled with her older children who ate all the bread and left nothing for Leah'le who was the youngest daughter whom the mother loved very much. Suddenly the door opened and Yudel Shamash came in from the Bais Hamedrash and asked Rishe what all the yelling was about. Rishe replied: "The young ones have swallowed all of the bread, the pigs, and what will Leah'le eat?" Here the tears began to flow from her always red eyes: "Hush, Hush", Yudel calmed his wife and told her good-naturedly: "Rishe don't get excited, don't yell, don't curse the children, they are already grown up, thank God. You may bring out the insolence in them and they will talk against you and you might cause them to transgress the commandment "Honor thy father and mother."

————

[Pages 65-72]

My Radzyn

Mendel Lichtenstein (New York)

For hundreds of years, life flowed peacefully in Radzyn. Jews lived safely and quietly. They married off their children, provided them with a livelihood and practiced the traditional Jewish lifestyle.

I do not know how the city came into being. How can one go back so far in a Shtetl hat has both an old and a new cemetery with old tombstones and two old Ohels? (Structures over the tomb of an important person). Maybe it came into being in a period when the landowner and some of the richer peasants were in need of traders, craftsmen and artisans so they invited them to come there and even set up a town for them. Where else can one see such a huge marketplace with long cast iron entrance gates on both ends and with so many shops in ornamented buildings all having one style of shingled roofs as if they had all been made by one architect? Even the synagogue, which was very old, was built in that style.

Everything is run in the old traditional manner. Every day of the week the marketplace is filled with wagons of peasants containing the produce that they sell. Later they are filled with the commodities such as kerosene, herring and clothing that they buy in the shops. However on Friday the market becomes quiet at midday. Slowly the peasants leave, the market is empty and the weekday retreats from the approaching guest, the Sabbath. The Jews dismantle their stands, the sounds of heavy bars let down over the doors of the closed shops are heard, and a heavenly silence reigns. It may be that in a side street there is a lone Jew. He is running home from the mikveh (ritual bath) so that he will not desecrate the Sabbath. In the houses however, everything is ready for the Sabbath. One can smell the fish and the candelabra are ready for lighting and blessing. When the beadle goes through the streets shouting, "Jews go to the shul (synagogue)" the Sabbath has settled down over the entire shtetl.

The Bais Hamedrash stood right next to the synagogue. It too was of massive size and very tall with large windows in the style of the Holy Temple. What was most beautiful was the external eastern wall that was taller than the roof, and shaped like a crown, and had two huge tablets that could be seen far away in all parts of the shtetl.

Houses in Radzyn
Painting by Manuel Lichtenstein (New York)

The synagogue with its temple like appearance inspired even more respect. It had a mystic holiness that made it into a place where one came only to pray. At other times one was afraid to set foot in it because of the souls of the dead who gathered within. Perhaps the little birds in the nests on the very high roof were really souls.

The Bais Hamedrash was very different. It was a community center where people came, debated, and got excited about various matters. The students stood out with their melodic high-pitched voices as they stood shaking and chanting all day over their Gomorra. They sometimes reached such high tones that it seemed as if one was trying to outdo the other. The Bais Hamedrash was like a giant music box from which the music spread over the surrounding fields through the streets and reached the market place. There were even times when it drowned out the sound of the church bells. This music comforted the Jews. They traded with it, they spoke with it, and it accompanied all of their moods. When it was sad, the melody cried and when the music was spirited it gave them cheer and courage.

However well we portray the shtetl itself, we cannot avoid speaking about the people of Radzyn. The Radzyners not only took from the world but also contributed to it. The town was famous for its students and intellectuals. It had something else, the virtue of hospitality. It is therefore no wonder that Reb Henoch made it his place of residence. Long before him the same thing happened with Shimon Daitsch who was welcomed here as a rabbi. Escaping from persecution in Germany, he came to Poland. He was a rabbi and a great scholar; he dressed stylishly like a German in a frock coat and a top hat and was persecuted and driven from wherever he came to. So he went from town to town until he reached Radzyn and there he stayed .He was welcomed with honor as Rabbi. He so cherished the town that he blessed her that she should not have any fires for a hundred years and in the worst case at least not more than in one house. In my time a fire occurred in two houses. I wondered how that could have happened. I was told that the hundred years must have gone by. For many years the sick and crippled came from faraway towns to visit his Ohel in the cemetery to ask him for forgiveness for the evils and insults that their forefathers caused him. Woe was to him who was cursed by him and happy was he who was blessed by him.

* * * * *

I came into this world in a time of great events and upheavals some were good and some were bad, but they were mostly bad. There was the War with Japan, the programs in Kishenev, Shedlitz and other places, the Revolution of 1905 and the (Mendel) Beilis Trial. All of these events caused me great fear and trembling as I took my first steps into life. Radzyn was so far from the railroad that no one could find her. Her streets were so quiet that at midday she looked deserted. When was there a noise that could be heard elsewhere? The nights were even quieter when the winds died down and the trees stood mute. The inhabitants huddled in their huts, closed the shutters and laid their tired bodies to rest, forgetting their problems of making a living and other worries. Great worldly events do have their echo. Even though Radzyn was far from the war with Japan, there was some connection.

Suddenly, like thunder from out of a clear sky, there is a decree from the Czar ordering all army and emergency service reservists to report for duty that very morning. The whole shtetl was on its feet immediately. The weeping and wailing reached seventh heaven. It also woke me up. I open my eyes and no one is at home. I am drawn to the street and run with the crowd to the market place where there is a group of people surrounded by all the townspeople. They stand there pale, as if crippled and half-dead. Many of them are older Jews with long black and gray beards, who are more suited to being grandfathers. Here they are being taken away from us to be sent off to the war. I am moved when I see their sad looks and their wretched broken wives and children. I will never forget their shrieking and wailing.

* * * * *

The programs, too, reverberated in Radzyn. Fortunately we got away with only a scare. At that time I was a student of Mendel the Moreh Halacha (Religious Judge). One morning I showed up at the Cheder (Boy's Religious School.) and was informed that there is no school! There is a great commotion. The Rabbi and his wife are packing to make a quick get away. They look at me with surprise. Have you not heard that there is going to be a program in the town today? Without delay the Rabbi and his wife are sitting in the wagon together with other Jews. They are fleeing to Kotzk to save their lives. When they got half way all of Kotzk was there. It turned out that the rumor "that there will be a progrom" had reached Kotzk too and the Kotzkers were fleeing to Radzyn. One group looked at the other shamefacedly and without saying a word turned their wagons around and went back home. I did not have the pleasure of a few free days from school.

* * * * *

The "Revolution" was imported into our Shtetl. The young people brought it with them when they came home on the holidays from the big cities. There weren't any bourgeoisie and there was no proletariat here. There was a class of poor people, so they agitated among them. They threw around all sorts of slogans not knowing exactly what they meant. They called meetings in the woods because they were afraid to do so in the streets.

However, the Bais Hamedrash was a very suitable place for such gatherings. It happened that in the middle of the prayers someone would bang on the lectern and one of them would get up and make a speech. Guards who stood by the door and did not let anyone out protected the speaker. If anyone protested he would get a knife in the ribs. Actually no one understood the speakers. Words like absolutism, obscurantism, abdication and democracy did not penetrate their minds.

The youth, most of whom were poor and oppressed, were enthusiastic about the ideals of the revolution. Many of them were ready to sacrifice themselves for it. They went to agitate among the peasants despite the great danger involved. The educated and intelligent ones went to the people and some Jews and the non-Jews extended a brotherly hand. However these meetings did not always end up peacefully. Once, when our young people went to Czmierniki to agitate, the local dark hordes were incited, and they attacked the speakers with scythes and cut two of them to pieces. The victims were Leibel Moishe Mates' son and the brilliant student Mendel Finkelstein.

Rabbi Mordecai Yosef lived in Radzyn in my time. He was a handsome man with a red beard that shone like gold in the sunshine. He had a pleasant face that sparkled with kindness and amiability. Like his father Gershon Henoch, he valued learning and talent. When Israel Tikochinsky made a deck of cards by hand, the Rabbi bought it from him. When Ben Zion Greenboim, a revolutionary and atheist, accompanied by Lozer Firstenberg, went to the Rabbi to ask for a contribution to help those who had been arrested for political activities, he welcomed them politely. He had a long talk with Ben Zion about worldly philosophers and writers, and he complimented him, adding that it would not hurt if he looked into the Jewish books.

The Rabbi also knew me well and often asked me about my painting saying "Paint, paint but not Christian pictures". I once said to him "When the inspired artist draws doesn't he praise God in the same way as by chanting prayers? He did not reply, just shook his head in the affirmative.

* * * * *

Protest of the silence
Painting by Manuel Lichtenstein (New York)

Our group of talented young men all started out in a very auspicious time when the earth seemed bountiful and the atmosphere warm. We sprung up as if over-night. We could have grown and grown if not for World War I. That storm tore us up from the roots. I had just gotten a scholarship of 2000 Rubles to go to Paris to study. Some of the others, too, had similar opportunities. Just when I was about to leave the war broke out. In the end, all of us, with the exception of Nathan Shwalbe, stayed behind in the shtetl. For us, this was a step backward and an obstacle to our development. Under the threat of war and the constant fear of being taken for forced labor, there was no chance of progressing. Later when we got used to the situation and despite the fact that the Germans made life difficult for us, we managed to make the best of whatever cultural autonomy that was allowed.

For a long time Radzyn had a large Yiddish lending library, thanks to which a popular intelligentsia was created that awakened hidden talents among its members. We founded a dramatic club where we presented varied literary works and arranged for lectures. For these events we used the municipal theatre which had been closed for Jews during the Polish and Russian rule despite the fact that it had been built by Jewish money.

A large number of talented people belonged to the group; Nathan Shwalbe a well known Polish and Yiddish journalist, Ben Zion Greenbaum, Shlomo Zuker (Radzynski) a Yiddish writer, Yisroel Tikochinsky a talented painter, his brother Mordecai a humorist, Henoch Applebaum a talented actor and Yoseph Daniliak a lyric poet. Shlomo Weingarten can be added to this list. He was a quiet, many-sided talent, a mathematician, inventor, etcher but he was especially known for his phenomenal memory. Having read a book one time he could repeat every bit of it by heart on the next day. The writer of these lines was also a member of this group. Unfortunately, the Nazis annihilated most of its members. Radzyn was a good nesting place for born talents and important people. It was so in the next generation too.

* * * * *

After the German defeat came the Polish rule with persecution and terror against the Jews. On the first night after they took over, they killed thousands of Jews on the roads and in the villages. In the village of Brave, near Radzyn, they killed a whole family of six. This murder caused great grief to everyone. They became very depressed. On the day of the mass funeral everyone closed their businesses and old and young Jews participated. The large mourning mass gave it the appearance of a giant protest. However, the terror continued. Jews were beaten on the roads, their beards were cut off and in many cases they were thrown out of moving trains. People became discouraged and lived in constant fear of death. There was no one to complain to or where to protest. From every Jews lips there was only one expression "Jews, we are lost. Run away from here..."

* * * * *

I loved my shtetl and also loved Poland. When the time came for my leaving Poland, I did not do so willingly. The situation had reached such a state of affairs that I had to pick up and leave. It was a dark night when I left my shtetl forever. Traveling on the long road to the train the sky suddenly turned red. Someplace there was a conflagration. Tongues of flames flashed across the sky gradually covering a larger area. That told me something. Maybe it was symbolic that in later years the sky would again be red day and night from the flames of the Nazi ovens where our relatives were burnt. I would prefer singing songs in praise for my shtetl and tell more romantic stories about it. However my heart is filled with grief and pain, and I would rather tear my garments, wear sackcloth and ashes and cry and mourn for everyone and everything that we have lost.

[Page 73]

Radzyn Portraits

by Abba Danilak

1. Life Style and Sources of Income

Radzyn did not have any great material wealth. With the exception of a few wealthy Jews, most of the others earned their living from the surrounding peasants who were their only source of livelihood. The craftsmen provided the peasants with clothing and footwear and in return bought their produce, which they shipped to the big city of Warsaw. From there they brought back kerosene, sugar and salt which the peasants needed. The Jews had a very low standard of living. Bread and potatoes for the family were, as they were in all the Polish Shtetls, the basic staples. Clothes were considered a luxury. Despite this, one rarely heard people complain. 'That is the divine will', they would often say in a pious tone, as if to console themselves.

Shops selling all kinds of goods surrounded the most centrally located market place in town on three sides. The fourth side was open to the courtyard of the castle and from there a road led to the train station. From early in the morning until the evening, the peasants from the surrounding area parked their wagons and unhitched their horses there and purchased equipment and other necessities. The shops provided the peasants with everything from a needle to building materials and agricultural machinery.

This source of livelihood created ghettoes within the ghetto. Tailors settled around the market place and formed a tailor's alley. From early morning to late at night the whirring of the Singer sewing machines blended with the sounds of the voices of the young apprentices singing dreamy songs. Here second hand clothing dealers prepared wholesale lots of long jackets and pants for the peasants at the fairs. The shoemakers had their ghetto on the school street. The smell of the peasants' rough leather drifted over the whole street and irritated the nostrils. Through the open windows the sound of the hammering was mixed with the sad sounds of interrupted High Holiday melodies. It was as if the stitchers wanted to sew their own troubles and sadness into these melodies. These hard working Jews were not great scholars, but they never missed a public prayer service. Quite often, between the Mincha (afternoon) and Maariv (evening) prayers, they would sit by the long tables in the Bible Readers Shtibl (hut) and eagerly swallow chapters of the Chumash (Pentateuch) with commentaries by Rashi, or from Ein Yaakov* as they were presented by the Moreh Hora'ah (religious judge) Reb Chaim Asher. He was a short, thin, refined, Jew who lived his life according to the Shulchan Oruch (The 'Set Table'- The Code of Jewish law) and who existed on 'Kav charuvim' (a 'handful of carobs') from one week to another. He was very strict in matters of the dietary laws. The housewives avoided going to him for rulings about kashrut and preferred going to the town rabbi. The latter was more practical, and maybe because the Sabbath was approaching, or for other reasons, he would be more liberal in giving kashrut approval for their chickens and pots. The Bible Readers' Shtibl was their study center and they had great respect for their teacher, Chaim Asher, and worried about guaranteeing his livelihood.

The commercial sector consisted mostly of scholars who had formerly boarded with their in-laws. They boasted about their erudition and had no contact with the everyday hard working Jews. So as not to lower their esteem in the town, they never showed themselves at the Bible Readers Hut.

* Ein Yaakov-a collection of legends from the Talmud collected and interpreted by Rabbi Yaakov Ben Shlomo 1449-1816.

They were mostly grain dealers or owners of small shops. These Jews could often be met in Batai Hamedrash (Houses of Learning) sitting in deep concentration while poring over thick Gomorra volumes, or sitting in circles listening to news from the wide world.

2. The Radzyner Koptchakes

Radzyn is located very close to the border between the Ukraine and Poland, half the way between Brisk, by the Bug River to the east and to the west the nerve center of Poland, Warsaw, by the Visla River. The main roads leading to the Ivangorod military fortress in the south and the famous Fortress of Brisk in the north intersected in the town. For this reason the city of Radzyn long served as a strategic middle point in Polish Russian encounters. The most important battles of the last century between Polish rebels and the Russian Cossacks took place in the surrounding forests. To guard this important strategic point, a Russian Army unit with its horses and artillery stationed behind the town. This created a shtetl within a shtetl and served as a source of income for the local residents.

Even before the arrival of the railroad the town served as the center of the food trade between the Ukraine and western Poland. Whole herds of cows and oxen from the Ukrainian Steppes were driven through the town to the German border. Here in Radzyn they were handed over by their Ukrainian herders, with their white linen shirts hanging out of their pants and straw slippers, to Polish gentiles. In the big house of the Danilak family, which served as a passage way from one main street to another, there stood a giant scale on which the arriving livestock was weighed. From here they were driven directly to the German border. With the arrival of the railroad this source of livelihood disappeared from the town.

The fate of a city can be compared to the fate of a person. The caprice of the Russian engineer, who was responsible for planning the location of railroad lines, determined the fate of the town. The lord of the great fortress of Radzyn was a staunch Polish patriot. He, Shlubowski, so the story goes, refused to properly entertain the dirty Russians. Therefore the engineer had the railroad track laid about four miles from the town through the town of Bedalno so that Radzyn was completely excluded from the railroad map. To get to the city of Radzyn one had to go to the carriage drivers. These Jews had carriages with springs over the wheels and leather roofs that could be raised or lowered at the request of the passengers. Their purpose was to carry passengers back and forth to the railroad. The other wagon drivers, the so-called 'koptchakes', were backward and remained stuck in the past. They had large families and were brave, broad shouldered Jews, good fighters of whom the non- Jews were deathly afraid. There were many occasions when they split open the heads of ' Esau's children' (non-Jews) using the poles from their wagons. There were uneducated liquor swilling people who never spoke, but bellowed like animals. They cursed, but never missed putting on their phylacteries and quite often managed even to squeeze in an afternoon and an evening prayer. The Kronenbergs, with their high, straw bedded wagons covered with white linen covers on wooden poles started out on the long road to the big cities with sacks of grain and flour and came back from there with wagons stacked high with salt, sugar, kerosene and iron.

One met them walking by the side of the Polish roads with their horses and creaking wagons in rainy, stormy and snowy weather. They kept warm by beating their hairy breasts with their muscular hands. Sometime the air was rent by the sound of a whip echoing through the fields and woods as they happily make their way to a roadside inn. The horse and the whip they inherited from their fathers and they bequeathed them in turn to their own flesh and blood.

Therefore on Saturdays and holidays they felt unhappy. They would slink into the Craftsmen's Bible Reading Hut to pray. They knew that their place was by the table near the door. They looked jealousy and enviously at the Jewish craftsmen who sat up front near the fasting-thin body of the Religious Judge swallowing every word that issued forth from his mouth whether it was the interpretation of a certain passage or a tiny bit of moralizing aimed at them. These otherworldly sounds reached back to the furthest table. The dense air and the strange incomprehensible words from the mouth of this holy Jew beclouded their dull minds. Afraid of dozing off, they sneaked out one by one from the holy place. The fresh outside air sharpened their senses. The dejection and inferiority which they had experienced but did not digest, spread through their bodies like a bubbling broth. For a while they considered what they had just experienced and unable to quiet their anger, they went home quickly to their wives.

3. The Hachnasath Kalah Association (Bridal Dowry Fund)

During Jewish celebrations such as weddings, circumcisions and the like there were sometime unusual incidents. In the middle of the celebration the door would fly open and strange looking figures appeared. Wearing green shirts and green hats with green visors, like those worn by the peasants, and with wire masks on their faces, they arranged themselves along the walls. There they stood silently like lead statues, without greeting the celebrants and not even acknowledging the presence of the other guests by a shake of their heads. They stood as if they were waiting for something to happen. Their sudden appearance in the room and their strange conduct did not did not upset anyone. Many of the guests did not even cast a glance at them, as if they were expecting them. Who are they? Why had they come? They plunked down on the table big tin boxes with the large lettering: HACHNASATH KALAH as if to declare to everyone "We have not come as beggars, we have come to collect a debt!" To marry off Jewish daughters, whether they were orphans or only daughters of poor families, was always an acute problem in the old country. A dowry and outfitting the new couple were often the main impediment to consummating the marriage. Official couriers or just ordinary Jews often traveled around in the cities and towns with letters printed on parchment from their hometown Rabbis testifying that they are suffering and needy and have a grown daughter to be married off and that all Jews were obliged to help them.

However in his hometown, such a middle class Jew would, out of embarrassment, rather put on a disguise than stretch out his hand to ask for money for his daughter's dowry. However, since the dowry and support came to considerable sums they constituted a very heavy burden for a poor family that God had blessed with daughters of a marriageable age. Fathers and mothers did not sleep nights, and turned their eyes toward heaven searching for help. How to help the needy quietly and secretly? The hard working craftsmen, those, who belonged to the Bible Readers Shtibl, were the ones that asked this question. It was they, under the direction of Rabbinical Judge Reb Chaim Asher, who formed the Hachnasath Kalah organization.

There were such organizations in many Polish towns. What was unique about the one in Radzyn was that its rules included one stating that both the collection and distribution of the monies be carried out in complete secrecy. This cardinal regulation made it possible for the organization to function normally for a long time. An elected committee of five people decided whom to help and by how much. Any member who dared to reveal this information was immediately expelled from the group. Every member was obliged, when his turn came, to get into a strange costume and go to a celebration to collect money. Since Jews were embarrassed to go collect money and circulate among women, they put strange masks on their faces and stood silently for the whole time so that they would not be recognized.

They did not come only to take money but also to compensate the guests and the bridal family. They injected a degree of solemnity into the celebration. According to an old tradition in the town, every wedding ceremony took place in the synagogue courtyard. The groom and the bride were marched there from their homes accompanied by the sound of music. It was these peculiarly dressed friends with their strange uniforms and blazing torches in their hands that led the parade. Two of these Jews walked in front and two followed behind. In the courtyard they placed themselves around the wedding canopy, and each one stood by one of the poles with a flaming torch in his hand. The crackling flames from the kerosene wicks drove away the nighttime darkness and spread light over the bride and groom.

They carried out their assignments from beginning to end perfectly without letting out a sound from their mouths and without a movement of their heads, like true artists. They valued the holy good deeds that they performed and the citizens, too, showed their appreciation by filling up their tin boxes with copper and silver coins. However the haughty students from the town's elite did not want to join this group. They considered it demeaning to consort with common craftsmen. They also did not like the non-Jewish costumes.

One time each year this group got its reward. This was on Tu Be'shvat (the fifteenth day of the Hebrew month of Shvat) the day of a big feast. The preparations began some weeks prior to this date. For three weeks the wives of the members were busy fattening the geese that they had bought. After the geese were slaughtered, these women put on thick linen aprons made from sacks and plucked the geese. They worked well into the wee hours of the night so they could share in the honor of participating in the feast.

On the Fifteenth of Shevat, after the evening prayers the audience sat around the long tables and relished the roasted geese whose smell wafted out through the doors into the street and stimulated the taste buds and appetites of the passers by. The strong 90 proof whiskey added warmth and courage. The common people ate and drank like drunkards. However, while sitting at the table they did not quarrel or fight. They concluded the meal by wiping their fat covered lips and a reciting a crackling benediction. On the way home each wished the other that God help him find a mate, and dowry so that they would not need to ask for the help from the Hachnasth Kalah organization. A resounding drawn out 'Amen' shook the air and drifted far out into the street.

————

[Pages 79-80]

Moishe Smolasz

(A Radzyn Legend)

Shmuel Daniely (Tzofit, Israel)

Only by a sandy snakelike path that led from the shtetl and was bounded on both sides by old poplar trees, could one reach the small hut standing alone in the forest surrounded by tall, majestic pine trees.

In a small low room, built cellar like into the earth and covered with a dirt roof, lived a small, thin Jew with a black beard. His eyes were so friendly that they could soften the cruelest of beings.

He had no mother, no sister, and no wife. He lived alone and lonely in the forest where he was born and where he came from no one knew. This was the way he lived his life. The trees were his only real friends. He told them his most intimate secrets and feelings. When he finished his prayers to the Holy One, the forest would become silent. In the middle of his prayers the trees would slowly and quietly bend their spiked tops and whisper his secrets each other. When he finished they would bend and to ask God in Heaven to accept his prayers.

He was rarely seen in the shtetl. He came only for the holidays. He was called Moshe Smolasz* because he would draw tar from the trees and sell it. When he did come, before the holidays, the whole way that led from the shtetl to the forest was lined with groups of different people, women with small children on their hands, old blind Jews leaning on their canes with grandchildren leading them. These were poor people who waited for Moshe.

When Moshe would come to the shtetl he was accompanied by wagons filled with food for the poor. He was also called Moshe The Provider because he helped support the few poor people of the shtetl. All of the income from his hard work he would give to the poor. When winter came he would buy up boots and jackets and on Chanukah distribute them to the poor children. In this way Moshe lived alone in the forest for fifty years. When asked why he had never married he had one answer. "I don't want to defile my body'. His greatest pleasure was only the holidays.

*Smoleh = Yiddish for tar.

Suddenly difficult days came upon Moshe. The work in the forest ended and he had no way of earning a living. The little money that he had saved he continued distributing to the poor until he had none left to buy bread, and he died of hunger.

It was on one of the days of Passover Eve, during a terrible windstorm and in the midst of a driving rain that Moishe Smolarz's soul left his body, which remained lying on the dirt floor, covered with a cotton jacket.

* * *

On that same holiday eve the poor stood on the road that led from the shtetl into the forest arguing about every wagon that set out saying 'that is Moishe's wagon.' They stood there till the evening when a peasant in a strange wagon came by and announced to them that Moishe had died. A terrible cry went up among the poor and spread quickly to shtetl of Radzyn "the Lamed Vov'nik (one of the 36 hidden saints) of the Forest has passed away."

[Pages 81]

Songs From My Home
Meir Segal (New York)

Sadness. A child's life –
Now again you go before me
The wind has already gone silent upon the earth
And the evening twinkles above snowy graves.

The clouds are thick above the sky
Twisting, white and lumpy
And I between earth and clouds
Also in such misery.

All rivers forged into one
The cold night approaches
Above the forests, thin streaks
Of the weary, setting sun.

The expanses grow larger
The fields wider
Frosty whiteness in the air causes a shiver
But everything is still open
Remaining so sadly open
My heart closed up in the forest's storm.

In the forest's storm
To God I pray.
Now I too am wrapped
In the evening's shape.

Across the fields I gather together
The colors into a single blue,
Between eternal birth
And eternal death.

Night. Snow has blanketed all the roads.
Branches quiver in the clear dazzle.
Such a snow fell once before.
When father carried to the field
His dead son in his slender, white hands.

O, stooped father at his child's grave.
Your head gray, tears flow from your eyes.
Soon the snow will cover
The field, the stone with white.

Father has returned from the cemetery

With an extinguished lantern and a boot full of snow.
At the frozen window, a flickering light,
And bleak mourning on two empty beds.

Late at night.
Father in the corner, in grief, in silence:
God, on the same day you gave him to me
You took away his mother.

Early in the morn father prayed.
Packed up a sack full.
Prepared for a journey-
With staff in hand, with *tallith* and *tefillin*.

Casting a final glance home
Silently opening the door.
Two pairs of sad eyes look after him.
Out from under the blanket...
He's left for a foreign city
To become a *cheder* teacher for poor children.
His beard is gray from grief
And has soaked up his tears.

The day cloaked the village
In homesick light. –
Father, what you've lost –
We, your heirs, have sought. –

Only graves are deep in winter,
And mother's stone – the largest.
We want to play with her stones,
My little orphaned sister.

Radzyner Chasidism

The Rabbi's Court

Abba Danilack (Toronto)

1. The Rabbi's Returns!

In the early days of the month of Elul (the 12 month of the Hebrew calendar, Aug. Sept.) the mornings are cooler and the sun weaker. The last of the high walled peasants' wagons, filled with freshly harvested grain from the fields, glides through the streets. The late comers, with their sparse, half-empty sheaves hurry from the fields to the barns as if ashamed.

It is on those days that the Rabbi's Court comes to life. During the whole summer, since the Rabbi left for the warm baths in far away places, it had sunk into a tired quiet slumber. The neighborhood, as if by some artifice, accompanied him. Occasionally the dead silence was broken by the dull sound of the iron handle of the pump that stood proudly in the middle of the court and delivered water from the depths to the whole neighborhood. Jews with small prayer shawls draped over their bare chests hurried to this pump. The Jewish women, with fat stained calico dresses and headscarves, carried jangling empty buckets. The clanging of the iron pump handle rents the tired silence and water from the depths of the earth pours forth noisily and cools the hot air. With bent backs, they drag the heavy full buckets on the way back, leaving a wet snake like trail behind them.

However, with the arrival of Elul, the sounds of fall begin to be heard. A whole row of stables clatter open and the Rabbi's wide coaches with the springs above the wheels can be seen with their dusty harnesses hanging on the walls on iron hooks. All of the equipment is dragged out to the middle of the court, aired-out, cleaned and polished by the non-Jewish watchman. A smile spreads on the thin, wrinkled, leather like faces of the Jews passing by and their eyes showed inner joy, when they notice the watchman's work that was a sign of the imminent arrival of the Rabbi. Soon economic activity in the town would pick up. The news of the Rabbi's arrival spreads quickly through the streets and alleyways. In the poor homes the Jewish women begin thinking about the hens, eggs and the like which will be carried into the Rabbi's house to his wife Hadassah, may she be healthy, who never argues about the price.

The news was received with a special joy in the Rabbi's Bais Hamedrash (study house) that stood opposite. Since the Rabbi went away, the neighboring Jews have been reluctant to come to recite the afternoon and evening prayer in public. Even in the Beis Medrash they run through the prayers hastily and audience feels as if it was in mourning without the presence of the Tzadik

Hador (the Most Righteous of the Generation). The special half bench half chair, Elijah's Seat, that was the place where circumcisions were preformed on generations of Jewish children, stands there as if abandoned. Without the Rabbi as godfather, no one brings children to be circumcised and the ceremony is performed at home.

The whole dynasty - the Rabbi and his daughters and his sons-in-laws- was spread out comfortably in buildings scattered over the whole width of courtyard that was hidden behind a big white wall. In scores of windows the long absent and forgotten sunlight shimmers again. Suddenly the curtains are pushed aside, the windows opened and red faces of the women appeared who with their strong and muscular arms cleaned, washed and polished the wide rooms with their massive white covered furniture.

A few of the first Chassidim arrive. They are local residents, with brown tobacco stained nostrils and mustaches, sucking on the stems of their pipes, a suck and a spit, a spit and a suck. They have arrived early so as to be the first to see the radiant face of the Tzadik (holy man) and to have the privilege of being the first to shake his hand.

The pale Gomorra-boys, (young students) with braided ear locks tucked behind their ears and with narrow cloth hats on their heads, with long coats and with trousers tucked into their boots, now feel uncomfortable. All summer they relished the juicy cherries and other fruits stolen from the Rabbi's orchard which stretched behind the wall and far away to the river. Now this comes to an end. A furtive rogue gloomy look creeps into their eyes. How will they be able to look the Rabbi in the face after such mischievous pranks?

On a gray, foggy morning Zalman'ke, the Rabbi's coachman, marches into the hungrily courtyard leading the two chestnut brown horses by the reins. He is going to hitch up to the Rabbi's coach for the trip to the train station. Half-sleepy Jews, with prayer shawls) under their arms walk slowly with measured steps, to prayers. When they see what is happening in the courtyard they straighten up their backs and push a finger into their cold beards pulling out one whisker at a time while thinking about how they will greet the holy Tzadik.

———

On that morning of the Rabbi's return, the gates to his courtyard stayed open longer. Jews from the town, the Rabbi's Chassidim, grain dealers and ordinary rural peddlers exchanged their greasy coats for their Sabbath caftans and proudly, with their fingertips tucked under their black linen belts, walked with measured steps to the Rabbi's courtyard. There they sat on the benches or lay on the grass awaiting the arrival of the coach. A solemn silence reigned with no one daring to say a word so as not to desecrate the holiness of the moment. Suddenly, as if a storm had blown in, the, whole congregation swayed, left their places and ran wildly toward the snakelike footpath close by the gate. What moved them was the clatter of horses' hoofs on the cobblestones of Warshava Street. The rubber coated coach wheels made the dull sound of the horses' hooves stand out. The horses swept like a whirlwind through the streets as if they felt the importance of their mission: they are carrying the Holy Rabbi and not just any ordinary person of flesh and blood. With pride and envy they rushed through the open gates into the courtyard. With foam on their mouths they come to a sudden stop opposite the Bais Hamedrash near the rows of standing Jews. The first one to jump down from the coach was Zalman'ke. Beaming with joy he threw down the reigns and ran around to the carriage door. From now on he will often take the Rabbi for an afternoon stroll around the fields and woods. That means more livelihood at home, more silver coins in his pocket and more drinking whiskey at the tavern. Zalman'ke opened the coach door quickly and revealed the Rabbi in all his glory. The smile that appeared on the Rabbi's pink full face with its high furrowed forehead and shining gleaming beard, filled the surrounding air with happiness and delight. His blue eyes with their mild compassionate look of wisdom and understanding of the whole the universe, took in the rows of weary, pitiful faces of these small town Jews. For a few moments he thought about the far away Marianbad in the Austrian Empire that he visited recently and that was frequented by royalty and dignitaries who came to revel in its salty water and where wealth and worldly pleasures had contaminated the air. How small and unimportant the hunch backed, sad Jews appeared! However seeing relatives and friends spread warmth through his whole ample body and breathing heavily he took his first step forward. The whole crowd, too, pushed forward each hoping to be the first to return his greeting. Callused, veined and trembling hands waved in the air. The Rabbi with his down like pointy finger tips barely touched the outstretched hands but this touch was enough to cause a tremor in the assembled crowd as if an electric current had poured a pleasing warmth into all their limbs. This was the way that the Shchinah, The Divine Presence, would be received.

Having finished his welcome greeting the Rabbi hurries to the steps of his family's house where his wife and children longingly await him. The shamash (sexton) trails after him carrying two heavy satchels containing the Rabbi's talith (prayer shawl) and tefilin (phylacteries) and his manuscripts, the most precious jewels in the Rabbi's the house.

Even though the sound of the Rabbi's steps long faded away, the throng remains standing as if they were glued to their places. That is the power of the radiant appearance of the holy Tzadik.

That evening, the Bais Hamedrash came to life. The holy books that stand in rows in open bookcases stretching from the floor to the ceiling collected and fondled by generations, attract renewed attention. The old dusty and yellowed pages of the Talmud and books about Kabbalah are opened, their four cornered letters pronounced with fresh enthusiasm. A dissonance of speaking and singing rents the air and float into space over woods and fields. Old and young sit by the dusty books, rock back and forth with their bodies and study God's laws. Young boys, with falsetto voices and a sparkle in their eyes, follow twisting Rashi letters. (A special kind of Hebrew script used for printing Rashi, Reb Shlomo Yitzchaki's commentaries on the Bible and the Talmud.) Aristocratic young people, desirable youthful bridegrooms with just the first signs of a beard, rock back and forth while brushing their hands over fat-bellied books while humming one of the Rabbi's old melodies. Older Jews, whose minds are on serious legal problems or on Kabalistic writings, chew the tips of their beard, and with dull blank expression, look into an other worldly sphere of only mind and spirit. Suddenly a keen open-minded Chassid, in a fit of spiritual ecstasy and with a book in his hand, begins pacing back and forth from one end of the Bais Hamedrash, back and forth for hours as if he hopes to catch the thin thread of Divine Thought. A knock on the lectern, which stands in the middle between the four columns, interrupts all thoughts. The whole congregation straightens its belts and surges forward. At the rear door of the Bais Hamedrash that leads directly to the Rabbi's room they come to a stop as if ordered to do so. At that moment the door opens, and in the intense dead silence one could actually hear the rustle of silk and satin as the bright figure of the Rabbi appears in all its glory. The wide silk stripe in the middle of the satin garment, which closed up to the neck and ended in a two-pointed collar, transformed the priestly long coat into a holy garment. The sable shtreimel, (Fur edged hat worn by rabbis and Chassidic Jews on the Sabbath and holidays) brought recently from abroad, shines like fine gold, blending together with his bright red face and the gold blond beard. All eyes follow the Rabbi's movements. With benign steps, he moves over to his holy corner by the. Eastern wall and begins to sway in fervent prayer.

After mincha, the afternoon prayer, the crowd lines up in rows and the rabbi walks, short winded, between them. By chance, he puts his gentle hand on a strange shoulder whose owner then gladly follows him. This means a longer stroll around the courtyard and a talk about Torah and worldly affairs. The Jews go home happily, eat a warm supper, and thank their creator for having lived long enough to come into contact with this brilliant form and creative source. It was as if the Shechina (Holy Spirit) has descended from the high heavens and had come to rest in the human form known as the Radzyner Rabbi.

2. The High Holidays

A.

On a foggy gray morning a hunched-up Jew with nimble feet, Laizer the Sexton, strides through the Jewish streets. Two short and one long thump of his hard rod on the closed shutters informs the sleeping inhabitants that it is time to get up and recite the Slichot prayers! (Prayers asking for forgiveness that are that are recited every morning between Rosh Hashanah and Yom Kippur) In the dead silence of the night, his steps resound like the echo from an empty barrel, and then disappear into space. Small flames flicker in the windows, and the dull sounds of sliding bolts are heard. Sleepy bodies of men and women, some with small children at their sides, slink out to the Bais Hamedrash. A cold damp early morning breeze strokes and cools the warm bodies. The dreamy nighttime world disappears and the whole Jewish congregation treads on muddy trails and footpaths on their way to Slichot. (Penitential prayers recited on the ten days between Rosh Hashanah and Yom Kippur). From afar, the half-lit lamps in the Bais Hamedrash cast their light through the unshuttered windows as if to show the way for the whole congregation. One by one, they slip sleepily into the building and look around as if they were strangers, rubbing their eyes against the sudden assault of the blinding lamplight. Suddenly a flood of bright, shinning light covers the whole atmosphere, as if by some forgotten magic. This happened because the assistant beadle, Moshe, straightened up the wicks. The first minutes of the Slichot prayer come closer.

The door opens wide and noisily as a bursting sack, pushes through the narrow opening. The head of a man, Mendel Danilak the bookbinder, can barely be seen under the sack filled with his merchandise. A dull thud awakens the half-sleeping Jews. It is caused by the contents spilling out on the long table that stands by the door near the ritual table. All year round only poor people or itinerant beggars who, during the day go from house to house use this table. During the night it serves them as a bed. On it, Mendel the bookseller leisurely arranges his holiday prayer books with their shining golden bindings as well as ordinary storybooks written by observant Jews. Having arranged his merchandise, he turns around to face his audience. He stands still for a moment. On his yellow leathery face his long blonde mustache hangs down into his long pointed blonde beard that hides his pale lips. From under long wiry eyebrows and his furrowed forehead an angry look appears in his blue eyes. Thoughts run through his mind. Is it worth sweating and panting under the heavy load for what would surely be very small reward? Instead of announcing his merchandise he remains silent and stares as if in some dream world. It is pride that keeps him from becoming a cheap merchant! He knows that he is a bookbinder with wide horizons. His work is appreciated by the Rabbi himself, as well as by Chassidim from the big cities of Lublin and Warsaw that buy the old Rabbi's writings and send them to him for binding. But he also knows that his fate to become not only a talented and artistic bookbinder, but also an ordinary bookseller is determined by divine providence. Looking at the gathering of the rich, satisfied, Chassidim raises mutinous thoughts.

A bang on the lectern interrupts this chain of thought. The Rabbi has come in and the Slichot prayer begins. A forest of heads rocks back and forth and the compressed air is filled with sad groans: "Yours is both the body and the soul".

B.

Ever morning and evening, as the High Holidays draw near, excited carriage drivers disgorge loads of Chassidim from the steps of their narrow carriages. Jews with black, blond, and gray beards and sidelocks walk with their luggage, some to more respectable lodgings, others to temporary ones set up for the High Holiday period. The owners are veteran tenants of the tumbledown, crooked huts who move up to the attic. They make their beds in the hay and straw while their creaking beds down below are turned over to the honorable guests. Their wives cook and feed the guests, and the added income will suffice to support their families half way through the winter. After catching their breath, the Chassidim head for the Rabbi's house to receive their welcome greeting. The air is suddenly filled with silk and satin caftans, belts and fur edged hats. Rich big city Jews, business leaders, and lumber merchants exchange their spacious homes for the crowded huts and creaking beds. Now they walk pleasantly, as suits reputable gentry, to the Rabbi's court. Young spirited Chassidim block their way with passion flickering in their eyes while rushing ecstatically to meet the Rabbi face to face. But as the Chassidim come closer to the Rabbi's house the more humble and dejected they feel. Humbly and with inner satisfaction they present the Rabbi with a hand written request and a fat coin.

(P93) In the sexton's house, which borders on the Rabbi's private reception room, the air is saturated with tobacco and smoke. The rows of chairs are crammed with thoughtful Chassidim sitting and writing their requests. Circles of Chassidim crowed around Chaim Barishover the Sexton and swallow his tales. He traveled with the old Rabbi to foreign lands and cities to search for the snail. He captures the audience with his fascinating stories.

Coming out of their interview with the Rabbi, the faces of Chassidim beam with internal radiance and grandeur. For a long time the sounds of the brilliant conversion with the Rabbi rings in their ears. Words of consolation or clever advice for seemingly hopeless moments are balm for the chassidic soul. Uplifted, they stride back deeply concerned with deciphering the meaning of the only hinted at, never clearly defined, words of the holy revered Rabbi.

C.

During these days the courtyard is transformed into a Jewish market. Local and visiting merchants spread out their wares, prayer shawls, scull caps etc. on overturned boxes near the stone footpath. Especially attractive to the passers by, are the many colored, soft linen shoes worn by Jews on Yom Kippur in place of their regular shoes. The local fruit dealers display their finest produce hoping to reap a substantial income from the crowds of Chassidim. The fragrances spread through the air stimulating the taste buds. The juicy shiny yellow grapes that come from far away places across the seas are the most stimulating. They appear in the Shtetl only once a year between Rosh Hashanah (New Year) and Yom Kippur (Day of Atonement) and then disappear completely. The only reason for importing them is to make it possible for the Jews to recite the Sh'hechionu (Thanksgiving) prayer on the second night of Rosh Hashanah. The bunches of grapes lie there majestically as if realizing their importance. The customers do not dare to touch them but have to be satisfied only with looking at them until that special day and moment. Outside, by the Bais Hamedrash, the carpenters are busy erecting, a half circular wall from blocks and linen near the eastern wall of the house. The Bais Hamedrash was incapable of accommodating such a large number of additional guests and participants and so many are forced to pray outside under the open sky. Not only did the Court change on those days, but so also did the whole Shtetl. It was as if a storm had blown through the town and destroyed its quiet, easy going, reasonable quality. Noise and commotion infect the inhabitants. A strange power overcomes everyone, young and old, male and female. It is unusual to see someone strolling leisurely. Everything is hustle and bustle. Every man, woman and child is busy serving the crowd of recently arrived Chassidim. The rustle of linen and satin is heard in all the Jewish streets and alleys. A non-Jew who happens into the town and sees the tumult is utterly perplexed. With dismay, he looks around at the strange looking creatures with their twisted beards and sideburns, spits and mumbles some words in his native tongue and moves away as quickly as possible. Special dishes, prepared for the big city eaters, send pleasant odors drifting from the Jewish homes. Red-faced excited women, with greasy aprons and twisted caps, race from their homes to the food shops and back again. Young girls, with roguish light in their eyes, steal wanton, playful glances through the open doors at the youthful young men. Blushing, they whisper one to another and burst into animated laughter.

When night settles, the sounds from the Rabbi's Court ring through the air. The young Chassidim are busy chanting their lessons; the sweet sounds of their voices carry far and echo back from the far-away stone wall that surrounds the old holy place on the other side of the river. (The Jewish Cemetery-see map)

D.

There are two Ohels (Structures over the tomb of an important person.) in the Old Cemetery. One, that is built of stone and very neglected, covers the grave of Reb Shimon Daitsch, the well known Hassidic Rabbi who was the patron of the craftsmen and the ordinary Jews. The tailors and shoemakers of the Shtetl maintain the Ohel. On white winter days one would often meet Tuvia the tinsmith plodding through the deep snow, struggling against the snowy wind which tries to push him off the road and force him to go back to the town. Tuvia struggles with all his might to continue on his way. He never fails to fulfill his obligation to light the" Eternal Light" both during winter or summer. The Ohel is always open to the neighboring ordinary people whose hearts cling to the cold stone. Rivers of troubles and tears pour into space and force their way toward the heavens where they demand accounting and change.

Opposite is the other Ohel, maintained by the Chassidim, with its big pump and piles of kvittles (written requests) that cover the gray stone. This is the Ohel of the Rabbi's father Reb Gershon Hanoch, may he rest in peace. Chassidim from near and far come here all year round to unburden their hearts. Every visitor leaves a substantial fee that benefits both the oil for the Ohel as well as for the caretaker Boruch Hirsch who is famous throughout the city. He is a joker and live wire. At the local weddings he appears in a calico Turkish uniform and with his artistic talents and his famous Cossack Dance, he makes bride and groom and all the guests happy.

On the eve of Rosh Hashanah, when long rows of hundreds of Chassidim on foot and in wagons make their way to the Ohel, on this holy day his look changes and becomes very serious. Jangling the long Ohel keys, he lets the visitors enter one by one. They make a turn around the high walled tomb while saying prayers for the dead. Then they drop a kvittel to the revered Rabbi while mumbling secretly to themselves. Having unburdened themselves to the cold stone, their mood becomes lighter. Contentedly, they place a final payment in Boruch Hirsch's hand, and go, exuberantly into town to make final arrangements for the impending holiday.

From then on, the light in the courtyard is never extinguished. As soon as the sun prepares to hide its face from the town, Mordechai the Sexton, with the help of his non-Jewish watchman, lights the lanterns that surround the newly erected linen wall. Immediately, bright flames spring up all over the length of the courtyard. When night falls, a forest of heads, praying outside, rock back and forth under the open sky. Their voices, broken and painful in "Let Thine awe", (From the evening service of eve of Rosh Hashanah) are surrounded by the stiff impurity of ringing of the church bells, as if the devil, camouflaged as dead iron, had taken upon himself to disturb the Jewish prayers. The dense metal sounds force their way into the air shrieking as if trying to deafen the living sounds of the prayers that issue forth from thousands of hearts and are directed to God's throne. Eventually the bells humbly surrender their shrill echo and sheepishly disappear into the deep black night. Soon silk scrapes against satin, hands are joined by happy voices wishing a Happy New Year rent the air. The prayers overcome the devil!

The lamps of the Bais Hamedrash burn late into the night and the doors and windows remain wide open. The Chassidic audience is tightly packed into the fetid atmosphere. Now the table is set. The Rabbi sits at the head of the table dressed in a grayish-white satin costume. Around him, in two rows, sit the older highly respected Chassidim. The Rabbi tastes something from one of the dishes that have been set out then pushes away the plate. This means that the rest is Shireim (leftovers). The old respectable Chassidim surround the table and with hands and fingernails, spear pieces of fish or meat straight into their mouths licking their greasy fingers. The young Chassidim stand frozen into their places around the margins of the hundred year old, thousand pound bench, holding on to the ceiling with their hands. They look with envy at the older Chassidim who have the honor of sitting close to the Tzadik. The Rabbi delivers his teachings in a falsetto-nasal voice while continuing to eat. They listen with bated breath so that they won't miss a word, a sound, or even a movement. The Chassidic teachings are expressed not only in words but also in movements and in the ability to repeat exactly what happens at the Rabbi's table.

The only Chassid blessed by god was Aaron Z'elekover from the town of Zelekov He was tall and erect and from his noble aristocratic face one could discern his breeding. His high forehead and penetrating look, and his measured steps arouse respect for his scholarship. The large nobleman's eyeglasses on his nose added charm to his refined look. He is the center around whom small groups of Chassidim gather to hear him repeat what the Rabbi has said around the table. He is blessed with a sweet high- pitched voice. His sincere pleading, especially on the mornings of the High Holidays, is famous throughout the area. Upon leaving the Rabbi, the Chassidim take home with them enormous spiritual baggage consisting of the Rabbi's newly pronounced teachings and newly absorbed nigun (melody). This equipment gives the Chassidim sufficient spiritual support to last a whole year.

3. Tchelet and Controversy

The most important factor which unifies the Chassidim and for which Radzyn was famous in the whole Jewish world was the Tchelet (azure dye).

The Rabbi's orchard, with its trees of various fruits, stretches for a long distance beyond the wall all the way to the river. Even though a fence that has a locked gate surrounds the orchard, everyone considers it as being in the public domain and the fruit free for the taking. Those who benefit most from this situation are "the bright young boys" who steal into the orchard shake a tree and came out with hands full of red cherries or with green sour gooseberries. They do not consider this a sin nor do they feel any pangs of conscience. They know that the orchard is public property!

Two wooden huts look down from between the trees on the other side of the wall. They are usually closed and rarely was anyone seen entering them. They are silent witnesses to a stormy past era. On the outside they are identical. However, the first glances through the dusty windows reveals different interiors and for what purpose they were erected. In one there were piles of large and small jars and bottles of all sizes. The smell that emanated from there reminded one of a pharmacy. It comes from medicines and chemicals. The other hut is a fully equipped workshop with all sorts of mechanical equipment ostensibly for a laundry. However both huts serve as scientific laboratories for the old Rabbi Reb Gershon Hanoch, of blessed memory, who was half doctor and half chemist and a great genius. Here carried out his experiments with the aquatic creature called the Chilazon (snail) to reveal the ancient secret of producing the blue dye. From the time that The Temple was destroyed the Jews stopped wearing a blue thread in their prayer shawls. According to the Talmud these threads were dyed in the blood of a snail found in the Mediterranean. From that time on, according to the traditional explanation, the snail disappeared and appears only once in seventy years. This stubborn genius challenged this accepted tradition. In order to do that he studied chemistry in German books. In the same way, he studied medicine, gave medicaments and wrote prescriptions like a qualified physician. In order to carry out his plan he went to Trieste on the Mediterranean and brought back a large quantity of snails to his far away, Radzyn. Here the snail will get its due and with his blood and some additional chemicals will again grace the prayer shawls with heavenly blue fringes. Hidden in an inner room, a large jar was set up in which the many hairy legged snails, the size of a kittens, were soaked in chemicals.

The Rabbi entrusted the secret of the art of converting the blood into blue dye to his trustworthy assistant, Yehoshua Barishover. He was a short, full, red-cheeked Jew with wise eyes, who was well combed, and always neatly dressed. He became and remained the chemist of the court. He was not a great scholar, rather more of a Maskil (follower of the Enlightenment) who was tight lipped and whose aristocratic appearance engendered great respect. In addition he was the bookkeeper of the court and carried on its correspondence in beautifully scripted letters and envelopes. His work in the Tchelet laboratory created an additional source of income for the court. Everyone who wanted to wear a blue fringe had to come and pay him a fee.

The great disturbance that the Tchelet created in the learned Jewish circles caused great grief and sorrow to the Rabbi. In order to calm his agitated colleagues he published one book after another about the Tchelet question. However, this did not calm the storm nor convince his agitated colleagues. Things remained as they were. His supporters, however, did weave a blue thread into their prayer shawls. As a result the Radzyn Chassidim became famous in the whole Jewish world. Everywhere, Radzyn Chassidim could be easily recognized by blue thread in their prayer shawl. In the beginning the opposition to the Tchelet produced quarrels in many cities and towns, especially in Radzyn. The Mitnagdim, (opponents of the Chassidim within Orthodox Judaism) who always looked askance at the chassidic leadership and their strange antics, now saw in the Tchelet a deviation from Jew tradition. They saw any agitator for the Tchelet as an offender.

———

In the Eighties of the Nineteenth Century what happened in Radzyn was a repetition, on a smaller scale, of what had happened to Reb Zalman Schneor of Ladi. There was a river in the middle of the Shtetl upon which stood a water mill, which belonged to the Rabbi. On one dark night, as bad luck would have it, the entire mill went up in smoke and fire. All that was left were the charred pillars covered and protected by the water. An informer appeared, and the old Rabbi was locked up in the Radzyn jail for sixteen days during which he never stopped studying or let the pen out of his hand. He was known throughout the scholarly world for his great compositions such as 'The Laws of Purification', 'Ohels' (see above), etc. He utilized the short time that he was imprisoned to write another book, a commentary on the book by Reb Eliezer The Great called 'Life Styles'. From that time on as a reminder of the time he passed in jail he was referred to as "The Life Styles". With his passing, the controversy slowly faded. His replacement, Reb Mordechai Yosef Eliezer, was a peace seeker. With his deep wisdom and radiant appearance he managed to win over the Gerer Chassidim who had been the greatest opponents of the Tchelet in his father's time. However the Shtetl of Radzyn remained divided. On one side were the Rabbi's followers, the Tchelet wearers, whose center was the Rabbi's Bais Hamedrash, while the other side were those whose center was the Communal Bais Hamedrash.

All year round, the Rabbi's white wall, the tallest of all the buildings on the street, proudly overlooked the whole town and attracted respect. The rooms were wide and roomy with many rows of windows that not only attracted light and sun, but also were conspicuous in the town for their holiness and awe. Every Chassid or ordinary Jew who passed over the threshold of the sexton's house felt the atmosphere of spiritual exaltation, of Torah and the Divine Presence. One room was designated as a lounge for welcoming guests. Twelve heavy armchairs stood around an old stiff oak table covered with white cloth. The doors rarely opened and it was even more rare for an ordinary everyday Jew to get a glimpse of what went on there. The only one who had a foothold there was Chaim Barishover, the Sexton, who went in every morning and dusted the furniture. The place smelled of mustiness and age. Those who did have free access to the place were mostly non-Jews. The important town officials who would sometime pay a visit to the Rabbi would be received there. The sober sounds of foreign languages that escaped through the windows signaled that there was an important reception taking place to help some individual or the whole community

Purim Nights in the Rabbi's Court

Once a year however, the serious holiness of the place suddenly disappears. It takes on a more mundane appearance and is converted into a theatre hall. This is during the Purim night meal, when masked Purim Shpielers (Purim Players), dressed as non-Jews with weapons in their hands, come to entertain the Rabbi and earn their due reward. The doors of the reception room are flung open, the table disappears, and the chairs are arranged around the walls as if waiting for the unusual event happening once a year. Suddenly the clamor and tumult of the bright young men is heard as they burst in to announce the arrival of the band and run from room to room, the very same rooms from which they were excluded all the rest of the year. They are followed by ordinary curious Jews who shuffle in bashfully, step by step, as if not to desecrate the holy atmosphere with their sinful bodies. After them come the Purim Players, one after another, with hasty steps as if they wished, by their non-Jewish gait to frighten the scared bearded Jews. Opposite the open reception rooms stand the women lined up to see the Purim Shpiel. Their gaze meets that of the men because on Purim night it is not considered frivolous or lewd. We are commanded to get drunk on Purim so we can't be too pious!

A group of artists marches into the broad hall and take up positions at its center waiting for a signal to start the first act. Who are these odd creatures with their strange gait? Some of them are yesterday's Bais Hamedrash boys such as Zishele the painter and cantor, Godl's Yentshe, Yoel the son of Yentsche Godel's, Boruch Hirshes' son together with craftsmen's apprentices. The latter have visited the Yiddish Theatre in the big city of Warsaw and brought with them a new repertoire of snappy songs, which they have included in their Purim performance. The majestic Achashverosh stands dressed in his royal robe and flirts with Queen Esther. (A man dressed as a woman because "hearing the voice of a woman is like seeing her in the nude.") Even Viazata, one of the ten sons of Haman, stands there with a group of household servants. The bright young men surround them and curiously examine the pants with the gold stripes and the tinkling swords. They try to touch the attractive pants, and when they are met with a harsh look from under a mask of make up accompanied by push from a muscular hand, they move as far away as they can.

Silence, The Rabbi is coming! This is announced in the hoarse voice of Chaim the Sexton. As if by magic, the tongues are silenced and the Rabbi appears. He breaks out into a big smile when he sees the large crowd of Chassidim, ordinary Shtetl Jews, Bais Hamedrash boys and Cheder (religious school for young boys) children who have gathered there. He sends his mild loving look in all directions as if wanting to quiet their frightened looks. The Rabbi sits in his place and the performance begins. The acting and love songs that are not kosher all year round for pious Jews' ears are made kosher on this night even for the Tzadik himself. The performance often produces hearty laughter in the audience and the voices of men and women blend together into a harmonious symphony that no one sees as improper. The Rabbi himself laughs heartily as if he is an ordinary member of the audience.

Now comes the second act called 'The Little Tailor'. Zishe, the leading actor, crosses one foot over the other and spreads out his piece of cloth intended for making a kaftan. A lens hangs from a string attached to two strings from both ears. In one hand he holds a needle and in the other a thread. As he struggles to insert the thread into needle, his sweet falsetto voice flows into the air bemoaning his faith:

A little tailor sits on high,

Sewing the waist of a kaftan;

With one leg crossed over another,

He sings a sugar sweet tune.

A pleasing tenderness envelops the audiences who for the moment forget their everyday worries and delight in the magic of theatre.

It is long past midnight when the performance ends and the Jews leave intoxicated by this non-Jewish pleasure. However, they know that only on Purim night can they loosen the reins and allow the body to taste earthly pleasures. Tomorrow total holiness will reign again in the court.

Radzyn Chassidim
Right- Rabbi Mendel Danilak (Einvinder); Left- Rabbi Baruch Hirsch (Appelboim)

[Pages 111-115 and 112-116]

The House of Izbitsa and Radzyn
The evolution of prayer music in the courtyard of the *Admors* ("Our Masters, our Teachers and our Rabbis") of Radzyn

By M.S. Gshuri (Jerusalem)

1- Rabbi Mordechai Yosef Leyner of Izbitsa

The founder of the Izbitsa-Radzyn dynasty, Rabbi Mordechai Yosef Leyner (May His Memory Be for a Blessing), a strong and distinguished personality, was amongst the prominent disciples of Rabbi Simcha Bunim of Pshisa, and the close friend of Rabbi Mendel of Kotsk. After the passing of the *Tsadik* ("righteous one") of Pshisa, Rabbi Mordechai Yosef was among those to proclaim Mendel as his *tsadik,* and to become his assistant.

However, he was also the first to leave him later on, causing the irreversible chasm among the *Chasidim* of Kotsk. During the Days of Awe of 5600 (1840) he sojourned for the last time in Kotsk, remaining there until after *Sukot.* During that holiday, in which the split was decided and also the tunes of the *Simchat Torah* processions could not resolve the dispute. Since that dramatic visit, his followers came out against Kotsk *Chasidism,* and gathered around their new *Tsadik,* who settled in Izbitsa. The storm of that dispute continued to intensify and it was responsible, in a great part, for the desecration of the *Chasidim's* good name.

While still close to Rabbi Simcha Bunim of Pshisa, tradition has it that, following their initial meeting and exchange of *Torah* wisdom, they decided to challenge each other. Rabbi Simcha Bunim told Rabbi Mordechai Yosef: "Let's stand next to each other and see who is the tallest". Then said the *Tsadik:* "For now, I am taller than you are. But you are very young, and you will still grow". This comparison did not refer to their literal height, because, in all truth, the Rabbi (Simcha Bunim) was as tall as a palm tree, and his disciple was short. The reference was, in all probability, to their spiritual height. It was also clear that the comparison did not apply to knowledge on the field of prayer melodies (*Nigunim*), for even without making it truly a cornerstone, the *Tsadik* knew how to appreciate and value it, whereas Rabbi Mordechai Yosef's knowledge of tunes was limited (See Rabbi Gershom Henekh's introduction to the book *The House of Yaakov,* Genesis, Warsaw, 1850).

The holy war between Kotsk and Izbitsa, and the unraveling of the close spiritual ties between them, did not affect the matter of the tunes. In Izbitsa, they did not wander far from Jewish melodies. Their strong attachment to them was reinforced even more after the split from Kotsk, and after they dissociated themselves from empty tunes and from those who did not emanate from a Jewish source (some of which were very popular in Kotsk). However, the preoccupation with prayer melodies did not occupy an important place in lzbitsa's dynasty, and its treatment of it was not serious. Indeed, the musical emotional decibel was low. This passive tendency toward melodies was not particular to lzbitsa, but a continuation of the same attitude that existed towards it in Pshisa and Kotsk. (Even the melodies for the Days of Awe, which more or less fit the spirit of the day, were devoid of energy and flexibility).

Therefore, *Torah* and melodies did not dwell in harmony amongst the *Chasidim* of Poland. In places where *Torah* prevailed, melodies did not, and where *Torah* was not foremost, singing was strong. Pshisa, Kotz and Gur were the *chasidic* centers of *Torah*. Their *Tsadikim,* Rabbi Mendely and Rabbi Yitzchak Meir, were amongst the great *Torah* scholars, but could not carry a tune while praying, and therefore needed those who could, in order to reach the hearts of those who heard the prayers. The *Tsadikim* of Kotzk and Gur reserved for themselves the right to enjoy the most beautiful prayers by asking the able cantors to repeat them twice or even three times. This proves that even in those places, melodies were important. In Izbitsa, no care was exercised in the selection of melodies- as they were considered sponges to dry the tears. In Pshisa, the approach to singing was better than in Kotzk: they did not strictly adhere to the essence of the Jewish origins of the melodies, but did not dare to accept, openly, foreign tunes borrowed from the theatre. Izbitsa followed Pshisa closely.

Rabbi Mordechai Yosef did not make use of the melody's purpose to awaken feelings: he was much too busy studying *Torah*. And if he blazed the trail for the ascension of the dynasty, the fact should be attributed to his influence and energy, and to his righteousness and scholarship. Melodies and cantors he treated lightly!

The book *Mei Hashiloach (The Water of the Shiloach)* which he wrote, was more than a simple introduction to literature. It was the first of the works of that dynasty. And despite the fact that it was written in summary form, it was considered a seminal book and the gate opener to the literary edifice of the dynasty. In his introduction to the *Beit Yaakov, Bereshit (The House of Yaakov, In the Beginning),* his grandson, author of *Orchot Chaim,* confirms his grandfather's brief style, and the fact that he only touched upon the essence of the topics, without providing long explanations. Their descendants wrote many works which provoked great excitement and upheavals in the world of *Torah* and *Chasidism* because of their new approaches and nuances. Except for two places, the matter of the melodies did not get any attention: he connects the journey of Moses and the Israelites ("and Moses led Israel") to Miriam the Prophetess' *Song of the Sea,* saying that after Moses saw that Miriam sang the song, he understood that the moment had come to leave the place. This is how the Almighty's way is viewed as a factor on the influence of the renewal of *Torah's* words in Israel. At first, the influence is felt by the hearts of the great and the *Tsadikim,* and then it continues until it reaches the hearts of the women. That is the place where the renewal is completed, and a need for new insights into the *Torah* arises. And this is the way it happened in the realm of the Song *(Shirah:)* first, it appeared on Moses' lips, and later in those of Israel's. And after Miriam responded "Sing to the Lord because He is exalted above all", it is said: "and Moses left", indicating thus that they had nothing else to achieve there. The chapter is closed, and now there is room for renewal (Exodus, Chapter 15, v. 21).

In the same way he spoke about dancing in a circle, so that no one person is closer than the other. To this kind of even-handed dancing, where no one rises above his peer, referred the sages who said that one day God will make a dance for his *Tsadikim.* The *Tsadik* maintained in his book that in Israel no one is higher than the other when God is in their midst. That is, He is in everyone equally *(Korach).*

Dancing was very popular among Polish *Chasidim,* with no exceptions and, undoubtedly, the *Tsadik* of Izbitsa also participated, having been able to observe, from close by, the personal equality reflected in the dancing, which gladdened his pure heart.

He had many disciples, among them his son and heir Rabbi Yaakov, Rabbi Yehuda Leyb Eiger, and Rabbi Tzaddok Hacohen Rabinowitz, who served in the courtyard of the *Admor* of Lublin, and for whom the preoccupation with tunes was foremost.

The *Tsadik* only served 13 years, and passed away in Izbitsa on the seventh of Tevet, 5614 (1854), leaving behind two sons: the first-born and heir to his throne, Rabbi Yakov of Izbitsa, and Rabbi Shmuel Dov Asher of Biskowitz.

2- Rabbi Yaakov of the "House of Yaakov"

The stormy controversy between Kotzk and Izbitsa abated somewhat in the period of Izbitsa's second generation, in Rabbi Yaakov's time. He "widened the main gate, as much as that of the Temple", and put his dynasty on a more sound basis. He was a great *Torah* and *Kabala* (Jewish mysticism) scholar, and devoted all of his time to his studies. There is no doubt that, with his exceedingly pleasant voice he could have excelled also in the singing, and that he could have thus expressed his inspiration, but obviously he feared that doing so could weaken his study of *Torah.* For that reason, he ordered the *Chasidim,* and only the most talented among them, to sing the melodies, to go in front of the ark, and to officiate as cantors.

The *Saturday* gatherings represented for him a spiritual combination of melodies and *Torah* wisdom. At his table on Saturday, he requested (after the blessing over the bread and before the eating of the fish) the singing of many of the Lurianic melodies, because of his *Kabalistic* spiritual connection to their composer. Indeed, singing came before the eating of the fish. The Rabbi would also expound on *Torah* every Saturday and holiday meal, between courses. On the Saturday evening meal, he prescribed the singing of *Kol Mekadesh* (All Sanctify), *Menucha Ve'Simcha* (Rest and Happiness), ending with *Ya Ribon* (God, Master of the World).

On the Saturday day meal he would say before the ritual washing of the hands- *Asader Le'Sudatah* (I Am Readying for the Festive Meal), and ordered the singing of *Baruch Hashem Yom Yom* (Blessed is God Every Day) up to *Emunim Notzar* (Faith Was Created), *Baruch El Elyon* (Blessed be the Exalted God), and *Yom Ze Mechubad* (Glorious is This Day). At the third Saturday meal, before washing his hands, he would open with *Atkinu Seudata* (The Festive Meal I Will Prepare) and, after expounding on *Torah*, he would order the responsive singing of *Bnai Heykhalah* (Children of the Temple). The cantor would stop after two stanzas, and the assembled ones would respond. Afterward, they would sing *Mizmor Le'David, Hashem Roi'* (A Psalm of David, The Lord is My Shepherd), and again they would sing, responsively, *Yitzaveh* (He Commanded), followed by *Dror Yikrah* (Freedom Will Ring) and *Yom Shabbat* (Saturday). The gathering would end with the Grace After Meals.

After the evening prayers and the recitation of *Havdala*, he ordered the singing of *Amar Hashem Le 'Yaakov* [God said to Jacob]. But, while sipping the *Havdalah* wine, he would whisper himself, with his pleasant voice, *Eli Chish Goali* (My Lord, Hasten my Savior). He would slur the passage *Khavi Kimat Rega* (Hide Yourself Briefly), convinced of the promise that trouble and worry will soon pass, allowing for the advent of a time of grace. And while he sang *Be'Motzaei Yom Menucha* (At the End of the Day of Rest), he would repeat many times the words *Nache Amcha Ke'Av Rachman* (Guide Your People as a Compassionate Father).

The *Seder* of the Passover *Hagada* added much to the holiday. The gatherings were enhanced by the melodies which were sung, by request of the *Tsadik,* line by line, and by the cantor as well as the participants.

Rabbi Yaakovs' book about the Torah in the House of Yaakov is one of the most important works, qualitatively and quantitatively speaking, about *Chasidism* in Poland. Three parts were printed, with long intervals in between, while the rest can be found in manuscript form. In the book, Rabbi Yaakov postulates a seminal idea about religious singing, which is very telling about his affinity to the subject. His thesis is that the sun and the moon function by force of their singing and praise, and that they shine the power of their light on the world while moving around its orbit. But that it has been proven that, when they stop singing, they are rendered motionless. When Joshua wanted to stop the movement of the sun, the sun stopped singing, and thus it did not have the strength to continue turning. The force of the song makes the grass sprout and grow. To summarize: the song is the root of everything and represents God's influential force. It is as though life and death are in the hands of the song and of its sphere of influence.

The *Tsadik,* with the assistance of King David, found a way to allow foreign tunes, as the king brought instruments from Gat (in the Philistine area) to play in the Temple. He dedicated a psalm "For the Leader, upon the Gittith" (Leviticus). Is it possible to see in this a way to allow Western melodies and the theatre into *Chasidism,* or it is possible that the allowance pertains to instruments alone?

And what is the connection between happiness and song? Happiness hints at a time when man is immersed in pleasure, and his soul expands by a supreme force, whereas song alludes to a contraction that is completely cancelled in his relation to the heights, without remains. Thus, he also differentiates between song and praise. Song exists in the moment that the creature expands forcefully and extols the Supreme influence on himself. Praise hints the opposite, that the creature recognizes that there is no other force in the world, except for the Supreme one, who does it all *(Shemini).*

The *Tsadik* finds a double song on Saturday *Mizmor Shir Le'Yom Ha'Shabat* (a song for the Saturday) as every good thing is multiplied in it. According to the *Midrash,* (the homiletic interpretation of Scriptures) all Saturday things are doubled. Its *Omer* is doubled, its sacrifices and its song are doubled, because indeed there are two degrees in every Saturday undertaking *(Shemot).* And there is a difference between a psalm *(Mizmor)* and a song. The psalm attests to an internal light, whereas the song shows an encompassing light. The psalm hints at a reduction, because the removal of the branches from a tree is called, in Mishnaic *(Torah)* language, a *Zimur* (same root as *Mizmor),* whereas song hints of expansion. On Saturday, these two are included- *Mizmor* and song *(Emor).*

This differentiation between *Mizmor* and song is repeated numerous times in the book, in different versions, a fact that causes much surprise. However, the differentiation itself between the two musical terms shows that he tried to penetrate the recesses of the vocal musical world, and to examine carefully and decipher the lofty sounds, at least linguistically.

While checking the *Gemoreh (Bava Metziah,* Ch. 25) or the second and supplementary part of the *Talmud,* which provides a commentary on the first part, he found that song is round, encompassing everything equally (Rashi said: "round as a bracelet") and alluded to the fact that all Israel are equal, and there is no reason for arrogance.

The Zimrah- (the singing) has an intimate connection to the declaration "Shem Elyon" and "to sing to Your lofty Name"- the place where the Creator, the Lofty one is hidden from human eyes- one must elevate one's voice in psalm, that is to reduce oneself and to pray. Prayer sheds light on the darkness *(Be' Shalach).*

The study of *Torah* was as popular as the loveliness of the melody. The violin that hung over King David's bed hints that *Torah* wisdom was planted deeply in his heart, so much so that even at midnight he would play by himself, even unknowingly *(Shemini).* One of the improvements that occurred during Rabbi Yaakov's time was, undoubtedly, the intensification of singing, as per his instructions. *Chasidim* knowledgeable in playing conducted the singing in the courtyard, under the direction of the *Tsaddik,* a fact that contributed even more to the wider discrepancy between Izbitsa and Kotsk.

Rabbi Yaakov was summoned to his eternal resting place on the 15th of Av, 5635 (1875). He was survived by two sons: the eldest, Rabbi Gershon Chanoch of Radzyn, and Rabbi Avraham Yehoshua Heshil, who settled in Chelem.

3- Rabbi Gershon Chanoch Leyner of Radzyn 5599-5651 (1839-1891)

The Radzyn dynasty was not a remarkable one. Despite its spiritual strength and its initiatives, it cannot be considered but a straight continuation to that of lzbitsa's.

The first *Tsadik* of Radzyn, the grandson of the founder of the Izbitsa dynasty, (and one of the very interesting characters among the T*sadikim* of Poland), was alert and experienced, an erudite and powerful debater, great in *Torah* scholarship and wisdom, multi-talented, a prolific writer, and a man whose eyes were open to every phenomenon of life. He acquired *Talmudic* and practical wisdom, and provoked much admiration and surprise for it. He was a Rabbi in Radzyn but, after the passing of his father, he received also the mantle of *Tsadik* of lzbitsa. Everyone saw his talent as a divine gift given to a meritorious man for his deeds. Rabbi Gershon Chanoch was also daring and energetic, and it was the combination of all of these qualities that made him great.

Rabbi Gershon re-introduced an old *Mitzva* (commandment) which had disappeared after the destruction of the second Temple: the color blue in the fringes of the praying shawl *(Talit)*. This became the last of his daring innovations. To this end, he established a laboratory in Radzyn, with a variety of dying equipment, and the special worm that grows in a snail in the Mediterranean, on Italy's shores. He published his findings, as well as the clarification of the rules pertaining to the snail and to the color blue, in three books: *Secrets Hidden in the Sand* (its third edition appeared in Lublin in 5664-1904); *A Thread of Blue* (Lublin, 5664-1904) and *The Blue Eye* (Warsaw, 5653-1893.) These publications caused uproar among some rabbis who opposed his findings, and a literary controversy ensued. In addition, he tried to introduce serious amendments to the law of *Eruvin* (the Saturday walking limits) in the city. In his book *The Gates to the City* (Warsaw, 5652-1892), he expounds on the subject.

Indeed, his knowledge was multiple and varied, not only on *Torah* and *Kabala* wisdom, but also as a chemist, linguist, poet, in medicine, etc. In the field of music, he did not demonstrate more initiative than his predecessors. But he was still interested in the matter of tunes. He acknowledged their importance and their need in life, even without considering them as possessing a wide practical or *Halacha* scope.

The problem he addressed regarding saying a blessing upon hearing a melody, was a very interesting one. Only one who could examine closely the function of the human senses could also bring up the following question: why is the pleasure of sound (upon which you are not to bless while hearing the strings of a violin or a harp for instance) different from the pleasure of fragrance, upon which you do bless?

He based the argument on the fact that sight and smell, while not concrete, are sensed and felt by the eye (like a tree or a fragrance,) and that the smell that emanates from them is, indeed, real, whereas the sound is not felt concretely and is not essential. Therefore, as the sources say, one does not need to bless the sound *(Orchot Chaim).* This is not to say that he ignored the attraction of the melody, and while expounding on the power of instinct in life's pleasures, he took into consideration its bowing to the pleasant sound that "will sing and take possession of the hearts and that will worship the hands that strum the harp or play the violin" (from his introduction to *"The Eye of the Blue"*).

The origin of the duty to honor God with one's throat was not very clear. The ones who supported it, based the commandment on the phrase "Honor God with all your Treasures", and on the *Psikta* (collection of legends) of Rabbi Kahana that says: "With all your treasures, (with which you were endowed), one of them being your voice. That is, if you had a pleasant voice, and were sitting in the prayer house, stand up and honor God with it. But, where is it written that "With all your treasures" is synonymous with "your voice"? He refers to Rashi's commentary on *Mishlei* 3 (Proverbs): "don't read with your treasures, but with your throat". And to emphasize the duty to sing even more, he brings a quotation from the *Zohar,* the *Kabalistic Book of Splendor* (Jethro, 93): "Honor God will all your treasures, with your endowments, with the joy of the music come before the Lord" (10 Words About *Chasidism, Orchot Chaim.)* On the other hand, he did not like those who rushed to sing or to perform in front of the ark to boast and show off their voice. He would say: "a glutton is a crazy man" *(Sod Yesharim,* Secrets of the Upright, ch. 40).

And yet, a man's pleasant voice reveals "delicate qualities", therefore he appreciated a person who possessed a nice voice. Once, when sojourning in Yosepov, in connection with the publication of his book *Sidrei Taharot (*The Order of Purification], he heard- while lying on his bed at dawn- a pleasant voice: "Arise, awake, go forth to join in the work of the Creator". The voice penetrated one's heart and disturbed the sleep. He arose, washed his hands and inquired after the caller with the special voice. When he was told that he was the city's beadle, he summoned and talked to him, because he found he liked him. Since then, he sent him *Matza* money from Radzyn every year. The *Tsadik* realized, after his conversation with the beadle, that his pleasant voice matched, indeed, his pure heart. (*Dor Yesharim*- The Generation of the Righteous.)

His followers, who hasten to enumerate his general knowledge, tell that once, when walking in the outskirts of Paris, he heard the sound of a piano emanating from a third floor of a house, and noted that the player was half a tone off. He distinguished between the length of the tones- a high level in music. Indeed, he had an absolute ear. He was also said to have known to read music, to which he devoted much attention.

He knew what to adopt and what to discard. He found that love songs represented a bad influence for young women, to the point of leading them astray (see his introduction to *Orchot Chaim).* In order to remove the obstacle, he took it upon himself to publish educational books with songs of appropriate content, and with a Jewish, folk-religious feeling. However, the project was never implemented because of lack of time.

He was very careful not to drink much with the gentiles, neither be present in their weddings and other celebrations. He did not see any incentive in participating in the dance and song of the gentiles, and in observing them in their excesses. However, in a *Mitzvah* celebration, both dance and song are major components, and it is incumbent upon everyone to participate.

He knew how to differentiate between celebrations. He would say: "ignorant Jews are happy on *Simchat Torah* because they finish the reading of the *Torah*, and we are happy on *Shavuot* for beginning it".

There were no changes in the fields of music and dance during the period in which he was a *Tsadik.* At the end of the Passover, after the afternoon prayers, he made everyone repeat three times: "The Passover meal has concluded", trying to end the season with singing before facing the regular week and toil anew. During the Days of Awe, and indeed during all other holidays, cantors led the prayers, but the right to blow the *Shofar* on *Rosh Hashana* he kept for himself.

The book *"Beginning of Wisdom"* was one of his favorite ones, and he would read it in bed, before falling asleep. There is a single article in the book that deals with the song of the spheres and tells of two men who went to India to hear the song of the sun (which is closest to the earth there). Only one of them returned, deaf, while the second one died from the power of the song. The fact that he cited that article in his book *"Eye of the Blue",* attests how much he reflected on it.

In connection with the supreme singing, he contents himself repeating in his books the ideas already expressed by his father, either in somewhat different words or in more detail. His original ideas are few. He said that in "the song of the celestial bodies" and in "the song of all creatures, one can find the confirmation of His existence, as they all act in response to Him who dwells above. The sun works, in its own rotation around the world, by the power of its song. The song of Israel includes the actions of all creatures, because not another creature recognizes the loftiness of the one who dwells above, as Israel does ('Secrets of the Righteous', on Passover).

In the last *Rosh Hashana* of his life, he directed the singing of *Shir Ha'Maalot, Esa Eynai Le'Harim* (the Psalm: I will lift my eyes towards the mountains), and readied himself to die without fear.

He did not live long: he was only 51 at the time of his death. He passed away on the fourth of *Tevet* 5651, (1891) and left behind many manuscripts. Radzyn is his sacred burial place.

4- <u>Mordkhe Yosef Elazar of Radzyn</u>

And the calm days returned, as it always happens in a second generation of a dynasty. Rabbi Mordchai Yosef Elazar, the son of Rabbi Gershon Chanoch (and his successor in Radzyn), continued what his father had started on the matter of the blue fringes and in his activism, and was much respected in rabbinical circles.

One of his books, *"The Splendor of Yosef "* (Warsaw, 5695-1935) which was printed after his death, contains new *Torah* and *Talmud* insights. On the matter of the melodies, he relied on his grandfather's opinion that singing reflects the face to face contemplation of God's light (Yaakov's House). He himself never sang at his table, and the order of the songs remained as it had been during his father's time and in the hands of the *Chasidik* experts. The melodies were not many. Their neglect was noticeable, and because of this lack of interest, singing waned in Radzyn.

During the First World War, the *Tsadik* moved his residence to Warsaw, where he continued to serve devoutly until the 26th of *Shvat,* 5689 (1929), when he passed away. His son, Rabbi Shmuel Shlomo, succeeded him, and devoted himself to the integrity of the Radzynian line of *Chasidism.*

Tunes at the Rabbi of Radzyn court
Written by Chanoch Appelboim

**Tunes at the Rabbi of Radzyn court
Written by Chanoch Appelboim**

Yisrael Kotzker Goes with the Rebbe to Find the Snail

Israel Kantor (Haifa)

(Rabbi Reb Gershon Hanoch and the Gabbai (treasurer) Yisrael Kotzker travel to Italy to search for the Tchelet (azure dye) snail-- as I heard about it from my father Yaakov Ben Yisroel Kantor z"l). Yisroel Kotzker HaGabbai (The Treasurer)-that was his nickname and that is what the Chassidim called him because he came from nearby Kotzk. His duties in the Court of the distinguished Rabbi Reb Gershon Hanoch in Radzyn were important and respectable, because in those days the Court was a sort of miniature state in which he filled the jobs of both the Prime Minister and all of the other ministers. First he was the treasurer and responsible for running the money raising campaigns and collecting the money. This was a very delicate task and had to be carried out with wisdom, diplomacy and tact because it was important to know from whom and how much. to take. After all it could not be expected that the Rabbi himself should be involved in such mundane matters. In addition, the Gabbai had to balance the expenses of the Rabbi and his family, maintaining the house and courtyard, receiving guests, etc.

His second function was to act as a sort of Minister of the Interior for both the religious and civil administration. His third function was, what is called, in these days, Chief of Protocol .He was the one who decided who would be first to meet the Rabbi, who would sit next to the Rabbi at the table, and who would be honored by being called up to read from the Torah etc. Tact, diplomacy and good relations with everyone were the necessary characteristics of the person who filled these positions. Therefore, it was not surprising that when the strange idea of going out into the world to search for the "Techelet" snail occurred to the Rabbi, his Gabbai, Reb Yisroel Kotzker, should accompany him.

I do not know how the idea was conceived or how it came to fruition, but one can imagine what a great a stir this daring idea created. It caused ferment and clashes between friends and enemies between Chassidim (Followers) and Misnagdim (Opponents) and even among his own followers. How is it possible for the Rebbe to go out into the non Jewish world, to countries that are strange to him, among peoples whose language is foreign to him and to be absent from his court and from his disciples and from Jews for such a long time? What about observing kashruth? What will he eat and what will he drink? If at least he definitely knew where he could find the snail! On one hand, there was the healthy logic of his Chassidim and on the other, that of the Rebbe who stuck to his plan.

Even today, with the perspective of seventy- eighty years, it is difficult to picture these two Jews going from city to city, from village to village, mostly by wagon, since there were not always railways, dressed in their Chassidic attire, with the Shtreimel (fur edged hat) and black Capote (long garberdine coat). It is hard to imagine their tribulations while searching for places where they could find kosher food and a safe place to stay.

Try to imagine them after reaching Italy, their destination, wandering around morning after morning for many months. How strange they must have appeared to the non-Jews who saw these two going a back and forth along the seashore, stooping down from time to time to search for something, day after day? They ate only bread that they baked themselves and drank water only from their own utensils.

When, after many tribulations they finally found the location of the snail from which the desired Techelet could be extracted, they enlisted the help of the local non-Jews in gathering it up. When they accumulated a sufficient number of sacks, they loaded them onto wagons and returned to Radzyn. That was no small accomplishment going from Italy to Radzyn by wagon, carrying their heavy and holy cargo. Imagine how they looked when they returned to Radzyn after such an exhausting trip and the reception they received from the Chassidim and the reverberations of their accomplishment in the Jewish world.

This however was not the end of the tale. In order to produce the Techelet from the snail it was necessary to perform complicated chemical experiments. For this purpose the Rebbe set up a small factory in his courtyard and he himself found the necessary formulae. There are very few people, even now; who are capable of finding them.

When the Rebbe passed away, people came from far and wide to accompany him to his final resting-place. Reb Yisroel carried out his responsibilities to the very end. It seems that there and then he decided that his tasks in this world were completed. On the day after the Rebbe passed away he too returned his soul to his maker. The Chassidim saw this as sign from heaven and so they buried him next to the Rebbe. There they lie one next to the other Rebbe Gershon Hanoch the discoverer of the Tchelet and his Treasurer Reb Yisroel Kotzker. In life and in death they were never parted.

———

[Pages 115 - 119]

The Rabbi Who Shook Up Poland

Y.Y. Trunk (The Morgen Journal)

The Radzyner Rabbi, Reb Gershon –Chanoch, carried on a single handed crusade against all the rabbis and respectable Jews of Poland concerning the Blue Tzitzes (ritual fringes} and the Chilazon (snail) fish which he had discovered in the Mediterranean Sea, He was a grandson of the famous rabbi Reb Mordechai-Yosef from Izbitzeh.

Reb Mordechai –Yosef was one of the first and most important of the Kotzker Chassidim. He did something that was very unique in the whole history of the Chassidic Movement. Chassidism was based on the authority of the Tzadik (Revered Rabbi) and the belief in him and his good deeds. On Simchat Torah of 1840, Reb Mordechai-Yosef rebelled openly against his Rabbi from Kotzk. The rebellion took place in Kotzk itself while the Kotzker Rabbi was still alive. Reb Mordechai-Yosef declared himself Rebbe and demonstratively left the court accompanied by almost all of the Chassidim who were in Kotzk for the holiday. They left together without even saying good bye to the Kotzker Rabbi and went to Mordcai-Yosef's hometown Izbitzeh.There he set up his own rabbinical court.

This revolt was shrouded in great mystery, and Polish Chassidim did not stop talking about it. Reb Mordechai-Yosef was of a restless, temperamental nature. The main reason for his revolt was as follows: The Kotker Rabbi carried his individualism to such a degree that he began avoiding people and became unusually scathing. He locked himself into his room and rarely allowed any Chassidim to come in. His words sounded like biting aphorisms that bristled with deep contempt for human wisdom. The wildest rumors spread about the Kotzker's "shut in" years. These unusual contradictions in the Kotzker's ways strengthened his authority and mythical powers among some of his followers. Even the more shadowy sides were transformed into great hidden lights. When they were near him, they felt as if they were in seventh heaven, despite the fact that seven locks closed this heaven to them. They saw in the Kotzker's behavior mysterious holy ways far from the understanding of ordinary mortals but with great symbolic meaning. Some of the Chassidim, however, could not and did not want to understand the secretive old Kotzker Rabbi. They were particularly opposed to his withdrawal from any close relationships with his Chassidim. By his every step he displayed his fear of the wider world. Many of his followers among the Kotzker Chassidim became uneasy. They began to feel sharp pangs of dissatisfaction, as if they were sheep without a shepherd. The essence of Chassidism was based on a very strong feeling of brotherhood.

As I have already mentioned, the Izbitzer (Reb Mordechai-Yosef) was of a restless and colorful nature. On top of that, he was a great conversationalist who loved to carry on discussions preaching Chassidism. He maintained a very brotherly relationship with his fellow Chassidim and was always full of chassidic enthusiasm. He thought that he had been ordained by heaven to leave the Kotzker Rabbi and to become the leader of these neglected Chassidim.

We have very little information about that period and just how this very unusual. Izbitzer's revolution was prepared. This dissatisfaction and the absence of Kotzker hospitality alone were enough to create this revolutionary atmosphere For his part, Reb Mordechai-Yosef did everything he could to make this dismal atmosphere even more depressing. Being a master conversationalist, his discussions with the Kotzker Chassidim, who came to him with curiosity and yearning, had great influence on them.

From the Kotzker study hall came strange undenied rumors that served to electrify the atmosphere and upset his already uneasy followers. Very unpleasant stories circulated that surely did not fit reality since the Kotzker Rabbi, an outstanding scholar, still remained very orthodox.

Whatever the reason, mutiny was in the air. On Simchat Torah, after the meal, Reb Mordechai-Yosef with the congregation that was in Kotzk went down to the Wieprez River that lay behind town. It was here that the Reb Mordechai-Yosef often carried on discussions with groups of his followers. The discussions that Reb Mordechai-Yosef carried on that Simchat Torah on the banks of the river with his followers must have been very pointed and decisive. What was demanded was action, namely breaking all the ties with the Kotzker Rabbi. Reb Mordechai-Yosef was the victor, his demands were met. When he came home with his followers that evening, everyone knew that on the morrow it would happen. The Kotzker would be abandoned and left by himself without a living soul. A new doctrine was kindled in Izbitzeh.

This is how it happened. The next morning, after the end of the holiday, Reb Mordechai Yosef with all of his followers left Kotzk for Izbitzeh without taking leave of the Kotzker Rabbi.

The news of the revolt in Kotzk spread rapidly to all Kotzker shtibles (study huts) in Poland. Almost all of the Chassidim were going over to Izbitzeh. Interestingly enough, the majority of those who left drifted back to Kotzk later, one by one, .It turned out that the daring step taken by the Izbitzer Rabbi had exceeded his capabilities. He became exhausted and began to falter. Those Kotzker Chassidim who had joined him began to desert him. They broke because the Kotzker Rabbi 's renewed internal authority.The majority returned to Kotzk and became even more devout Kotzker followers than they had been before they left. The Kotzker Rabbi's eccentricity now became very attractive to them. The whole revolution resulted in the creation of yet another chassidic sect, Izbitzeh, which later moved over to Radzyn. Mordechai Yosef no longer played the important role he had played in Kotzk, that of being the head of opposition.

When Reb Mordechai-Yosef passed away his son Reb Yaakov took over the Izbitzer throne. He had none of his father's characteristics. Reb Yaakov was of a quiet, lyric- poetic disposition. His book, "Beis Yaakov" is one of the most enchanting books in all the literature describing the spirit of Chassidism.

Much of the characteristics of Reb Mordechai-Yosef reappeared again in his grandson, Reb Gershon-Chanoch. He lacked some of the mystical enthusiasm and the visionary Kabalistic view of everything that characterized his grandfather. He was his antithesis; Reb Gershon-Chanoch was a thoroughgoing rationalist .He did however inherit his very combative nature. Reb Gershon- Chanoch's temperament did not have the proper surroundings for expressing itself and what bothered him most was that he was not equal to his grandfather. He wanted to be new, original and subversive. Gershon Chanoch provoked fierce opposition This, however, did not frighten him. He always undertook audacious projects. For example: As is well known, the Mishnah (a collection of post-Biblical laws) has six Sedorim (the Orders into which the Mishnah is divided) of which only four have their own Gomorra (Commentary) Reb Gershon Chanoch undertook the gigantic task which should have required the work of many generations. He wrote and published one Masechta (Tractate) .The Rabbis admired the audacity of this undertaking.

Then Reb Gershon Chanoch did another thing that exploded like a bomb. In the Talmud there is a passage saying that the blood of the Chilazon (snail}, from which the blue color used in dying only one of the eight Tzitzit (fringes of the prayer shawl), floats up onto the surface of the Mediterranean Sea only once in 70 years. One must have great expertise to know the exact hour of its appearance in order to catch it. This was one of the secrets known only to the High Priests in the Temple and was lost after its destruction. The subsequent generations were forced to do without the blood of the Chilazon in the same way that they had been forced to relinquish animal sacrifice.

The news that a dye producing fish is found in the Mediterranean Sea, especially in the Gulf of Naples, reached Reb Gershon-Chanoch in Radzyn. Nowadays this type of dye-fish is found in every major aquarium. Gershon Chanoch did not hesitate. He betook himself to Naples. There he saw the dye fish and declared that it is the long sought after Chilazon.

Once again Reb Gershon Chanoch caused a great stir. He astonished the Jewish World, this time with something that simply did not seem logical. How could this be the same Chilazon that appears only once in seventy years and that only the High Priests in the Temple knew how to anticipate their appearance and to catch them? Reb Gershon Chanoch showed that the Chilazon fish that he had brought all the way from Italy carried a blue dye in its gills. This would make all the other fringes unkosher. This caused the polemic against the snail to turn loud and acrimonious.

Reb Gershon Chanoch was not the type of person who could be easily frightened off. He appeared in person and in print to defend his daring discovery. He attacked the whole world with erudite casuistry using quotations from the Talmud and from Later Sages and other authorities, to prove that he was correct. A tremendous controversy flared up in the Polish rabbinical world with the followers of Reb Gershon Chanoch on one side and all the other

Chassidic and Rabbinical world on the other. On the command of Reb Gershon-Chanoch, all of his Chassidim began to wear blue Tzitzit. They were attacked and even beaten by the other Chassidim, especially by those from Ger who were followers of the Kotzk dynasty and who vigorously opposed Reb Gershon Chanoch. Gloom covered those Polish shtetls where there were followers of Reb Gershon Chanoch. Some were denied a livelihood. Women divorced their husbands and whole families broke up. There was great ferment. The written and vocal diatribes against the Rebbe however, had no effect on Reb Gershon-Chanoch. He remained convinced that this was the genuine Chilazon. He aimed his attacks mostly against the followers of the Rebbe from Ger. The Gerer dynasty was of direct descent from Kotzk. This may have been the psychological motive which drove Reb Gershon Chanoch to take up the struggle so as to be equal to his grandfather.

The only rabbinical authority in Poland that Reb Gershon Chanoch acknowledged as being higher than himself, and from whom he swallowed many a bitter pill, was Reb Yehoshua'le Kutner. He accepted everything from him both pleasant and unpleasant. He would often come to visit Reb Yehoshua'le with respect and circumspection

When travelling to Tshechotshinek for a health cure he would always stop in at Reb Yehoshua'le Kutner. Reb Gershon-Chanoch would not wear the usual fur-lined coat worn by "respectable Jews" but instead wore the plain grey traveling coat. In this too he was different. The Polish Rabbis and "respectable Jews" put great emphasis on the traditional forms of attire.

This was Reb Gershon-Chanoch. He was an individualist who always went his own way. In every detail he showed the uniqueness of his nature and shook up the Chassidic world.

———

[Page 120]

The Rabbi and the Colonel

by M. Ben-Shmuel (Tel Aviv)

It happened in the time when the Czar of Russia ruled over all of Poland including our shtetl. For strategic reasons the Russians built military barracks to house soldiers. Among them were some thirty Jewish recruits who came from far away Russian districts, some of whom were members of the military band. In their free time some of them would come to the shtetl to spend time among Jews enjoying being in Jewish surroundings. The permanent meeting place was by Yaakov Fligel the Cantor's house.

One time on Passover Eve, when the military authorities released them to spend the holiday among Jews, the late Reb Mordechai Yosef invited them to the Seder with the Chassidim. When they returned to the barracks after the holiday their colonel, the battalion commander wanted to know how they had spent their holiday among the Jews. When they told him that they had all been invited to the Rabbi, where food and drink were plentiful and that they had all sat around one table, he found this very unusual. How could they have prepared food for thirty people in a private home, and what about the cost? The Colonel was so impressed by this unusual event that he immediately ordered the band to go to the Rabbi's court after the holiday to express his thanks for the hospitality extended to the soldiers, and so that the joyful Jews of the town could be entertained by military music!

The colonel accompanied the orchestra as did the officers and their wives and all of them together enjoyed the whole evening. The Chasidim were very excited and Zalmen Dematshever, a happy Jew was especially excited by the unusual visit. In a moment of excitement, he quickly poured a bucket of water on the floor (a way of making it easier to dance on a wooden floor) and broke out gracefully in a dance to the accompaniment of the military band.

From that evening on a friendship was created between the Rabbi and the Colonel and they met often. Through the influence of the Colonel, the Russian priest of the town was drawn into the group. Since the priest knew how to speak Hebrew, the conversations between the priest and the Rabbi took place in that language. When this became known in shtetl the Jews saw it as a sign of the coming of the Messiah. "It is no small matter, that the priest speaks the Holy Tongue!".

**Radzyn Chassidim- the leaders of the community
Right- Leibel Nachtigal; Left- Yisrael Wienderbaum (Dzshabak)**

(As told by Henichel Appleboim)

[Pages 122-123]

From Those Days

by M. Ben Shmuel (Tel Aviv)

In the days when Reb Mordechai Yosef lived in Radzyn, his Chassidim who lived there near him and were directly influenced by him were not conspicuous in their zealotry, their outer dress, or their everyday life style as was customary in other places.

This is the way they lived in the town most of the year. However when holidays, especially the High Holidays approached, and Chassidim came to the Rabbi from many other places, they stood out in their dress, their behavior and were more fanatical about everything. The guests usually looked down on the local Chassidim as being lenient in observing the commandments, deviating from straight and narrow path and being undisciplined. On those days in which Chassidim from all over streamed into the city a typical Chassidic atmosphere enveloped the town.

The addition of a large group Chassidim to the town created certain tensions between the guests and the local inhabitants especially between the youth, and the children of the local Chassidim. The visitors queried: How do they dare to make changes in the accepted life style by shortening their earlocks, reducing the length of their long coats and shaving beards that have just begun to grow? The visitors often brought pressure to bear on the Rabbi not to be so lenient toward the youth who visited the Beth Hamedrash of the Chassidim and who had become immoral. This pressure created tension and disorder as well as turmoil in the social life of the young people.

As has been noted, the young local Chassidim began to display signs of slackening in the observance of the accepted customs. However, since they were still tied to their parents, they continued frequenting the Beth Hamedrash on Sabbath and holidays to study a chapter in the Gomorra which began to serve as camouflage for reading the newspaper. (The reading of newspapers was still considered a deviation from the straight and narrow path.) Some of the fanatics could not accept this situation and a violent struggle broke out which even led to blows being exchanged and expulsion from the Bait Hamedrash. (This was a very radical step.) The youth, despite their being freed in spirit from the influence of Chassidism, fought obstinately for their right to frequent the Bait Hamedrash of the Radzyner Chassidim.

With the normal Jewish social development, these young people who were children and grandchildren of passionate Chassidic parents, were captivated by the different youth movements that became the basis of the national and the social movements. They joined them bringing with them their inherited ardor.

———————

[Page 123]

The Golden Chain

by Leib Rochman

The Golden Chain of the Radzyn Rabbinical dynasty that spread over many generations was broken off in the days of Reb Shloime'le, the last of the Lainers.

For three years Hitler's gangs stormed through Poland. In the spring of 1942 the news spread of the destruction of the Jews under all sorts of terrible circumstances.

Reb Shloime'le, the last of the Radzyn dynasty, was unable to rest. He locked himself up and did not allow anyone in. The strange sounds that issued from his room tore the hearts of his household. In a few days he changed so, that he was unrecognizable.

When his beadle opened the door one morning, a resolute Reb Shloime'le stood before him. It was recognizable that the Rabbi had new strength and courage reflected in his eyes. He ordered that some of his closest and most important Chassidim should be summoned quickly. He remained locked up with them for a long time. What they talked about, no one knew. Only later the news flashed like lightning among the Chassidim: "The Rabbi orders everyone to go into the forest to join the Partisans in their resistance! "

Special messengers carried the Rabbi's message from settlement to settlement, from ghetto to ghetto. They talked about it in whispered voices and the Chassidim began to prepare secretly. Reb Shloime'le then ordered that all Jews fast, rent their garments, remove their shoes and lament before the Almighty. However the news was leaked to the exterminators that" the Radzyner Rabbi...partisans...fast ...etc." everything that should be said in a denunciation.

The next morning the Chassidim learned that the Gestapo was looking for the Rabbi. In the morning they hired a carriage with a good team of horses and sent the Rabbi, by all sorts of back roads, to Waldawa near the Bug River that divided Poland from Russia. Waldawa was a city in which there were many Chassidim who were followers of the Rabbi. The Rabbi was hidden by one of those followers. The Gestapo searched for him for weeks but could not find him.

Suddenly in the middle of a bright day, a grayish green uniformed gang with wild red faces surrounded the ghetto. They set up machine guns as if preparing for battle. The Jews became alarmed and began to think about hiding in cellars or attics, but before they could do anything, firing started from all directions and dozens of holy Jews were lying dead in the streets. At the same time a fat red face appeared at the Judenrat and announced that if the Radzyner Rabbi was not handed over they would shoot all the Jews.

Entreaties would not help. A Chassid came running and threw himself on the floor of the front room of the Rabbi's house and wailed: "For Heaven's sake Jews, we are damned. They want the Rabbi and if they don't get him that will be the end of all the Jews."

For a moment all were silent, everyone sat stiffly and silently. Suddenly the sound of the voice of the old Reb Yaakov Wolf, the beadle, was heard. "Silence Jews! Do not speak loudly so that the Rabbi does not hear. I will go. I am now the Radzyner Rabbi!"

No one uttered a word. Reb Yaakov Wolf quickly took out the prayer shawl and robe from the velvet bag and said to the Chassid: "Go quickly so that they will stop the shooting. The Rabbi will come soon."

The Chassid slipped out of the house and Reb Yaakov Wolf disappeared shortly after him. Later Reb Yaakov was seen on the Mikveh (the ritual bath) street. After he had immersed himself quickly, seven times in the bath, he drew on the prayer shawl with the fringes over his shirt, put on his outer garments, and recited the Vidui (Confession) prayer. Then the old sexton and Chassid Reb Yaakov Wolf went to the market place and turned himself in to the villains.

Laughter echoed through the market. The red faces beamed with satisfaction. Later a single shot announced to all the Jews in the cellars and attics that the Reb Yaakov Wolf had breathed his last breath in purity and holiness.

———

The secret of Rabbi Yaakov Wolf's tragic death and martyrdom did not reach Reb Shloime'le from Radzyn for many weeks. However the Gestapo's intelligence did find out about it. Suddenly on one clear day the barbarian gangs with machine guns again surrounded the Jewish section of Waldawa by the Bug River. Again there were new martyrs lying in the streets. The Gestapo informed the Yudenrat that they knew about the ruse. They knew exactly what the Radzyner Rabbi looked like and in case of deceit all the Jews would be shot without exceptions.

The town was dark. The Chassidim thought about what to do, but there was little time left. Every minute brought new victims. A group of the older Chassidim got together and knocked on the Rabbi's door, went into his room with fear and trembling and stood there in complete silence.

Reb Shloime'le who was seated with his face to the table turned around to the door and seeing the Chassidim with their pale and darkened faces, jumped up:

" Tell me quickly! Is there more bad news?"

They all sobbed out "Holy Rabbi, Holy Rabbi"

"Tell me immediately" said the Rabbi as his heart beat quickly.

"Holy Rabbi!" all of them sobbed "We are in gloom "Yankel Wolf's sacrifice was not accepted."

"What?"

"They want the Rabbi!" the elders sobbed. "They want the Rabbi as a sacrifice."

"Me ?" The Rabbi barely managed to say.

"Yes. They have been searching for you for a long time here in Waldawa. There have already been victims. So Yaakov Wolf went and told them that he is Radzyner Rabbi. We thought that would bring calm. Now it seems there has been an informer and there are many more victims. They want the Rabbi! If not, they are ready to murder and kill" The old Jews sobbed like small children "Oh Holy Rabbi."

The Rabbi became white as chalk. He stayed silent for a while and then said. "I have been ready for this for some time. But Yaakov Wolf...one must be ready for such trials. But Yaakov Wolf ...if that is God's will...".

The Rabbi began to run around the room from corner to corner murmuring to himself: "It is a great thing to be a sacrifice to God. Not everyone experiences it. Our parents never experienced it as my Yaakov Wolf did."

One of the elders dropped down to the Rabbi's feet- "Holy Rabbi."

"Yes" the Rabbi said as he turned aside "Yes we must go quickly to prevent further victims."

He ran from corner to corner as if looking for something while mumbling. Was the Rabbi praying, or making a confession, or just telling his forefathers that the Lainers' Golden Chain was severed?

It did not take long .He dipped seven times in the Mikveh, put on his white Izbetzeh linen robe and the prayer shawl with the wide collar and the first blue fringe that belonged to his grandfather and his father's caftan. Then Reb Shloime'le turned himself over to the tainted hands. The sound of a shot announced that the last of the Lainer's Golden Chain had been gathered unto his forefathers.

———

[Pages 127-128]

The Unbroken Blue Chain

by Mordechai Tannenbaum (Tel Aviv)

When one enters the synagogue during the services one can sometime see among the worshippers some who have a blue thread in the fringes of their prayer shawls. These are the Chasidim from Radzyn, a small town in Poland whose remarkable rabbi, the late Reb Gershon Henich Lainer, was the first to renew the commandment of including a blue thread in the fringes of the prayer shawl. This commandment had been forgotten for most the Exile. According to the laws of the Torah, one blue thread should be included among the eight threads of the fringes. This thread was dyed in the blood of a snail that that is found on the shores of the Mediterranean Sea. However, the long wanderings of the Jews from place to place made it very difficult to obtain the snail and the commandment of the blue thread was neglected.

The late Reb Gershon Henich, who was one of the great geniuses of his time and also a man of science with very original ideas, was very doubtful of fringes without a blue thread. He decided to correct the situation. It took a lot of effort until he achieved his goal .He made many trips to the shores of the Mediterranean Sea till he found the snail that is described in the Mishnah and by Maimonides. Once he found the snail many difficulties presented themselves as the blood of the snail was black, and it was not easy to produce the blue dye. Therefore the rabbi set up a laboratory, and after a number of attempts, he succeeded in producing the blue dye. Thousands of his Chassidim began wearing the blue thread in their prayer shawls. Among them were the Breslav Chassidim whose rabbi Reb Nachman foresaw the revival of the wearing of the blue thread and instructed his followers to do so in the writings that he left.

This innovation created a stir in Chassidic and Torah circles, which was echoed in the questions and answers of the rabbis and even reached Hebrew literature. With the outbreak of World War II and the execution of the last Radzyn Rabbi Reb Shmuel Shlomo z'l (May he rest in peace), the grandson of Reb Gershon Henich z'l, by the Nazis, the source of the blue dye dried up and the blue thread became rare.

Right after the end of World War II, Radzyner Chassidim in Israel made a serious effort to renew the production of the blue dye. Unfortunately, no one was left alive of those who had participated in making the dye. However, after many attempts, a snail was found on the beaches near Haifa that suited the description in the books by the Radzyner Rabbi However, they ran into many problems. The blood was enclosed in a special sheath and it was necessary dissolve the blood before dying because the blood became hard as stone when removed from the sheath. After it was dissolved it became necessary to boil it with different acids that cleansed it until the blue color appeared. . The

Radzyn Chassidim applied to the chemists of the Hebrew University, the Weitzman Institute and other laboratories to accomplish this. Lo and behold! What the Radzyner Rabbi accomplished with primitive methods, these chemists were unable to accomplish with their sophisticated equipment. In the end they gave up and unanimously decided that it was impossible.

The Radzyner Chassidim did not give up easily and eventually achieved their goal when Mr. Shpizeisen, a Radzyner Chassid, immigrated to Israel. He had worked in the dying trade for twenty-five years, had fled to Russia when the war broke out and ran a chemical enterprise. When he arrived in Israel he confidently spent nights and days performing many experiments and finally saw results! At a festive ceremony in which the Mayor of Jerusalem Mr. S.Z. Shragai, himself a Radzyner Chassid participated, he triumphantly displayed the results. The snail was cut open, the blood was boiled and liquefied and after the addition of acids a thread from the fringes was dipped in while the spectators waited very tensely to see the results. Behold! The mayor of Jerusalem removed a glistening blue thread! It is hard to describe the joy of all those present who recited the Shechionu (thanksgiving prayer) and who saw this as a sign that 'the Blue Chain 'remained intact. (From Hebrew daily 'Maariv')

[Page 131]

Life and Youth

In Your Streets Radzyn

Yitzchak Cnaanii (Kopeck) (Tel-Aviv)

Seven days of travelling on land sea and a period of over twenty years, that is the distance that separates you from me, Radzyn the place where I was born. Through those 20 years in which men's nations' and the world's fate unfolds, you rise and appear before my eyes in all your clarity, alive- as if I left you only yesterday. It's enough to close my eyes for a moment, to feel you with all my being. The smell of the endless forests, the green fields with the tall grain, the ancient palace with the croaking of the frogs in the ponds surrounding it, the quiet stream, that passed by its side- all this is your exterior fabric, in which your dignity dwells. And inside?

One of the "Hashomer Hatzair" groups in Radzyn

At the crossroads close to the town stands a post and on it arrows pointing in three directions: 27 km to Lukow; 18 km to Kotzk; 1 1/2 km to Radzyn. I will not linger on the rest of the neighboring towns like Miedzyrzec,

Czermierniki, Wohyn, Komarowka and others that also contributed their share in shaping Jewish life in the whole region. I will start my tour at the sawmill. Since my late father was a dealer in lumber and wood, I often visited there, and it made a deep impression on me. The two large bench saws swallowed up giant logs and noisily spewed out boards and planks which were sorted into neat piles. Most of the laborers who performed these tasks were non-Jews, but I only remember the two Jews, Michael Rosenfeld and Shmuel Fast who worked there for many years. They typified the hard working Jewish day laborer and played an important role in the slogans about proletarianism, productivisation etc. that so influenced us, the Pioneer Youth of those days.

Musicians- Radyn theme
Painting by Moshe Appelboim (1886-1931)

Mostly Christians populated the outskirts of the town, although there were a few Jews among them. The town itself began with the theater building, which because of its size stood out among the other buildings even though it, too, was built of wood. Inside there was a roomy auditorium with a large stage and backstage area. I remember the first motion picture show after word got around that "at the "Luzion" they are showing snow, despite the fact that today is a summer's day." The stage was used mostly by school and other amateur dramatic groups. This is the place to mention two very theatrically talented people: Motel Vineapple and Hannibal Appleboim (who is with us in Israel) who showed great initiative in this field. They kept the town in a state of theatrical tension for most of the year. For weeks and sometime for months various parties and groups prepared plays. This was followed by the sale of tickets (the income was devoted to good causes) and finally to the performance itself and the discussions that followed it. They performed Shalom Aleichem, Peretz Hirshbein, Ansky and others. I cannot summarize this section on the theater without mentioning the Purim Shpiel "The Sale of Joseph" which was performed by the shoemakers and of which they were very proud.

The Polish Library was the other institution on this part of the street which attracted young people and some of the Polish speaking Jewish intelligentsia. I remember two small rooms, one of which served as a sort of waiting room with a large picture of Jesus on the wall. The other room's walls were covered with books with black bindings. The librarian, a pleasant looking Christian woman, was dressed in black as if to say: "My books and I are one."

Across the street and behind the city hall there was a big blue building, the Rabbi's house. Rabbi Fine was a very respectable looking figure in his turban, who, standing next to his short wife who wore pincnez glasses and a long black elegant coat, commanded respect. From here on, the population consisted only of Jews living in small wooden houses on both sides of Warszawska Street. I will point out a few of them. There is the building that housed a mangle. The women would drag heavy bundles of clothes on their backs to be ironed by the heavy weight of a wooden box filled with stones while at the same time exchanging the latest gossip. They told a story about the owner of the house, Reshke'le, whose husband went out one evening to close the shutters and disappeared. A few months later she got a letter from him from America. Her partner in the lot was Eliyahu Haim Tennenboim the builder. Despite the fact that his son and daughters were members of the Bund (Jewish Socialist Party), we respected him for being one of the two or three builders who actually built houses. In the next yard, they produced oil which they sold in a store at the front of the house. Two girls who lived in this house immigrated to Israel. Their brother was the last Jew to leave Radzyn. After experiencing the Nazi tribulations and long wandering, he finally reached Israel. Next to their house stood that of Dr. Petrolivich. This was a villa built of stone and surrounded by a blue fence covered with an abundance of flowers, vegetation, and trees. All this was guarded by a loyal, gigantic dog who reacted to anyone's touching the fence by barking loudly. We, the children of the adjacent house, were attracted to the doctor's yard because of its cleanliness and beauty even though our own yard was wonderful. It contained flowerbeds, young pine trees, and a patch of varied fruit trees all of which played an important part in the memories of my early youth in my father's house. This is the place to mention our neighbor Beryl-Leib Appeloig, a tall and very unusual person, a man of science, a graduate of the faculty of philosophy of Vavelberg Polytechnic School in Warsaw who lived in the other apartment in our house. He was a member of the city council and gave private lessons. His hobby was scientific books which he read even on his way from his house to the store. Across from our house stood that of Michelovsky, a wooden villa of an unusual style with a large garden with an ornamental pool. This house was purchased by a Jewish family from the village of Vela-Savinska who were forced to move to the city because of a pogrom .By the way the, mayor of the town, who was a drunkard and caused great embarrassment to his wife and children, lived in this house.

Yaakov Kopietz
A councler in "Hashomer Hatzair" and one of the organizers of the first training farm in Izchess. Graduated with honours from the teachers seminary and taught untill his last day. Died young while making arrangements for his immigration to Israel.

A printing press was located in a house near ours, and the sound of the machines could be heard from a distance. After every third thump, a poster or copy of a municipal announcement slid out from under the press. The owner of the press, Yaakov Lazer, a very honorable, reserved person, was a member of the city council and an ardent follower of the Radzyner Rabbi. It was told that his son Yoel was a Communist and when the Russians came close to the town he seized the "keys to the town". Later, when they retreated, he joined the Russians and disappeared into the wilds of Russia .The next neighbor was a non-Jewish industrious peasant and anti-Semite Pruchnitzky. The picture of him, bare footed, with his pants legs rolled up and a scythe on his shoulder going or returning from the fields cast great fear on us children and has remained engraved in my memory. Behind the house, there was a big lot where the horse traders gathered. It was a very lively place on market days. The meeting with the non Jewish buyers and sellers running up and down with the horses to try them out, the hand shake and beer drinking when the deal was closed, were characteristic of this place.

On the steps in front of this house sat Shuchmacher the Communist, a short thin and terminal sickly looking man usually reading a newspaper. Across the way stood a number of miserable buildings whose walls were whitewashed. Behind them there was a U shaped alley. Among those who lived there, I remember two shoemakers the sound of whose hammers could be heard late into the night. One was Shmuel who had a silent look. The other was the father of Hershe'le the Angel who was always annoyed and angry. I also would like to mention Shoshanah the milkmaid who could be seen dragging her heavy milk cans. My late father's lumberyard was opposite the crosswalk to Ostrowiecka St. Behind it stood Yisroel Hersh Kavebloom's bakery from which the odor of freshly baked bread could be smelled from afar. On Saturday morning there was heavy traffic of women and children who came to take their casseroles of cholent (a bean stew for the Sabbath) from the oven. This bakery was in the home of Reb Yaakov Moshe, a shrewd clever witty Jew. Tzvi Koppelman, the founder and a leader of the Hitachdut (Socialist Zionist Party), lived here too. A joke about him and his fellow worker and party member Uziel Wiesman made the rounds. It was said that they prepared themselves for immigrating to Israel by studying bee- keeping, but instead of immigrating they both got married and continued working in the flower mill. "Instead of immigrating and getting themselves black doing agricultural work, they continued working in the mill and stayed white." Above, in the attic, lived the Patshek family, a mother with five beautiful daughters. One of them married the well-known artist Moishe Appleboim and settled in Katowice. This house was considered very "romantic", singing, accompanied by a mandolin, could be heard from afar until late into the night.

By turning ninety degrees to the right, you go up an unpaved road that leads to the barracks used by the soldiers in World War I. Later it housed war refugees and in the end it housed the elementary school run by Balshatziac, a non-Jew who was very knowledgeable about nature. He was a good friend to both his Jewish and non-Jewish students and was a "righteous gentile". His wife however was an Anti-Semite. Beyond the fence that surrounded the barracks stretched the old, abandoned and neglected Jewish cemetery with its rough stone gravestones. Two graves of famous departed, built in the form of small buildings, stood out. This road passed over a stream on a wooden bridge next to which there were usually many women, up to their knees in water, washing clothes. Near the bridge stood a building that served as a public bathhouse during the German occupation and later became a studio for the fireman's band. On summer afternoons, many Jews could be found bathing in that section of the river between the threshing buildings owned by non-Jews. There was always the danger of clashing with the shkotzim (young non-Jews) who would wait and interfere with our getting out of the water. While we stood there naked, they would attack us with mud and stones from the opposite bank. This usually ended up with one of our boys going naked to the other bank and chasing the fleeing shkotzim thus allowing us to get dressed and leave.

"Hakoach" football (soccer) team

On the left of the bridge there was a green meadow maintained by Reb Mendel (Danilak) who was both bookbinder and farmer. I think he was the first Jewish farmer I ever knew. Beyond the meadow, on a ramp located between two frog filled pools, stood a thatched booth where the finest of Jewish youth gathered on summer evenings to sing and discuss books. An intimate and romantic atmosphere was created that served as the basis for a Zionist youth movement. One who stood out from this group was Pearl

Kiettelgisser who worked all day in the large garden (the Rabbi's orchard) preparing herself for working in agriculture in the Land of Israel. She was the first of all the girls to immigrate to Palestine paving the way for many more to follow in her footsteps.

At that time, at the end of World War I, there was a group of "Poele Tzion" ("Workers of Zion") and "Tzeire Zion" ("The Young of Zion") that spread the idea of cooperatives. They rented a room in Reb Legible Reichenberg's house, and with instructions from a carpenter began to produce kitchen chairs sold to homeowners. Some time later a co-op food store was started in the same room. An adjacent building housed the "Bund" ("Jewish Socialist Party") center. Among its outstanding members were Shmuel Itzl Meir Goldes (a leader of the fire brigade), Leitzeh Gelibter and Velvel Tennenboim. Later on Pshenitza and others joined. Yehoshua the builder, a very proud proletarian stove repairman, lived some three lots down from there. From there I remember a women with two orphaned children, blind from birth, who aroused great pity in us and for whom we often served as guides. Further down the road, there was a fenced-in empty lot with a very tall post with rungs going up to the top which served as a look-out post for the fire brigade. On the opposite lot there was a stationery store belonging to Pessach Yehoshua. The door would open accompanied by the ringing of a bell, and only after a few moments a salesperson would appear, either Chanoch or Shmuel or their mother. The store was crammed full of books and stationery, and was the only one of its kind in the town.

Following "Flower Day" for a public institution

A few steps down from there stood the Rabbi's house, court and the Beis Medrash (study hall). Behind it stood a blue hut where the Tchelet (a blue dye used for dying the ritual fringes) was produced. "The big house" stood opposite. The old timers told many tales about that house. I will only mention the darkness in the entrance passageway, which forced you to feel around in the dark to find a door for entering. Different craftsmen lived there: Yisrael the building carpenter, a short Jew with a short rounded beard some of whose pupils are now in Israel and are noted for being good carpenters. Opposite and facing it stood Reb Boruch Hersh Appelboim's house. Women and children came there with their fowl to get a "kvittel" (note) to the shochet (ritual slaughterer). Beyond the lane that led to Ostroweicka St., stood Alter Blichovitz's house. He was short, spoke slowly and had a heavy watch chain across his chest. He was a skilled mechanic who educated all of his sons to be workers. It was a pleasure to watch him wholly concentrated on repairing a sewing machine, the peak of mechanical knowledge by the standards of the town at that time.

The house behind that one belonged to Moishe Berman. The house was very low as compared to its inhabitants who were all very tall. He was a tall, well to do Jew with a white beard and looked very patriarchal as he strode leisurely to the synagogue. What was special about his son, Chanoch, was that he wore a black Russian shirt on weekdays and on holidays and led a very modest life He lived in Israel for a number of years and passed away childless.

In the stream near Yossel the soap maker (Lichtenstein)

The city hall stood opposite. This building was very different from all the others: heavy, gray and built of stone with massive windows. Sometimes the representatives of the Jewish community, Lazar, Appeloig, Z'laza, Greenblatt, Kleinboim and others were seen sitting at the tables inside.

The house of Shvalbeh the photographer, who was known to us youngsters from our class pictures, stood near the city hall. He was the father of Nathan Shvalbeh who was a famous journalist in Poland.

Then came the Christian orphanage, the pharmacy, and the church, which stood in the center of the town and was bordered by the three main streets. Behind the church, in the priest's courtyard there was a well (the priest's pump) famous for its good water. People came from all parts of the city to draw water for brewing tea. Then came the "Midlarnia" the home soap manufacturing workshop. It was a very picturesque place, a low sunken building surrounded by some old wooden huts that stood on wooden posts reflected in the water. By the way, the son of the soap maker, Mendel Lichtenstein, eventually became a famous artist who is now in New York. (A number of his drawings appear in this book). This place, between the huts, attracted many bathers in the summer. To pass this part of the river from the huts to the bridge ("between the posts") was a sort of swimming test. These were burnt wooden posts sticking up from the water that were left over after a fire destroyed the flourmill that once stood by the river.

Rabbi Leizer Zigelman
Among the most respected members of the community and renowned Torah reader. Served as Shofar blower and prayer song leader in the synagogue for many years (1867-1942).

The "new" cemetery was located about two kilometers from the city along the road that ran from the further end of the bridge to Czermierniki. This was the source of the curse used by the ordinary people "You should go already on the Czemiernicki road," meaning to the cemetery. Beyond the bridge there were two giant ponds teeming with frogs whose croaking blended well into the surroundings of rows of ancient trees, the old house of the landlord, and the murmuring of young couples who spent the late summer evenings here. The ponds were intersected by two ramps .One was used for learning to ride bicycles, and the other was sort of the end of the world for us young children. The ramps met on one side with the road to the government hospital, and on the other side they connected up to the palace.

"Beit Tarbut" evening school students with their parents and Daniel Parsky from America

Many legends circulated about this palace. No one knew who built it and when. What was known was that its owner was the wealthy Lord Shlibovsky who was often seen riding through the town in an unusual carriage drawn by two glorious horses. My father told us of the impressions he had of his visits to the lord's house where he went in connection with his buying lumber and other business deals. As mentioned, it was a very ancient building built in the old square style with two giant gates. Eventually it was adapted for use as the district offices. Beyond the palace, in the direction of Miedzyrzec, there was a park that covered an immense area surrounded by a high wall. Inside were thick trees with winding paths between them, and a giant pool that attracted many young people and froze over in the winter. Beyond the wall was the road to Miedzyrzec with its promenade on the one side and the "square" (a sort of municipal garden) on the other, with a closed up Orthodox Church in the center. The high school, the post office, Shlomo the Smith's workshop, Leskovsky's machinery factory and a windmill were located here. The big flourmills were also located here. The owners were three rich Jews from whose wealth the poor also benefited.

Yakov Blachawitz
Teacher in the "Tarbos" school for many years; among the most dedicated educators of Zionism and Hebrew

The busiest spot was the two market places called "The First Market" and "The Second Market". A lane filled with small stores connected them. On market days peddlers and merchants from the surrounding towns came here with their stalls, as did the peasants from the neighborhood with their wagons. Together, they completely covered the whole area.

This is the place to mention the stores of Moishe Appeloig who sold cigarettes and tobacco, Kiseleh (Yekutiel) Lichtenstein who sat by the door of his hardware store reading a book while waiting for customers, Ahre'le Lurkis who one bright day switched from being a tobacco merchant to being a textile merchant and Mushkat's restaurant which was patronized mostly by non-

Jewish porters since no self respecting person would eat in a restaurant. After that, there were a number of hat shops, one of which was known for making the hat fit the customers head by the hat-maker inserting fingers between the head and the hat so that it was always a perfect fit. Here there were also a number of ready-made clothing shops and Shaul Henich's saloon from which the voices of its drunken customers could be heard

Beyond those buildings were those of the Second Market with two wine shops, that of Yossel Zita and that of Beryl Nachman Laizers who kept the peasants supplied with alcohol. Further along in that row, was Yosef Dovid Wolf's haberdashery store and Itshe Meir Rav Azshes paint store.

Here too, were the stores of Chaim Burker, Beryl Shtrik, David Lomka, and Chaim Gelerman who was an official and delegate of the Jewish National Fund for many years. Across the way, were the storerooms and hardware store belonging to David Lichtenstein and Shimon Kleinboim. This was a very fancy store with a telephone, cashier, and bookkeeper. Laizer "the watchmaker's" (Zigelman) shop stood in the corner of the market. Reb Laizer was a short Jew who was considered an expert in his field and was often invited into homes to service large wall clocks. He also gave great pleasure to the congregation when he read from the Torah on Sabbath and holidays.

Travelling to Israel: this time it's Menucha Idelman

Kozia, Szkolno, Kotlarska and Kalen Streets were partly paved roads without sidewalks that branched off from the two marketplaces. Ordinary people, mostly craftsmen, shoemakers, tailors, coachmen, owners of vegetable gardens and the like inhabited these streets. The Bais Medrash (study house), the synagogue, the Hassidic study house, the different cheders (the Jewish religious elementary schools), the public bath house, the school and the fire station were all located here.

**The first elections for the Polish Siem following WW I
At the house of Lea'le Kleinman**

I remember the bais medrash and the synagogue from the Sabbaths and holidays when Jews would come there to pray. They were both high stone buildings with large windows that stood out among the low wooden houses and were visible from a distance. The western side of the bais medrash served as a center for the ordinary people: storekeepers, artisans, coachmen, porters, etc. who usually prayed in the first shift. The more "respectable" class of citizens, shopkeepers, merchants and observant Jews who were close to the religious officials, could be seen on the eastern side. An itinerant preacher or a Zionist official from the Jewish National Fund or the Keren Hayesod (Palestine Foundation Fund) would appear there and would be seen the next day going from house to house accompanied by a local official to solicit contributions. The synagogue was used mostly for praying on Sabbaths and holidays. The building was clean and well taken care of, and the atmosphere was festive. I remember the very artistic Torah ark, the colored glass windows and the women's balcony from which sighs or sobs could occasionally be heard. It is worth mentioning by name the various "shtibles" (small prayer huts): "Chevreh Mikra Shtibel" (The Bible Reader's Hut) The Bialer Shtibel (The people from Biala's Hut), the "Kotzker Shtibel" (the followers of the Rabbi of Kotzk), the Artisans Shtibel, etc. The public bathhouse and the mikveh (ritual bath), which was used for ritual immersion, were located behind the synagogue. On Friday evening the "everyday Jews" would gather here on the high benches among the steam vapors uttering groans of satisfaction while flogging themselves with the famous "bezemel" (whiskbroom). The Jews would come in here pale and with a bundle of clothes under their arms and leave clean and with pink cheeks, their sidelocks spread out and wrapped in their capotes (long black coats), a feast for the eyes.

The public toilets, not noted for their cleanliness, were located behind the bathhouse.

The area between Kotlarska and Kozia Streets and the Beis Hamedrash was inhabited mostly by coachmen, porters, shoemakers, and tailors It was covered with wooden huts, abandoned old wagons, and a jumble of buildings, horse stables, barns and chicken coops. The place was impassible for most of the year as everything was immersed in mud that surrounded two puddles of stagnant water covered with green muck. Two shoemakers, Hersh Leib Putzig and Tzalkeh controlled this area. They were both tall Jews, excellent craftsmen who marched in front of the fire brigade parade, and played the leading rolls in the traditional shoemakers performance of "The Sale of Joseph". Liquor was not uncommon in these houses whose windows were almost on the same level as the earth outside .The moving sounds of Jewish folk melodies being sung or played could be heard late at night accompanied by the banging of hammers.

The different "cheders" (Young boys' religious schools) were an important part of this neighborhood. Here was "Lozer's Cheder" for beginners. He was a broad shouldered red faced man with a long beard who terrified us children. Then there were the "Yossel Glutz's, Itche Kune's and Pinchasel Melamed's Cheder" for advanced students. "Hershel Lipe's Cheder" was for even older students, a sort of institution of "higher education".

The institution that later succeeded in attracting the majority of the youth was the David Lichtenstein School. It was named in honor of a leader who had been the head of the Jewish community for many years. Here there were a number of teachers dedicated to educating the younger generation and whose mission in life was ensuring the existence of the school. Worthy of mention are Blachovitz who was the first zealot for Hebrew in the town and its flag bearer all his life, Yehoshua Freedman, the Bible teacher, Rachlis, p.143 the math teacher and the language teachers Yehudit and Menucha Lichtenstein and others. The school building was made of wood and was located on Skolno

Street. It served as a center for youth many of whom, as members of the youth movements, made their way to Israel. Hebrew courses for adults, dramatic groups, Zionist meetings etc. also took place there. Yehoshua Lichtenstein, one of the leaders of the local Jewish intelligentsia, who exemplified the period, lived in that building.

From the corner of Kotlarska and Kozia St., I can see the house where Yosef Dovid Wolf and Itsche Meir Burshtein lived and in which I was born. (We later moved to Warshavska St.) This house was known for its social and Torah activities. On the bottom story, many visitors and family members could be seen around a long table, carrying on friendly discussions and arguments. Above, on the second story, Reb Itsche Meir could be seen bent over a Gemora with his tobacco box next to him. On Kozia Street, I remember Vinderboim's house with its grocery store that was a center for the young people thanks to all of his children, who belonged to "Hashomer Hatzair". ("Young Guards" a Zionist youth movement.) There too was Hershel Mandleboim's famous grocery store. He later immigrated to Israel together with his whole family. They were followed by the their neighbors, the family of Chanale the Sticher (Adelman). Here is the place to mention the two shochtim (ritual slaughterers) "the Big Shochet" and the "Small Shochet" whose names suited them.

Yitzchak Shlimak
Among the respected members and supporter of the community for many years

The offices of the Jewish Community were in a building that stood in a large empty lot on the side. This was the realm of the affluent David Lichtenstein. This house was the center of activities for the Jewish community although not always in close contact with it. Worthy of mention were "perpetual leaders" led by Reb Israel Vinderboim (his grandson Levi Vinderboim served as the secretary of the community for many years). Two other buildings that were located at the end of Kozia St. are worth mentioning. First there was the house of Akiva Rubinshtein with its big garden. He was an aristocrat who had little involvement with the people and with community affairs and was only interested matters of culture and education. The second house was that of Motyia Bashes Katznelbogen, a God fearing, Torah learning Jew, who spent most of his time studying the Talmud and educating his children to traditional Jewish life style. When one of his daughters when on Hachshara (a farm where young people trained for life in Israel) he came there and took her home by force.

The end of Kozia St. was connected to Ostroweicka the main street by an alley. Here at the corner stood Leah'le Klayman's house. She was a widow who owned a nice cigarette and tobacco shop. By the way, her son in law introduced the first taxi into the city that competed with the coachmen who carried passengers to the railroad station. I remember very well the coachmen's glee when he did not know how to start the engine and he had to ask the passers by to push him. The adjacent house belonged to Mendel Klayman. It was a two-story building of unplastered red bricks. The bottom story contained a store that sold kerosene and salt. The peasants, who came into town and sold their produce, (butter grain etc.), would come to this store to stock up on its goods before returning home. The next door was the electric company office. Here one could see Lichtenberg the bookkeeper, a feeble looking Jew who sat bent over his ledgers with a colored pencil stuck behind his ear. The entrance to the flourmill was located behind this house. Varied agricultural machinery, remnants of the big machinery warehouse belonging to Yehoshua Lichtenstein, stood in the front part .The entrance to the mill was inside the back of the second lot. People white with flour and the continuous roar the machines were all an integral part of the scenery. All of this bordered on David Liechtenstein's magnificent two-story house with its garden of ornamental and fruit trees.

The owner of the house was the head of the community who had a very keen sense of control of everything. He raised a large family. His oldest son was the first to flee and come to Israel after deserting from the anti-Semitic army. Among his other children it is worth mentioning Michael Lichtenstein, a sensitive and sickly young man, who died while still young. In the evenings, one could see young people sitting on the sidewalks in front of the house and engaging in friendly conversation. Ostroweicka St. continued on from here under a different name "De Kleine Gass" (The Little St.) David Kleinman, the petroleum dealer whose son and daughter came to Israel, also lived in this house. A number of grain dealers lived in this house including Hershel and Henich Punchiak the leaders of the Tzeire Tzion. It is also worth mentioning Shlimak's house. One of his sons was a prominent soccer player and was in charge of activities connected with this sport for many years. His second son was a founder of Hashomer Hatzair (The Young Guards). One of his daughters became the only Jewish teacher in the government school. An unpaved path to Nedzink led from the corner of Lichtenstein's house, passing through an area inhabited by non-Jews, through which we finally reached the soccer field. Nachum Yekel Brezers "the Petition Writer's" house stood not far from here. Yekel Kantor, the bank clerk, lived in the front of the house. He was a Zionist, very devoted to public service who in later years left the city. Across from the vacant lot stood the house of Label Nachtingel, one of the city elders. His son Nissan was an important watch manufacturer in Switzerland. One of his grandchildren was among the first to reach Israel. "The Kugele" a smith standing by his anvil could be seen through the window of a dark room in a dilapidated building. (By the way, his son reached Palestine right after World War I and passed away in Haifa not long ago after having lost his son in the War of Independence). Through another window Yitzchak Butman, with a growth above one eye, could be seen standing by his sewing machine. Behind that is Pincus's house sunk partly into the ground. Opposite was Eliyahu Shteper's (the sticher's) house and Neche Kupliak's small store all of whose goods could be packed into one sack. After that came the house of Reshke who was one of the two or three Christian families on the whole street. (By the way, Reshke's boy Adik spoke an excellent and fluent Yiddish). In the yard was the Herbst family that had the only cowshed in the middle of the town. Opposite was Yekel Gershun's barbershop. He was also a paramedic, who was very proud of his profession and considered himself almost a doctor. He took great pleasure in saying with special emphasis: "In our medical profession". His wife was Freidel the Midwife and his daughter was Felinda the manicurist. (At present in U.S.). Yekel Buber's store was in the yard. I remember the lane leading into Warszawska St. and just behind that Yisroel'ke Gottesdiner's store where he sold ice cream and soda. This was a meeting place for the older petite bourgeoisie young people. ("Give me a half of glass of soda water with syrup"). Next to that was another soda shop belonging to Aaron Knop with an altogether different clientele, mostly craftsmen, laborers and ordinary people. Here I should mention their unfortunate, mentally disturbed daughter called "Die Shtumeh" (The Mute) who ran around the streets barefooted and dressed in a sack frightening the children. It was reported that she was the first victim of the Germans when they entered the town.

After that I remember the Feivel'eh "Putter's" (Butter's) store with its primitive scale made from two pieces of board and a rope, with stones that served as weights. His capote, (caftan) the table, everything was soaked in butter. In the adjoining house was the bakery of Greenberg who was a tall thin man whom I remember as the head of the Cohanim (High priests) at the prayers in the synagogue. Itsche Levenstein's "Tsheineh" (teahouse) was located in the same building. Here people stood in line with their kettles to get tea on Sabbath morning or noon. It is worth mentioning his son, Israel, who was one of the strongest athletes in town.

From there we reach the bank which was a large central two-story building opposite the churches. Milson the Christian's pharmacy and Bonk's pork shop were on the first floor. Shimon Kleinboim, the father of Moshe Sneh, occupied the apartment on the second floor. He was an ardent Zionist who served as chairman of the Zionist Organization in the city. He was also a member of the city council and was very devoted to serving the community. The bank, which was located on the same floor, but in the second wing of the building, also served as center for community and Zionist activities. I remember its director Simcha Goldwasser (who succeeded the above mentioned Yaakov Kantor) who was a Zionist activist and a leader of the "Hitachdut". I also remember Rachel Richter, Menachem Appleboim, Simcha Reichenberg and others. Across the street behind Reshke's house were Kevelboim's bakery, Hershel Yiskar's barbershop and the alley that led to Kozia St.. Here I would like to mention the Goldwasser house with Mattiyahu the Zionist activist and his two sisters Nechama and Freideh who were both seamstresses, and Hershel Tikatchinsky the newspaper distributor. Not far from there stood a number of two-story stone houses with Motel Wineapple's barbershop. Here a number of a certain type of well to do adolescents gathered for a friendly chat and entertainment thanks to the barber shop owner who, as noted, had a strong connection, to the stage. There was a posh non-Jewish restaurant there too, and next to that was Natan Turkeltoib the rich lumber merchant's house. Yakel Nussboim, who was a partner in flourmill, lived on the second story. There was also Nachum Fullman's gas station and the non-Jewish store belonging to the two Letz old maids as well as the grocery store on the corner that belonged to Zalmen Mechel. Then I remember the lane leading to Kozia St. with two butcher shops and the textile shop belonging to Yeshiyah'le Zilberberg and Nathan Turkeltoib. The wine and beer store belonging to Fishke Turkeltoib was located in that same building and further along that row of buildings was the haberdashery store belonging to the fat one-armed man whose son Yechiel Hoftman went to Palestine but later immigrated to America. Then there was Henya'le Bracha's store and Mordechai Kokosh's (Neiman) barber shop that was followed by the shop of Shimon and Elka Kupitz, and Diamant's hat shop. Behind that stood the glassware shop belonging to Zabidovitz and at the end Yeke'le Blumenkop's bicycle rental shop with the big clock in the window.

This clock, together with the pulse of the whole Jewish town, was silenced forever in the light of day by the evil bloody hand.

Yaakov Cantor
Of the Jewish bank founders and its first manager.Typical Zionist activist and
good friend of the young generation

[Page 149]

My Shtetl

Levi Vinderbaum (Tel-Aviv)

Yiddish literature is called 'small town-ish' because most of it was devoted to describing life in the small shtetls. It celebrated its hidden beauty, the beauty of its Jewish traditions and the extraordinary small town characters. We really did love our shtetls both for better and for worse.

The life in my shtetl was suffused with family-like warmth. Everyone knew what was cooking in his neighbor's pot. We knew each family through and through and knew all the details, all the gossip.

Participants of "Flower Day" for the "Tarbut" in Radzyn   5668 (1928)

We called everyone by his own name followed by that of his father or mother. Otherwise, it was impossible to know exactly who was being referred to: Reb Itshe Meir of Reb Azshes, Bear's Reb Moishe Laizer, Chaim Eidel's Zalmen Mecheles, Reb Laizer the Watchmaker, Yisroel Dzabak (The Frog) etc.

Radzyn was one of the most appealing of the Jewish Shtetls because together with its small townishness it was also was big townish. First, it stood on a high cultural plane. Life was not fanatically religious or limited, as was the case in many other shtetls. Its leaders were wise and cultured people: for example Shimon Kleinboim, Shaul-Henich Rosenwald, Chaim Yitzchak Gelerman, Yisroel Vinderboim, Yishaya Zilberberg, etc. Therefore, there were relatively few public quarrels.

A religious school in Radzyn
With guest Chaim Goldberg from America (Top row, second to the right)

The Radzyn Chassidim were different from the Chassidim of the surrounding Shtetls. They were happy, well groomed and liked a song and a dance. Utilizing every opportunity to down a glass, they would slap each other on the back wishing each other Le'chaim and thereby driving out all anxiety and melancholy.

The Radzyner Rebbe was definitely different from the rabbis of the neighboring chassidic dynasties. He was more cultured, worldlier, and more humane. It was a well-known fact that Reb Gershon Chanoch (The Radzyner Rabbi), in addition to being a genius in Jewish studies, was also well versed in science as well as in medicine. I remember my grandfather telling me that the Rabbi would write prescriptions that the non-Jewish pharmacist would accept. The Rabbi could also play on a number of musical instruments.

Radzyn produced a number of famous people, journalists, actors, painters and political leaders.

Radzyn was proud of the fact that in later years it sent the best of its young people to Israel to help build the land. Despite the very difficult conditions they faced there, with a few exceptions, almost none of them returned.

The market street after the big fire in 1929

In later years, before World War II, heavy clouds covered the quiet life of our Shtetl. With fear in their eyes, the Jews faced the impending future. The Polish Government instituted a policy of extermination aimed at the Jewish population. Their situation became unbearable. The activities of the Jewish Communities were severely curtailed. The government would eliminate from the communities' budget any sums intended for Jewish cultural activities. The social welfare needs grew rapidly. Jews began to consider seriously how they might liquidate everything and go to Israel. The horrible events arrived suddenly and devastated the last hopes of the Jewish Shtetl. They extinguished forever all hopes for an attractive Jewish life at home.

May the mute curses of the annihilated communities and of the unlived lives descend forever like a tempest onto the heads of the executioners of our people and our shtetl.

[Pages 152-155]

In The Shadow Of Our Town

(A Bundle of Memories)

Simcha Reichenberg (Tel-Aviv)

I was not present in Radzyn, the home of my youth, during that stormy, wrathful period. I was not a witness when you downed the cup of poison in the terrible time of the Nazi inferno. From a distance I followed with excitement and concern those loathsome days of the past. I hoped to see you whole again carrying on your regular life style as you had for many generations. Then the curtain was raised and the terrible scene was revealed. Together with the former majestic Jewish Poland, her deep roots and broad genealogy, the Jewish community of our town had sunk in the depths.

On the general demographic map, our town was a tiny and unimportant dot. However on the web of the diverse Jewish life in the Zionist Pioneer movement it played an important role.

Even in the traditional Polish-Jewish world of numerous 'rabbinical courts' and 'shtibles' of the different rabbis, our town was famous for very special Radzyn Chassidim and for their unique 'blue thread'. I remember when we were still boys how we stole on to the Rabbi's garden and into the hut that stood there. We went in and watched how Reb Yehoshua Keitelgisser tended this 'blue' and dyed the threads for the prayer shawls with it.

In my childhood I heard many stories about the life style and customs of the various Chassidic types who came from afar to live in the town so as to be close to the Rebbe and enjoy his words of wisdom. Our house served as a lodging place for these Chassidim. About one of them, Yehoshua Meir from Piotrokov I heard the following story. He was a wealthy Jew who in his old age handed over all of his affairs to his sons and went to sit far away from his family to be near the Rabbi. A special room with a big bookcase was allocated to him. He was awake most of the night studying and looking into the books. Toward morning he would go to the synagogue, spend some time with the Rebbe and then go back home. Then he would doze off for a while, wake up and continue studying and learning.

When I recall those times in the Twenties after the end of World War I, I see myself with a group of friends sitting in the house of Reb Mendel Hersh Lipe's and studying the Torah. The room was small and the sun's rays rarely penetrated its darkness. We would sit there from morning to evening. Only once a week did we leave for a couple of hours. That was on Wednesday. That day was market day in the town. Our teacher's wife had a stall where she sold manufactured goods and on that day he would go out to help her watch over it so that no one would steal anything. Therefore, those hours were a real holiday for us when we would close our books, go out and loll around, and make as much mischief as we wanted.

When did the Rabbi delight in his pupils? When he would be invited to come to one of their houses and there repeat everything that we had recently learned. If the pupil from that house passed the test and could answer all the questions and solve all the problems, the Rabbi was happy because he knew that the student's parents might reward him with a coin. However, if the student did not pass the test the Rabbi would remain angry with him for a long time.

Members of the "Yehuda Ha'Macabi" youth group of "Ha'shomer Ha'tsair" in Radzyn

Not far from the cheder of Reb Mendel Hersh Lipe's, there was a school known as Dovid Fishel's School which fascinated us boys very much. We also got news about the existence of youth movements in the town about which we knew very little. I remember that one winter evening Chaim Shlimek, whose brother was also a student in the Cheder, came and told us about the existence of such youth movements and invited us to join. The Rebbe wanted to prevent our leaving but could not do so because of the fervor of our craving to do so. One day we threw off the bonds of the Cheder and went to study in Dovid Fishel's School.

Our town existed and developed despite the disappointing and hostile regimes that began with the Endeka (National Democratic Party- an anti-Semitic party) and continued on during the reign of Pilsudski and the Senatziah and up until the pogroms in Brisk and Pshitik. All these were stations in the unending social and economic struggle of the Jews of Poland who did not have factories or warehouses that could employ large numbers of workers and clerks. Most of the Jews were small, independent merchants or craftsmen and a small number were day laborers. The occupations that could be acquired were limited to tailoring, shoemaking, hat making and carpentry. It did not take long before reality and ideological considerations led to the conclusion, as it did in most of the Polish towns, especially among the young people, that there was no future in the small towns.

The idea of leaving the small towns, to move to the big cities or travel abroad to build a better future began to penetrate. The young people who were members of the 'pioneer youth movements' looked for places on the world map to which they could immigrate.

Members of the youth group "Shahar" of "Ha'shomer Ha'Tsair", Sivan, 5685 (1925)

At the head of the movements in the town that offered a clear choice to the youth stood 'Hashomer Hatzair' ('The Young Guards') which attracted the best of the 'pioneering youth'. The unusual combination of sporting and social activities, together with education and preparation for a life of labor on a kibbutz in the Land of Israel was what drew the young people to join this group. On hot summer's when I went out to get a breath of fresh air outside the town I would meet many groups in a corner of a field a meadow or in the woods sitting and discussing the movement and its activities. This movement stood at the forefront of activities for the community. Members of this movement were among the first immigrants to 'The Land of Israel' in the 1920's and later were the leaders of the increased waves of immigration in the 1930's.

Among the other parties it is worth mentioning the 'Bund' (Jewish Socialist Workers Party), that carried on political activities, had a clubhouse and maintained a very good library.

Most of the middle class citizens were members of economic and mutual aid organizations such as The Merchants Association, Craftsmen's Association, etc. In the center of the economic life of these organizations was The Jewish People's Bank. It served all segments of the Jewish community, responded to all requests for financial help and was a democratic institution in every sense of the word.

———

Was our town different from the hundreds of other Jewish towns in Poland? Yes, our town was different from the others beginning with the revolutionary change that the Radzyn Chassidim introduced and which stirred up the whole Chassidic world against them. It was different because all the public social and personal forces that were hidden in it bust forth from time to time into the general public sphere. It was also very different in its restlessness and its refusal to conform to the routine and accepted ways and its view of the cruel reality and its constant attempts to change it. It was also very different and superior in the way in which the Zionist Pioneer organizations contributed to it numerically and qualitatively. These were its principal characteristics.

May we who grew up and were educated in its reality, which has since faded and disappeared, know how to preserve its sparks that so stimulated our desire for life and creativity.

———

[Pages 156-159]

Memories Of Radzyn:
During And After World War I

Abraham Zigelman, Tel-Aviv

Radzyn was not a very big shtetl, but it was very well kept. It was clean and polished and full of life. Compared to the surrounding shtetls it was very developed both in commercial and in social and cultural matters.

———

The Cultural Organization, which was founded in 1916, made a very strong impact on the town. It was then housed in the beautiful house of Molly-Chavah. Actually this organization was founded by the Bund but attracted wider circles. It's activists were then Yisroel-Meir Tannenbaum, Avraham Shuchmacher, Moshe Rotshtein and others.

The Radzyn Library was also under its aegis, and its name was changed to "Shalom Aleichem" the same as that of the cultural organization. Actually the library was founded in 1902 by an altogether different group of people that included Yehoshua Lichtenstein, Akiva Rubinstein and others.

The young people of Radzyn saw the library as a well of knowledge and drank deeply from it.

In the early years of World War I, the town advanced in a number of unusual areas thanks to the initiative of David Lichtenstein and others. These areas created a flow of energy and enthusiasm. The first of them was electric lighting. The transition from the dimness of kerosene lamps, in both the houses and on the streets, to the bright electric illumination pushed the town forward. People got together more often, social life improved and people began to see life in a much brighter light.

Of no lesser significance was the establishment of the first modern Jewish school. Jewish children studied and knew not only the Bible with Rashi's (Rabbi Shlomo Yitzchak 1040-1105) Commentaries but other subjects and languages. They began learning the Hebrew language and were the first children in the town who spoke the Holy Tongue.

The schoolteachers were those who introduced modern and progressive education not only for the children but also for the adults. The first one to do this was 1) Yaakov Blachovitz a former student of the yeshiva in Wolozneh who was very well versed in the Talmud. He was the first one to who began to educate the younger generations in the spirit of Zionism and Hebrew. 2) Yehoshua Freedman who was a typical modern schoolteacher who taught the Bible and other Jewish subjects. 3) Leon Rochles who came from Rovno and turned up in Radzyn and for many years taught Polish and German as well as other general subjects. He also was a social activist and for many years contributed to the development of the Jewish youth. In the early years the school was supported by Benzion Lichtenstein and his sister Yehudit Zakalik (both in Israel today) children of the late Yehoshua Lichtenstein the well known cultural activist.

"Ha'Chalutz" branch in Radzyn, Lag Ba'Omer, 5694 (1934)

When the war ended, and the Jewish parties began their political activities, Radzyn became the center of all the surrounding shtetls. In 1919 there were a number of important political parties in Radzyn. There was the Bund that numbered hundreds of members and was the largest party at that time. Then "Tzeire Zion" (Young Zionists) and the "Poele Zion" (Workers of Zion) with their youth movements began to take the lead. This was the beginning of party discussions, big election meetings and mass meetings. Every party tried to attract people to it and every Jew was a member of some party. The General Zionists', the Mizrachi (Religious Zionists) and Agudath Yisroel (Ultra Orthodox) Party too, were established. It was freilich (merry) in the town....

"Tzeirey Zion" (Young Zionists) Radzyn on a commemorative tribute to Dr. Chlenov (1920)

The 'Hashomer Hatzair' (Young Guards) movement played an especially important role and had great influence on the youth. At the head of the movement was Dovid Rosenbaum (now: Hanegbi), Yitzchak Zeligman, Motke Gottesdiner, Chaim Shlimak, Shmuel Danilak, Yaakov Rosenfeld and others. The young people were educated to Zionism and pioneering and most of them found their way to Eretz Yisroel.

The Poele Zion S.Z. (Workers of Zion- Socialist Zionists) had a great success with both the youth and the adults many of whom immigrated to Israel. It also carried on great political-cultural activities. At its head stood Gershon Henich Pontshak and others.

A donation card for "Ezrat Cholim" ("Help for the sick")

One cannot write about Radzyn without devoting a few lines to the Radzyner Rabbi, Reb Chaim Fine. He was a clever Jew, full of Torah and wisdom, who also had a European education and was very refined. He never discouraged or insulted anyone and did not meddle into the affairs of others.

I remember standing in the synagogue on Rosh Hashanah after the morning prayer when a number of 'respectable Jews' went up to the Rabbi and asked him to say a few words of morality to the young people. He did not think very long and said "Nu and what about my son Yankel?" They did not reply because they knew very well about his son's behavior, when he came back home from Eretz Yisroel (The Land of Israel) on a Saturday morning.

[Pages 160-161]

Teachers of Small Children, Leather Whips and Youth

by Zanvil Zaltzstein (Rishon L'tzion- Israel)

My first teacher was 'the little Rabbi' and his name suited him very well. He was a small, thin Jew with a yellow beard and sideburns who cast fear on me when I first crossed the threshold to the Cheder (religious school). In a small room stood a long table with benches on both sides, on which there sat some twenty little boys of my age, four to five. At the head of the table sat 'the little Rabbi' with big leather whip in his hand. This whip made such a terrible impression on us children that from the first day we hated the Cheder. In addition, exactly opposite this Cheder stood the Lichtenstein School, later called the Tarbut School. How I envied those children who attended that school! They had a break on every hour when they would run out and play happily while we had to sit all day in our classroom and study. For the smallest misdemeanor 'the small Rabbi' showed that when it came to matters of thrashing he was not inferior to the 'big Rabbis' such as Loser Melamed ('Loser the teacher) and others.

On the rampart near a side gate of the Radzyn castle

Loser devised the brilliant two whips system, one for meat and one for dairy. This is how it worked .The boy who was called up by him to be whipped would have to declare what he had eaten that day. If he had eaten dairy he would be whipped with the dairy whip. If he had eaten meat he would be whipped with the meat whip.

'Pinchasl Melamed' had an idea that in addition to whipping he would announce that a slap was on the way .The one who got the slap was usually the one who least expected it. Among us boys it was also told that Itshe Kines grabs the pupil by the ears and lifts him up to the ceiling and performs other such 'pleasurable' acts.

My only desire at that time was that my father would take me out of the Cheder and send me to 'The School'. But there was no possibility for this to happen. My father believed that 'The School' led to apostasy. 'Yes a little knowledge of reading and writing is useful but can be learnt in a few hours in the evening '

———

When the Sabbath arrived there was a great desire to go to the 'New Bridge' on the highway to Vishnitz or on the ramp by the castle. However that was the time when we had to go to the Bais Hamedrash (study house) to learn together with Shmuel Bear and Avraham Pinkus. There was an agreement between our three fathers that every Saturday one of them had to teach the three of us in the Bais Hamedrash. This was not so terrible in the winter, even though it meant that we could not go skating which we enjoyed very much. However, during the summer Sabbaths it was very difficult for us to go to learn. The streets were deserted and quiet with not a soul in sight. Our parents were having their after Cholent (a traditional Sabbath afternoon dish) nap. The young people did not nap. Not far behind the town near the ramp by the castle, behind the tall thick trees, the Jewish youth of Radzyn sat absorbed in newspapers and books. Groups of Jewish youth sat hidden, so that they could not be seen, and learnt new subjects very different from those learnt in the Bais Hamedrash.

In the evening, when the sun began to set in the west, the whole group of young people began making their way back and began their stroll on Ostrowiecka Street. At that time the women dragged out the chairs and benches in front of the houses to observe and discuss everyone. Opinions were expressed as to whether this boy is suitable for that girl etc., will anything come out of this or that match or are they just 'dragging' around together without any purpose, and other such important questions. The older generation appeared, little by little, on their way home from the Batai medrash and Shtibles to perform the Havdalah Ceremony (that marks the change from the Sabbath to weekdays). However the young people did not want to return to the weekdays so they strolled in the streets and continued their discussions late into the night.

Episodes From The
Jewish Worker's Movement In Radzyn

by Tzvi Liberson (Hadera, Israel)

In 1905, Russia and the other occupied territories seethed like a boiling kettle. The opponents of the monarchy prepared to overthrow the Czarist rule. The Polish people struggled to gain independence. Among the Jews, the Bund (Jewish Socialist Party) mobilized the working masses in the struggle against the Czarist despotism and for Jewish national and socio-economic demands.

Our town was not an exception. The Bund organized action groups, the so-called "Fives". The first ones who laid the foundation for the Bundist movement were one of Chaim Borver sons, Shmuel Meicher, Yaakov Peretsovitch, Eli Chaim Miller's daughter (Tennenboim), Chaim Simcha Nievieski, Shmuel Prizant, Roiselle Lichtenstein and many others.

In that same year the first strike by the tailoring workers broke out. Their conditions were unbearable. They worked sixteen hours a day .The bosses employed them from Pesach to Succoth in slave-like conditions. The first strike broke out because of a conflict in Yaakov Meirwasser's tailoring workshop. Velvel Adelman (Katshuveh) who worked there was the first one to strike. All the master craftsmen backed Meirwasser and fired all the workers. The Bundist parties in the surrounding shtetls supported the Radzyn tailoring workers.

A group of friends from the "Bund" party

When the peddlers of old clothes would come to the fairs in Miedzyrzec, Lukow or Parczew, the local Bundists would prevent them from unloading their wares and forced them to go back home. Once, on the spur of the moment, the peddlers went into Raizeleh Lichtenstein's house, beat her up, and took the Bund Party's official stamp. When they took the stamp they thought that the strikers would be defeated. Some of the peddlers, however, went to the police to denounce them. Nevertheless, the strike continued on and the peddlers saw that their livelihood was affected, so they broke down and sat down to negotiate. The tailoring workers then managed to win better conditions. The peddlers were forced to cancel the accusations that they had made before the police. This first economic success strengthened the Bund. All the workers saw that they had strength and that much could be obtained through unity.

The Bund not only confined itself to economic activities. It wanted to get even with the priest from Czemierniki who made an anti-Semitic speech in the church. The speech was also aimed at upsetting the solidarity between the Poles. The Bund in Radzyn decided to assassinate the priest. The attempt was not successful; the Christians carried out a pogrom on the Jews and killed Kupershmit, a Radzyner Jew. Shmuel Meicheren hid out and after a few days barely managed to escape from Czemierniki.

After the Czermierniki affair and after the failed revolution in Russia, came 'bloody Wednesday' in Warsaw (when the Czar's provincial governors carried out a Pogrom on the workers movement in Warsaw. Blood flowed in the streets and many of the leaders of the workers movement were hanged). These were followed by so called reaction years. There was a truce in the worker's movement in general as well as in the Bund, Radzyn included. This truce lasted almost until the outbreak of World War 1.

In 1915 the Germans and Austrians occupied the Polish territory. Radzyn belonged to the Germans. The war was a serious obstacle to the activities of the Bund. The Germans would round up the healthy men and send them to work in the forests. Police and military terror raged against the population. The Germans instituted a special 'Shperen Hour'. That meant that it was forbidden to walk in the streets at night and other such limitations. Despite that, in later years (1917-1918) a non-political literary circle was formed and many Bund members belonged to it. The circle engaged in arranging literary evenings, study groups devoted to Jewish writers, literary discussion groups and the like. Among those who belonged to this group were Ben Zion Greenboim, Shlomo Tzucker, Yechezkel Greenblatt, Mendel Lichtenstein, Yitzchak Butman, Moishe Shaiyeh Rotshtein, Yisroel and Meir Tennenboim, Avraham Leib Wassermann, Avraham Shuchmacher, Chanina Vetshtein, Aba Danilek, Yosef Danilak, Ben Zion Lichtenstein, Yehudit Lichtenstein, Moshe Zigelman. There was also a group of Yeshiva students that belonged to this circle. They still wore their 'Jewish hats' but when they got to the meeting room which was located in Malichava's house, they removed them. Many different political parties, the Bund, General Zionist, Poele Zion, etc. later emerged from this literary circle.

The founding meeting of the Bund in that period took place on the Vishnitz highway near the 'New Bridge'. Two German soldiers, who were Social Democrats, participated in this meeting, which was illegal. This was a renewal of Bund activities after a long period of dormancy.

On the morning of November 11, 1918 tension was felt in the shtetl. The Germans were apprehensive and soldiers patrolled the streets. The soldiers stationed near the Rabbi's house were packed and ready to flee. Tension was felt among the Poles too. The Polish Legionnaires wanted to disarm the Germans and take control. They waited for the proper moment. When the Germans began to leave, heavy firing broke out. The Legionnaires tried to disarm the Germans but the later resisted. Then the German mounted military police rode through the streets, firing continuously. Legionnaires and Germans fell, as did one Jew, Yosef Rabinovitch. The Germans left the town as if hurrying to go home.

The regime was now in the hands of the Poles. The first Polish government, actually a worker's government, was formed in Lublin. The Polish people breathed more freely and the Jews, too, felt better. The Jewish parties became legal including the Bund which became a force in the town. There was an immense upsurge of political and cultural activity in all of the parties. The Bund opened its first center in Shimon Danilak's place. A series of lectures on political economics took place there as well as lectures on natural sciences. The Bund also established cooperative of providers of basic necessities and its own bakery. Later an evening course for illiterate adults was established. There was a very strong desire for knowledge among both the youth and the adults. The first demonstration by the Bund took place on May 1, 1919. Yisroel Meicher marched at the head carrying the Red Flag. It started out from the 'courtyard' by the park where the Polish Communist Party joined them. The wagon was left standing on Ostroweicka Street and Yisroel Meir Tennenboim delivered a fiery speech from one of the balconies.

Just before Passover of the same year, the Bund organized a strike of the women who worked in matzo production. They worked 16 to 18 hours a day from very early in the morning until late at night. The Bund decided to put an end to this situation. The employers were forced to give in and the workday was limited to eight hours.

The Polish-Soviet War broke out in 1920. The Polish authorities arrested many labor leaders, and the Bund headquarters were impounded. Among those from the different parties who were arrested were Yitzchak Butman, Leon Rachlis, Moishe Laizer Pessachovitz, Shmuel Kimmel, Leibel Nissenboim, Yechezkel Greenblatt, Yisroel Tennenboim, Loezer Appleboim, Ziltshe Wiseman, Moishe Shayeh Ratshtein and others. All those who were arrested were sent to the prison in Dambia. The arrests made a grim impression in the town. In effect, the most capable people were imprisoned. After the Soviet-Polish War all those who had been arrested returned. While the town was temporarily occupied by the Soviets, the Bund carried out certain administrative functions in the town. When, after seven days, the Soviets left the town, many young people from labor movement left with them. Later many of them came back from either Russia, or from along the way.

With the return of those who were arrested, the activities of the Bund and of the Poele Zion were renewed and the social and political activities revived. In 1921 there was a split in the Bund in Poland. Part of the Bund was influenced by the Russian Revolution. The Bund split into two groups, right and left. On the left were the so- called Comm-Bund. Because of this split the most active part of the Radzyn Bund joined the Comm-Bund. They were the actual founders of the Communist movement in Radzyn.

Despite the split, the Bund remained a significant organization in the town. Zukunft, (Future) Bund Youth was founded in 1922-23. Among the organizers were Shlomo Kashtenbaum, Yaakov Melinasz, Shaul Lifshitz, Leitshe Gelibter and Lippe Wassermann. In that period the Bund established a Needle Workers Association, a library and a dramatic circle. In 1924 the Bund together with the Left Poele Zion established 'The Yiddish School Organization'. The school opened in the home of Leah Kleinman. The Bund brought the best speakers to Radzyn. It was more active in this than the other parties.

Two delegates, Yechezkel Greenblatt and Shmuel Kimmel, represented the Bund on the Radzyn city council. Later it was represented by a woman activist Leitshe Gelibter, and Shlomo Rosenfeld a youthful leader who was considered one of the best speakers in the town.

In 1925 the Bund, together with Communists, carried out a strike of all the mill workers. It lasted two weeks during which the mills were closed down. The Labor Inspector was forced to intercede and the strike ended in a victory for the workers.

In 1927 there was a new split in the Bund and more than twenty Radzyn Bund members went over to the Communists. This split was mainly among the members of Zukunft, Bund Youth, and the Communists again gained significant reinforcements.

The Bund continued with its activities, and although some new young people joined, it lost strength. It lacked the leadership that could educate and lead the new young people. The Needle Workers Association too, ceased being a force in Radzyn because people could not make a living in the needle trades and they had to go to Warsaw to do so.

In the last election to the city and the community council before the war (World War II) the Bund got a greater proportion of the votes. It remained active until the last minutes before the outbreak of the war that demolished the Bund together with all the rest of the Radzyn Jewish community.

The foundations for the Communist movement in Radzyn were laid by the already mentioned Comm.-Bund or even earlier by left leaning Bundists who just happened to be in the Bund at that time before the split. The foremost leaders of those who considered themselves Comm-Bund were as follows: Avraham Leib Wassermann, Avraham Shuchmacher, Velvel Tennenboim and Leibel Tzucker. The later was considered a good speaker and propagandist. He was the real leader of the Comm-Bund.

In the beginning the group was divided and did not belong to the Communists. In general, the Polish Communist party did not belong to the Communist International because of its extreme leftist orientation that Lenin fought against at that time. The Radzyn Communists did not participate in the first elections to the Polish Seim (legislature). That was the position taken by the Communists in Poland. They expressed their stand by propaganda against the parliament. They covered the walls of the town with slogans. A slogan that was displayed on Shkolna Street read: "Town and country proletarians Unite! "

Officially the Communists in our town began their activities in 1921-22, after the Polish section joined the Commintern. The first Needle Workers Association that was established in 1923 under the Communists influence was located in the home of Moishe Ravniak (Bruder). The secretary of the association was Avraham Shuchmacher. This organization led a campaign to improve the conditions of the needle workers. It also had a section devoted to the needle workers apprentices. This association was utilized for Communist propaganda and lectures on current events. The association became the center for all the left oriented workers in the town.

As time passed, the police became interested in this trade union organization. Informers revealed its Communist activities. In 1924 the association was shut down and its activities moved to into private homes and onto the streets. The Communists carried on propaganda among the peasants in the surrounding villages and distributed literature there. In town they pasted slogans against the government on the walls and hung red flags on the telephone wires. Thus the Communist movement again began to attract the attention of the police. The police assigned both special uniformed and plain clothed personnel to observe these activities. However the police did not succeed in uncovering any conspiracies at that time.

In 1925 a new meeting hall was opened on Shkolna St., this time as the headquarters of the leather workers' trade union, but was utilized mostly for Communist propaganda purposes as well as for the needs of the leather workers. There were discussions about political problems almost every Saturday. The main leader of these discussions was Yudel Borochovsky. Whenever Yudel spoke the hall would be filled to overflowing. Announcers stood outside and repeated his speech. At that time Borochovsky was an official of the Central Committee of the Polish Communist Party. He came to the Party from the yeshiva and in his speeches he used quotations from the Bible. He liked to engage in debates and to challenge his opponents. Woe was to anyone who tangled with him in a debate. So the police would lie in wait for him and were frequent guests in his house. However, they rarely found him there.

Elections to the municipal council were held at that time in 1925. The Communists appeared in the elections under the banner of the Leather Workers Union. Their candidate was Shimon Gansky who was not a politically attractive person. He could not even sign his signature and was being taught to do so in secret. There was no other candidate who would agree to stand, because such people were often targets for arrest. The Communist movement at that time was not so much interested in its representation on the council as it was to show its strength, and so it did. It got more than six hundred votes. However, Shimon Gansky did not bring it much esteem. He would sit there like a deaf mute. The Polish reactionary members had pity on him and the police did not bother him because he was not dangerous.

In 1926, before the month of May, Zanvel Zaltzshtein was arrested for carrying illegal May Day literature to Miedzyrzec. Usually such literature was sent directly from Warsaw to Miedzyrzec. Because of a Communist omission that road was heavily patrolled. Therefore the road that went to Miedzyrzec through Radzyn was chosen. The task was conferred on a certain member Zaltzshtefenikein who was going to Mezeritch with Yantel the wagoner. That road, too, was heavily patrolled, and near Kanklevntizeh the wagon was stopped and searched. The literature was found and Zaltzshtefenikein was put on trial. In court he acted very bravely. He sang Communist songs and shouted out anti- government slogans. He was sentenced to five years in prison.

On the thirteenth of May 1926, during the Pilsudski rebellion, Yudel Borochvski came to Radzyn and gave an order that every member should be prepared to leave his work, go into the streets wait for further orders. The situation was very unclear. In Warsaw the Communists, led by Varskin, were fighting alongside Pilsudski. In Radzyn the police were confused. The telephone connections with Warsaw were disconnected .The Communists expected to get an order any minute to take over control of the town. However this never came about.

In 1927 Yudel Borochvski was arrested together with a whole group of Jews and non-Jews from Radzyn, Vohin and the vicinity. They were arrested as the result of an informer. The group, together with Yudel, sat in jail for over a week. On Friday they were informed that on Saturday Yudel would be taken for the last time to the investigating magistrate whose office was in Dovid Liechtenstein's house. The Communists decided to free Yudel at any cost and prepared a raid. There was only one problem to be solved, namely, how could they inform Yudel of the plan so that he could be ready. They tried many different ways to do so without success. Because of that, the whole plan failed despite the thorough preparations of many of its details. Borochovski was not psychologically prepared and at the proper moment he could not flee. His feet became paralyzed. At the trial he was given five to six years in prison. After spending some time in the Sedlitz prison he was given temporary release because of his lung disease. He used this opportunity to flee to Russia where he was again unlucky. During a purge of Communist Party membership there, he was arrested and accused of being in the opposition, was exiled and disappeared.

Avraham Shuchmacher occupied a very honored position in the Radzyn labor movement. He came from a poor home and nevertheless he became a famous labor intellectual. He came to the Bund like many others from the Yeshiva during World War I. Later he joined the Com-Bund and he became the first secretary of the trade unions section. For a certain time he was the secretary of the trade unions in Likoveh .His greatest accomplishments were in the field of cultural activities where he also founded dramatic groups. In the last years of his life he was the secretary of Manual Workers organization. He died young (in 1928 or 1929) partly because of the years of hunger that he had experienced.

Matel Pshenitze- on the left

The name of Mottel Pshenitzeh must be added to the list of capable activists. He began by being active in the 'Youth League Zukunft' approximately in 1923. By profession he was a tailor. His father Yankel Pshenitzeh was a veteran Bundist who wanted his son Mottel to become a musician and bought him a violin. Motel's ambitions were different. He read a lot and wrote stories. In 1925 he joined the Communist movement and founded a youth group of some twenty young people and taught them Marxism. In 1932-33 he moved to Warsaw where he continued his literary activities. He joined the ranks of young writers and attempted to have a book of his, stories published. However he lacked the financial means. After great efforts he had the book published ('Fine') in which there are many descriptions of life in Radzyn.

In 1927 there was a split in 'Hashomer Hatzair' ("The Young Guard" a Socialist Zionist Youth Movement) and a group left the organization led by Shaul Ackerman and Moishe Hochbein. For a certain period the group could not decide where to go. Both the Communists and the Bund tried to attract them. Speakers from both parties tried to entice them. Finally some of them joined the Communist movement.

In the last years before World War II, the Communists, after a certain period of stagnation, again became a significant force in the town. Again a few more activists from Hashomer Hatzair joined them. Sometime in 1933-34 Yoel Lozer set up a party printing press with Polish typography. It was a rather primitive press but could print small proclamations. In that way the Polish Communists issued their own proclamations signed by the Polish Communist Party. When the anti-Semites in Radzyn urged the Polish citizens to boycott Jewish businesses, the Communists in Radzyn issued a proclamation saying, "Buy wherever it is cheaper."

[Pages 173-175]

The Jewish Craftsman
And His Organization

by Tzvi Liberzan (Hadera, Israel)

After the Germans were expelled in 1918, there was a revival of the social life of the town and the founding of many economic institutions, and workers' professional organizations as well as independent Jewish political parties. The Jewish men began to think about their own organization, which would include all the Jewish craftsmen. Their desire for their own organization was influenced by a number of reasons:

1. The Jewish artisans needed their own representatives in the Jewish Community Council to protect them from heavy taxation.
2. They wanted their own representatives in the Credit Bank
3. They were influenced by the psychological moment. They wanted to go along with the momentum of the developing social life of the town at that time.

Formally, such an organization came into existence after the Polish-Soviet war when it was called a Craftsmen's Organization. It included all the independent craftsmen, tailors, shoemakers, tinsmiths, bakers, dyers and watchmakers. The largest trades were those of the shoemakers and tailors and they were also the most active. The headquarters of the Craftsmen's Organization was at that time in the home of Sarah-Feigeh Berman and its first secretary was Abba Danilak.

The organizer of the tailors was Avraham Nissenbaum the best tailor in town. He devoted a lot of energy to this task. His main goal was to reduce the competition between the tailors. He wanted them to institute fixed prices, however he did not have great success. Later he moved to Brisk and the tailors in Radzyn lost one of their best organizers. The organization also mediated conflicts between the second hand clothing merchants and the tailors who worked out of their homes.

The shoemakers were more successful at that time. In 1924 they founded the Leather Cooperative that sold leather and other materials of use to the shoemakers. This store was in the middle of the market place in the center of the town. The bookkeeper was Simcha Lieberfreint. At the beginning things went well for the cooperative. The merchandise was brought from Warsaw and the turnover grew regularly. However, after three years the coop was liquidated because of poor results. The shoemakers called meetings to discuss how to reduce the fierce competition, at least, partially, however these had no effect.

When Abba Danilak went to Mezeritch (and later abroad) the post of secretary was taken over by Simcha Fest (today in Poland) and Itzel

Gottesdiner. In approximately 1925 the Craftsmen's Organization was moved to the beautiful house of Hershel Handelsman that he had purchased from Akiva Rubinstein.

The organization was also involved in cultural activities. Among others, they formed a dramatic group. Its first production was a popular piece 'The Sale of Joseph' which was presented exclusively by shoemakers. A second dramatic group was established that recruited talented men and women from all over the town. The director of this group was Avraham Shuchmacher. When Itzel Gottesdiner left for the Land of Israel, Avraham also became the secretary of the organization. Among others in his group were the three daughters of Hershel Handelsman, Feige, Heni and Ite who were very talented actresses. Other participants were Meir Migdael, Velvel Vishkovsky and others. They often performed in the surrounding shtetls and the income from the performances was devoted exclusively to the Craftsmen's Organization.

Avraham Shuchmacher also developed an intense program of activities for the organization .In his time the artisans got one of their members, Motel Smetankeh, into the city council. He worked very hard to reduce the local taxes levied upon the artisans. In the Credit Bank they were represented by Yosef Appeloig. They also had representatives in Gmilat Chesed (Free Loan) Association. Members of the organization were also on the appointed income tax committee where they represented the Craftsmen.

In later years the Bund tried to establish a Socialist Craftsmens' Association. However the attempt to tear away members from the old Craftsmens' Association was not very successful. Except for some inveterate Bundists, no one left and the Bundist Socialist Craftsmens' Association remained a fiction.

After the death of Avraham Shuchmacher, Akiva Lichtenberg became secretary. He was followed by Yitzchak Butesman's son. That was the way that the Jewish artisans carried on their activities for some twenty years, campaigned everywhere for their representatives, maintained social and cultural activities and fought for their existence up until the final moments of the life of Polish Jewry.

[Pages 175-179]

Interest Free Loans

by Dov Katzenelbogen (Tel-Aviv)

A cold winter morning descended on the market place. The crystal-like snowflakes that fell worried Rabbi Yitchak, the owner of the haberdashery store, lest the heavens were against him." Just today of all days the snow is coming down so heavily! Who knows if any peasants will show up on a day like this?" Reb Yitzchak had gotten up and opened his store early. Therefore unlike his usual custom, he prayed the morning service with the first Minyan (prayer quorum) that was composed of ordinary people, the porters, craftsmen and the mill hands, who had to go to their work early. He joined the early risers today because he had many important things to attend to. First, he had to pay his promissory note to the Polish Bank due today. He could no longer postpone paying the non-Jews, because the Polish bank was not like a Jewish bank. Second, today he had to pay the hundred gold coins to Yaakov the carpenter, interest free loan from Yaakov that he had promised to repay on this day. If he did not keep his word, it would be very embarrassing, even though he was a learned and God fearing man, to hear the complaints of the commoner who was very successful financially. He also had to pay the tax collector of local authority who, although it was very early, was already running around in the market. Surely he would come into Reb Yitzchak's store and he would have to give him at least an advance. Where could he find all the money in one day? And now with the snowstorm, very few peasants' wagons could reach the town and among those that did, no one came to his store. It was two hours since he had opened it, and he was still worrying about where his help would come from.

He stood in the door of his store and pondered his situation. Reb Yitzchak understood that everything in his store did not really belong to him, that there was a heavy debt on everything and that he subsisted only on loans and credit. Would he be able to maintain his reputation which was all his strength and fortune and on which everything was so dependent now? If he lost the trust that most people had in him what then? A shudder passed through him at the thought of it, and a sigh like prayer burst forth from his mouth. "Do not let my enemies rejoice and do not lead me to shame and disgrace. Do not make me dependent on gifts from human beings". While he was thinking about this, he remembered the morning prayer and how he had found himself in a Minyan that was not his and not of his class. How these ordinary people honored him and immediately asked him to go up to the Holy Ark and lead the prayer. This he refused to do, because he wanted to be one of them. Really, was it not better to be one of them? He was very impressed by their prayers. They were very different from those of the respectable Jews who sat in the front row closest to the eastern wall and who considered themselves the privileged of the Holy One. They bring to the house the joy of self-satisfaction and as a result forget the commandment "Know before whom you stand". Their prayer is like paying off a loan which the rich do without effort. Can it be compared to that of the poor that he witnessed this morning? How intense was his desire to be one of them and to do what they do after the prayers, to go to the sawmill and load heavy boards onto his shoulders and to earn his bread by the sweat of his brow, even though it is a poor man's loaf. In his mind's eye, he saw himself sitting among common people, his colleagues during the day, in the synagogue for the evening prayer. He sees himself organizing Mishnah (Oral Law) studies group and also teaches them Torah. But then he immediately remembers his oldest son Mendele, who is a genius, sharp witted and erudite and knows Mishnah. Is he not entitled, because of his erudition, to become the husband of the daughter of a scholar? Both his daughters, too, were beautiful and had arrived at a marriageable age. Would he marry them off to a boor or an ignoramus? Reb Yitzchak mind returns from its earlier thoughts and he sighs. "For them...for them".

Thus lost in his thoughts, he is suddenly awakened by the sound of a heavy male voice, that of a peasant who stood at the entrance to his shop. Reb Yitzchak was happy to see him, invited him in and gave him everything he wanted. Then the bargaining about the price began. At the beginning the peasant was very stubborn but as the negotiation continued he added to the price little by little until he satisfied Reb Yitzchak who was now ready to close the deal. Suddenly it occurred to Reb Yitzchak: "Isn't this as if Elijah the Prophet appeared at the hour of need dressed as a peasant?" However, he soon became disappointed when the peasant called in his wife to come consult with him, and then the peasant turned down the offer. Time passed and Reb Yitzchak became nervous. At least if his wife were here, he could go out for a walk around town and find an interest free loan. He was angry with his wife because today of all days she was late. Then he remembered her duties at home. In addition to helping him in his difficult business she also rigorously supervised the housekeeping. Memories of the distant past pass before him. He remembers their wedding day as if it was yesterday. His wife was from a good and wealthy home and, as an only daughter, was spoiled by her parents. Ever since she moved in with him, she did not experience a moment of plenty. Despite that she never complained and just did her duty in both the house and the store. Stubbornly, quietly and despite the shortages, she managed to balance the household needs without diminishing the family honor...and he sometime scolded her! Then he is so filled with contrition that he cannot look at himself. When he raises his eyes to look into the distance, behold what does he see but the figure of his wife coming out of one of the lanes. From afar he recognized her by the colorful scarf that was wrapped around her hips, the one that she had woven between their engagement and their wedding. It was still in good condition despite the forty three years that had passed since then. She walked proudly and calmly, her hair neatly combed, her shoes polished. The basket she carried, which she had made in the evenings, added to her dignity. However, she did not carry it for ornamentation only, but to put the supplies that she bought. She goes close to the entrance to the store kisses her hand and touches the Mezuzah that is attached to the door post and goes in saying: "Good morning". Reb Yitzchak, who is excited by her movements as if seeing them for the first time, turns his head away from her so that she will not see his excitement and without looking at her says: "It is good that you came. I must go out into town", and disappears while speaking.

When in the street, he shakes off all his previous reflections and thoughts because now his day's work begins: to find new sources for the loan that will make it possible for him to get through the day. Time passes and since only two hours remain before the bank's closing, Reb Yitzchak decides not to take any further chances and decides to apply to Rivka. If she does not have the money, she won't rest and will go to her neighbors and friends until she finds what she is looking for. However, it is not very pleasant to disturb her and so he has left her as a last resort.

––––––

Moshe Avman, a maker of ready-made clothing, lived in the Second Market near Shalom Pinkas's store. He made his living by going to the market days in the surrounding near and far towns to sell his clothing. In the days when there were no markets, he sat at home and sewed and prepared the clothing to sell to the peasants. His wife, Rivka, in addition to being a housewife like all the other women, would also help her husband by doing such things as making button holes, sewing on the buttons, ironing and finishing off her husband's handiwork. In addition to all this she was also the financial manager of the business and would worry about raising the money needed for her husband's trips to Warsaw to buy cloth and about paying off his promissory notes on time. Not only did she worry about paying of their promissory notes but also knew when the notes of all her friends and acquaintances and of those who did business with her came due. As the time passed and the situation worsened, so the number of her friends and acquaintances increased. Not only women of her status came to her house, but also respectable and intelligent men. However, their attitude to her was different, and they usually came to the back door so that their apprentices would not see them, since it was not normal to carry on negotiations with a woman. They would open the door and say: "Good morning Rivka", and that was all. Rivka would come out and say "Yes Reb Yitzchak, Reb Yosef etc. I will come immediately".

The man would wish her well and go away feeling certain that Rivka would show up at his shop with money from an interest free loan. At such moments Rivka was very agile. With one hand she would wrap her heavy wool scarf, known as a Fartsheleh, around her and go out. Sometimes she would turn her head back toward the door and say to her husband: "Moishe, I left the meat cooking on the stove. Pay attention to it and stir it from time to time so that it does not burn". Moshe would answer in a mocking but amused tone: "All right I will be a housewife", to which she replied vigorously "I don't have time for you. Just stir the meat. Did you hear?". "I heard I heard". However, whenever his wife went out on such a mercy mission, he was forced to stop his work. His conscience bothered him without his understanding why. He understood his place in the world by the worktable and the road from his house to the Bible Study group in the Tailor's Synagogue, to which he went twice every day. All the rest of the concerns and worries, such as purchases, loans, bills and coins, he left to his wife, because there was no one like her for handling such complicated matters. Her own problems were not enough for her, so she went out of her way to help others including many well- known people who asked for her help. Moshe quickly awakened from his musings and continued with his work all the while thinking how proud he was of his wonderful wife. Then because of his excitement, he began quietly humming a tune as he pushed the needle.

When going around the town to help others, Rivka recognizes no difficulties that will prevent her from returning home without what she was looking for and disappointing those who were dependent on her. She goes into every place and, if it is necessary, promises to return the loan within a day or even within two hours. Her promises have a reputation for dependability everywhere. In such situations she acts very vigorously and hurries to give her takings to those that are waiting for them so that they may still make it to the bank. She then catches her breath, and, in a short time, goes out again to find new sources for loans in the two hours left to her to fulfill her promises.

This time it was Reb Yitzchak who headed for Rivka. As was suitable for a man of his status, he went in by the back door, delivered his message and turned around and went back to his store. Now he walked slowly and calmly but was dissatisfied with the success of his mission today. The feeling he had was one that that he had felt before, such as when, in times of need for Sabbath supplies, he would withdraw money from his daughter the seamstress' savings that were intended for the purpose of...

He approached his store and his wife, who was very well acquainted with the hardships involved in his transactions, seeing the peaceful look on his face, allowed herself to ask him what is happening. "I went to Rivka", he answers, lowering his voice. She needs no further explanation .He checks the cash box to see what has come in during his absence-very little. Now both of them know that their deliverance depends on Rivka's arrival. He takes out his pocket watch, when his wife is not looking, and casts a quick look at it. Time is short and if she doesn't come soon...? However that is impossible, Rivka never disappoints people, he thinks to himself.

Rivka appears on the run and breathing heavily hands over the money.

[Pages 179-181]

The Founding Gathering of the Poaley Zion (Zionist Workers' Party)

by Tzipe Rosenfeld (Ness Ziona, Israel)

On a summer Saturday afternoon in 1917, while strolling on Ostroweicka Street with Friede Reichenberg, Shmuel Falshspan and someone else, whose name I cannot now remember, joined us. They handed us a small brochure: "The Contents of the Borochov Program" and invited us to a meeting on the following Friday.

The Germans were at that time well established in Poland and people were not allowed to be in the streets after nine o'clock in the evening. The organizers took a great risk by scheduling the illegal meeting later in the evening in Chaitsche, the woolen scarf maker's house, located near the German Headquarters which were then located in Mali Chava's house.

When we came to the meeting on Friday evening, we met many Radzyner young people there. Among those that I remember were Shimon Berman, Chanina Gellerman's brother-in-law, Sarah Zussman's father, Moshe Koptshak, Weingarten, Chaim Be'r Shpigel, Chiel Goldwasser, the two Finkelshtein brothers, Leah Berman, Toibtshe Richter and many more. A speaker from Lublin came to the meeting, and his speech made a great impression on us.

But then something unusual happened. It seems that the Germans found out about the event and in the middle of his speech they surrounded us and all the participants started to run away. I, together with Freide, had to run from one end of the town to the other, all the way to Warshavska St., all this when it was forbidden to be in the streets after nine o'clock. We were then 16-17 years old and very frightened. We ran through all the Beth Hamedrash (Jewish seminary) gardens until we reached home more dead than alive. On Saturday morning I heard that all the participants from Radzyn managed to run away, and only the speaker from Lublin was arrested and sent back there.

Early on Sunday morning Leah Berman came running and informed me that we must run away and hide because they are searching for all the participants. I remember that Freide and I put on shawls, such as those worn by non-Jewish women, so that we would not be recognized, and went to our garden where we spent the day the rest of the day. This was the beginning of the Poaley Zion in Radzyn. After that we began be recruit new members, and our meetings took place each time in a different location.

Leon Rachlis- of the first Hebrew school teachers and one of the leaders of "Poaley Tzion" ("Zion Workers")

"Poaley Tzion" group

When the party became legal with the retreat of the Germans from Poland in the year 1918, our headquarters were located in Nachum Goldfarb's place. From that time I recall that when a certain member, Tabatchnik, came from Warsaw to speak he was met by Bund members carrying sticks.

At that time a number of new committees, cultural, technical, etc. were created. Shimon Berman, Leon Rachlis from Rovno who was a teacher in the Yiddish School and Shlomo Mushkat were on the cultural committee; Chaim Ber Shpigel, Chiel Goldwasser, Hershel Tzukerblatt were on the technical committee,

When the first elections to the Polish Seim (parliament) took place, the Jewish community became activated. There were three Jewish lists, two of Workers parties and one General list that was composed of all the civil parties. We then had a strenuous struggle against the "Bund" in Radzyn and throughout the country. Despite that the Poele Zion in Poland succeeded in electing one of its members, Dr. Yitchak Shiffer as a deputy to the parliament.

I now remember the name of the speaker that we brought to Radzyn for the elections. His name was Shurek. As was then usual with big meetings, he spoke at the Bais Medrash and made a strong impression on the audience. After his speech in Radzyn, he took sick and died in Warsaw. Shlomo Tzucker then wrote a song about him that all of Radzyn sang.

———————

[Page 182]

Poaley Zion in Radzyn

by Shprintze Gottesdiner (Tel-Aviv)

The real beginning of the Poaley Zion in Radzyn started in 1916 before the split into Right and Left. At that time the Poalei Zion already had its 'worker's house' where the party members met and discussed and dealt with various problems. They also started evening courses for adults which were taught by Leon Machlis

In 1926, I was already an active member in the youth movement. Shlomo Mushkat and others were its leaders. The youth movement was then established by the so- called "Borochov Groups" but consisted of younger age groups. Together with the older members we carried out various educational programs. The members from Radzyn helped establish party branches in the surrounding smaller towns. We also brought lecturers from the center in Warsaw to speak about literary, scientific and mainly political subjects. Poaley Zion also participated actively in the Yiddish Schools Organization and established, together with the Bund, the first Yiddish School in Leah'le Kleinman's house.

We participated very actively in the municipal and parliamentary election campaigns that took place at that time. In our discussions we often clashed with our opponents the Bund, the Communists and the right wing Zionists. We heatedly discussed our program that was very complicated and far from easily understood. How did Borochov put it? "To be a Poaley Zionist, you have to be half a philosopher". However we succeeded in explaining his teachings properly. Yes, all the questions that at that time seemed so complicated and difficult were eventually answered by the passage of time and life itself and today seem so ordinary and understandable.

The Poaley Zion stood steadfastly by their ideals, those of the Labor Zionist Movement.

[Pages 183-188]

Gottlakes

(Descendants of Gottel Lichtenshtein)

Abba Danilak (Toronto)

1. Dovid Fishel's (Lichtenshtein)

A conspicuous proud large white wall stood out among the gray, moss covered houses and spread out and covered half of the market place. From early in the morning until late into the night the clang of iron and clatter of metals rang through the air and echoed out from there to get lost among the far away fields and woods. A row of brick steps led up to the entrance. On either side of the steps stood, like metal sphinxes, two huge anvils on which the metals were cut or fashioned .The profusion of iron and other building materials attracted the attention of the poor unemployed Jews who passed by. With great awe and respect they cast a glance at them and humbly continued on to the other end of the market place. This was the only shop in town where bearded Jewish employees waited on customers. Out of great respect and with lordly dignity, the peasants who entered removed their caps apprehensively and barely managed to get their Polish "good morning" out of their mouths. Often huge wagons and lordly carriages drove up to the works, loaded up piles of iron and other materials and headed back to their lordly estates in the outskirts. Jewish customers often felt uncomfortable there and often avoided this wholesale concern. The servants, who constantly ran up and down hustling and bustling, looked askance at the Jewish penny customers who got in their way. The oldest son of the "Gottlakes", Dovid Fishel's served the wealthy customers. He himself was imbued with an unusual business sense and blessed with an unusual source of energy that not only perpetuated the fortune but also expanded it. In his quest for material wealth he reflected the spirit of the time. He also tried to introduce other branches of modern industry. In this way he provided both the landowners and the peasants with all the latest technical inventions and modern machinery and completely changed the life style in both the town and in the surrounding countryside.

His crowning achievement, which required great ambition and industrial ingenuity, was the introduction of electricity. This last accomplishment almost completely changed the appearance of the town and the surrounding area. This increased his importance in the eyes of the inhabitants and together with his restlessness increased his prestige far and wide.

Not being a great student, formal studies did not impress him. He looked with disdain at the Torah stuffed Jews and felt closer to the hard working Jews of the town. With his tall figure and his humble behavior he made a great impression on the ordinary Jews. He spoke in a style, which they easily grasped and understood. His homespun jokes brought forth hearty laughter and made them consider him one of their own. However, from time to time outbursts of his inherited aggressiveness repelled those who came into contact with him

He completely reformed the communal life of the town. He overturned and modernized the established, generations old arrangements and modernized them, to suit them to the spirit of the times. His inherited daring and forcefulness as well as the trust of the ordinary Jews stood him well so as not to fail in the new revolutionary era. In the middle of World War I, he established a Modern Hebrew –Yiddish school where Jewish children learned both the Bible as well as non-religious subjects. His practical business sense more than his intelligence made him dare to establish such a project to which he donated a house that he owned. In place of 'Melamdim" (teachers of traditional Jewish subjects), he invited modern experienced teachers and tried with all his might to improve the school and make it more attractive. With the introduction of this new educational system he caused a break with the established, hundreds of years old, educational system. In this way he prepared the ground for a new generation of nationally conscious young people who became permeated with the pioneering spirit of Zionism and immigrated to the Land of Israel.

2. Yehoshua Lichtenstein

Left: Yehosha Lichtenstein - a typical culture activist, establisher of the Jewish library

Right: Ester Finkelstein (Lichtenstein) - the director of the Jewish library for many years

On the other hand, his brother Yehoshua personified the Jewish intellectual. His refined appearance, the golden eyeglasses on his nose and his closely trimmed beard bore evidence to his education and worldly knowledge. With the turn into the 20th Century, strange rumors about a Zionist movement in the Jewish World began reaching even the most remote shtetls of Poland. Jews shrugged their shoulders, not understanding the meaning of these strange rumors about a Dr. Hertzel who was wandering around the royal courts wanting to bring salvation to the Jews even before the arrival of the Messiah. Pious Jews immediately shrugged their shoulders saying "nonsense, another Shabbtai Tzvi !" and spit three times. On the other hand, their rich genteel sons-in-law were captivated by the idea and searched for followers among ordinary Jews. In this way they created a narrow circle of enlightened young people, who with the help of booksellers subscribed to Hebrew periodicals and books. This was the first Enlightenment literature that reached the town and was passed from hand to hand. The main initiator of this group was Yehoshua Lichtenstein. He, however, set himself a much higher goal in life, which was to spread scientific knowledge among the backward Jewish youth. He collected the appropriate books and opened a lending library in his own house. In this way, there was added to the book packed libraries of the Batei Medrash (religious seminaries that had served Jewish youth as centers of religious learning for generations), a new cultural center in the town. Thus he opened the eyes of the youth to the greater world and stimulated their desire for education and science. Observant fathers struggled tooth and nail against these forbidden, non-kosher afflictions. They often tore the books out of the hands of their sons and daughters and threw them into the fire. They convened meetings to denounce this apostate who was tearing away their children from the true Judaism and poisoning their minds with heresy and threatened him with excommunication. However he inherited the same forcefulness of his brother. He was not easily frightened and continued his struggle with the fanatic and ignorant zealots. Some time later his job was taken over by his niece, David's daughter, Esther. She threw herself into the work with zest and moved the library to her home. Thanks to her energy and efforts the cultural center grew in size and quality. A new generation grew up of intelligent and cultured youth. For this generation the atmosphere in Radzyn became too constricting. Spurred on by the thirst for knowledge the educated young people strove to go to the larger centers where they enriched their education and culture. Others went out into the world to live as free people in a free world.

3. Shimon Kleinboim

The third branch of the family, that contributed more than a little to the cultural upsurge among the town's young people, was the brother-in-law of the above mentioned Dovid Fishel and Yehoshua, Shimon Kleinboim, the bookkeeper of the family business. With a gentle friendly look on his face and a quill behind his ear, he sat, underneath the office, which was built on a high platform, busy with papers and surrounded by books and papers of various of colors. One could immediately discern that this was the realm that he ruled alone. His brother-in-law, David, got lost in this labyrinth of numbers and therefore left the art of numbers to Shimon the aristocrat. Having brought from home a large supply of both Jewish and non-Jewish knowledge, Shimon immediately captured an honorable role in this aristocratic family. His manners and behavior created a barrier between himself and the ordinary Jews. He strode around in the streets like a stranger among strangers. Despite his stiff cold behavior his heart was open to Jewish pain and problems. Because of his straightforward thinking, he was favored by the city government. He used this to obtain favors for individuals as well as for moderating between the non-Jewish city administration and the Jewish community. In order to alleviate the bitter situation of the small businessmen or craftsmen, he contributed greatly to the establishment of a credit union. Like a real public servant he threw himself into this activity with his whole heart and soul. For many years he devoted his time, energy and knowledge to supporting this important institution. He was the most revered, important, and recognized leader in the Jewish community between the two world wars.

[Pages 188-191]

Nathan Shwalbe [1]

Nachman Maizil (New York)
(Excerpts from a longer article)

Nathan Shwalbe was one of the first and most important of Yiddish and Yiddish-Polish journalists who, from the very beginning, specialized in one realm, journalism. He was a journalist with very open eyes and ears for the political questions and problems that he constantly studied and researched, always only from primary sources. From his youthful years, after graduating from the Reali School and studying in Krakow University, he was associated with well-known, dependable Polish-Yiddish newspapers. From the very beginning, he carried out important journalistic assignments and missions. He did so with great competence and responsibility. The development of Jewish political and communal life, in Poland, was rife with jealousy and had many open and secret enemies who were searching for any flaw that could be used to attack Jews and their politics.

He began his journalistic activities in 1913 before World War I when Jewish-Polish relationships were very strained. He was associated with important Jewish and Polish-Jewish newspapers during the German occupation and up until 1938. During this period he was an important correspondent for foreign affairs in these papers, as well as their correspondent in the Polish Seim, (Legislature) which was always an important arena for Polish Jewish interests and problems. He was also a special correspondent for the meetings of the League of Nations in Geneva. He wrote about all the issues raised there in a correct, factual and comprehensive style without journalistic affectation.

Such a talented Polish-Jewish writer, with so many important acquaintances and connections in the outer world, could have made a career in the greater Polish press, as was done by many other less talented journalists than Shwalbeh. However, deep down in his soul, he was firstly a proud Jew with a powerful attachment to Jewish life, and a natural, interest in problems of Jewish nationalism and in its future existence. Therefore, he always stayed in a Jewish environment and was friendly with Jewish colleagues. Whenever he was free, he was a regular visitor at the Jewish Writer's Club at 13 Tolmatzke St. Other Polish-Jewish journalists rarely 'stepped down' from their 'high positions' to visit this journalistic 'shtibl' which was more than a place to eat a meal. It was more a 'holy place' or a place of 'refuge' for the different writers, journalists, teachers, actors, artists, cultural activists, and just plain champions of Jewish literature and journalism. He stood out for his activity in the Writer's Union, which was crowded with people and was the center for literary-artistic disputes.

Just as in his newspapers so too at the Jewish Writer's Club, he never mixed into other matters. He never became agitated, or took on any official position in the leading Jewish institutions. He was wholly and completely involved in his political world and always tried to be up to date on all matters having any connection to his field, which was the political-social world.

The Jewish Seim (Polish Legislature) members gladly listened to the logical, practical opinions of Nathan Shwalbe that often could point, to the straight path out of a difficult political situation. Nathan Shwalbe, who was straightforward and unflinching, was often very useful in the struggle for Jewish rights. Polish political and journalistic circles too, listened to the opinions of their colleague, Nathan Shwalbe, who impressed them with his arguments and opinions. More than one pro-Jewish piece appeared in the Polish press thanks to the influence Nathan Shwalbe.

I have before me the protest that Jewish writers publicized in Warsaw on the 4th of September 1922 when the Polish Minister of Education closed six Yiddish צ.י.ש.א (Central Yiddish School Organization) schools for Jewish children. In that sharp protest in the Yiddish and Polish-Jewish press it said: "We protest against this violent injustice. The hand that was cruelly stretched out against the Yiddish school must be withdrawn" etc. Among the signatures of the 68 Yiddish writers, including many who were on the 'left', there appeared that of Nathan Shwalbe.

Here, it must be noted that if the Polish-Jewish press in all of Poland and especially in Warsaw was thoroughly nationalist and pro Jewish and pro Yiddish, it was to a great extent thanks to the quiet and resolute Nathan Shwalbe. Everything that was healthy and productive in Jewish life was near and dear to him.

Among the various Polish-Jewish writers, Nathan Shwalbeh, was the most modest and most Jewish and as such he will remain forever in the history of the Jewish press in Poland which has yet to be written.

Translator's Footnotes

1. For further details about Nathan Shwalbe's activity in the Yiddish and Yiddish-Polish Press see: Zalmen Raisin's "Lexicon" Vilna 1929, Vol. 4, Pages 308-309. Return
2. About Nathan Shwalbe- the beginning of the World War and the gruesome German occupation see: V. Segalovitch's book: "The Burning Steps" Buenos Aries, 1947. Pages 7, 8, 35, 39, 67.

Laizerkeh Szalasheh
and the Radzyn Amateur Artists

Henich Applebaum (Pardess Chana)

In the year 1901, or maybe even earlier, Laizerkeh Salasheh, who was a small and dark shoemaker with small dark eyes, and as agile as quicksilver, was never at home. He sat all day long in Menachem-Laizer's tavern, with all the coachmen waiting for someone to come in and order a drink and a bite for which Laizerkeh would have to pay by some kind of a performance.

He got together a group of shoemakers and tailors and began performing. They played 'The Shmendrick', 'The Old Father' and 'The Sale of Joseph'. All year long they waited for the good Purim and the beautiful Passover. Then Laizerkeh exploited all his talent and 'flew' around the whole town. First they went up to Fishel Moshe Gotttel's, then to Akiva Rubinstein and for a finale they went up to the late Rabbi, Reb Mordecai-Yosef where Laizerkeh showed what he knew. The Rabbi often said: "Laizer, Go to the big city, and you will become a Mentsh."

Drama group led by Hanikel Apellboim (first from the right), 1931

That was what really happened. One fine morning Laizerkeh left Radzyn and went to Lodz. There he was successful and he went on to Warsaw where he met Y.L. Peretz (famous Yiddish author and playwright) and became the great artist Laizer Zalasheh and later became a member of the famous Vilna (theatre) Troupe.

The Radzyner troupe of shoemakers and tailors were left like sheep without a shepherd and decided to continue performing "The Sale of Joseph". They continued doing so for many years until many of the actors passed away and with them so did "The Sale of Joseph".

---*---

In the year 1910-11 the play "Bar Kochba" was performed in Radzyn by intelligentsia of that period (p.192) that included Ben Zion Greenbaum, Yantshe Gottel's, Laizer Firshtenberg, Chanina Glazer, Mottel Goldwasser and others. Someone by the name of Kaminsky, a Jewish soldier who was stationed at the time in Radzyn, helped them. There was then no theatre building in Radzyn at the time so they performed in a horse stable on the Raientowka Street near Hershel the rope maker's place. However, despite the fact that no posters were posted, the shed was full of people. Everyone went to see the performance of "Bar Kochba". Even the local officials came. At that time women did not participate, so the cantor's boys choir showed what it knew.

There were almost no further theatre performances until 1915-16 except for "Tikun Tifferet" (The Grand Reconstruction) The boys from the Bais-Hamedrash (seminary) presented this dressed like Russian Cossacks with whips in their hands and speaking Russian. They could not appear in the streets for fear that the Russian police would chase after them yelling "Jewish traitors". Therefore they ran only through the back streets. They would go into a house and take up positions as if they were soldiers, and one of them would shout out in Russian "Musicians! Play the First Moscow March!" Then began singing with gusto. When they finished singing, one of them went up to the table and put a card on it on which was written "Chevrat Tikun Tifferet" ("The Grand Reconstruction Society") that had the stamp of the Rabbi and of the teacher on it. Another one went around and collected up a few Zloties, and then they rang a bell and disappeared like clowns.

[Pages 193-197]

Hashomer Hatzair in Radzyn

Emanuel Tor (Kibbutz Negba-Israel)

In this survey I want to tell about the development of the branch of Hashomer Hatzair ("The Young Guards") in our town and about the Hashomer youth, who even at that time, contributed greatly to the development of the concept of 'Zionist-Pioneering self realization' among the youth in our town.

From the very beginning, our path was not paved with roses. We had many opponents on all sides. First there was a fierce argument between our parents and us. We did not succeed in convincing them that the only solution to our problems was our territorial concentration in the Land of Israel. We warned them for a long time, pointing to the approaching holocaust, but all this were just a voice in the wilderness. They were unwilling to listen to the younger generation. Therefore there was no choice but to wave the flag of revolt in front of our parents. We told the young people: "Do not listen to your father's moral principles."

That was on one side. On the other, were the socialist and anti-Zionist parties that appeared in the Jewish community and waged a strenuous campaign for the souls of the young people of our town. Who can ever forget the unending political agitation and arguments? However, in the end, our prognosis, that viewed the land of Israel as the historic homeland of the Jewish people and the place for its territorial ingathering, was victorious. In those days it took much strength and courage to stand up and fight for our just way, which today is almost unchallenged even by its opponents.

Let us now recount the activities of our branch of Hashomer in our town. As a result of this prognosis, we educated the youth toward a new life, one of labor and toward a new culture, which eliminates the burdens and fears that had become symbolic of those times. We sponsored hikes and trips outside of the narrow confines of the town. We hoped that the clean, pure air of the country would penetrate into the bodies of Hebrew youth. Our aim was to heal the body of the Jew. For that purpose we sponsored summer camps that also served to prepare for the founding of agricultural training farms. However, many mocked us: "The "Shomrim" are playing at being "soldiers..." they said.

How was this to be done? How to mobilize the financial means for maintaining teachers? Despite the difficulties we managed to maintain evening Hebrew courses. I must note with pride and praise the devotion of those teachers who worked hard for this goal and strengthened the Hebrew schools. The Hebrew language was heard. The young people began to sing Hebrew songs and to read the newspapers that reached us from Palestine and in that way learned about what was happening in our homeland.

"Hashomer Ha'tzair" members on a hike

We collected money for the Jewish National Fund, the Keren Hayesod and other funds. I still remember the cynical derision when we came to empty out the National Fund collection boxes, but we were not ashamed because we saw this as one of the pioneering tasks to which we educated the youth. This was in the period in which there was almost no immigration to Palestine. The mandatory government issued only a very small number of certificates so that there was no choice but to immigrate to Palestine by other means.

----*----

The history of the chapter of Hashomer Hatzair in our town begins with its founding close to the end of the military actions in 1920. It was among the first branches that began functioning in Poland. At first various other scouting movements influenced it. Slowly but surely, its own particular method was established becoming the foundation of our movement, and brought us to where we are today. As already noted, there were difficulties even at that time. The struggle over the soul of the Hebrew youth was bitter. The other movements such as the 'Bund' and the 'Communists' fought against us fiercely offering a different solution to the problems of the Jewish people, and influenced to a great extent the ideological unrest in our ranks.

"Hashomer Ha'tzair" "Prachim" group, "Kfirim" battalion

I remember the arguments that took place inside our branch at the end of 1924 about the ideological way of the Hashomer Hatzair movement. In the end we overcame the deviants even though many of them left our ranks. The older members managed to overcome this difficult situation, and as a result the beginnings of immigration to Palestine, the so-called 'self-realization' began.

I remember the immigration to Palestine of the first members of our branch. How we envied them! We who were very young took over both the leadership and educational direction. The period was the one of immigration. At that time every member understood what 'self realization' demanded of him. It was not enough to declare that you are a Zionist and a pioneer. Pioneering means self-realization in all walks of life.

There were various elements among the youth in our branch. Some came from well-to-do homes, some from religious homes, and some were children of merchants, etc. and some even from partly assimilated homes who had studied in Polish secondary schools. All of these elements affected the development of our chapter. Therefore it was necessary to merge all these elements into one strong bloc.

"Hashomer Ha'tzair", a group on the occasion of a friend's departure to Israel Tevet, 5686 (1926)

In the early years of our existence no working class youth joined us. They were not attracted to our way. With the passing of time, this youth, too, was attracted to our movement and a united bloc including all elements of the Jewish youth in our city was created.

On the seventh anniversary of the founding of our branch, in 1927, its leaders produced a booklet called "דרגא" (The Ladder) that was an authentic expression of the fulfillment of our aspirations. In it we found true literary expression for the activities of our branch at that time. After that anniversary there was a changing of the guard in the leadership. The older generation immigrated and those that had been pupils up to now took over the leadership. The younger generation took charge vigorously and carried on with the activities. New problems appeared such as preparing a new generation of leaders, leaving for agricultural training, etc. At that time the Hechalutz (Pioneer) Organization was formed. To summarize: The 30's were years of intensive activity and efforts in our branch.

The time for our Aliyah (immigration to Palestine) arrived. The younger generation took over and continued on faithfully along the same course. However the Holocaust and W.W.2, that destroyed most of our people in Poland, extinguished the light of our dynamic Hashomer branch that had carried on broad and blessed activities through which many young people found their way to the Land of Israel.

"Hashomer Ha'tzair" Leaders of the "Kfirim Bar Cochva" battalion, Nisan 5683 (1923)

"Hashomer Ha'tzair" group, Sivan 18th, 5684 (1924)

[Pages 198-199]

The Amateur Stage of "Hashomer Hatzair"

M. Ben Shmuel (Tel-Aviv)

With the awakening of communal life in our town, after the end of the German conquest at the end of World War I, many political organizations of different types were established, among them different youth movements. There was an outburst of activities in all facets of social life: expansion of the existing libraries, sports organizations, cooperatives, trade unions etc. Political antagonisms grew. The youth were caught up in a desire for social and political solutions for the rest of the world and for our people. Amidst all of this craving and search for change in the world and for the Jewish people, an important cultural nucleus was created in almost all of the youth movements affecting the cultural life of the town, namely dramatic groups. Such groups were organized in all the youth organizations from Hashomer Hatzair to the Craftsmen (with their performance of "The Sale of Joseph").

Every production of any one of the dramatic groups, including both its preparation and its performance, was an important event in the life of the town. The audience at these performances which was always large was mainly made up of the supporters of the political line of the performers. Therefore these performances served as an activating factor in the cultural life of the whole town.

Many theatrical talents in Hashomer Hatzair were revealed in these performances. I want to mention two of them Rachel Lazar and Lichtenstein, who were later murdered by the evil Nazis.

I remember that once one of the actors, Yaakov Z'alaza from famous Vilna Troupe, came to our town. The members of Hashomer Hatzair utilized the opportunity to meet with him, and he agreed after a number of meetings when he was convinced that these amateur actors were capable of performing the play successfully, to prepare a production of the play "Der Dorfsyung" (The Country Boy) by Kobrin. After a few weeks of preparation, the play was performed under his direction and with his participation. This production was of course very successful and was the ultimate accomplishment in this field in our town.

רבותי, בערב היום הטוב הזה על־הבמה אליהם, וילר שולוצער־פזעטדרעדרפטיאן, פראפ טביעיו.

Drama group of the "Shomer Ha'tzair", Radzyn 1925

Youth music band

[Pages 200-202]

ד ר ג א

תרפ״ז - 1927

(The following article has been taken from "Darga" (The Ladder (above) which was published by the Hashomer Hatzair organization in Radzyn in 1927 on theits seventh anniversary. They picture both the vigorous and effervescent life of the youth in our town.)

About the Educational Activity in the Hashomer Hatzair Branch in Radzyn

Y. Zeligman

It is important to point out that in our movement in general there was for many years a tortuous and misleading social education that brought us, in addition to some useful experiences, some serious crises that cost us a lot of blood. This happened as a result of the actual blurring of our social goals on one hand and the fear of the leaders who were "afraid" of creating "socialist restraints" on the youth on the other hand.

With the crystallization of the essence and the framework of our social position in both Israel and in the Diaspora and the accumulation of educational experience, our educational path took on more and more the suitable form and content.

Those who are acquainted with the conditions in the provincial towns and especially of those in provinces knew that most our youth are under the negative influence of their home environment which was in many cases anti-Zionist. They were always filled with 'doubts' and 'questions' about our way and as a result they did not believe their leaders. Therefore there was a need to prove to our pupils that we were not hiding anything from them including the truth about social problems, the political system, and its future.

As a result of this method of uncompromising socialist education we flourished in Radzyn. We tried to give our people not only a romantic longing for a moral life and a strong desire for social justice but also the scientific basis for social theory and socialism. This brought the young people to believe in our seriousness about the above and to believe in the justice of the solutions that we offered to social problems.

Hashomer Hazair – a scout group (1927) with the participation of Radzyn natives and those of the surrounding towns

We succeeded in the area of "Chalutzic education" (education for a life as pioneers in Israel) and there were many reasons for this success the most important of which were: a. the continuing immigration of our members and b. their social status.

The persistent immigration from our branch had strong and continuous influence on the enthusiasm of our younger members for 'The Land of Israel' and was a very important educational element. All of the discussion groups, parties and camp fires were nothing compared to the immigration of one person especially if he was a group leader who was emotionally bound up to his younger pupils.

First there was the tradition of handing down the leadership from older to the younger and their following in their footsteps, all of which started first as a dream and ended up with the actual parting from brothers and personal acquaintances.

The son, who understood the economic changes and saw the economic changes in which the families of our members found themselves, their shaky financial basis with the father who carried on meekly and with inertia without the possibility of assuring the family's welfare, became fiercely critical of the traditional way of life. Together with casting off of the sickly "Menachem Mendel" impetuosity came great dissatisfaction with the whole meaningless culture.

From inside this intellectual confusion and its ensuing spiritual emptiness burst forth the redeeming-enslaving word of complete personal salvation and the cultural renewal through "Chalutziut" (Zionist Pioneering).

"Hashomer Ha'tzair" - the Shomrim that received third rank, 5683 (1923)

[Pages 203-205]

About Our Development

Ch. Shlimak

I don't want to tell only the historical facts. I would rather give you a short review of our ideological development during the different periods.

Seven or eight years ago we were a group of young boys who had just felt the breath of the free world after the loosening of the last knots tying us to the religious school and shtibl. (Small Chassidic prayer hut). We were free! But after a short period of being filled to the brim with freedom, the mind again began to search in all directions. What to join? How to take advantage of this opportunity? Where to invest our natural enthusiasm?

The bench for studying the Talmud was too crowded; the well-trodden path to the 'education bench' was too low. We put an end, once and for all, to personal 'ambition' in all of its forms. But we did not know what to do with ourselves after that.

"Hashomer Ha'tzair" - an Older Group

For a long time there had already existed somewhere the source of a particular youthful creativity that we had somehow not heard about-

"Hashomer" ("The Guard"- A Zionist Youth Movement), We looked into the 'record books', learned the 'commandments' and started working. We started with "scouting". We the 'book worms' went out into the fields and woods. Out there, far from the city, the group leaders, all them outstanding young men, must have exposed the innermost weaknesses that we were ashamed of. We felt that here, in this place, we held the control of our lives and that here is our home. But in what direction should we go? We could not continue to be influenced only by the early cult of the scouting. Our unrest drove us further. "Where to?" was no longer the question. It was clear that "Hashomer" was the answer to that. But where do we go further with "Hashomer"?

"Hashomer Ha'tzair" - in honour of the emmigration of the head of the group to Israel. "Tzofim" battalion "Mishmar Ha'emek", Adar, 1932.

A group called 'Hatchiya' ('The Rebirth') was established which in eight months forged a nucleus of leaders for the organization. New people were added, some of whom unlocked the secret of their up until then silent, but plainly rebellious, souls. At that time, the first "Seniors Circle" was established. I remember that long period as being a great and beautiful dream. Though we called ourselves "the Seniors Circle" we were only children!

I remember the lively gatherings where our young spirits blossomed. We loaded all the pain of being both human and Jewish on our backs and thought about salvation. But we still saw everything only in our own personal mirror. I am the center of everything! Although we planned to make the whole world a happier place through our principles, we measured everything only by our own personal standards.

How innocently and honestly the good Yaakov, our group leader, would project before for us the picture of our future lives in the homeland in the "Small Kvutza" (small collective).

Now we can evaluate it objectively. We were a group of people who had reached the age of doubt and clung to the idea of collectivism but from purely individualistic reasons. More than once we even reached a doubtful pessimism. The habitual question at our meetings was: "What is life?". The answers were always romantic outbursts, natural romanticism! The influence of the first Seniors group covered everyone and everything. Even the meetings of the 'Kfirim' (Young Lions) were saturated with this legendary format through which we saw the Land of Israel, the commune and our future, in general. Also, in those months, the immigration of our members to Israel began and grew.

---*---

"Hashomer Ha'tzair" – a girls group

With the collapse of the first Seniors Circle, through immigration to the land of Israel, a distinct crisis developed in the attitude of those who remained behind. It began with personal ambitions and ended with a reevaluation of many of the strongly established norms in our lives and work. The doubts about the dreamt-up youthful plans, the search for personal happiness among the adults, together with the fact that more and more of young people had lost their experienced leaders by immigration, caused them to fall under the corrupting influence of the "street'. All of this together called out in us a revolt against locking ourselves up in our own realm and even against the realm itself ! Days arrived when everything blistered with the longing for unlimited horizons. It was not only a change in our ideological activity or a sudden change in the ideological outlook; it was a link in the greater chain of our psychological development, an absolute and unavoidable link. It was a massive revolt of the individual against himself, when self hate leads to losing oneself in the whirlpool of maddening communal activity.

At that time some of the more restless among us, who were more affected by their psychological inner conflict and went as far as denying the essence of the movement, were torn away from the course of their rebellion. At the same time, the organization, that had been guided in its most critical moments by its healthy instincts, began slowly and step by step carrying out a process of reshaping itself in the spirit of newly emerging currents.

After somehow limiting the spontaneous eruption, and on the background of the educational activities (which had already for some time become the focal point of the movement's activities), a new foundation was laid which guaranteed further development along quite different lines.

Instead of the inflated individual pain, the essence of the national and social questions was stressed. The Land and the Kibbutz (collective settlement) were no longer oases for helping the individual, but healthy solutions for the sum of all the national and social problems that confronted us and were the essence of this latest period. Self-realization was no longer understood as being only the expression of "the chosen people syndrome" and its negation of the surrounding reality which drives people to 'escape' and to isolate themselves. It was understood as being the only conclusion to be drawn from our way and from our serious intentions with the ideal of Zionism and the acts of social pioneering.

This is the short summary of our intellectual development in Radzyn.

[Pages 206]

Out of the Furnace

(from a Journal of a training farm)

...I was abandoned, exposed, and a combination of anger and productivity guided me. Now my time has arrived. I miss the law as a frame to protect me. I will press my arms into my body; I will seal my mouth with my fist, not to sin easily. Man is his word and his motion. This is my credo today for me and him and her: for all of us. I believe in the inner impulse that brought together to this place every man and woman, and I see in it the enormous strength which calls us to a complete and decisive nakedness. None of us enjoyed the popular reward, not a single remnant from the past.

I focus my sight in the countenance of A's beautiful face, devoid of expression, and with a sympathetic heart I witness his private moments, his self-contempt at his own banalities- a contempt mixed with anxiety and sorrow- as he tries to raise his character to overcome the confusion and nature's habits.

"Hashomer Ha'tzair" - a Hachshara (trainiing) group at Oschesh farm

With spiritual arms I will embrace all my brothers, because their broken bodies and their patient silence in the day were like pure spring waters, but they tortured themselves lying on their planks at night. And their fragmented conversations, confessions almost, were whispered in my ear, thirsty for their trembling soul and their divine fear: will we fail? At every step a jackal sneaks in, lying in wait, rooted in our guilt. But if our heart is empty and beats in its quest for purity, for a re-birth, what will we do if it delays its coming?

The jackal that waits in ambush possesses seven eyes, sometimes is the image of a nice tree and furrow, and other times shrewdness and fullness of life. Everything reports a momentary light and the termination of purpose. And much, much more...

In those first days, we will gnaw with our teeth at the essence of our heritage. We still have fashioned nothing new, our own miracles, and we have to stem the tide with seven- fold force: with rhetoric, motion, a fluttering of our eyelashes from the past- surrendering to Satan.

Oy, my brothers! Not all of you are true to your essence today. But I am sure that, even unknowingly, this thought crosses your mind, a thought that reflects the crisis, the birth pangs. We burned the Rome and Babylon of our souls, but in our new poverty we must painstakingly gather the slivers of our soul...

As though I had a top secret which they fear, I will walk among the terrified to gather their thoughts. Maybe some of them will think to call a meeting or request a lecture. But I have nothing to say...I feel the fatigue of my instincts, which became soft and unstable like children's bones. And if I appeal to my common-sense, I also find it weak and agitated. It travels wearily thousands of moments and paths, caresses them but does not stop to acknowledge them. Like a tree whose branches are many but his roots are few, I yearn for the ground, for a spring flowing with strength.

I have nothing now, except for the conscience of the poverty I suffer, which propels me to what is coming. I did not come here with pre-conceived notions. I only believe in the honest steps with which I approach my own self. I will try everything again, collecting all my principles.   And time will engrave my good deeds.

What are lectures for? And what can they say? I so fear routine words like "a new life and a new society". They say:" a unique social creation". When I reflect on it I am surprised at the ease with which they pronounce the phrase, which we have to repeat. Man lost his way, lost his path in his private life. He yearns for redemption. Not the redemption of Nirvana, that sets world on fire in its storminess, but liberation from the complications caused by the deterioration and exaggeration of individualism, a liberation that will bring an accomplished and perfect society. This creation, this cultural innovation that represents a future religion, cannot happen without the painful revolution of thousands, which will last moments, days, generations...

Even Christianity, in its redemptive aspect, did not appear in the world through a legislative meeting of priests, but out of the human suffering of the disciples of John, the Baptist, and the colleagues of Papanotius, the Nazirite, at the shores of the Nile.

Out of the intensity and the delving into life itself, out of the difficulty in the common experiences, based only on the free will of the purpose of the existence of the body and soul of our society...what is the matter to be dealt in the gathering I hear it is already talked about?

A man is born with much effort, overcoming stumbling blocks. Let's look at the feelings of his lofty birth. Let's shake in fear...but let's not talk much...

David R.
Austriana-Radzyn, Tammuz 1927

"Hashomer Ha'tzair" - the leaders of the "Bar Kochva" batallion, Radzyn, Nisan 5685 (1925)

[Pages 208]

The Ascender (Poem)
L. Vinderbaum

The riser like a moon-wanderer
Over the cliffs spikes, and into the night
On the crowning tips of the treetops, he looks into the future
The sun shines on the luscious fruit
Towards the sweaty plantings of the heart
Every cliff from your [illegible]
With rousing laughter
The last dreams will be broken on me
And a noble's shadow will pass by each tree.
It won't stay so happy here forever – your dream,
Know, wanderer, that under rocks and shadows
 There are only shining old [illegible] from fire in [illegible]
Sleep, thick breath of dried up wells
Rise up far away [illegible]
  [illegible] Rise up [illegible]
Over Chava's barren fileds
Mercy cannot flourish: Hate!
Spread out over rocks and shadows
Waiting for their beloved Messiah
Who will say Kaddish over today's day? – - -
From the learned countings
Somewhere, in the swinging path goes "where to"
It is not worth it to grant him the days!!

[Pages 211-220]

Destruction and Extinction

The Beginning of the Storm and the Extinction

Abba Lichtenshtein (Tel-Aviv)

The situation of the Jewish community in Poland was not very easy from the very beginning of Poland's independence in 1918. Two possibilities faced the Polish rulers: to develop and industrialize the country so as to drag it out of its backwardness by transferring its lands from the land owners to the peasants and thereby improving the situation of the working class, or to leave the country in its economic weakness and to accuse, the three and a half million persons of the Jewish community as the source and reason for the evil and suffering of the Polish people. The rulers of Poland chose the second of the two possibilities. They nurtured the hatred of the Polish people for the Jews. Anti-Semitism in all of its forms was the daily occurrence for the Jews of Poland.

It became especially conspicuous in the period during the treaty of friendship between Hitler and Pilsudski and his successors. Economic boycotts and even bloody riots became every day events. There were such riots in Pshitik, Brisk in Lithuania, and in Minsk-Mazowieki and other towns and villages. All this was the result of the inspiration given by the Germans to the Jew haters in Poland. The latter carried out their mission faithfully.

In our town Radzyn too, in the days before the outbreak of the war, gangs of pickets from the N.D. Fascist Phalanges lined up on the sidewalks opposite the Jewish stores and workshops and shouted wildly at the top of their lungs "Poles, buy only from Poles! Boycott the Jews! Jews, get out of Poland!" The Jews became frightened when even the best and most intelligent Poles were swept up in this current of Jew hatred.

The situation changed in the beginning of 1939 with the election of Hitler and his demand for the western territories of Poland. Then it became clear to everyone that a bloody storm was approaching. However the storm of Jew hatred abated. It became clear to everyone that the bullet and the bomb would not differentiate between nation and race but spread death and destruction equally over everyone. Then it became the desire of the entire population to stand up with all their might against the storm and to prevail against it. However it was too late, since the mistakes of the leadership had determined that the fate of the nation was enslavement, and that of the Jews living there was extinction.

Poles and Jews demonstrating against Hitler's demands regarding Western Poland

Life in the town, even in the last months before the beginning of the storm, moved along its usual path. People worked hard as they always did, despite a feeling of depression, but they still hoped that the war would not break out. Hitler would not dare to attack Poland with its thirty five million inhabitants. They believed in the strength of the Polish Army and could not imagine the power of the Nazi Army. There was general complacency.

The weather was fine, the fields and the gardens were in full bloom promising a plentiful harvest. Their intoxicating odors reached all the way to the city streets in the evenings. The young people hiked on foot and on their bicycles on the roads surrounding Radzyn. The people wanted to believe that all would be well. The months of May, June, and July passed and harvest time arrived. From morning until sunset, wagons piled high with golden sheaves of wheat and other grains passed through the town. The ears of corn were bursting with grains. Then came the second cutting of hay. In the orchards the branches of the trees hung low from the weight of fruit.

On Saturday we spent many hours in town in the magnificent palace garden. We walked around between the rows of lilies looking at the sparkling waters of the lake. On the bank stood a small boat that some mischievous children were trying to untie from its moorings and sail to the opposite end of the lake.

---*---

The palace stood in all its glory, with its windows wide open. From the right wing, the clatter of a typewriter in the regional offices could be heard. From the central annex, which housed the post office, the voice of the telephone operator at the switchboard could be heard saying "Hello! Hello! This is Radzyn! Radzyn speaking!"

In the afternoon hours the Jews, who had finished eating, preferred a stroll in the nobleman Shlobovski's garden, which was public property rather than the traditional nap under covers. Mothers came with their children in baby carriages to enjoy a rest in the fresh air and a friendly chat. Everything was natural, traditional and wrapped in pleasure and tranquility and no one expected the storm that was brewing over our heads.

---*---

However, the seriousness of the situation was well known among the ruling circles and they initiated defensive actions nationwide. The government propaganda began working full steam to arouse patriotic feelings of the population. From the pages of the newspapers and from the walls of the buildings a famous motto shone forth: "We must be ready, strong and united."

In Radzyn, as in all of Poland, money was collected for national defense funds. Jews contributed generously believing innocently that the arms and planes that will be obtained through these funds will help them in time of need. Courses in first aid and especially anti- aircraft and anti-gas were organized. Everyone, both Jews and non Jews, participated in these courses. This was something new. In the same course there sat Jews with beards, ear locks and wearing capotes (traditional long black coats) and next to them 'shikses', young Polish girls. As was mentioned before, the danger threatened everyone equally.

July passed and the month of August arrived. The political-diplomatic activities in the European capitals, as well as in Warsaw, reached a feverish pitch. We thought that something serious was about to happen.

One morning, just after the arrival of the newspapers, groups of people could be seen gathering in the streets, peering at the papers, and standing there to read them as if they were looking to find an answer and a solution to the question that was bothering them and keeping sleep from their eyes. Will war break out?

When I went out early in the morning on Thursday the 30th of August, I saw large signs that read "Partial mobilization of reserves." The city became panic stricken.

A few hours later men began streaming toward the railroad station to report to their army units. Sighs, crying, and farewell kisses echoed through the streets. None of the conscripts knew if or when they would ever return home. The war became a reality.

The next day Radio Warsaw broadcast a call and orders for a general mobilization, and on Friday the 1st of September, the Germans crossed the borders and invaded Poland.

We were located some 400 kilometers from the western border of the country, and we felt almost nothing during the first three days of the war. However on the fourth day, early in the morning, a warning siren sounded and everyone scrambled to find cover from an air raid.

However, it turned out the Germans had more important targets to bomb than the town of Radzyn itself. These were the airplane factories in Lublin and Biala Podlaska, the railroad junction at Siedlce, Lukow etc. They would fly over, flight after flight, in their black bombers, like birds of prey high in the skies of Radzyn, without dropping any of their deadly cargo on us for the time being. The quiet that had reigned in the town disappeared suddenly and forever.

Terrible news reached us about the weakness and defeats suffered by the Polish Army and the strength of the invaders. We found out that there was already a serious a shortage of heavy weapons and air power and also a lack of organization and a general laxity. The roads and paths were filled with army units fleeing in panic eastward from the West. Together with the army, hundreds of thousands of refugees, among them government officials and ordinary citizens, fled from the western areas. Vehicles loaded with the movable equipment from important scientific institutions and from the universities of Posen and Krakow arrived. The flood of soldiers and refugees grew from hour to hour. The roads were too narrow to accommodate such traffic advancing in four columns or more. The refugees, tired, hungry and thirsty filled the city streets and vacant lots. The supply of food for the city began to run out, and there were very serious problems of distribution. There was no bread.

The Germans had already penetrated deeply into Poland, besieged Warsaw and incessantly bombarded the most important centers of the county. They bombed the roads surrounding Radzyn daily. The movement of the army, the evacuees and the refugees stopped completely during the daylight hours for fear of the German planes. Everyone hid out in the forests and grain fields and filled the villages and estates that lined the roads. Panic broke out. There was complete disorientation and disorder. When night fell, the roads were again filled with thousands walking and riding eastward in an unending stream. The town was completely blacked out. The refugees wandered around in the town like shadows in their search for food and lodging. Tired and hungry, they would fall asleep usually on the sidewalks and near the buildings that were already filled with refugees/guests who had reached Radzyn before them.

On the 7th of September the Central Command in Warsaw ordered all men to leave the area of Warsaw and to go eastward. Masses of ex-Radzyner, who had been living in Warsaw, came back to Radzyn. They told about the horrors that the Germans had perpetrated on the whole population and especially on the Jews.

The Polish radio was silent. The newspapers had not reached us since the second day after the war broke out. We learned what the Germans were doing and what lay in store for us only from the Jewish refugees. However there were some Jews who thought to themselves, &147; surely the devil cannot be as black as they paint him."

On Friday the 8th of September there were frequent alarms that came almost one right after the other. We hid out during most of the day in the fields and gardens that surrounded the city. The German planes flew over our heads with frightening and ear splitting noise. When they spied any army unit they rained down a shower of machine gun fire on it. There were no real bombings that day. They came on the following day.

It was a beautiful day; the sky was clear and the air pure. It was one of those lovely early autumn days for which Poland is famous .We hid out in the fields and gardens surrounding the city for most of the day. German planes flew over us deafeningly. Already in the early morning, a number of planes appeared in the sky, swooping down low in the suburbs where most of the granaries belonging to the Radzyn farmers were located, and set them on fire. The wooden buildings that were full of grain and straw went up in flames. Despite the great danger involved, many people ran to the fire to try to save whatever was possible with the voluntary fire brigade leading the way. A crowd gathered there which was just what the murderous pilots were waiting for. Suddenly they returned, flew low and began firing on those trying to extinguish the flames. We scattered in all directions and hid under any cover that we could find in the vicinity. The result: more than ten dead and many more wounded, both Jews and Poles. Among the Jewish victims was the veteran fire fighter Shmuel Kimmel.

Some of the German bombers seemed to have chosen Radzyn as their target for this Saturday to do whatever they wished. We lay down in the fields and the grass so that the murderers would not see us from up high. Everyone feared for his life and in his mind was the thought "Will I live until the evening or will I be hit by a bomb?" Suddenly we heard the humming of the motor of an approaching bomber and the dreadful and deafening shriek of the bomb exploding on the earth. When the plane flew away a bit, we raised our heads slightly so as to see from which direction the flames and clouds of dust were coming from the target that had been hit.

There was no effective anti- aircraft protection in the important centers of the country and of course not in Radzyn. The city was completely neglected so the German pilot-murderers could do whatever they wanted. Every once in a while you could hear the rattling of a lone machine gun but that was like the buzzing of a fly against the roar of a lion. That was the balance of power in all parts of the country. The planes finally left the city skies at sundown and we left our hiding places. The results of that day's bombardment were terrible, many were killed, and many houses were destroyed especially in the vicinity of the palace which was the pilots' main target. The telephone poles and lines were destroyed, and the town was left completely without any communication with the surrounding area. Many of those who had sought shelter in the garden by the castle were killed .Many others who were killed were just enjoying a stroll in the gardens and did not have time to run away. Most of those killed were youths; among them were Boruch Blumen, Daniel Sodberg, the two Saltzman sisters, as well as some others.

Almost all of the population left the city on that Saturday evening. People tried to find hiding places in the surrounding villages especially in those located in forests and far from roads. My family chose the village of Ulshabnitzeh which was located in the forest on the Shlubovski estate. I said "almost all of the population." There was however a small portion that did not leave the town during all those difficult days. They were mostly the older citizens who refused to leave their homes. They did not want to go out into the country, even if only for a few days. There were two reasons for this. They were religious people who believed that one could not escape from fate or death. The others were people who were bound to the town of their birth and who argued that: "Here we were born, here we lived, here we raised our sons and here we will die if so it is willed". Every attempt on our part to convince them to leave with us the younger people was futile. They refused to go with us some weeks later when we fled eastward away from the Nazi conquerors.

Even the remote village of Ulshebnitze was already filled with Polish refugees from the west who had tired of wandering. The peasants received us with a smile, sold us food and arranged places for lodging. A number of army units were stationed in the nearby forest. During the day, we wandered idly about the town. At night we would go on foot to Radzyn to see and find out what went on there. On Sunday and Monday (10th and 11th of September) nothing special happened in the town. The houses were closed and locked. Even more refugees filled the streets. In their search for food they broke into most of the food stores and restaurants, but these were already empty. At one o'clock in the morning they broke into the cellar of a wine and liquor store and found a treasure. The bottles passed from hand to hand everyone wanting to take an intoxicating swig. Most of the bottles were broken even before the corks were removed and the pungent smell of alcohol filled the street.

When we came to the village before dawn on the Tuesday night (12.9), we were told that during the day there had been a heavy bombardment. Many houses were destroyed; most of them new ones that had been built recently in place of those that were burnt in the great fire 1929. The fire from this bombardment spread and no one even tried to extinguish it. We stood by baffled and apathetic. Together with us stood the famous reporter Shlomo Tzuker who worked on the editorial board of the Yiddish newspaper "Haint" ("Today") in Warsaw. He was born in our town and had arrived as a refugee.

Between us we whispered: "What will be? What should we do?" Tzuker stood there dumfounded just mumbling: "Night over the face of Europe."

We returned to the village just before sunrise. The date was Wednesday the 13th of September. At noon a German plane suddenly appeared in the sky over the village and began firing its machine gun. We fled to the fields and jumped into a deep pit. The sound of a strange explosion reached our ears, and at the same time flames arose from the straw roofs of the houses. The fire spread with the speed of lightning through the whole town.

All the possessions of these hard working peasants, in which they had invested many years of hard labor, all the produce that was in the silos and some of the domestic animals were destroyed in half an hour! We wandered around the site of the fire helpless and confused. The fire had also destroyed the few possessions that we had taken with us to the village. That same night we returned 'home'. All over the horizon we saw fires from every direction both near and far. It was as if the whole country was burning.

Rosh Hashanah arrived. Almost no prayers took place. The Germans were already present in the vicinity. Although Warsaw was still defending itself, the fate of the whole country was to surrender.

Part of the Jewish youth had left earlier. My friends and I were preparing to go eastward to Russia when we found out that the Red Army had crossed the Russo-Polish border and was nearing us. There was no limit to our joy.

On the evening of Kol Nidre we sat and listened to the radio and got news that filled our hearts with endless joy. The German broadcasting station announced that the district of Lublin, up to the eastern banks of the Vistla River, was to be under Red Army rule.

Joy and gladness reigned over us. We were happy that we would not have to leave our homes and flee. That the Red Army was coming to us meant freedom not only for the Jews who lived east of the Visla, but since it was due to reach the eastern suburbs of Warsaw, for the Jews of the entire west of Poland. This was because it gave them the opportunity to move eastward and escape from the claws of the Nazis. The Russians had already reached Biala Podalska, Mezritsh and Sedlice. One unit had even reached Radzyn.

In those days something happened that caused additional Jewish casualties even though the actual fighting had stopped. A lone unit of the Polish Air Force that had not managed to flee was stationed on the estate of the Prince Chetvarshinski, a noted Jew hater. On one Saturday they went into the town and began firing in all directions, killing and wounding Jews

We waited in eager anticipation for the Russians to enter the town that was lacking any sort of governing authority in the last days of the Polish rule. To our great disappointment an agreement was signed giving the Lublin district over to the Germans. The Russian army began retreating eastward to the Bug River. Widespread depression took hold of the town. We prepared to leave and move eastward.

The last battle between the Germans and units of the Polish army took place in those days in the vicinity of Radzyn. The commander of the Polish army at the time, General Wilhelm Orlich-Rickman, dug in with his troops between Radzyn and Kotsk. He fought with blind stubbornness and refused to surrender. Did he really believe that there was a chance for any sort of success or was it just his heroism? For a number of days, the roaring of cannons still reached us, but the general's power grew weaker and weaker. His soldiers fled dressed as peasants and the general himself was taken captive. Warsaw, too, surrendered and the Germans ruled all of Poland.

---*---

The first German unit reached Radzyn in the beginning of October. It was composed of armored forces, motorcycle troops and the 81st Infantry Battalion. The roar of the motors deafened the town. Proud and polished, the Germans filled the town and cast fear and trembling over the Jews. They established their headquarters in the most magnificent building in the town, that of the Jewish Bank. There they flew their flag with the swastika on it that looked, from a distance, like the claws of a bird of prey.

The Jews tried not to go outside if there was no urgent reason to do so. The Germans began to search the houses and play all sorts of tricks on their inhabitants. The Jews were taken immediately to different hard and repulsive work and absorbed many blows. The goods that the Germans found in the stores, cellars and houses, they distributed among the non-Jews free of charge. After some time these regular army troops were replaced by the Gestapo. The Gestapo, terror, violence and fear reigned over everything.

---*---

A group of my friends and I left the town of my birth a few days after the Germans arrived. I cannot describe the terrible feeling I felt on leaving my dear homeland when we sat down in the wagon and headed eastward. We left behind us Poland under the rule of the night.

With the help of a boat belonging to a peasant, we managed to cross the Bug and we started walking. We stopped when we reached a Russian Border Police unit. We greeted them. They returned the greeting and asked, "Where are you from and where are you going?" We answered, &147;We are Jewish refugees and are fleeing from the Germans to the Soviet Union." The soldiers looked at us seriously and questioned us some more. They demanded to know what was in our bags, where we want to settle, etc. In the end they became less serious and broad smile spread over their faces and they said: "Go, go in peace. The road is open to you." This was what they said at that time to the thousands of Polish Jews.

Meanwhile night fell. We did not know the way and we were tense and tired, so we decided to spend the night in the fields and to continue on to Brisk in the morning. We lay down under a tree in the field and slowly dozed off, depressed by the fact that our relatives remained behind in the bloody land

----*----

At that time Brisk d'Lita was one of the centers for Jewish refugees from Poland. The city was bustling with Jews from all parts of the area west of the Bug. The meeting place of the Radzyners was Shalom Hirshbein's restaurant. He was also a Radzyner. Most of the refugees stayed with relatives and friends. Whoever did not have a place to sleep did so in this restaurant, some on the tables and some on the floor. New refugees arrived from Radzyn daily. They told us about the hardships and atrocities that the Jews there were experiencing.

We stayed in Brisk for a few weeks. The authorities opened an office there to arrange for the refugees who wished to, to find all sorts of work in Russia itself. A friend and I signed up. One day we boarded a long train, and together with hundreds of other Polish Jews, left Brisk and traveled to the northeast.

Up until June of 1941 there was a postal connection between us and our relatives in Radzyn. These letters contained a very few lines and were written in Polish. However anyone who could read between the lines understood how terrible the conditions were under which our bothers and sisters lived under the Nazi's. For hours at a time I would hold these envelopes and post cards in my hands turning them over from one side to another. I read them a second and a third time, looking again and again at the postmark as if this dumb paper, that came from afar, was a living part of the relatives who had remained there. Would I ever see them alive again?

---*---

Only seven long years later, years filled with unending longing and suffering, did we return to Radzyn. I jumped down from the wagon and ran to the house in which I had lived with my parents and grandparents. I could not find it. The house had completely disappeared! The whole lot was covered by an onion patch.

I looked around and started walking, hoping that I would find someone. In the end I found a few Jews, returned refugees like myself, who were also wandering around the city like orphans. The Jewish Quarter, which included Szkolna, Kozia and Kashiwa Streets as well as two market places, was completely destroyed. There was hardly a sign that there were once buildings here and that not long ago such intensive life had throbbed. The Great Synagogue, the Bais Hamedrash (Seminary) and the wonderful Rabbi's Courtyard, all were destroyed. Even the castle was burnt.

Most of the non-Jewish Polish residents of Radzyn survived. Even the anti-Nazi political activists, whom the Germans had arrested and sent off to Auschwitz, returned home when the Nazi rule collapsed. Although they had seen how the crematoriums had swallowed daily tens of thousands of Jews, how a whole people, including the young and old, were destroyed, they themselves had returned home. Just the Jews had disappeared from the face of the earth. I wandered confused through the streets of the town, and could not believe what I saw, but it was so. I stood for hours on the sidewalk in front of my grandfather Gad Levenstein's house. Maybe this is just a bad dream? No this is the terrible reality. There were no Jews in Radzyn! Polish Jewry had disappeared.

These were the days in the month of May that are warmed by the sun, when the lilacs bloomed and the fragrant acacia sprouted. Every morning the Radzyn farmers took their herds out to pasture and returned in the evening at sunset raising clouds of dust over the roads. Life moved along in its normal course. On Sunday thousands of worshippers crowded the Catholic Church and its surrounding courtyard. The delightful sound of its organ bursts out from the church and filled the surroundings with beautiful chords. The audience joined in. That was the way it had also been years ago. Now only the voice of the Jews had been silenced forever!

The scorched market in Radzyn

[Pages 221 - 226]

The Beginning of the Catastrophe

Rachel Zaltzman-Freter (Ness-Ziona, Israel)

*Dedicated to my unforgettable mother, father, sisters and brothers and to the
entire Freter family.*

The entire summer of 1939, without knowing exactly why, everyone had a
premonition that something unusual was about to happen. It was rumored
that Hitler would declare war on Poland despite the 'good relations' that
existed at that time between those two countries.

Sad to say, that premonition was fulfilled. On that Friday morning of the
first of September 1939, the sad tidings traveled lightning fast through the
whole shtetl. It was immediately reported that that within a few hours the
German Army had penetrated deeply into Polish territory. Outbursts of crying
were heard from all corners and everyone ran in the direction of the People's
Bank to the bus station where all reservists were getting ready to leave for
active duty. There were heartbreaking scenes of men parting from their wives
and children .The war had become a fact.

In the first week of the war our shtetl remained quiet although everyone
lived with great foreboding. We all understood that no good could come from
Hitlerism. On Friday, the eighth day of the war, a German plane flew over the
shtetl followed by a Polish plane that downed the German one. We
immediately understood that the German revenge would be vicious.

Early on Saturday morning I, together with all the other children in my
family, was sent by wagon to a neighboring village. Our parents promised us
that if Radzyn was bombarded they would come to us. No sooner had we
crossed the threshold of the peasant's house in that village than we heard the
sound of bombs falling on our shtetl Radzyn. I will never forget that cruel
Saturday. The peasant's house shook even though the village was far from our
shtetl. We then all ran out of the house and into the forest. There too, the
exploding bombs shook us up.

We could hardly wait for night to come and for the bombardment to
subside so that we could go back to the shtetl. We were overcome by shock
when we reached it. There were giant craters in the streets and no people to be
seen. Everything was going up in flames and there was no one around to
douse them. The whole place was deserted. For quite some time we ran
around until we found our parents. We found out that the Germans had
bombed our shtetl all day, and that there were many casualties. It was
interesting that this mass bombardment had an immediate effect on the
survivors. From the very beginning, we understood that these casualties would
somehow get a proper Jewish burial but what was unclear was how we would

end our days. We could not imagine then that 'the cultured murderers' would develop techniques which would send millions of people to the crematoria.

The days following the bloody Sabbath where very quiet, too quiet. The streets were literally dead. Rarely did one see a soul running through the streets to get to his home.

———

Suddenly rumors began to circulate that it was not the Germans who would occupy Radzyn, but it would be the Red Army which would occupy the whole eastern part of Poland up to Warsaw (The Vistula River) Suddenly there was a feeling of relief and an increase in traffic It was reported that the Russians had already reached Mezeritch. After a short wait, a Russian Intelligence unit arrived in Radzyn and began distributing arms to the local Communists both Jews and Christians. They armed the county commander and carried out a number of 'activities'. The town came to life.

However this did not last more than a few hours. Another Russian unit appeared and announced that the Russian Army would not reach Radzyn as the border was being moved back to Brisk. Anyone who wanted to join them there is invited to do so. The Russians provided special trains, on which there was enough room to take an unlimited quantity of baggage, for transportation to Mezerich.

Naturally the first to leave were those who had some part in the few hours of 'Red Rule'. Again the streets became deserted, and fear crept over everyone. Shots were heard and there was a new Jewish victim. The anti-Semitic Endecja (The Peoples Nationalist Party) went on a rampage.

When these disturbances died down, the Jews began to think of what to do. Should they flee or should they remain in their place? Most of the young people decided to flee to Brisk, not only the pro Communists or Bundists (Jewish Socialists), but everyone who felt that he had strength left. Married middle aged people also fled. Their wives helped them by deciding to stay behind with the children since they thought the Germans would have pity on them.

———

The black day arrived. The German Army arrived in town accompanied by a band. The citizens were called on to welcome the military with enthusiasm. With broken hearts, we left the house and went out to the street. The band played happy marches and our hearts were heavy.

The next morning there is a temporary Polish police force that went from house to house ordering that the shops be opened. Willy- nilly, they were opened. Little by little, people appeared in the streets and life began to return to normal. The Germans appeared in the shops and said that there is no reason to be afraid of them. In a few days they are leaving for their permanent position and will be replaced by the SS personnel who are 'very different'.

In a couple of days the Regular Army units left and were replaced by the SS hooligans. Immediately they showed off what they were capable of. First, they went into the synagogue and took out the Torah scrolls and unrolled them like rugs all over adjoining streets, Kotlarska, Shkolneh, Kazshe and others. They ripped up other holy books and spread them over the streets. Then they drove the people out of their houses to witness all of this. Can one imagine the terrible pain?

The next morning they led out the Radzyner Rabbi Reb Shloimele z"l together with the other prominent Jews and honored them by forcing them to chop wood. Azshe Abman turned to the SS man who was directing this spectacle saying that he would like to substitute for the Rabbi. The answer he got from the German was such a beating that he was forced to stay in bed for a long time.

On another occasion they grabbed Jews and dragged them to the banks of the river near the soap factory and drove them into the water with their clothes on. When they came out of the water, dripping wet, they were harnessed to a wagon and forced to pull it through the streets of Radzyn. The visors of their caps had to be turned backward and their faces smeared with mud. During this brutal performance, on that rain soaked autumn day, many Jews were tortured and one, Manish Pshenitzeh, was tortured to death.

The next morning, the SS rounded up older bearded Jews, among them, my grandfather Hershel Freter (Shtein), and ordered them to bring water to their headquarters so they could wash up. After they finished cleaning up they poured the dirty water onto the water carriers. Then they shaved off half of their beards not forgetting, at the same time, to cut off half of their faces.

My grandfather returning home half-dead did not speak. Each one of us stood in his corner choked with tears. In the end my grandfather spoke up: "No children, the situation is terrible. We must run away. You children are young. Go and save yourselves."

Until that moment the whole family had remained in its place. No one had the courage to speak up and say that he wanted to run away and leave the older members of the family. Grandfather, having said what he had said caused an upheaval. My father, the oldest son, (the whole family lived together with my grandfather) asked, "who is leaving?"

After few days of qualms and anguish, I packed my meager bag and left my home.

———

With great fear we reached the house of a peasant in a village near the Bug River. Our plan was to cross over the river to the Russian side. After another sleepless night we found ourselves, on the next morning, on the Russian side.

We start walking in the direction of Brisk. On the way we were stopped by a Russian patrol which took us to their commander. After questioning us, they announced that they were sending us back to the Germans. We begin to cry, declaring that we would not go back not even if they shot us. After some negotiation they brought us some food and also tickets for Brisk.

The Nazis burning Jewish holy books
First to the right - Yisroel Windenbaum (Jabak); left - the second - Moshe Abman
(a tailor); the third - David Karman (Shlep)

That evening we arrived in Brisk by train. The impression that the town made on us is hard to describe. In one moment we had left hell, and in another, entered a bright happy city. One could move about freely with head raised and death did not lurk on every step.

We went to the Radzyner 'hostel' in Brisk in Hirshbein's Restaurant. That is the place where, all who like myself had fled Radzyn, and had not left on the first transports to work in Russia, met.

An old Razdzyner acquaintance of mine invited me to stay with him. However I did not want to desert those who had suffered the same fate that I had, and refused the invitation.

We left for Russia, and arrived at our place of work on a holiday, November 17th, the anniversary of the Russian Revolution. The whole city was celebrating. We were invited to a very nice restaurant and served the finest dishes. This very polite reception we received was like a balm after the persecution we had experienced in our shtetl. The next morning they gave us housing and arranged for us to work. The work was 'black labor' to which we were not accustomed. In the beginning it was a bit difficult, but little by little we got used to it and it went well. Later we learned Russian which was very useful to us the whole time we were in Russia.

My great ambition was to go back home. Who could have foreseen that when my dream came true, six years later, there would not be one single soul that had survived?

Shkolna Street in Radzyn. On thre right- a German taking photographs

[Pages 227-244]

The History of the Destruction (1939-1945)

Yehoshua Rosencrantz (Kibbutz Shuval, Israel)

1. The First Panic

I will not spend too much time trying to describe the feelings of the majority of the Jewish people on the day that the war broke out. Let me just say that together with the fear for the future that threatened the Jewish population, there was also a sort of joy, that sprung from the belief that in a few months the terrible German tyrant would be driven out of our country, and that would bring an end not only to our suffering, but also to that of our brethren in Zvonshin, the suffering of the Jews of Czechia, Austria and Germany.

People looked to the sky and waited for the appearance of the British and French planes. The German bombers did not appear during the first week. When they did appear in the skies above the town, some of the inhabitants still joked about them. However, after nine days they stopped making fun of them and most fled to the nearby villages believing innocently that the enemies' bombs would not reach them.

I do not know whether to call the number of casualties in the first bombardment large or small. The whole concept of "massive casualties" changed in my mind during the five years of suffering. Then, on that Saturday of the ninth of September, there was a tragedy that no one could predict. I remember that I ran as if crazy between the trees in the municipal garden and near the pond and ran into a man muttering and wailing. He was wailing over the smashed bones of his brother Avramke Sudberg. Everyone hid behind the trees. For many months they had taught us in courses on self defense against bombing that "The women and children should hide under the trees in the city and especially under those in the municipal garden. The men should stand in the attics and watch and if a bomb fell to seize it, throw it into the street, and cover it with sand."

Wonderful advice!!! But the bombs did not wait for anyone, they just exploded. Fires burned in all the surrounding neighborhoods. I especially remember that which went off in a neighborhood called Marainke and another in Landzinak. Following their instructions, the municipal militiamen ran to help the different neighborhoods. Then, a shower of bullets rained down accompanied by a hail of destructive bombs. Among the fire fighters and their helpers who were killed was Shmuel Kimmel, an official of the "Bund" and a member of the municipal council, and one of the Blumen brothers, Boruch. A few others people were killed whose names I cannot recall.

That night the townspeople spread out into the neighboring villages but after a night or two they returned to find violence plunder and destruction in their homes and especially in their shops. Tremendous destruction was caused by the German bombers but seven fold greater was that caused by the retreating Polish army and Polish 'guests' who emptied out the Jewish homes.

2. The Soviet Episode

They came, but before that we had to experience many cases of fear, joy and despair that followed one after another. One day they came into Mezritsh which was only twenty seven kilometers from Radzyn. The soldiers of the Red Army were welcomed there with pomp and splendor. During the next ten days they managed to move forward some twenty kilometers in the direction of our town but for some reason they could not manage to cover all of the short remaining distance.

On the morning of second day of Succoth, a small convoy of Red Army troops halted near the road that leads from Visnitz to Kotzk, about two kilometers from the town, but no Red Army soldier entered the town. There they stopped and talked for some time to some of the residents who had come to welcome them. Koshitzki, a teacher in one of the Polish schools, who had on that day organized a Red Militia of Poles and Jews, delivered a passionate speech. In that militia there were people from the underworld as well as people from the suburbs who were known Communists. I remember how Pinkus and some of his friends got keys to the city hall, to the electric works, etc. In one of the buildings Comrade Yoel hastily drew a Red Flag and put up a number of slogans. However we did not get a chance enjoy these scenes for very long. Suddenly panic broke out and the sound of shooting was heard coming from the other end of the street.

The firing and the panic continued on for about half an hour. I looked down the street from the attic of my house. Companies of Polish soldiers ran down the street with machine guns in their hands, firing into the houses. After close to an hour, everything became silent. When we went out into to the street it became clear to us that there were two Jewish casualties. One was a young man of sixteen, Daniel Sudberg the son of Chanina and a relative of the Daniel Sudberg who had been killed on the day of the bombardment. I do not remember the name of the woman who was wounded. Among the dead there were also Poles who were members of the Red Militia.

Two days later, at noon, we listened to the radio broadcast from Germany that announced the signing of the agreement between Ribbentrop and Moscow in which the Red Army would retreat to the Bug River.

This was an unbearable blow. People did not believe it, nor did they believe it when they heard the same thing on Radio Moscow. Innocently they sent a protest to the local headquarters in Mezritsh asking; "can this be possible?" The answer that came back was; "When the Red Army puts it feet on territory, it never leaves it again." But after one week the Red Army quickly withdrew from Siedlce, Mezritsh, and Biala and retreated all the way to Brisk.

At the same time a division of the Polish Army under the command of General Kalbers was encamped near Radzyn. It dug in between the towns of Parchew and Kotzk, and fought the Germans. It's attacks were successful. The Poles advanced, drove the Germans back and took prisoners. However this situation did not last very long. The Germans attacked and the surrounded Polish Army that had begun to retreat to the road to Kotzk.

That evening, we learned that the Polish residents of the city had hung pictures of The Holy Mother near their houses. That was a sign that Kalber's troops had decided to take revenge on the Jews and the Red Militias. A deadly fear descended on the city. Many groups of young people left for Mezritsh on that night to join the Red Army in its retreat to over the Bug River. In the city itself, popular militias of a hundred people or more were organized that stood ready to defend lives and property. I do not know how things would have developed without these popular militias. It is a fact that the Polish underworld was set and ready to rob and destroy. On that same night there was a battle between the Poles and the Germans. The Poles retreated hastily through the villages in the direction of Demblin–Riki. For a few additional days the rear guard units of the Polish army still controlled the town, and only at the end of October the German army entered the town.

3. The Germans Arrive

When the Germans first entered there was a surprise of sorts in store for the Jewish residents. The orders to vacate homes were served to the Poles first and it took some two weeks before the orders for the first expulsion of Jews was served. It ordered the Jews to abandon the whole area of the two market places. This whole area, consisting of one and two story brick buildings, was emptied out within twenty four hours and immediately the Germans began destroying it. With the help of Jewish men and boys, who were abducted for this purpose by the Germans, all the store houses, toilets and kitchens that separated the northern from the southern bloc were destroyed. A wide path was cleared from Yossel Zita's gate to the building that bordered the alley which was well known to the local residents from the great fire. There was now a wide passageway for vehicles to pass from Mezritsh Street. Of course, walls were destroyed and rooms were converted into garages. Here I would like to mention that my mother, of blessed memory, went, with a few other women, to ask them not to demolish the buildings but live in them the way they are and to give them warning before they began to confiscate them. The answer was: "Get out of the way you Jewish pigs. This is not yours anymore. Yours is the place where the dogs relieve themselves!" Close to the issuing of the evacuation order, another order was issued by the local headquarters leveling a fine of thirty thousand zlotys on the Jewish Community. It immediately became known that ten important people were taken as hostages. The fine was paid immediately and the hostages released.

Despite all this, relative quiet reigned for a few weeks and commerce picked up. Grocery stores and markets selling pork and bakeries sprung up supported by the German customers. They would enter the stores and restaurants buy something and strike up a conversation. To the ordinary German soldier, it did not matter that this was a Jewish owned restaurant. When the storekeepers were ordered to post a sign saying "Jewish Shop" many of the soldiers advised us to take down that "rubbish".

However, the situation began to change when the S.S. arrived. They began showing off their bravery. First they broke into the Beth Midrash (seminary) and the synagogue on one cold wet day and paved the courtyard with Torah Scrolls in the mud. They grabbed a few old Jews and tore off their beards, abused them and ordered them to dance on the Torah Scrolls respectfully. On the 3rd of December, a number of wagons arrived from the nearby town of Levertov filled with Jews sitting on their belongings who told us that all the Jews had been driven out of the town. We became very frightened. At the same time Landrat von Pinkerfeld was appointed regional commander for Radzyn and Levertov. If he did that there, the same fate awaited us. That same night a decree arrived ordering that, within a week, Radzyn must become Yudenrein (devoid of Jews). It is not easy to describe the panic that ensued. People ran helplessly from place to place. It turned out that the order had been handed to Dovid Lichtenstein and he was made responsible for its being carried out. People started lobbying him to intercede and to get the order cancelled. After two days, a terrible stench of favoritism and money rose from the whole affair. Certain craftsmen and their families were allowed to remain. People were willing to pay money to be allowed to remain, and there was a possibility that most Jews would be allowed to do so. But why did that not happen? For you to understand this, I must explain another matter.

4. The Expulsion to Slovatich

On the day, when the Russians withdrew to the Bug River, there was a sharp difference of opinion among the Jews in the town. Some held that we should exploit the situation and flee to Russia as long as the borders remained open. Others felt that there was no danger in living among the Germans. Look around and see. People are coming back from Brisk in a terrible condition. There is no housing and food there and there is sickness. It is true that here there are all sorts of terrible orders, but it is still possible to live here and who wants to abandon his property? There were also others, and they may have been the majority, who believed that the Russians would return soon. The retreat over the Bug River is only a matter of a few days and they will return in a day or two. But meanwhile, the flow of people who had decided to leave their property grew. Sometime whole families did so. On the other hand, the return of Nachman Yiddel Sudberg with his whole family made a great impression. He had been on the Russian side and told horrible stories. The effect of his stories had barely worn off when the exact opposite happened. One clear morning it turned out that Chaim Zuckerman, a well known wealthy man, left all of his property and fled at night together with his family to Russia. The reason for his doing so was a libel that guns and ammunition had been found in his house that he had abandoned on orders from the Germans. After this, the 'immigration' to Russia picked up. In those very days when the above mentioned expulsion order was issued, instructions were received to go to the small town of Slovatich (near Domchevoh) on the safe side of the Bug River. There were also promises that it would be easy to cross from there into Russia.

I was in the long line that left Radzyn, on foot and in wagons, on the 8th of December 1939 heading in the direction of Slovatich. That same night, the first snow of the winter fell and did not melt until the beginning of April. At the entrance to the town stood German gendarmes who usually confiscated all of the refugees' belongings but sometimes left them everything, all depending on their mood. Where did we get the horses and wagons? The local peasants smelled a good deal. We paid up to 1000 Zlotys and sometimes even more for the trip. That amount, at the beginning of the war, was a huge sum. That was the way that many families, including that of Rabbi Fine, left for Slovatich. Others scattered among the other towns and villages in the vicinity. Three hundred families remained in Radzyn.

It is worth describing the life of our Radzyner in that remote town, Slovatich, where the mud reached up to our knees. Its low ramshackle buildings and its Jews looked like something out of the stories of Mendele Mocher Sforim. However, the Jews knew how to get rich in a few short weeks, since the town was located at the easiest and most important crossing point over the Bug River. When we got there in the evening, we were housed in the synagogue. There was no one who pitied us or invited even one family to their home. I was shocked by the attitude of these people. Aren't they Jews, or do they only think about making a profit? I don't know how things would have worked out. No committee was set up and everyone worked on his own and paid heavy sums for housing. Those who could not afford to, continued living in the synagogue for many days.

On the same day that we arrived, the Border Police arrived and closed the border. From now on you had to sneak through the border thus endangering your life. The paths for smuggling contraband were well known to the local inhabitants. The water in the river froze, and the ice formed a bridge of some 150 meters. On the other side Russian Border Police were stationed. A number of strange events took place. There were people whom the Germans kidnapped, fed, and led back to the middle of the river, so that they could go back to the Russians from there. When the Russians got their hands on them, they locked them up for days, starved them and sent them back to the Germans while firing in the air so that the Germans would notice. It happened that a Jew, who had been detained by a Jewish border guard (a Russian soldier), started speaking to him in Yiddish. The guard listened to everything and with a nod of his head expressed his agreement, and at the end added that he was sorry that the Soviets had assigned him to duty on that day, but the Jew had to be returned to Germany.

At that time there was a fundamental change in the direction of stealing across the border. The people who fled because of the cold and filthy living conditions there, began to return. There were also traders in contraband who smuggled in goods and brought back a lot of money. Among the returnees, were a lot of people from our town. I still remember the evening when my father and I were ready to depart. After a prolonged inner struggle we reached the conclusion that there was no basis for waiting. Although the local municipal committee had sent off telegrams to Stalin and Kaganovitch about the condition of the Jewish refugees in Slovatich, no one deceived themselves about the results. Therefore, we were ready to start out on the road to Russia. Our guide also sat at home waiting. At sundown a Jew with a thin unshaven face came in to us and asked for a place to sleep. He was an acquaintance of ours who had just recently returned from Russia and started to tell us all the horrible stories. He had lived in Brisk in a dark cave and made lots of money a couple of times but in the end fell into a trap. Fortunately, they took only his goods and released him. "In Brisk" he said," there is hunger, life is not life and everyone wants to go back." We did not go out that night !!!

On the night of the 14 of June 1940, the Germans decided to destroy the bases used by the smugglers .On that one night, forty five innocent Jews were killed or imprisoned, among them two from Radzyn, Mordechai Naiman ("Kokosh the Barber") and his daughter's husband. Many families decided to return to Radzyn. Others decided to go to Mezritsh, among them my family. From then on I spent my war years in Mezritsh .

5. I am in Mezritsh

From the very beginning we suffered greatly despite the fact that in Mezritsh itself, everything was "blooming". Fashion was flourishing. Men's fashion consisted of officer's boots, riding britches and a pretty "dshukika". More than half of the town's inhabitants wore this costume. It was hard to get by and we made do with whatever we could earn each day. My father and mother became grain traders in the local market. Most of the ex Radzyner met in the Mezritsh market that was, strangely enough, open to everyone until the summer of 1942. There were very few Radzyn families, only about 20 in the town. They were in constant touch with Radzyn as long as that was possible.

6. We Go Back To Radzyn

In the spring of 1940 most of the families returned to our town, Radzyn. Understandably, there were no Jews living there on the main streets anymore. Everyone settled in the Jewish quarter that included Kalon, Kroiah, Shkolna and Kashiva Streets. There was no closed ghetto during that whole year and even up to the fall of 1941 the Jews were permitted to walk around in any of the streets and even to go outside the town. They were permitted to go to small villages and trade, as much as was permitted, in such confiscated goods as fats, eggs and butter. People did not go hungry. The Yudenrat stood at the head of the Jewish community. We will discuss that in a separate chapter.

Radzyn Jews in the Meseritz ghetto

The problem of Jewish workers in Radzyn arose with the arrival of the Germans. The Germans would grab anyone who passed by, to do a day's or a few hours of work and then release them. Sometime, during the day, they would beat them. However, in some cases it happened that they were fed well and sent home. This situation caused a feeling of permanent insecurity. However, this changed for the better when obligatory labor for all the men and for whole families was proclaimed that required of them to give a day or two of labor (sharvak) every week. They would work in army neighborhoods chopping wood, cleaning the yards, sweeping the city streets and in the winter clearing the snow. Of course, they were not paid for this work but it happened that eventually a permanent job developed. Certain people preferred to pay the sharvak tax that was between two and five zlotys. The Yudenrat paid this money to permanent workers who survived on this money. The labor contractors preferred permanent workers. The latter enjoyed many possibilities, a work place convenient for trade (on the roads near the coal mines), the possibility of trading with the German soldiers, etc. In this way those who were not craftsmen and did not have jewelry or other goods left over from before the war, managed.

The situation of the craftsmen was very different. They 'flourished' in the early years. Expert shoemakers, a small number of building workers and metal workers all found permanent and lucrative employment from the German soldiers and their officers. They also did very well from the Gestapo personnel, sometimes even reaching to the point of luxurious living. The third class consisted of those who had goods, jewelry and assets from before the war. Then there were people who risked their lives and went out to the surrounding towns and villages and sold manufactured goods or shoes, ready made clothing, bedding, etc. They brought back with them oils, flour, etc. and sold them in Radzyn and this was the way they lived.

There were two small, semi-legal stores that existed for some time. One carried groceries together with other small, everyday necessities and was owned by a number of pre-war shop owners. The other was the restaurant belonging to Rav Beryl-Nachman-Laizer's that was located in the "Hassidic Bible Readers Hut" located near the Beth Midrash (Seminary). The 'famous' craftsmen were Mr. Yissachar Kashmacher the tailor and Tzelke the shoemaker as well a few other shoe makers and tailors whose names I cannot remember. Oh yes, the leather stitchers Moshe Edelman, Flatzman and some others, the builder Moishe Rothstein, the glazier Shue Glazer, and a number of smiths. The attitude of the authorities to the Jews was that of "Yekes" (Germanicly correct). They related to every one individually and to the Jews among them according to the orders that they received from their superiors. Although every German officer, soldier, or Gestapo agent had his own 'informer' or a number of them with whom he maintained a good relationship, this did not help those Jews when an order came down ordering the agent to do otherwise. There were many cases of abuse during work hours. The response was an appeal by a member of the Yudenrat to the commander of the Gestapo. This was helpful, sometimes. This was the situation and these were the relations for about two and a half years until the summer of 1942 when the Holocaust and destruction of Polish Jewry began. Before I begin to relate the story of the Holocaust in Radzyn, I would like to tell you about some interesting events that took place in the town.

7. The Yudenrat

Yudenrat! The name alone is enough to awaken feelings of hate and contempt toward the people who were its members. That feeling is justified in most cases. But it also happened that the members of the Yudenrat were merely mediators between the local German authorities and the Jewish community, and there were rare cases where they actually acted in the interests of the local community. The Yudenrat in Radzyn belonged to those rare cases where most of its members were devoted to the needs of the public and to its welfare.

Its leader was a very old man of seventy, Dovid Fishl's (Lichtenstein). Who did not know this man, who was the president of the community for many years? Who did not know this bitter and unfriendly man? It seems to me that in the years before the war, when I was still a child, they really hated him in the town. Maybe this was because of his being very rich, the owner of much property, the town millionaire. Maybe he was hated by the petit bourgeoisie, the small shop keepers, the artisans and the workers because he ruled the community forcefully for many years. It was a fact that he was not friendly and few people came in and went out from his home (if there were any at all). Already in November of 1939 he was summoned by the commander of the Gestapo and ordered to find a contribution of thirty thousand gold coins. He himself gave ten thousand out of his own pocket and organized contributions for the rest of the sum. In that way he saved ten people who were being held as hostages until the money came in.

After the expulsion, he was ordered to organize the Yudenrat. He gathered together the best people in the town who were known before the war as public leaders and Zionists. These included Simcha Goldwasser a Zionist activist and the manager of the Jewish Municipal Bank; Yaakov Blechowitz, the principle of the Tarbut Hebrew School, and a Zionist activist, Shimon Kleinboim; and Mr. Eliyahu Shineman, a well known Zionist activist who had been chairman of the Jewish community a few years before the war. If I am not mistaken, there were also the gentlemen Chaim Yitzchak Gellerman a Zionist activist and the representative of local branch of the Jewish National Fund; Moshe Appeloig a local merchant known for his pleasant temperament and his cleverness and the sons of Dovid Lichtenstein, Sender and Shimon Lichtenstein. Only Avraham Blumen, the former Revisionist (radical right wing Zionist party) leader, of whom it was said that he entered the Yudenrat by 'divine will', was usually referred to unflatteringly.

All of these members fulfilled their duties devotedly and with great concern. Especially active was Dovid Lichtenstein who interceded with the authorities and helped solve many unpleasant situations. Strangely enough this old man was liked everywhere that he appeared. I heard someone tell that the commander of the local Gestapo, a high ranking officer, called him 'the old Jewish Prince'.

Mr. Shimon Kleinboim, who was active in Joint Distribution Committee, arranged for help for the Jews in the neighboring towns of Lubartow and Lukow. The activities of 'The Joint' in that period makes interesting reading but, unfortunately, I do not have any information about its activities and about those of Mr. Kleinboim in our town.

The above mentioned Avraham Blumen, who was for a time the director of the labor office of the Yudenrat and its vice chairman, was very active, but not always in a positive way. I know of many cases where he acted with contempt and superiority toward the needy. However, there were also many cases where he acted in the public interest by his lobbying. I witnessed with my own eyes his attitude to the ordinary people. It was said about him: 'I am Avraham

Blumen—Stay away from me." This is the place for me to relate something that happened to my father and to me that throws light on the attitude of the 'other kind 'of Yudenrat activists.

My father and I were in Mezritsh. In July of 1940 all the men there were ordered to report for forced labor in the half open camps, to work at regulating the flow of the Kazashne River that flows from Lukow through Mezritsh and Biala Podlaska to Brisk. The camps were spread out in a number of places in the villages along the banks of the river and in Biala itself. We therefore fled to Radzyn, and since we had work certificates from there, we tried to find work through the labor office belonging to the local Yudenrat. From here we could be sure that they would not look for us to work in Mezritsh. At any rate it was self evident that as refugees who were now living in a neighboring town this little help would be forthcoming from the Radzyn Yudenrat. However Avraham Blumen demanded money, a lot of money, which would go into his own pocket, for making such an arrangement. After that my farther appealed to Dovid Lichtenstein and other officials, but they sided with Avraham Blumen. With resentment, we paid a small sum to the Yudenrat.

I do not want to make a comparison between the Yudenrat in Radzyn and that of Mezritsh. In the latter, too, there were people who were devoted to serving the public good. However those were very few and very weak. The members of the Jewish Police were both greedy and demanded respect. First and foremost they worried about their own good. They were responsible for carrying out orders for work assignments, accompanying people to their designated place of work, and later to seeing that they did not walk on forbidden streets. They were also responsible for supervising the sanitary conditions together with the sanitation committee of the Yudenrat and especially the supervision of the compulsory labor.

If my memory serves me correctly the following were members of the Radzyn Jewish Police: The commander was Avraham Blumen. The others were Yisroel Meltzer who hade been active in the Hechalutz Movement, (An organization for training young Jews to be pioneers in Palestine) before the war, Yitzchak Wolf, Beryl Lichtenstein, an active member of Hechalutz, Zelig Blumen and a few others. Most of these people fulfilled their duties with devotion and responsibility, while their being in the police gave them the possibility to live comfortably and enjoy many luxuries.

8. Suffering, Informers and Women

From what I have written so far, it might seem that the Jews in the town of Radzyn did not suffer at all until the day of the annihilation, as if they never suffered hunger, cold and abuse. However compared to other ghettos in Warsaw, Lodz, and in the cities of eastern Poland, the situation was bearable, but it would be a mistake to think that there was no abuse of the Jews. Order after order to abandon blocks of buildings, to contribute money or gold etc. were issued. The first violence was, as I have already mentioned earlier, on

November 1939, when the first company of the S.S. burst into the synagogue, ripped up the Torah scrolls, tossed them into the mud and ordered the Jews to trample on them while dancing on the scrolls reverently. Then they cut off the beards of a number of Jews (of whom I remember Yaakov Yisraelkes' Hochman) with their own hands. In that same month there was the case of Shimon Kleinboim who was dragged out of his bed in his pajamas one morning and chased through the streets of the town, beaten with sticks and stomped on. He recovered eventually and even went on to fill an important position, but that day of abuse left its mark on him. In the beginning beatings, during and after the work day, were very common. Later when the work was better organized this became unusual. In the winter of 1941-42, on Christmas day, an order was issued confiscating all furs and parts of furs from those used for decorating sandals to blue fox pelts. As if the furs offered to them were not enough, they searched the houses and during the search they abused the inhabitants, stole things and killed the widow of Mordecai Naiman who fell, as I have already mentioned, in Slovatich two years earlier. That same summer an order was issued demanding that the inhabitants provide two kilograms of gold or its equivalent. In the intimidation connected with this order, five people were killed

Here a very interesting incident took place. Whereas in other cities this action was carried out on the initiative of the Gestapo, here in Radzyn the members of the Yudenrat got the order saying that an order had come down to include five victims in every place where this 'golden action' took place. I don't know how these five elderly victims were chosen to be a 'human contribution'. Neither do I remember their names, with the exception of one, Rotenberg the husband of Malkah (called 'Cossack'). One of the actions carried out by the Germans were house to house searches. Two or three Gestapo members were enough to turn the house upside down. It must be admitted that in most cases they knew where to search as the result of information garnered from informers. Who were these informers who collaborated with the Germans?

When I met the survivors after the last deportation and liquidation from Radzyn in Mezritsh, many of them told me that the Germans had a number of 'loyal Jews' only one of whom operated in the open. However, before I begin describe him and his deeds, I would like to say a few words about collaborators and informants as I saw them in another place. First, most of the informers came from the underworld and were notorious even before the war. Among them the Nazis found their most loyal allies. This was true in Mezritsh and Warsaw as well as in all the cities and towns all over Poland .In most cases these people had a fair amount of control over the community and influence with the Yudenrat either as leading members or as 'officers' in the Jewish police force. However this was not the case in Radzyn. That same fellow called Bar Yoel, despite the fact that he was 'respected' by the Germans, had no influence on and also no connection to the appointed Jewish community institutions. Anyone who did not know him before the war and did not see him during the war years, could not imagine what the Germans were capable of doing to a person, promoting one of the worst people to be a commander who could determine life or death. I do not know the names of other informers although there were others, no doubt.

Rabbi Yaakov Lazar- that is how the peoples' faces looked...

There were also a number of women, especially girls, who had close relationships with the Gestapo. There is one case that I know very well because I heard it directly from one of the girls. (Permit me not to mention her name.) Back in the summer of 1940, Mr. Turkeltoib's house was searched. This girl's family also lived in that house and she happened to be present during the search. They found gold and jewels and they began to beat the occupants while continuing to search. At that time the girl began to sing a beautiful German song. She sang and whistled very beautifully. The leader of the search started listening, honored her with a smile and entered into a conversation with her. As a result, they took the jewels but left the people alone. From that moment a relationship developed between the sixteen year old girl and the Gestapo officers. They would visit her in her home, and spend time with her there. She, however, did much for the good of the community. Many punishments, imprisonments and fines were cancelled at her request.

I met her in the winter of 1943 in Mezritsh. She had been one of my best friends before the war, so she confided in me revealing all of her secrets I felt that what she told me was true. She told me about cases of cancellation of jail sentences etc. as the result of her efforts. Others verified what she had told me.

9. Annihilation and Liquidation

In this chapter I will focus on annihilation and liquidation in Radzyn that began on the morning of Monday the 20th of August 1942, and was completed on the 20th of December of the same year, with the transfer of the survivors to neighboring Mezritsh. Now their fate was the same as that of the people in Mezritsh.

At sunrise on Monday, the Gestapo together with the Shufu (Uniformed Security Police) gathered together all the Jews of Radzyn on the lot between the synagogue and the beth midrash (seminary). The whole operation was carried out under the command of the officers of the Yuden Farnichtungskollege (Extermination of Jews Group.), special units with special powers against which even the highest ranking officers of the Wermacht, the S.S. the Shufu, and even the Gestapo could not appeal. These were units that got their powers directly from Hitler. I was a witness when documents signed by Goering, or his highest ranking colleagues were retuned despite the fact that they were sent to the officer in charge by the colonel of the Security Police.

However, there was room for negotiation, a sort of 'Jew trading' between the local headquarters and the commanders of the operation. The extermination order allowed that a minimum number of 'necessary' Jews remain in place without their families. It seems that in Radzyn the lobbying and influence of the local commanders was very strong and they succeeded in leaving four hundred Jews behind, legally. The first of those put aside were members of the Yudenrat and Jewish police. After them came skilled craftsmen chosen from a list, together some one hundred persons. After long negotiations they managed to add a number of close and even some not so close relatives of 'important' people. Altogether this added up to the above mentioned number. All the rest...

I was not there during the 'selection' as I was living in Mezritsh. On that very day I was working on Count Pototzki's farm which was located on the road that led from Mezritsh to Radzyn. A Polish fellow called me and the two of us went up onto a roof near the road. The entire convoy of the Jews from Radzyn passed before me. I was shocked. They traveled in wagons accompanied by a small number of Polish policemen. Almost all of them were in wagons loaded with all their belongings and driven by Polish peasants.

Two days before that, I left my house in Mezritsh to go to work and did not return home to sleep there. In Mezritsh we knew that on Tuesday the third 'annihilation march' would take place. My sister and mother were already hidden out in a place that had saved us on two such previous occasions. I believed that this would be true again this time, even though it would not be the last such event. I gathered up my courage, put on a metchyovke -Polish hat, and went down into the town. I saw them herding the Jews into the ghetto which had no guards on the inside. They were free inside the barbed wire fence and even outside there were only guards by two gates. Through a hole in the fence I entered the ghetto and went up to the hiding place and told my mother about the transport that had arrived from Radzyn. We went outside and brought Moshe Appeloig's family into the house. Pesseh Appeloig and her daughter ate lunch washed up and combed their hair. From the conversation we learned about the pace of the operations and that there would be no additional extermination operations. We also found out that Fisher, the commander of the Gestapo, had solemnly promised that there would not be any further exterminations there, and that the ghetto in Mezritsh, one of the twelve in the principality, would continue to exist, and anyone who reached it should feel fortunate. They believed that he was not lying...

We asked her to go hide with us, but she refused. If there will really be such an operation and they find her in a hiding place she preferred to die on the spot. She must have seen similar cases with her own eyes in Radzyn. She would not hide!

We went outside and tried to convince people to look for a hiding place, but not all of them listened to us. However, many did hide. About an hour later, I returned to my place of work. That night firing and yelling was heard frequently from the direction of the ghetto. I understood what was happening. I lay in the attic. Since the place was a farm owned by Christians and under German supervision, I was sure they would never come there. I looked outside through the cracks. The road led to the train station where during the morning hours, some two thousand people were loaded onto freight cars.

S.S. Sergeant Fritz Hehen, Commissar in charge of the Mezritsh ghetto for the Radzyn Gestapo, was the most tyrannical of them all. Interestingly, this wolf was quietist on his home grounds. The Jews of Radzyn feared him, but he never did them any harm, yet he did murder many Jews in Mezritsh and Lukow. These two towns were especially detested by him for some reason. In Mezritsh he even killed Poles. At the time of the transport from Radzyn to Mezritsh on Monday, he suddenly appeared in a car at the half way point, stopped two wagons, and killed their passengers with his own two hands. I found this out from one of the Jewish policeman a few days after the destruction of Mezritsh. They were summoned to the Radzyn road and took back with them two wagons loaded with some seventy corpses who had been murdered by him.

That week Fritz Hehen did not appear in Mezritsh. When he did appear after a number of days, one of the stars on his epaulets was missing. It was told that he had been reprimanded and demoted for the killings, by his commander Fisher. That was a result of the vigorous intervention by Dovid Fishel's (Lichtenstein). After a short time, Hehen was transferred to another district, and when he appeared again on a visit to Mezritsh he told one of his police colleagues there that the 'old bastard' from Radzyn had really 'fixed' him, but that he knew how to get even with him.

If a stranger had come to the town at that time and looked around him, everything would have seemed fine and as if nothing had happened. To the usual worries about finding work and making a living, a new ugly phenomenon appeared that could possibly be partially understood under the circumstances: the search for the fortunes and properties of those who had been deported or annihilated. After the annihilation of the Jews came the annihilation of the Jewish fortunes. Those who were left behind were forced to work collecting up the possessions from the houses, sorting them out and bringing them to the Nazis. Maybe it was understandable that some of these people who had endangered their lives collecting up the property thought "instead of giving it to the Germans I will take it for myself". Others, again, were looking for a way to provide themselves with long term sources of income.

In the beginning of November, new rumors began to circulate among the few remaining survivors. Someone brought an item that had appeared in a German newspaper saying that the Jews who survived after the annihilation campaign of the summer and fall months of 1942 would be sent to twelve ghettoes, one of them Mezritsh. It was known a long time before that the final evacuation of the ghetto would take place on the 20th of December, but the inhabitants would not be liquidated only transferred.

Loaded with bags, bundles, suitcases and all their household belongings, the Jews from Radzyn arrived in Mezritsh. In their honor the ghetto had been enlarged. Three lanes had been added in the "Shmultzubizneh" the Jewish neighborhood of poor, ramshackle houses.

The crowding then reached its peak. I did not visit all the homes of all of my townspeople, but I would like to describe a one room apartment belonging to one of the town's 'respected' citizens, one of those who would have managed well on the outside. Five families, more than twenty persons, lived in one spacious room: Mr. Shimon Goldwasser and his family, Mr. Mottel Vinapple and his family, the four Fletzman sisters, Mr. Yaakov Blechovitz and his family and for some time, Israel Seltzer and his wife. I knew this house because I had visited it often and a dismal picture of life under those circumstances became engraved in my memory. These people had means and were not poor or hungry for bread.

I saw a room in which thirty persons lived. Maybe this large number itself was not so frightening, but the sanitary conditions were so appalling that it is hard to describe them here. The condition of the streets and yards were such that had never been seen before. There were piles of excrement and filth, rags, windows that had been torn out to be used by important people, scenes that when I recall them, I am still shocked. I never saw such horrible scenes even in the worst times in the concentration camps. Is it no wonder then that in the winter of 1942-43 two thousand five hundred out of the four thousand inhabitants came down with typhus-fever. One day I found ten sick people in the same yard that I described above! But life again went back to normal and no one died of hunger. People found work paving the roads and engaging in a little illegal trading which was very dangerous.

Radzyn Jews in the Meseritz ghetto

Alongside the Yudenrat in Mezritsh, another Yudenrat, dealing with the Radzyn refugees, was established. Arrangements were made for buying bread without a ration card and even as many potatoes as you wanted, something that, I think did not exist in the rest of Poland. In that same period, very broad social services were introduced. To this day I do not know where the necessary means came from. These social services included medical care, the free distribution of potatoes and financial support. At the head of the Yudenrat were Shimon Kleinboim and Yaakov Blechovitz. They and their assistants stood out for their understanding and their readiness to help, something very rare are in the Mezritsh Yudenrat during the whole period of its existence. May these people be remembered always for their willingness to serve the public without making any personal profit.

Since I have mentioned Mr. Yaakov Blechovitz, I would like to dwell on some other cases that will provide us with an answer to one of the most biting questions always asked of me here in Israel: Why did the Jews not flee to the forests, to the Partisans, to Polish friends, to hide? Today the answer is very clear. We knew very well the attitude of the Poles toward the Jews. Here are some typical cases. After the first big liquidation Avramke Sudberg and his wife went to Polish 'friends' in the country. After staying there for a number of weeks and paying a lot of money, they disappeared. Later it turned out that they had been murdered in the forest by their Polish hosts. The police wanted to notify the Gestapo about the case. Dovid Lichtenstein advised them not to publicize the case at least among the Germans. His argument was that the information should be kept from those circles so that they not become aware that Jews were fleeing to the country to hide out. The second case: Yaakov Blechovitz and his family did not join the four hundred Jews who left Radzyn. They thought that Mezritsh would only be a way-station in the new march to extermination in Treblinka. Three weeks later, on Christmas Eve, their tracks disappeared. Later I saw them silently enter through the gate of the ghetto. I stood there and could not believe my eyes! Could these be the same people that I had always known? Now they had rags wrapped around their heads and their clothes were tattered. The faces of the dead were more attractive. Through a conversation with their son Aaron, I learned the following appalling details. They had gone to a far-away village to Polish "friends". They left all their possessions there and paid them a sizable sum. This time the "friend" was a real friend. He did not hand them over to the Nazis nor did he kill them. He was just worried about their living in a room in his house lest some undesirable person might see them there, so he put them up in the silo. There they set up their beds, there they got their meals, one during the day and one at night. From there they did not see the light of day or sunshine for two continuous weeks. The only information that reached them there, and which they could not be sure that it was true, was that the that all the Radzyn refugees living in Mezritsh were living a comfortable life, and some even say that it is the most privileged ghetto. They felt that they would not be able to survive for long under these circumstances and one day their friend led them back to Mezritsh. It was during the time of the battle for Stalingrad and the Jews felt a spark of hope in their hearts when the Russians began advancing rapidly. Suddenly they halted for weeks or months near Karkov, near Izium and darkness and depression again descended on us.

As I have already mentioned, Yaakov Blechowitz was one of the heads of the Radzyn Yudenrat in Mezritsh. A number of Radzyner decided to open a restaurant in Mezritsh (a few already existed) so as to make a living. They were: Eliezer Weisman, Chaya Blechovitz (the wife of Yaakov Blechovitz) and her sister-in-law Hentziah Wolf. What was the justification for this restaurant in this small poor ghetto? Its justification was the good meals that it prepared for the people from the ghetto "aristocracy" such as the members of the "Jewish Police", members of the Yudenrat and for the rich, whose only concern was finding a comfortable place for playing cards while enjoying a good meal. In Mezritsh there was no shortage of people, who had accumulated wealth and property, and who ate tasty foods, such as eggs, chickens and other things that the ordinary Jews had seen only two years before and whose taste they had forgotten. These were smuggled in by road laborers who risked their lives when they went to towns and villages on the 'Aryan' side to trade. I, too, was among them even though I do not look at all like a 'Sheigetz.' (Yiddish expression for a non- Jewish young man). A German did not look closely and could not recognize one. The biggest problem was getting out and coming back into the ghetto in the dark of night. The second problem was that I and the others were closely watched by the Jewish police from Mezritsh. You had to pay them a special 'tax'. They usually confiscated my goods when they caught me. The restaurant to which I brought my goods did very well because the prices were very high. I often brought lots of smuggled butter and chickens and often even tasted their good dishes.

At that time word began to reach us about the revolt in the Warsaw Ghetto. We felt that it was the revolt before the before the final liquidation. We could not follow all the developments. The survivors of that uprising found us in the Mydanek concentration camp.

At four o'clock in the morning of the 1ˢᵗ of May 1942 the ghetto was surrounded by S.S. Judenfarnichtungs Troopen (S.S. Special troops for Liquidating Jews). They celebrated the First of May over the bodies of hundreds of victims. On the next morning they found me and my family in the attic that had not failed us many times in the past. This time they found it. This indicated to us that they had searched very thoroughly. On the empty lot on which they collected us, we found out that on the previous day some two thousand persons had been sent to Treblinka and that we were destined to be sent to Mydanek. Everyone sat down on the filthy square as bullets sliced through the air as if on a battlefield. The victims covered the whole area. Not far from me lay the bodies of many of my dear friends. I recognized my friend Aaron and his father and mother. Chana Berman, a girl from Radzyn, yelled to me when she recognized me from a distance: "Oh Shia Shia, they have killed my Yankele right in front of my own eyes". They continued bringing people from all the corners of the ghetto.

After two days of traveling squeezed into in a closed car for hauling cement, and without a drop of water, we arrived at Mydanek together with two hundred other suffocating people including my father who, as long as he could, dragged along after me and my mother. My mother and I felt good as did my younger eleven year old brother. Only my father...

In the selection process in Mydanek my father was placed with the sick and weak and I, as a young man ,was placed among those able to work, my brother among the too young to do so, and my mother, as a young women capable of working, was ordered to leave my brother. She refused and was beaten, left, and never returned. My father too did not return. Only I remained, an orphan, together with some two hundred and seventy men and about the same number of women. That is all that was left from a transport of a thousand two hundred souls. The rest, may their memories be holy unto eternity.

10. In The Camps

I met very few of my townspeople while I was in the four German camps: Majdanek, Birkenau (Auschwitz), Boneh and Buchenwald.

In Majdanek I once hauled five of my townspeople to their final resting place, after they had been beaten to death for stopping to rest and putting down their stretcher loaded with clay for a minute. I worked together with Moishe Klinkeh and Velvel Turkeltaub and a number of others in Birkenau, where I was sent for forced labor. Together with them, I took Moishe Klinkeh to the hospital from which he never returned. Velvel Turkeltaub passed away while working next to me. I, with three others, carried him on my back to the camp. Shaul Blumenfeld and his son Leibush who, for some time were better off (the son wrote poems and read them out loud in front of the Kapos (prisoners who were assigned to do guard duty inside the camp) and got an additional two liters of soup for himself and his father), were taken in the selektzia of the 15th of August to the crematorium. One day when I worked in the women's camp I saw Felitzia Hirshbein a young women in good shape, well dressed, and good looking. It turned out that she worked in a good workplace .That was the most important thing. I met the two sisters Freideh and Leah Berman who worked in the oil press. They looked well and were well dressed. I also saw the attractive Chantziah Sudberg who was sixteen years old at the time.

My condition, too, improved for many months, and I did not suffer hunger nor did I lack clothing. I had opportunities to help others and did so. But after that, I again became almost critically ill and felt very weak after an attack of typhus smallpox. But I was lucky and recovered. It was not only luck that saved me but also the constant striving to improve my conditions and to survive no matter what.

I met Yosef Schupak in the Boneh concentration camp where he was working as an electrician and did not suffer any deprivations. I met him at a time when I was suffering hunger, and he often shared his bread and his soup with me. Among the ten thousand Jews in the camp there was only one more from Radzyn, Avram'ke Shuchmacher the son of Yaakov Shuchmacher, the teacher and newspaper vendor, who worked supposedly as a metal worker. Although his situation was not perfect, he did not suffer hunger. When I, too, became a metal worker, my situation again improved considerably.

A few days before the liberation from Buchenwald I met Shalom Kashemacher, a young man the son of Sheindel "Bartek", and Eliyahu Kupitz the fifteen year old son of Roisia Kupitz whose father now lives in Israel. The two of them disappeared from sight during the last days of suffering.

After the liberation I was the only one from my town left from all of the nearby camps, the only survivor.

[Page 245]

Hellish Experiences in the Radzyn Ghetto

Sarah Bashe Voyazsher (Paris)

The ghetto in Radzyn was set up in the summer of 1940. The Jewish population was separated from the non-Jews. Jewish police patrolled the boundary line so that Jews could not leave the Jewish quarter and enter the non-Jewish one. The main streets of the city, Ostrowieka, Pilsuckiego (formerly Warszawa) were reserved for non-Jews. The Jewish businesses on these main streets were taken over by non-Jews.

Right from the very beginning the Germans demanded that the Jews contribute large sums of money and it followed that only the wealthy could remain residents. Therefore there were many expulsions because of the Jews not being able to come forth with the sums that the Yudenrat continuously demanded of them.

The first such expulsion was to Mezritsh. Later they also sent Jews to Slovatich. My husband, my six year old daughter and I were in this last group.

On the first night after our arrival in Slovatich we slept outside. Only on the next morning the local Yudenrat gave us one small room for a number of families. This is the way we lived there, approximately ten families, in terribly poor conditions. The women did laundry for the local residents and the men chopped wood or did other physically difficult work. The Germans came to investigate the sanitary conditions and at the same time beat us mercilessly.

During our presence in Slovatich the Germans shot forty Jews, three of them from Radzyn: Mordecai Neiman and his son-in-law and Yitzchak Shpivak. My husband was fortunate that time in not being among those who were shot. When an S.S. man came to arrest him, my six year old daughter stood up and begged him not to take her father away. The child kissed the German's hands and said: "My father works very hard for the Germans. Look how sore his hands are from the work. I beg you do not take my father away." A miracle happened, the S.S. man left and my husband meanwhile remained alive.

When my parents in Radzyn found out about the murder of the forty people, they went to Dovid Lichtenstein and asked that he get permission from the Germans for us to return to Radzyn. He demanded a thousand Zlotys. My father managed to bargain him down to five hundred and we returned to settle in Radzyn.

After being in Radzyn for a short time, they arrested my father and my uncle, both of them tailors, because they found two dyed Polish Army overcoats that had been given to them by Poles for remodeling. They were sentenced to death by shooting. This time, I went to Dovid Lichtenstein and begged and pleaded with him. So we went together to the commander and I proved to him, by written documents, that the coats had been given to them by non Jews for remodeling into civilian overcoats. Thus, through great effort, I succeeded in having them released. The death sentence was replaced by a sentence of twenty five lashes. However, they were so badly beaten that that they had to stay in bed for two months.

Every night the Germans would visit Jewish homes and brutally beat the inhabitants. At that time I was living with Moishe Idelman who was taken out every night, and beaten mercilessly. One time my uncle Yaakov Leib Krein was dragged out of his house, beaten cruelly and had half of his beard torn off. They threw him down into the mud and trampled over him with their feet. That's the way life went...

In the fall of 1942, at the time of Succoth, the Germans posted an announcement in the streets that on a certain date all the residents must gather by the synagogue where a head count would take place. A terrible fear overcame the Jews. They understood that this was the end of everyone. The women wailed and quietly wrung their hands. Some Jews went to the Yudenrat and asked what could be done? Maybe they should try to run away? The Yudenrat replied that that they should all gather at the designated place and not be worried as no harm would come to them. The Germans just want to determine the number of ration cards they have to distribute.

At the appointed hour all the Jews gathered by the synagogue. The majorities were shipped off to Mezritsh and from there, on the next morning, were sent to the Treblinka death camp.

Only 320 Jews, who worked for the Germans in different jobs, were left in Radzyn. Among them were my husband, my two children and I. However, among those that were sent away were my parents. My mother with my youngest sister, Golda, came back to Radzyn, secretly, after they jumped off the train that was transporting them from Mezritsh to Treblinka. We had to hide them so that the Yudenrat would not find them.

Approximately three months later, the rest of the Jews were transferred to Mezritsh with the exception of thirty-five of them led by Dovid Lichtenstein. Seeing that there was no hope left, I went to a non-Jewish woman on Kasharan (St.?) to hide out. She agreed to my offer to bring her all my possessions, which I did, since I had no alternative. This was to be the last chance to save myself. After being with these non-Jews for one day, the children came down with the measles and she threw us out of the house. We went back "home." When we got back to Kazsheh Street, I saw many Jews, who had been shot, lying in the street. I then went to Dovid Lichtenstein and pleaded with him to give us chance to go to Mezritsh. By great effort we arrived in Mezritsh where a new hell awaited us.

In Mezritsh they put twenty of us Jews together in a room without any facilities, without bread and without the minimum necessary to exist. Then the Germans took us to work again. Everyday they came into the fenced-in ghetto and took out groups to work at different tasks. After being in the ghetto for few a months, a typhus epidemic broke out. Many people died including my youngest child.

On the 30th of April 1943 the ghetto was surrounded by German gendarmes armed with machine guns. The Jews tried to explain this by the fact that the next day was the First of May. However, a good friend of mine, a Jewish policeman, told me, secretly, that I should go home and hide because tomorrow there will be an expulsion. My husband did not want to believe this. He gave our child up to me in the attic in which we were hiding, but he himself did not attempt to hide. He was shot immediately in the market place. The attic in which we were hiding was also fired upon and a Radzyner, Moishe Zoiberman got a bullet in his side. Our hiding place was revealed by his screams. On May 2 some eighty of us from Radzyn and Mezritsh were sent off, some to Treblinka and the rest to Mydanek. My daughter and I were sent to Mydanek.

In Mydanek I met many Radzyners who had been sent there some time ago on earlier transports. They were: Yitzchak Heiblumzil and Beryl Koptshak, Simcha Berchat, Meir Steinberg's two daughters, Pesach Rutberg, Dobeh Rosenboim, Velvel Vishkovski and others whose names I do not remember anymore. Yitzchak Heiblume worked in a soap warehouse and would help all us Radzyners with everything possible. Itzl and Beryl Kaptshock, who worked in a kitchen, brought us food.

On the first day they showed us pictures of mothers together with their children. This gave us the impression that they do not annihilate children. My child bent down and told me that five minutes before her death she would still like to see her father. On that very same day, my dear eight and a half year old daughter, Miriam, was taken away to the gas chamber to be killed.

———

[Pages 249-263]

Five Years in The Abyss

(The Experiences of a Radzyner)

Sarah Ashman Zaltzstein (Haifa)

The Beginning

Hitler's attack on Poland on the 1st of September 1939 found me in Siedlce where I was working in a cousin's business. Already from the first days of the bloody war, Siedlce got its fair share of bombs from the German Air Force and of course there was no shortage of casualties. Especially horrible were the bombings on the 7th and 8th day after the outbreak of the war. All day, almost without interruption, they murdered the civilian population and set their houses on fire in the most brutal way. Then, almost all of the Jewish population of Siedlce fled to Lositch and to Mard, towns that were near Siedlce. Of course, I too fled with all the rest. But unfortunately, German planes sowed death and destruction there too. By a miracle we, a group of Jews from Siedlce, succeeded to get out alive from there and flee to a neighboring village when it got dark in the evening. A few days later I went back from the village to Siedlce, where the bombing had meanwhile stopped with the idea of going back to Radzyn. When I got to Lukow, I met the Red Army, but they announced that they were pulling back to Brisk and whoever wished could go with them. I, however, had meanwhile decided to go to Radzyn to see my parents.

When I arrived in Radzyn there was no authority there except for a civil militia with white armbands. Only a few days later S.S. personnel arrived and began their bestial pranks. First they set up a Yudenrat whose task was to send the Jews to Levertov and to Parchew thereby making Radzyn "Yudenrein" (Clean of Jews). Of course the Jews who had money bought their way out and those that did not have the means were transported by wagon. Along the way they were robbed of their last coins.

Sometime later many Jews stole their way back to into Radzyn. I, too, being in Parchew would often come to Radzyn with some produce. In those days the Germans in Radzyn decreed that the Jews leave the main streets and move to back streets such as Kotlarski, Kazshe and adjoining area. In this way a real ghetto was created.

In the Radzyn ghetto

Aktzia (The Campaign)

In Parchew, too, where I was living with my sister and brother-in-law there were tense and difficult days. The frequent deportations and requisitioning as well as the fear of being shot, threatened constantly. Therefore, we started thinking about preparing a hiding place. We decided to make it at my sister Devora's house. We moved away the bed and ripped up two planks from the floor. We cut the boards in half with a saw and made a small door that opened inward so that it would not be recognizable from the outside. We dug a not too large hole, covered it on top with the boards and moved the bed over it.

The frightful day of the "Aktzia" arrived. It was on the morning of a summer day in August of 1942 when the town was still asleep that the crackling of heavy gunfire awakened us. We immediately understood that something terrible was taking place. I went out near the house and saw that a few houses further away a tall Jew had been shot and lay dead by his house. I went back into the house and told this to my brother-in-law and sister, and we immediately went down into our hiding place. In that small hole there was not even enough room for even one person to sit down. But in this terrible situation we lay, all three of us, squeezed together for two horrible days and even partly managed to perform our human functions. Above us we could hear the coming and going of people in the house. They were searching for Jews and plundering. At night, as soon as we heard that everything was quiet around us, we opened the door of this living tomb, and I went out alone to inspect what had happened, figuring that if I was captured at least they would remain alive.

Outside, it was a dark, starry summer night. All around there was silence like in a graveyard without any sign of human presence causing terrible fear. I convinced myself that now there was no danger and went back into the house and called to my sister and my brother-in-law to come out and straighten out their limbs and perform their human functions. We washed up a bit as we were very dirty and then decided to go back down to our hiding place and wait for the following morning.

As we later found out, the plan of the Germans was as follows: On the first day they surrounded the town and under heavy gun fire, they began abducting Jews and transporting them to Treblinka for annihilation. After that, when they reached the required quota of people, they began to collect up the belongings from the houses. That is why they came into our house. As we lay hidden in our hole we heard them come into our house, collect up belongings and begin carrying them out to load them onto the wagons. While they were searching for the goods, they moved the bed aside and noticed the slits in the floor boards. They immediately understood that there was a hiding place here and ordered us to come out or they would throw in a hand grenade. Deathly scared, we climbed out of the hole and following their instructions went outside to the front of the house. A Volksdeutche (ethnic Germans who lived in Poland and formed units that helped the Germans.) drew out his pistol, aimed it at us and declared that now he would shoot us. My sister, Devora, began weeping loudly and asked the bandit that if he wanted to shoot us he should start with her and her husband and save my life, because I was young, only sixteen years old and healthy and could still work. A miracle happened! The German returned his pistol to its holster and ordered us to go get washed up since we were terribly dirty. He sent my brother in-law off to work and let the two of us go free. After that, we could move around more freely, because after a campaign there was usually a respite even though the Germans would occasionally arrest Jews and, without rhyme or reason, shoot them. We then started thinking about a safer hiding place, because we understood that another Aktzia would take place and hundreds of Jews would be sent to Treblinka to be executed. We then went up on the roof, made a double wall and prepared a hiding place.

The day of the new Aktzia arrived and it fell on Simchat Torah. We immediately hid out on the roof in the prepared hiding place and lay there for a number of days until they dispatched the transport of arrested people. We then found out that Parchew and the surrounding town must be made "Yudenrein" and that a ghetto would be established in Mezritsh for the Jews of the whole vicinity. The Germans announced that anyone who surrendered on his own accord would be sent to Mezritsh and anyone who would be found hiding out would be shot on the spot. We then left our hiding place on our own accord and were sent off to the ghetto in Mezritsh.

In Mezritsh

In Mezritsh we were packed into the synagogue like chickens and locked up together with the newly arrived Jews from Radzyn. Members of the Jewish Police together with some armed Germans guarded us. We had to perform our bodily functions on the spot. The dirt and the lice were unbearable. When you wanted a drink of water, you let down a pot with a sizeable sum of money in it through the bars of the windows of the women's synagogue. Then you would get back some water. Once each day the Germans opened the door and a long line formed. They would hand out small pieces of bread and some water. Of course the crowding was terrible, and the Germans then 'restored order' by shooting a few Jews every time.

Meseritz- after the hunt for Jews, being led to the train station (many from Radzyn)

One day, while I was searching among the hundreds of Jews that I knew, I found my father to my great joy. We fell into each others arms and wept like children. He took me in his arms the way one takes a small child and with fitful sobbing said: "My dear child, look under what circumstances we meet. Instead of leading you to the bridal canopy, I am a leading you to death!" I then answered: "If there is a God in this world how does he allow his Chosen

People to be murdered so brutally?" His answer was: "if that is his desire then that it is the way it has to be and it is forbidden to argue against it".

On the following morning they took all of us out of the synagogue and lined us up men and women separately and began preparing for our final transport to Treblinka. I tried to look for my sister Devora, who had just arrived from Radzyn, in the women's line. It turned out that she was just a few rows away from me. I then moved in her direction but I got a strong whack on my head from a whip, and I immediately lost consciousness. Then with my last bit of strength I managed to get to my sister Devora and stood near her. From the distance, I saw my father, for the last time standing in the men's line. However, he could not see us.

An order was given to march to the train station where freight cars were already waiting. They started loading us into them. I made an effort to find a place near one of the small windows so that I might be able to jump off the train. I decided that, come what may, I would never go alive to Treblinka! I was not the only one in the freight car who thought so, however, not everyone was lucky enough to be standing near a window.

In The Death Wagon

The freight car was crammed with women like herrings in a barrel and was closed hermetically. Those who were further away from the window choked to death slowly and were trampled on like rags. We, the fortunate ones who were near the window, (near me there was, in addition to my sister Devora, Zalman Mechlis' grandchildren, Yosefa with her sisters) collected on the palms of our hands every drop of moisture that ran down from the ceiling to moisten our lips. I was lucky that Yosefa's sister, Devora, had a small piece of a lemon which she allowed me to lick occasionally. When that gave out, we used our own urine to quench our thirst. We did not have any pot so we just put our hands underneath and made use of it that way.

Occasionally, when the train stopped along the way, the Germans would promise us a drink of water in return for money or gold. They would take the money but not give us any water.

When the train got near to Treblinka, we instinctively felt that our end was drawing near, and we had to do something. My desire was not so much to remain alive, knowing that everyplace was Yudenrein and there was nowhere to flee to, but at least to drink a lot of water before death. I began to prepare to jump from the train. I thought: If I get killed I won't need anything anyway. On the other hand, if I remain alive and the Germans capture me, I will ask them that before I die they should give me some water to drink.

I Jump From The Train

My sister Devora asked that she jump first and if she got killed I should jump differently. My dear sister Devora, in the last minutes of her life, she was only worried for my sake! I had already decided to jump. I dragged myself up to the small window. My sister and Yosefa Rubinstein pushed me up and when the train was traveling fast, about three kilometers before Treblinka, I jumped out. I immediately became unconscious.

I was awakened by the echo of a shot. I looked around and instinctively began to inspect my hands and feet to see if they had been injured. I was all in one piece. I also saw that I was lying on an embankment of sand. That was the reason that I had remained all in one piece. It was on a night in December of 1942 that I awakened, just as the morning dawned. In the distance I noticed shape of a small house with a well in the yard. My desire was that no matter what happened, I would be able to drink a lot of water. Immediately, I headed for the well, but I did not find a bucket and the trough was empty. There was not a drop of water anywhere, as if the only solution was to jump into the well. I went further and noticed a small place surrounded by a wire fence where water flowed from a small well. Quickly I threw myself on the ground, lifted up the bottom wire, crawled inside and threw myself on the water and drank until I ran out of breath. Right after that I heard the voices of a gang of drunken Ukrainians getting closer. I noticed that they were riding on a cart in the direction of Treblinka most likely to celebrate the arrival of the latest transport of Jews from Radzyn, Mezritsh and vicinity. I crawled quickly, under a tree with my head pushed deeply inside so that I would not see when they open fire on me. However, they drove by without noticing me, and I went quickly in the direction of the closest Jewish village Kosov-Telaki.

On the way, by the edge of the forest stood a small house in which a poor peasant lived with his family. I went in, and in return for money, got something to eat. They also allowed me to spend the night hidden in the stable and the morning to hide in the hay. They would not allow me to stay longer because, as they told me, they were afraid of the Ukrainians that visit there often. From them, I found out that there was still a Jewish ghetto in Kosov, so I started for there. I stole though the barbed wire fence into the Jewish ghetto. There I met many Jews who had jumped from the trains. Since Kosov was not far from Treblinka we understood that the Germans would not wait long to liquidate it. So a group of us Jews went through Sokolov to Siedlce.

We reached Siedlce safely and stole into the Jewish ghetto which consisted of ... one house. After spending a few days there, we went back to the Mezritsh ghetto. From there, a group of us decided to go Vohin so that we could get into the Parchew forest to join the Partisans who were there. In Vohin I met Leibel Schtzupak with his wife and children and also his sister Golda and her husband. All of us decided to go into the forest. However, we did not manage to do so because of the beginning of an Aktzia, so we ran back to Vohin where we were cursed and were all sent to the ghetto in Mezritsh again.

In Mezritsh Again

On the way I took sick with typhus. When we arrived in Mezritsh I, was left to sleep in the street with my sickness. The next morning my cousin from Mezritsh, Avraham Zaltstein, happened to pass by. I made as if did not see him but he stopped immediately and was very happy to see me and took me along to his home."What I will eat you will eat" he said. But I could not take anything into my mouth with the exception of a little water and saccharin, because I already had a high fever. My cousin did not want to put me into any hospital because there the Germans would shoot anyone sick with typhus. He and the others around him were insistent so I spent the whole period of my sickness with him.

In those days many Radzyners were shot, including my cousin Golda Zshita. Under different circumstances, my cousin, Zaltzstein, was also shot. When the Germans discovered a hiding place they started leading the group from there to the cemetery where they intended to execute them. My cousin grabbed hold of an ax, and with all his might, hit an S.S. man laying him out on the spot. Of course, a bullet fired by another German bandit put an end to my cousin's life. May his memory be honored!

The next day the Germans continued their search and declared that anyone who gave himself up would be sent to Mydanek. With that transport I, too, went there. While passing through Lublin, a large number of Radzyners came up to our train. They asked about us and seeing who we were, they gave us bread. Even while being in this transport, we began to make plans to escape. We began cutting an opening in the barred widows. However the Germans, at a certain station noticed this and with a few shots from inside put an end to our plan before we arrived in Mydanek.

In Mydanek

As we passed through the place on foot from the train station, we saw large pits and we thought that this is our end. But what happened was a little different. First the Germans carried out a selection in the place where we were gathered, men and women were separated and so were the young and the old. I was chosen to be part of a group of young girls who were to go to work.

We worked very hard dragging stones to build new crematoria so that they could cremate Jews in Mydanek. Selections took place often among us inmates. If they found anyone who had any sort of weakness, or even any sort of a rash on their body, they were immediately executed. On our first night in Mydanek we experienced the worst: all the men, women and children who were designated as not being fit to work were immediately put to death in the gas chamber and those left over were shot to death. In our barrack that housed young women and girls, no one slept that night. When we heard the terrible screaming of the victims, we began running from fear and pushed through the doors and windows. However the Germans, by the threat of shooting at us, pushed us back inside. Half way through the night, when the screaming gradually died down, we fell asleep exhausted. In the early morning when we woke up, we saw a horrible sight in our barrack. The bodies of two young girls, who had put an end to their lives, were hanging in two of the windows.

In Auschwitz

I have already mentioned the many selections that took place by us. The weak stayed in Mydanek to be annihilated and the healthy were sent on to Auschwitz. I was among those that were sent away. It was in the middle of the summer of 1943 when I arrived there. The first thing they did was to cut off our hair, housed us in separate barracks and gave us clothes. When I asked that they give me a dress to fit me better, I got the first slap in the face from the oldest inmates and my face swelled up immediately. Our first job was to tear out the overgrown grass in the fishponds. It seems that the grass interfered with the development of the fish. We would go into the water up to our necks and many of us became sick with malaria. The Jewish girls from Greece suffered the most from this. They died in great numbers. Every day we carried dead bodies back from work. Only when the size of our group became very small, did they move us to another place.

I will never ever forget that place. It was Bashezinke, one of the quarters of the Auschwitz Concentration Camp in which the crematoria were located. We lived in a barrack that was located a few meters away. Our job was to sort out the clothing of those who arrived on the transports and had been gassed and cremated. We had to stay inside and keep the windows closed when each new transport arrived so that we would not see the people going by to be exterminated. We would stand and look out through the cracks and saw horrible things that I don't have the strength to describe.

Once I saw a transport of Jews from Hungary that included many children. Two pretty little girls of about four and eight passed by our barrack that had flowers growing around it. They tore out two of them and sniffed them childishly. These little girls did not know that this was their last step on their way to the gas chamber.

The gassing was dreadful. The cries and lamentation of the choking gassed victims reached us. At first they were very loud, later they became less audible and little by little they stopped completely. Even today I think that I still hear those cries. They have followed me all my life and it is impossible to forget for one minute those gruesome days, weeks and years.

The nights were especially terrible. Oh! Those terrible nights in those barracks opposite the crematorium in Auschwitz! Where is the writer who can describe that awful hellish nightmare? Who can describe with his pen those horrible scenes? Anyhow, my pen is too poor for that.

Jews led to the furnaces
Painting by Manuel Lichtenstein, New York

Midnight! Everything is quiet and dark all around us. Through the small window in the toilet of our barrack I now see the smoking chimneys that are working at full steam. Together with the thick smoke, sparks fly from the singed corpses. The entire killing machinery of Auschwitz is now operating under full steam. In every spark I hear the last cry of a near one, of my mother and father, my sister and brother.

I tear myself away from the spot and run outside. A few hundred meters away I see another horrible scene. Huge flames flare up from big pits and one can see in the light from the flames how people carrying dead bodies and throwing them into pits. Those are bodies that the crematoria could not consume. The stench from the scorched bodies is unbearable. These scenes repeated themselves month after month.

The Resistance

It is interesting that in this midst of this gigantic death machine there existed and underground movement preparing for armed resistance. There was a Jewish girl from Tshechanov by the name of Ruzshke in the department that sorted the clothing of those who had been murdered. In utmost secrecy, she received arms from a Jewish girl from Warsaw who stole them from an arms factory in which she worked located in the concentration camp. Ruzshke would hide the arms under the tremendous piles of clothing. However, the Germans discovered them and the Gestapo interrogated them, using the most ruthless inquisitorial methods. However, they did not succeed to get a word out of the two girls. They then decided to hang them in public. They drove out all the inmates to the execution site so that everyone would see and be terrified. Meanwhile the Nazis observed everyone to see if anyone tried to make contact with the girls and in this way add to their list of candidates for hanging. The two Jewish girls, with heads held high and without betraying anyone, marched proudly to the gallows shouting "Zemsta!" (revenge) and breathed out their holy souls. For a whole day and night the murderers did not allow their bodies to be taken down. This happened at the end of 1944.

Resistance - Painting by Manuel Lichtenstein, New York

The Beginning of the End

At the beginning of 1945 there were frequent over flights by Allied planes. The Red Army got closer rapidly. The Germans begin to liquidate the death camps and prepare to move us to Germany. Our long march on foot to Germany began. In the winter of 1945 we are driven day and night on foot in the snow and freezing cold. Those that became exhausted and fell behind were shot on the spot. Now our desire to survive became stronger. We could already see the vision of the approaching liberation. Allied planes often flew over the route of our march. Then the "brave" Germans would mix in among us and throw down their weapons. We waved to the pilots. They did not bomb us. They obviously knew who we were.

We arrived in Ravensbruck. Here, we, a couple of thousand concentration camp designates were driven into a large roofless barracks filled with snow and filth. Hungry and tired, we were squeezed together. Infrequently, they would throw in a small portion of bread to us. However, this created such a crush of inmates that that we were almost asphyxiated. In the evening we stole raw cabbage in the vicinity and got severe beatings. After a few weeks in Ravensbruck, they took us in closed wagons to Malchow (Concentration Camp). As we passed through German cities while they were being bombarded we were also hit and had a number of casualties. From Malchow we went to Leipzig.

From Leipzig we began the painful trek on foot on the accursed German soil. During the day, we hid out in the caves because of the frequent bombardments, and at night we would march. The discipline gradually became looser as the Germans already saw their approaching downfall. The SS. men gradually ran away and were replaced by ordinary Reichswehr soldiers who accompanied us. Then it happened that many different and large groups would break off from us and go free. That is the way that I and ten other Jewish girls got free.

We went into a yard in a certain German village. On the garbage bin we found a piece of dried out bread which we grabbed and hid. We went into a German house. We met two Russian women who were working there. They promised to provide us with food and also arranged a place for us to sleep in the attic where there was straw. When the owner of the house went out to the fields they would cook potatoes and give them to us to eat.

After a short time in the village we found out from one of the two Russian women that the American army had already entered a nearby city called Ashof. We went there immediately. In that town there was a concentration camp. We went in and saw that the place was teeming with dead, some of whom had just died after the liberation. America and Polish military police stood near the food supply stations and distributed food and chocolate to the former inmates.

Thus the longed-for day of liberation for which we had waited for five years, enduring pain and suffering, had finally arrived.

Inspection of the Jews before their transfer to the train station

[Pages 264-270]

The Struggle For Survival

(As told by Liber Farbiash)

When the Germans proceeded to liquidate and exterminate the Jews from the cities and towns of Poland, I was, together with other Radzyners, in the Mezritsh Ghetto to which we had been driven from Radzyn. Together with hundreds of other Jews, we were transported to the train. There we were shoved, approximately one hundred people into a car that was covered with lime to make breathing more difficult. The crowding was unbearable. About seventy Jews died immediately from asphyxiation. The living tread on them and also on those that were still partly alive who could still breathe a bit but could not speak up. They would howl like animals or would pinch the legs of those standing on them. This was the way they expressed their desire for help. In order to calm their thirst they would wet one another's' lips with urine and that made them only thirstier.

The train moved along very quickly. At my feet lay my suffocated dead mother and my seven and four year old brothers. The living knew that they were being transported to the death camp Treblinka, so many Jews began to jump from the moving train, preferring to find their death under the wheels. I, too, jumped but as fate would have it, I would remain alive. This took place near Siedlce at midnight. On the way, I met Jews from Mezritsh, and we decided run back to the Mezritsh Ghetto. Along the way we saw many dead Jews who had been cut apart by the train wheels. With inhuman speed we managed to get back to Mezritsh before sunrise.

When we arrived in the ghetto, I went immediately to our flat. There I met my father who was all alone. When he asked: "Where are mother and the children?" I broke out into a mournful lament. Both of us wept for our nearest and dearest.

The Jews began to prepare bunkers in which to hide in case another cursed Aktzia took place. At the same time they began to bring new transports of Jews from the vicinity. A lot of Jews arrived from Radzyn among whom I found Moshe Edelman with a son and two daughters. I took the children into my bunker where we remained hidden for a number of nights. A few days later, when the arrests of the Jews ceased, we went out of the bunker. Eidelman's children, too, went back to their parents. But exactly on that same day the second Aktzia took place. During that Aktzia Eidelman's wife and children went to the woods near the city. On their way there they were all shot.

During the third Aktzia the Germans discovered my bunker. We were seven Jews in the bunker including my father. We were moved to the Beit Midrash where the Jews were rounded up before being transferred to the concentration camps. My father decided that by no means would he go to the concentration camp, preferring to die in this place. Two days later the Beit Midrash was surrounded by a unit of the military police, S.S. troops and Polish police. An order was given to leave the Beit Midrash. While leaving the place my father threw himself onto one of the S.S. men and began choking him. I went to help my father. Military Police tore me away from him but I managed to see my father lying on the S.S. man and choking him with all his might. My father was killed by a bullet to his head.

Near the shacks at the suburb of "Piaski" in Meseritz

We were led off to the barracks that were located on the sands on the way to Radzyn. There they would undress everyone and search them to make sure that they did not have any money, gold, or arms. Then they would transfer them to the railroad yard.

On the same day, more Jews were brought from Radzyn and I met Shlomo Migdal and Shlomo Lozer Fleiss. Shlomo Migdal asked me that if I survive and meet his daughter, I should tell her the place where he had hidden some money. The old Fleiss just stood there and cried like a small child because he had not had the honor of dying in his own bed. We all stood there as if we had been condemned to death.

In the evening we were led to the train and from there to Treblinka. I was in the same car with Migdal and Fleiss. I had decided to jump again from the train and asked them to join me. They, however, refused. They said good-bye to me and wished me success and that should I survive I should tell about these depressing times.

Jews kneeling and bowing

I did jump off. I lay on the ground with my eyes closed listening to the clatter of the wheels. When the train passed by I opened my eyes and saw that I was lying near a forest. I went in and slept for the whole night. In the morning I realized that I was not far from Siedlce. As I went further in to the forest I met seven Russian partisans armed with rifles. They told me that at night they would free the thirty thousand Russian prisoners being held not far from Siedlce. This seemed unbelievable to me. How could seven people, armed only with rifles free such a large number of people? All day I thought that maybe it was only a joke and they were testing me to see if I was not a spy. However, when night fell, I saw that they were making all the preparations for starting out. They did not have a gun for me, but they ordered me to do as follows: When they started shooting at the guard towers I should begin shouting loudly so as to make a commotion. I of course, agreed.

And again to the train station...

At about ten o'clock that night, we went out of the deep forest and moved by different routes to the vicinity of the camp. The night was very dark and around twelve o'clock we were close to the camp. The searchlights on the towers lit up all the surrounding area. However, we managed to get up close to the barbed wire fence. The plan was to shoot the guards and free the prisoners. One of the partisans gave an order and suddenly shooting broke out. I heard a heavy load fall from the tower. It was like the sound made by a tree when it is cut down. My heart was filled with joy. Suddenly the Germans on the towers turned the projectors in our direction and opened heavy machine-gun fire in our direction. Two of us fell dead and the rest of us went back into the forest. That night we did not sleep, being under the influence of what had happened and expecting a German visit. The partisans went away at midnight to find food for themselves, leaving us behind. I utilized their absence and again went in the direction of Mezritsh.

Along the way I was seized by four non-Jews. They tied me up, put me on a wagon to take me to Mezritsh and turn me over to the Germans so as to get a reward of four kilograms of sugar. I pleaded with them to release me and promised that I would give them my winter coat which was worth more than four kilograms of sugar. Their answer was: "We are four people. How will we be able to divide up the coat between the four of us?" However when I promised to add my boots they agreed, untied me and let me go. Naked and barefoot, I went off to Mezritsh on a freezing snowy day. The cold made me feel weak. My feet became two frozen limbs that gave me the feeling that they were two artificial limbs that were attached to my body.

When I got to Mezritsh I met acquaintances in the streets who told me that the Aktzias had been discontinued. All those now in Mezritsh would be sent only to work. That is the way it was. They sent us to repair sidewalks. I worked, along with many other Jews, in the German firm "Stuage" that repaired sidewalks and built new ones. However, after working for a month, the Germans carried out the fourth Aktzia.

On the night of that Aktzia, our foreman did not let us go home too avoid our being caught. However, the Chief S.S. Man, Fisher came from Radzyn and ordered that we be turned over to the transportation authorities and shipped off.

From 'Stuage" we were sent to the market place in Mezritsh. The order was that all the Jews must line-up and kneel down and anyone who dared get up would be shot.

In the evening we were taken to the train row by row. There were many Christians in the streets witnessing our black day. They 'parted' from us with a smile on their faces. The rows of Jews were very long with German Military Police and both Polish and Jewish police marching along on both sides. Again we were packed into the freight cars with the doors and windows locked from the outside.

We arrived in the Majdanek Extermination Camp. At the entrance gate we met the daughter of Dovid Zysman from Radzyn. I asked her what do they do here. However she did not answer. Meanwhile we were all led to the baths. There I again met a Radzyner Yudel Ravniak. I saw him sweeping the area around the baths and I tried to speak to him, but he, too, did not reply. A little later he came up to me, gave me a few potatoes and told me on which side I should stand during the lineup. I did as he told me. Our transport was divided into two groups. Both groups went into the baths. One came out, the one that I was in. The other was executed by Cyclone B gas.

—— * ——

I spent six months in Majdanek and after that I was sent to a coal mine in the swamps in Zaglembia. There we worked very hard while going hungry. When the battle front moved near to us in 1945, the Germans pulled out and moved us to Blachamri. I and two other Jews ran away and most of the others were shot along the way.

I went in the direction of the Russians. While running away, I came to a river. I saw Russian troops and heavy Russian tanks on the other bank moving to the western side. I walked along the bank of the river looking for a bridge to cross over. Along the way a German came out of one of the trenches and wanted to shoot me. I begged him to take me to his commander as I had something very important to tell him. After much pleading he fulfilled my request. I told all sorts of stories to his commander, and the end was that he ordered them to tie me up and lay me down on the bridge that was to be blown up by the Germans saying that it was not worth wasting a bullet on such a Jew.

They did as they were told. I lay tied up on the bridge like an animal for slaughter while the Germans made preparations to blow it up. All the facts of my struggle for survival ran through my head as if on a movie film. I had descended all the steps to hell and stayed alive. Yet here, when Hitlerism was about to get the final blow before its defeat, my body lay waiting to be blown up together with the steel from the bridge. My eyes overflowed with tears and I saw the blue sky as if through a fog.

Suddenly from the eastern side, I heard the sound of the heavy artillery fire. For a moment I turned my eyes to the water wanting to wash the tears from my eyes. However, my hands were tied to my back. From afar I saw the green trees of the approaching spring. A breeze smoothed my ruffled hair like a loving hand stroking a corpse to make it easier for him to die.

Unexpectedly, I heard a loud clanging of tanks approaching from the east. One of the tanks stopped near me. A soldier got out, cut the ropes and freed me.

———

[Pages 271-281]

Two Years in a Dark Pit

Sarah Fass

I was one of the last, if not the very last, from our Jewish community that left the town in which we were born in that terrible time for us. I can unfortunately say that with my leaving Radzyn I closed the doors to the Jewish community forever and took with me the most painful terrible memories: the sad histories of our close relatives and friends, the saintly souls on their final journey. I carry the picture of those days with me and it does not disappear. Therefore I would like to record some of my memories.

___*___

Shortly after the arrival of the murderous Gestapo in Radzyn, they suddenly came to my house and started yelling at me in their drunken voices that I should give them the "English Protocol". For the first few minutes, I did not understand what they wanted from us, and from fear I could only mumble "Meine herren ('My Lords') meine herren". The six Hitlerite bandits drew their pistols angrily and threatened to kill all of us if we did not hand over the pact that England had made with the Jews. When I began begging them that I knew nothing about it, while at the same time hugging my child who was shaking with fear, they angrily ordered that my Jewish neighbors should all gather in my house. They immediately dragged in my neighbors Henich Nussbaum from the town of Valasvinsk, his son Yechiel and the sick grandchild of his son Moshe, who lives in Argentina and also Henich's son from Kotzk, with his three children, who were in his house at that time. The Germans then ordered all the Jews to line up facing the wall and yelled at them,"Hand over the English Protocol and don't move or we will shoot you right away!" I happened to be standing close to the door and seeing how my ten year old son was shaking all over, I moved, almost unconsciously, and slipped out of the house with my child. However, in the street I remained standing. I thought: "Where can I dare go walking in the street so late at night without being shot by the military patrols?" Therefore, I went through the back street out into the fields nearest my house, so that I could hear what was happening to everyone in the house. I sat there stifling my child's crying and fearful about the fate of those left in the house. I sat that way the whole night, without hearing the sound of a shot. I calmed down and calmed my child who was shaking from the cold. At dawn, when the murderers too, got tired of this game, they left my house drunken and tired ordering that when they come tomorrow everything should be ready for them. In the morning, we were not in our houses. We went anywhere we could go. When the bandits came again and did not find any of us, they cursed us vehemently in front of our Polish neighbors but never came back.

___*___

In the winter of 1941 the oldest Gestapo-thief, Fisher, ordered that all Jews must immediately surrender their fur coats and fur accessories. The Jewish population, knowing that sooner or later they would be deported from Radzyn, wanted to keep their furs in case they would be deported in the winter. They all took their furs to Polish families who were their friends. Some of the Poles did not want to accept the furs saying that they did not want to be left with the last possessions of their unfortunate Jewish neighbors. However most of them accepted the furs with obvious pleasure, without showing any sympathy for their Jewish neighbors and added that it was better that the Poles get them rather than the Germans. One woman from Radzyn, Sarah Neiman, whose husband the Germans had already shot in Slovatich together with some fifty other Jews and was left with her two orphans, took her furs to hide by her good friend Katchky. He accepted them readily, but a few days later he informed the Gestapo and Sarah was arrested immediately and shot by the door of the detention building. This caused a great turmoil in the town. The whole Jewish population was so filled with pain they could not communicate with each other but, as if ordered, they all took back the furs from their Polish neighbors at night and threw them through the fence into the yard of the house where the president of the Yudenrat, Dovid Lichtenstein lived. When Dovid Fishel wanted to open the door in the morning he could not do so because of the piled up furs. The booty was taken away by the murderers in trucks.

After the frequent contributions of money and our last remaining valuables, when the Gestapo murderers knew that we had nothing more for them to squeeze out of us, and that we were are all physically broken and mentally exhausted, when almost the whole Jewish population existed on the little bit of soup that was distributed by the last remaining Jewish institution, the communal kitchen, only then did the oldest bandit, Fisher, begin carrying out his fiendish plan, the final curse on the Jews. In the fall of 1942, at five o'clock in the morning, they suddenly attacked the Jewish houses together with their live four footed dogs and with other, even worse two footed animals, foreign Ukrainians and local Poles who, with a terrible frightening uproar, drove the old and young, half naked Jews out of their old homes. The heart-rending crying of the small children mixed with the choked up wailing of the adults, mingled with the sobbing

and pounding of the murderers and the barking of the dogs, awakened the still sleeping Polish neighbors. The simpler and more honest ones immediately ran to the school yard where the Germans had driven the wretched Jews. The fences and the roofs of the surrounding buildings were crowded with curious Polish spectators. At the same time the majority of the Polish neighbors ran to collect the as yet not cooled off bedding and other items that were still wet with the tears shed by the Jews before they left.

The bandits meanwhile drove the helpless Jewish population into the Radzyn school yard. The leader, Fisher, declared demonstratively and with an amused look on his face, that from now on the Jews had no right to be in

Radzyn and all of the community properties were to be confiscated. Temporarily, the most necessary of its employees would be allowed to remain including the president, his colleagues and their families, altogether thirty-eight people. A few weeks later the Germans assembled them all in one house. It did not take long before all of them were murdered.

At that time I was living in a side street and therefore I was 'forgotten' by the bandits and they did not come into my house. However, hearing about what was going on in the town, I took my child out of the house without knowing where to hide. We wanted to run to the house of a Polish friend, however, they closed the door in my face. I ran wildly from house to house but everywhere they refused to let me in. Then I ran to the house of our old acquaintance the washerwoman named Akusht. She hid us out in her house and she herself then ran to see if everything had quieted down and if the murderers were not running around between the houses. A few hours later she came with the good news that my husband had managed to slip out of the hands of the Gestapo.

Late at night we returned to our house indifferently and apathetic to life and knowing that at any moment we might be noticed by the Germans or the local scoundrels. Being cut off from all the Jews, we became indifferent to everything that might happen. We stayed that way in our house for another couple of weeks. During that time, a number of Jews, who had not fallen into the hands of the Germans but had not gone back to their houses and were wandering around in the nearby woods, found out about my being in the house. At night they would come there to eat some hot food. Not knowing what lay in store for us on the following day, we would part cordially and choking with tears. At that time my sister Zlota's daughter Sarah, who had jumped from the train that was carrying them to Treblinka when it was only eight kilometers from the extermination camp, came running to us. She was then only fifteen years old.

The terrible sight of this heroic child and her half nude body, her short but horrible stories about what happened to our closest relatives in the last minutes in that freight car, her experiences running a couple of hundred kilometers ragged, hungry and fearful, froze our blood. Even at that time when we had already seen and heard about so much pain and suffering, the child's description exceeded our wildest imaginations and fantasies. We wept with her, but at the same time, in our hearts, we were happy that she had come at the right time since we were planning to go that very night to the nearby village of Biala to a peasant with whom we had already made an arrangement to hide our family survivors. My sister and her younger daughter Esther were already there. We had waited for a dark night without a moon to steal out of the town. Two days after the child's arrival, seeing that there was a danger of our being discovered, we, my husband and I, my son and my sister's child, went to the peasant in the village. There he had prepared a place in his barn for us to hide in. It was located in the middle of a hay stack that surrounded it up to the height of the balcony. The entrance to this 'dwelling' was through a hole in the earth in the pig pen near the barn, so that no one could guess that there, in the middle of the hay, lived six Jewish souls.

——*——

The peasant's farm was located in a colony outside of the village and was safer and more protected from the eyes of strangers. But little by little the peasant used up the hay for his animals until he got close to our hiding place. At the same time, there were frosts and it became impossible for us to stay there. Our plan, when we entered that hiding place was, like that of most of the Jews in that dark period, that the Russian army which was already advancing would in a month or two catch up to the Germans. That gave us the courage to carry on in such terrible conditions. But, seeing that the advance of the Soviets was taking longer than expected, and that there was danger of our being discovered, we thought up a new plan; to dig a pit in the earth and there spend the time that was left, according to our estimation, before the Russian Army's arrival. One dark night we started working and we managed to dig a pit with four corners into which we set up poles and covered the top with planks which we then covered with earth and topped with snow so that it would be unrecognizable. In the morning, the owner of the plot parked his sickle for cutting fodder for his cows there. In this way it was well concealed. We made the entrance through a hole dug in the earth of the pig pen, so that it was very difficult to push one's way into the hole. There we felt like half dead corpses, not knowing when it was day and when it was night. From that day on we were dependant on the peasant's hospitality for our survival, naturally for a very considerable payment.

At the beginning he would pass down bread to all of us every day. But every week the amount was less, until he started feeding us only potatoes in their peels, the way he fed his pigs. He claimed that he could not give us anymore. We understood that having squeezed everything he could out of us he was sorry about the whole business. But the longer it continued the stronger was our desire to live and see the end of Hitler which we all hoped for, this despite the severe hunger that we had been suffering from since the spring. At that time the water from the melting snow began to penetrate the earth together with the sewerage from the pigs who liked to lie near the opening of our pit. All this soaked the little bedding which we sat on because it was impossible to stand up in the pit. One could only sit or lie down.

That is the way the winter passed and the summer of 1943 arrived and still we could not hope to see an end to our troubles. One day, in the middle of that summer, our host told us that the Germans had ordered that all the Polish residents must leave the village immediately, and it was said that Germans were coming here to settle there. For us in the dark pit, things became darker yet. What should we do? Should we go out of the pit and go to a certain death after being captured by the bandits, or should we stay in the pit and die of hunger? We decided to stay in the pit and not to surrender to the Germans. Our peasant, before leaving his house let down enough bread and other food and water to last us for a number of days. Everything around us became deadly still. We were prepared to die of hunger in a few days. One day passed and then another and everything was quiet and we did not hear or see any Germans. On the fourth day we suddenly heard a loud noise, the sound of horse's hooves, and later the sound of human voices. We were sure that Germans were already living here. When we listened more closely we heard, from a distance Polish being spoken. We could not understand what was going on here. Soon we heard the voice of our landlord who went up to the opening of our pit and yelled in: "What? You are still alive?" It turned out that after three days went by, the Germans regretted their plan to settle Germans there and they told the former residents to return to their places. A ray of hope shone for us that we might survive all this suffering.

———*———

At the end of the summer of 1943 our peasant informed us that because his potato crop was not successful, he could no longer supply us with food and we would have to find other sources from which to obtain potatoes in the winter. It meant that we would have to go to other fields at night, dig up potatoes and bring them to him to cook for us. We calculated the danger involved in being seen walking in the fields at night. However, because we wanted to save our children, who at the time looked like pale thin skeletons, we started out on that dangerous course. We were very careful and everyone went alone and to a different part of the fields. We chose the darkest cloudiest nights. My heart shook with fear, and I held my breath as I pulled the potatoes out of the earth and gathered them into the sack, but I did not have the strength to throw the sack over my shoulder. On top of that, I often tripped over a stone and in falling let go of the sack. I got dizzy and lost my orientation, not knowing in what direction I had to go to get to the pit. Then I remembered that the treasure which I was carrying, the potatoes, could save us and make it possible for us to survive and I got the strength to overcome all the dangers that I saw in front of me. We prepared ourselves to eat heartily.

However, with every month that passed our situation grew worse. The peasant continuously cut down the amount of food and our children suffered seriously from hunger and looked terrible. My sister and I were very frightened about the fate of our children. We had already sacrificed much for them, and what could we do now to keep them alive? I decided for myself that I would endanger my life, and go to the nearest village where I had a friend, a good hearted peasant woman. I thought that she would surely give me some bread for the children. We hadn't seen bread for a long time. I crawled out of the pit so as not be seen by our landlord who would not have let me go out of fear for his own safety. In the evening I went to the neighboring village and was recognized immediately maybe because of my terrible appearance. It seems that they immediately recognized me as that terrible worldly creature the "Yude". This message spread rapidly through the village so that when l came to peasants hut, she asked me anxiously to leave immediately. She was afraid to give me anything. I started going back agonizingly, not thinking about the danger that awaited me but only about what would happen to the hungry children for whom I had nothing. Suddenly I heard an old man speaking to me: "Run away quickly! The administrator of the district told the Germans over the phone that you are here". As if suddenly being awakened, I remembered the danger that faced me. I went off the road, into the field and lay down on the earth. My heart grieved but I did not have the strength to cry. After lying there for a short time, I heard the sound of motorcycles. I heard the Germans shouting to the peasants as they drove their cycles back and forth over the road. Meanwhile night descended and I could not recognize the way back. I lay confused all night in the field. Late that night I heard the sound of shooting. I was beginning to get used to the thought that the Germans would find me there and I would never be able to go back to the pit. (After the liberation, peasants from that village told me that on that night there was a shoot out between the Germans and the Partisans who had come to the village that night). I lay that way the whole night until I saw the beginning of daylight. I raised my head and slowly began figuring out the direction to the pit. I moved slowly, partly lying down, until I reached our hiding place. Understandably my husband and sister had already started to mourn me being sure that I had fallen victim while searching for a piece of bread for our children.

—*—

The winter of 1945 was unbearable for us. We all felt that we were reaching the limit of our strength. The dampness of the pit got into our bones. The propped up beams and boards became warped. There was a danger that everything would soon cave in on us. We could not repair it, and we didn't feel that we had the strength to rebuild it in one night. The peasant too, did not want us to appear in the light of day because of the gangs of rioters who were wandering around in that neighborhood. So we lay on half rotten bedding while the water from the melting snow ran in over our heads. My son could not put his hands down normally because the skin and flesh between fingers and his hands were cracked. His groaning made us even more heartbroken. He could not even cry because all sorts of strangers gathered in the barn over our heads. We were tired of living.

However, our desire to live grew again when we heard that the battle lines were getting closer to us. The desire to outlive the murderous Germans was boundless. For a whole winter we could not get out of the pit because we did not have any warm clothing. When the spring arrived, without considering the danger to our lives, from time to time we quietly crawled out of our hole and went to a friendly Polish family who would give us some bread. Seeing that our children were strengthened by the small piece of bread, our instinct again drove us to go wherever we could so as to survive. To our great pain, my husband went once to bring us some food. This was ten days before the Germans were driven out of Radzyn. He was met by a gang of anti-Semitic hooligans who brutally murdered him. After my husband's violent death we broke down and became completely indifferent to everything that could happen to us. We believed that these gangs of local murderers would sooner or later murder us.

A few days later, I heard the loud roar of airplane motors and of bombs exploding. Realizing that the frontline was getting closer to us, we were instinctively afraid of asking our landlord about it. He too, while passing down our supply of potatoes, was silent. When we did hear the sound of horses' hooves and wagons and the noise of people, we understood that the army was passing near us but, not being able to hear the language that they were speaking, we did not know if they were Germans or Soviets. When it became completely quiet our peasant's old father yelled down into the pit that the Germans had gone and that the Red Army had entered Radzyn. He added, I do not know if you people have the "right to live" therefore I cannot let you out of here yet. We became more frightened, and the silence of our landlord added to our fright not knowing what he was thinking about doing to us. We, my sister and I, decided that we must leave the pit quietly without our peasant noticing it. But how can we circulate among people when we are half naked? All of our clothes were torn from the dampness. In town we had left some clothing with a Polish friend, so we thought that one of us should go to bring them. But in the light of the recent, still fresh, misfortune of my husband's death, we decided that we would not go alone, only all of us together. What ever happens should happen to all of us. So, early one morning, when the owners of our house were still asleep, we crawled out of the pit. This was already ten days after our town Radzyn had been liberated. We went, five unfortunate souls through the fields, avoiding the highway because we went with our emaciated bodies wrapped only in sacks. When the sun rose we first saw the death-like look that lay spread out on faces of our children. It was difficult for us to walk on our feet, and we had to sit down and rest every few meters, so that it took us a half of that July day to cover the distance of approximately five kilometers. Along the way we met a Soviet soldier who examined us anxiously. We asked him if we have the right to live. He answered: "By us, all people have equal rights". This gave us strength and we slowly moved closer to Radzyn.

Coming into town dressed in sacks and with our deadly pale faces and being the first Jewish souls who showed up in Radzyn after the Germans, the Polish passers by stared at us and moved aside. When we reached the house of our old Polish neighbor, a friend of our mother's, she looked at us and with fearful eyes, crossed herself three times and yelled out: "Oh my God, you are alive?" She received us cordially but was still scared, without knowing why. Therefore she took us into the barn were we stayed for a few more days.

Gradually, the accumulated layers of fear left our minds and we began to appear on the streets again. However every street, every house every stone or brick from the homes of Jewish acquaintances cried out to us and we wandered around like lonely orphans looking for the holiest of martyrs – the Jews from our beloved town of Radzyn.

The Parting

Sarah Basheh Vayazsher (Paris)

We, a group of girls from our town, came from Majdanek to Auschwitz in the beginning of August 1943. I ended up sleeping together with two girls, sisters from Radzyn, by the name of Lublinerman. After being there for only a few months, the first big 'Selectzia' takes place. Among five blossoming young women and girls who are taken out of our room, one was the youngest of these sisters. With great effort and suffering I somehow console the oldest sister Sarah, who would not allow herself to be consoled at all. Since then we became very friendly, virtual sisters.

After some time there was another selection and the barbarians took away the second sister when the Soviet planes were already roaring overhead. The parting was very painful. On that day we could not be separated. With terrible crying she asked at the last minute: "Sarah Basheh, I beg of you, never to forget me and may I be the last victim."

That moment remained inscribed in my memory, and I can never forget her words. Wherever I go and wherever I stay they are ringing in my ears. Therefore, I share them with all my Radzyners through our Yizkor Book.

[Pages 282-284]

In the Inferno Unknowingly*
(Reminiscences)

Chava Burstein (Ramat Gan)

It was night. I lay on the ground with my cheeks burning. A small amount of straw served as my bed. The cold from the earth penetrated my body, but I was hot, too hot. I twitched on the straw as if wanting to get rid of something that was bothering me. I did not close my eyes all that very long night. At daybreak I got up quickly, ran bare foot to the river and washed my hands a bit. My aunt had warned me that it was forbidden to prepare food without first washing your hands. A few minutes later I was standing on a small chair to reach a pot that stood on the stove and to boil up some coffee for breakfast. The house was completely silent. Everyone was asleep. I moved around the kitchen all alone. I was alternately hot and cold. My whole body shook. A pleasant odor rose up from the coffee. Dozens of times I had wanted to taste the coffee, if only one sip, but did not dare. I heard the sounds of the cows from the barn, and I knew that it was time for me to go feed them. However an evil instinct got the better of me this time and I tasted the coffee. It was very tasty and I wanted to taste it again. The coffee was very hot, so I waited for it to cool off a bit. Just as I lifted the spoon to my lips I felt a sudden blow on my cheek and saw stars before my eyes, and I fell down.

I don't know what happened after that. When I regained consciousness I felt a terrible burning pain in my back. I saw that I was naked and I saw black and blue marks on my hands, signs of the blows that I had absorbed. I was happy that I had not felt them at the time they happened and that I had not heard the coarse voice of the father of the Adamovitz family. Tears formed in my eyes and I wondered: "am I not a Christian like all the Christians so why do they humiliate me? Why do they beat me when other mothers pamper their children? Really, why do I call Zofiah "aunt", why isn't she "mother"? I did not find any answers to these questions. Even when they took me to church on Sunday and I prayed there for an answer I heard no reply. Once when my aunt Zofiah had guests, I had an inspiration: I summed up courage and asked my question. She laughed and answered: "Your mother is in heaven". Then she turned back to the guests. Now that I knew where my mother is I thought: "My mother will kiss me too, sometime". My mother now became a divine power. She, too, resides in heaven higher than Jesus himself !

—— * ——

Two years passed. The war had not stopped and the sound of unending artillery fire could still be heard. The Germans wreaked havoc on the inhabitants especially on the Jews. Once, while I was standing behind the fence of our farm, I saw flames. "Auntie"! I yelled. "Christ! What do you want?" my aunt answered angrily. I pointed with my hand in the direction of the fire.

The aunt ran quickly with me following behind her. I never saw such a terrible sight. The flames were billowing up from the farm of some distant neighbors. Breathing heavily we arrived at the burning farm and could see the Gestapo nearby "Damn them!" she whispered angrily, "They have set the farm on fire". Zofiah was angry that we had come here and she scolded me for having made us do so. The aunt went closer to the Germans and made as if she too was happy about what made them happy. The Germans talked with her and laughed. One of them even took me in his arms and gave me a whole package of chocolate, but I kept looking toward the burning farm. Through the window of the burning house I could see our Jewish neighbor with her small baby pleading with the Germans to save the infant. They made fun of her and promised that they would save her. When she saw Zofiah she began begging her to take the baby. However, my aunt for some reason did not dare to do so. I already knew, even though I was still small, that in such cases you don't ask questions. This was explained to me many times at home. One of the Germans stretched his hand out toward the baby and took it up with his fat hands. The mother thanked the German, now she could die. She stood in the midst of the flames, her hair caught fire and she was one big flame, then she let out a scream, and died. Laughter was the answer of the Germans to her bitter death. Mixed in with their laughter, you could make out the weak sound of the baby crying. I did not dare to cry. I had seen many such scenes and my aunt ordered me not to show any sign of grief. "To laugh" she said with her German laughter as she herself had just done. We stood for a long time by the farm. The flames died down. One wall was left. The Germans carried on a lively conversation with my aunt Zofiah. They were annoyed that the child was still crying .The German held the baby's legs in his hands. Its head was red and hung down low. It appeared as if they had hung it by its little feet. Suddenly the sound of the German's voice could be heard: "Do you want to see a show? This is the right time for it! "He went over to the wall that had survived the fire, raised his hand that was holding the infant, and with all his might, slammed the baby against the wall. The head of the child became a mashof >flesh and bones. The crying stopped and the voice that had annoyed those that were laughing was silent.

All that day those pictures flashed before my eyes. One time I saw the mother in the flames. Another time I saw her kissing the baby. At that moment I was jealous of the child. However my jealousy disappeared quickly when I recalled its fate.

It was night. The moon looked as if it had wrapped itself in a black robe inlaid with sparkling jewels. Far, far away I saw a small shinning star that looked as if it was laughing at me. There stood my mother in a snow white gown beaming, while the wind ruffled her fair hair.

---

* The writer of this item is a young woman who was a child when she was in the Nazi inferno. Her whole family was liquidated, and she was adopted as a niece to by her Christian "aunt". The girl herself, as well as her adult and child neighbors, with the exception for her "aunt" and "uncle", did not know that she was of Jewish descent. Return

[Pages 284-292]

With My Father the Rabbi Chaim Fine in Russia

Sarah Achicam-Fine (Tel Aviv)

A.

The outbreak of the war found us in the summer of 1939 on vacation in the holiday town of Nalenchov. My father agreed to join me there after much coaxing on my part. When the first news of the war arrived, panic broke out among the vacationers and they started fleeing back to their hometowns. With great difficulties, and after experiencing attacks by anti-Semites along the way, we arrived at midnight in Warsaw, the place where my oldest sister lived. When the whole family gathered together at her place, my father turned to us: "My children, the fire is spreading all over the world; I must go back home (to Radzyn) but you my dear children stay together." We started crying bitterly and begged him to stay with us in Warsaw. My brother-in-law asked him how does he dare at this time and after the bitter experience that we had on our way from Nalenchov to Warsaw, to go back to Radzyn ? All of our pleading was useless and he stuck to his decision: "My dear children it is absolutely forbidden and I cannot, at this terrible moment abandon my city!" At the last moment we tried to convince him to change his mind by saying that he had not abandoned his city at a time of danger, that it was only by chance that he was in Warsaw with his family. He stuck to his decision not to abandon his Jews whom he had served so faithfully for almost twenty five years. He went on his way together with my brother Yitzchak.

— * —

A few days later we found out that our city was already occupied by the Germans. I could not rest for a minute because I knew for sure that the first wrath of the Nazis would be directed to the leader of our community. (Later I found out that they searched for him and demanded that they be told where his hiding place was.) I also knew that my father would force his two sons Zanwill and Yitzchak to flee and to leave him to his fate. My fear was therefore very great, and I decided to return to Radzyn at any price. The main problem was the lack of transportation. However, by chance my sister found out that a carriage had arrived in Warsaw from Radzyn and was planning to return there immediately. My sister contacted its owner and he agreed to take me. That was on Saturday night. Already on my way to Radzyn, I had become acquainted with the Nazis who stopped the wagon after every kilometer and searched it. When they did not find anything they allowed us to continue on our way accompanied by a stream of curses. The trip took until Monday morning.

When I arrived in Radzyn I learned that my two brothers Zanwill and Yitzchak had fled from there on orders from my father and that he himself was hiding there. Menucha, our devoted maid, took me secretly to this hiding place located in a far away alley. After we made sure that that no one was spying on us, we went into a murky room where father was hiding. I realized that the man whom we saw there dressed in the clothes of a woodchopper was my father. He had wrapped his body in a coat that was covered with patches and on his hips had a belt made of simple rope. On his head he wore a wrinkled peasant's turban (Matzyovka) and his face was wrapped in a headscarf so as to hide the disgrace of his shaved beard. My father kissed me and broke out into tears. I tried with all my might to present an indifferent face and encouraged him to flee from the city.

At first I urged him to flee to Warsaw because that was the decision of all my sisters. He refused to do that saying that the children who were there had enough hardships and misfortune, and he did not want to add any further burdens on them. The second possibility, too, to flee to Russia did not satisfy him at first, but after four days of discussion, he agreed to my request that he should cross the border to Russia with me. Those were four difficult days. The city looked to me like an old cemetery. I did not stay even one night in our house but instead stayed with different neighbors and friends From time to time I stole up to our house silently to take out some clothing for myself and my father to wear along the way. First of all I took out the silk robe for the Sabbath and brought it to father's room because I thought that he would not feel right without this garment. (Afterwards when we were already in Brisk and he saw the robe he laughed and told me with fondness: "Did you think that the Soviets would invite me to serve as a Rabbi?")

When we were in our house for the last time I suddenly heard the heavy footsteps of a man coming into the room. "Where is father?" an old man leaning on a cane asked me. At first I was confused by fear and I began mumbling: "he... is in ...Warsaw." The man looked at me and spoke to me affectionately: "Your name is Sarah isn't it? I ask you to tell me the truth. I am entitled too and must see your father". It was hard to refuse this nice old man's request that, as it turned out later, was Reb Yisroel Vinderboim, an old friend of my father. His sincere desire was to see father for the last time. I cannot describe in words that parting meeting of these two old friends that met secretly. The picture of these two old men who hugged one and other, looked into each others eyes and did not let a sound out of their mouths was engraved in my memory. Reb Yisroel wiped the tears from his face, and without uttering a word, left the room. Now I felt that I could not hold out any longer, I simply could not find the words to comfort father after this dramatic meeting. I just stared at his face that had lost it human look.

The next day we started out. The distance from father's hiding place to the carriage was actually short but in my eyes it seemed very long. Anxiously we walked together until we arrived at the place. This was the first time in two weeks that father had gone out of his hiding place and seen the sunshine. He was very excited when we approached the carriage that was waiting for us together with all the passengers. After some hours of traveling we reached a remote village near the Bug River. Quickly we met a non-Jew, who, in exchange for the little money we had, took us on his boat to the other side. He let us off on the bank and left quickly. We hadn't managed to advance two hundred meters when a Russian military sentry appeared who signaled us with his hand to return immediately. After much begging and pleading he took us to police headquarters and from there we were allowed to continue on our way to our destination, the city of Brisk.

B.

We breathed a sigh of relief when after a number of hours we found ourselves on the train that was taking us to Brisk. It is hard to describe the joy in our hearts. I sat close to my dear father's body and kissed him and both of us broke out into tears that welled up from our happiness and thankfulness to the Almighty for the kindness which he has shown to us so far.

It was Friday. We arrived in Brisk at the onset of the Sabbath. I suggested to father that we go to the home of one of his acquaintances, however he refused absolutely "because his appearance was like that of a wood chopper" and preferred instead that we go incognito to a nearby hotel to spend our first night in a foreign country there. Somehow the people of Brisk found out that the Rabbi of Radzyn had managed to escape from the claws of the Nazis and had reached there. At the end of the Sabbath one of his old friends, Mr. Luria took us to his house after much coaxing.

And from Brisk we went on to Bialastock. After a few days my brother Yitzchak, who had arrived in Bialastock before us, managed to find work for me at the municipal hospital. He also managed, with the help of the local authorities, to get us a spacious room where we founded a new family nest abroad.

Father went back quickly to his regular routine, overcoming all the hardships, and took upon himself the important task of being the treasurer of our economy .He became friendly with one of the local rabbis whom he had known previously. He also found a group of old friends and acquaintances whom he visited often. Among them he found Mr. Motel Vinderboim formerly from Radzyn who stood out in his devotion to father.

Thus we passed seven months of relative quiet in Bialastock until the famous registration campaign carried out by the Russian authorities. To register everyone had to decide: to stay there as a Soviet citizen or go back to Germany. My brother Yitzchak became a citizen immediately after he came to Bialastock so my father also got a Russian passport. I, too, took the first steps toward doing so. According to the order that was issued, all refugees living close to the German border had to leave. Father, too, planned to do so and got an invitation from the people in Stolin to come to their city.

However this plan did not work out, because meanwhile they began searching for those refugees who had refused citizenship, or those, like me, who had not managed to obtain it. On one day nearly all the refugees were rounded up. I, too, did not manage to avoid the N.K.V.D despite all of my attempts to hide. They dragged me out of my hiding place in the hospital and sent me together with my brother Zanvil, who had recently returned from the city of Gomel where he had heard that father, in Bialastock, had been sent to the transfer point for those being sent to the Siberian forests. When father heard that, he decided immediately to give up his right to remain a free citizen and quickly packed up his meager possessions (in a bag that also contained a few holy books that he had recently managed to purchase anew) and reached the train station to join us and go together to the place of our deportation.

C.

So again we three found ourselves on the train being carried to the distant forests of Archangelsk in the north of Russia. After a journey that took two weeks, under indescribable conditions, we arrived at our destination and were put up, as were the other families, in poor, ramshackle wooden huts, there to begin life anew in a foreign land. Immediately we were assigned to different tasks that were preformed under the supervision of powerful guards. Of course the living conditions were unbearable especially since most of the deported could never get used to the hard work in the forests in such an extreme climate as that of the far North.

Because of his age, father was excused from working and spent most of his time studying the Torah, reading newspapers and books etc. in Russian. It should be noted that he was very well treated by the local authorities and the guards because they knew that he was a "Yibraiskeh pope" (Jewish religious official). The work supervisors and security guards were impressed with his knowledge of Russian and treated him very respectfully. Our life in the village was relatively quite satisfactory as father's true friends and acquaintances had remained mostly in Brisk and Bialastock and supported him by sending him packages of all kinds of goodies. Therefore we almost did not know what hunger was.

On Purim almost all the residents in the village, especially the senior ones, met at our hut and heard father read the Megillah. Father was very impressed by this event and with tears in his eyes remarked that it was a great reward for him to hear the reading of the Megillah even here in the desolate forests of Russia. (The Megillah itself he got as a present from one of his friends when he stayed in Bialystock.)

One thing distressed him very much when the winter ended: How will we manage during Passover? I tried to convince him that we had no choice here in this foreign country but to make do with a token Seder without scrupulously observing every one of the commandments, especially since he was a sick man, he should not have to suffer from this too. The whole situation bothered him very much but suddenly there was a real miracle: Right after Purim we got a package from Brisk from one of father's friends that contained matzo, raisins for making wine and other foods that were kosher for Passover. The friend had also packed into the package two 'Kosher for

Passover' dishes. Father got very excited and said: "In this package, I have found a Jewish heart!"

However, two months later, when the war between Hitler and Russia broke out and all this aid stopped, and all the connections with the outside world were severed. Now we placed all our hopes on the approaching defeat of Hitler (Cursed be his name!). The relationships at work got worse. The foremen bullied the refugees who were already working under terrible conditions.

D.

Then came the end to forced labor. At the end of August 1941, as the result of negotiations between Russia and the Polish Government in London led by General Sikorsky, an order was published freeing all former Polish citizens who were in the camps. It was declared officially that everyone was free to leave his place and choose any other place to live. Most of the inhabitants were at their wits' end and did not know how to choose a place. My father wanted very much to leave the place and its desolate forests. The reason being that the hardships of the last year had their effect and he felt that his life was drawing to an end and that he wanted fiercely to be buried in a Jewish cemetery and not to be laid to rest in the forests of Archangelsk. Because we had no money we had to postpone our departure until after the holidays.

Here I must relate a very sad happening, if not for which there was a possibility that the lives of father and of our small family might have changed for the better. One day word reached us through one of our village's inhabitants who worked in a neighboring one where there was a telephone that the local authorities had inquired if Rabbi Fine was still in the village. Our acquaintance, who happened by chance to have been in the telephone office answered, for some reason, that we had left the village and its surroundings. In retrospect we were happy with our friend's reply because we suspected that this inquiry was not for our good and maybe was connected with things that had happened to us in Bialastock. Two years later, after father's death, I found out from my brother Zanvil that that inquiry was for our good. This is the story: In the vicinity of a Tashkent and Buchara (My brother Zanvill visited there later) the Polish Regiment of General Anders was organized. One of the organizers was Attorney Marcus who knew father personally and offered him the position of Regimental Rabbi. That phone call was connected with that offer.

E.

We went on our way and after a long trip of tens of kilometers on a wagon, we arrived at the nearest railroad station Following the advice of an acquaintance, we had decided to go to the Caucuses in southern Russia, that being the most suitable place for father because of its warm climate. We hoped that there he would regain his health after almost two years of hardships and moving from place to place. However, the whole matter of the trip was not easy. We spent a couple of days in the station till the train heading for South

Russia arrived. Finally we managed, all three of us including my brother, to squeeze into a train heading for the city of Gorky near the Volga River.

Unfortunately, father's assumptions about the situation in the south turned out to be completely true. The trip to Gorky passed with us making many long stops in the various train stations. After the first such delay the two of us were forced to continue on without my brother. He, seeing that the train would be delayed for a long time at the station, went down into the town to buy food supplies for us. Then, suddenly, a signal was given and the train began to move. Father was so terribly upset that I could not comfort him by assuring him that he too would reach safety

However father's health got worse and worse. The inhuman conditions of our journey made him weaker and weaker, and his legs swelled more every day. In this situation, they suddenly informed us that we would have to proceed from Gorky by river transportation in steam boats. Not having any choice, we got off the train in Gorky to look for a place on one of the boats that sailed southward.

The city of Gorky, an important industrial center, was crowded with refugees from all corners of Russia. There was a well based fear that Hitler's troops would soon reach its gates. The nervousness of its inhabitants grew from day to day concerning the many refugees who were looked upon by all as being stumbling blocks in the way of the troops that flowed as reinforcements to the Moscow front. I tried going into a clinic to get medical help for my father and was met by a response that frightened me terribly: "How dare you wander around the town at this time?" was the doctor's answer. We realized how dangerous it was for us to remain there and lacking a place on the ferry that was about to sail, we were forced to board a tug boat that towed freight, that when father caught sight of it he said: "Why that's a coffin!" In the boat, between the freight, there were puddles of water that reached our knees. I sat father on one of our bundles while I sat the same way and held on to his two swollen legs that I placed on my knees. This is the way we sailed until we reached the city of Saratov.

F.

The cold and the dampness that flowed up from the river seriously affected father's health. He had the address of a relative who lived in Saratov ever since the end of W.W.1 and from whom we had often received packages when we were refugees in a village in the forests of Archangelsk. Father must have felt that his time for parting from the world was drawing close and he turned to me: "My dear daughter, I do not have the strength to continue. We get off here!" I tried to convince him that we only had two days left before reaching our destination, the quiet and beautiful city of Naltzik in the Caucuses. There he could regain his strength, but he was adamant. He explained that in Sartov there is a large Jewish community and he would be able to find a place to have a real Jewish burial .I understood his reasoning and gave in.

At midnight we got off the train. We were the only two people among all of the passenger who got off there and we were dragging heavy bundles that I saw as only being obstacles on our long and difficult way. I understood that we were heading to the house of our relative but father decided that he did not want to disturb those people at night and so we waited, standing in the waiting room of the station which was filled to capacity and we could hardly find one place to stand. I finally found one such place for father while I guarded our bundles on the outside.

Early in the morning I went into the waiting room to take father to our relative's house. Father said that he could not go into anyone's house in the condition that he was in without going to a bath house first. I accompanied him to a nearby bathhouse and from there we went to the relative.

The old wife of the relative, the husband was already at work, greeted us cordially and immediately made up a bed for father so that he could lie down on it to rest a bit. It is almost impossible to describe his relative's joy when he returned from work in the afternoon and recognized father. He was very pleasant and good hearted, and even though his living conditions and income were very meager, he gave us one of his two narrow bedrooms and promised to be our host until the troubles subsided. He added: "If Hitler, God curse him, does not reach Saratov first."

G.

Despite the relative quiet, father's condition got worse from day to day. I saw all the signs that father would not survive under these difficult conditions in a primitive Russian apartment where terrible cold prevailed and the walls were full of moisture. One of the greatest problems that stood before me was that of heating the room which did not have any heating stove and was heated only by a kerosene cooking stove that also served for lighting. The relatives supplied us with every thing we needed for father, but there was a difficult problem obtaining kerosene at that time. I had to stand on line all night so as to get a small can of kerosene in the morning when the store opened. I remember that on one of the nights when I left the line to peek into father's room and ask how he was coming along, he turned to me and said: "My daughter, when you leave the room, please wish me goodbye." He felt that his end was drawing near. I tried to believe that he would somehow still overcome his sickness, regain his health and we would leave Russia and return home. Nothing I ever had to do for father was ever difficult for me, therefore I decided to make every effort to get him into a hospital. That looked like a dream to me as all the hospitals were filled with wounded soldiers and it was impossible to imagine that at such a time they would let an aged citizen enter a hospital. Our relatives too, were not inclined to believe that possible and later, after father's death, I found out why. The private doctor, whom the relatives had once called in for father in my absence, had determined that there was no hope for him to survive. This they hid from me. However because of my great belief that father could still recover, I managed to convince the doctors in the Municipal Health Bureau to accede to my request even though I did not know how to speak Russian. I turned to them with a bitter and desperate cry:" Save my father! He is all I have left now that my entire family is in Hitler's hands and you know what that means." They understood my terrible pain and agreed to send an ambulance immediately to move my father to the hospital.

Father was already so weak that it was hard for him to speak. When I told him about the hospital he was surprised and almost could not believe what I told him. He knew that he was going to die. He did not eat a thing because he could not digest even the lightest food. I remember one incident that moved me very deeply: Two days before father was taken to the hospital, at a time when the living conditions were very difficult in Russia, a Jew appeared before us in our house with a slaughtered chicken. He had brought it on hearing in his town that the Rabbi of Radzyn was in Sartov and was very seriously ill. He emphasized a number of times that the fowl was strictly Kosher, "If the Rabbi will eat the fowl and the soup he will recover."

When father was taken into the hospital it became known in all the wards where there were many Jewish patients from among the refugees who had been hospitalized earlier. They were interested in his fate until the last minutes of his life. The next morning I was allowed to visit him for only a very short time. However, I succeeded in staying by his bed, which was located in one of the long corridors of the hospital, for three consecutive weeks until his passing despite the ban on being there, especially for a civilian whose identity was not certain.

Father did not survive, and at the end of the Sabbath on the 14th of Kislev he began to expire. My dear father barely managed to say "My dear daughter you will get to see good yet." When he could not continue speaking, he squeezed my hand, fell back on the bed and breathed his last breath. His final request was fulfilled when he was buried properly according to the Jewish law in the cemetery of the town of Saratov.

—— * ——

Thanks to my father, who was also my teacher and my spiritual guide on the difficult and complicated road of life I have the privilege, (with the help of my dear husband) to perpetuate my father's memory in these lines, and to thank (as was the sincere wish of my late father) all those who survived everywhere on their interest in the fate of my father at the time of his exile in the forests of Archangelsk.

[Pages 292-294]

My Return Home

Ethel Keitelgisser (Holon, Israel)

It happened in the year 1939, a few days before World War II broke out. I said goodbye to my whole family; everyone accompanied me out of the house. My religious mother quietly mumbled a few words. I only heard the word "Shomer Yisroel" (Guardian of Israel). Father went with me through Warszawa Street up to the bus station. He was silent all the way. There was already panic in the town and I was going home to my husband and children in Galitzia where I lived at that time. I embraced my father, we kissed and I went up onto the bus. When I was already seated in my place my father said: "If a war really breaks out, take your family and come right back. At such a time let us all be together, for God's sake".

___*___

Fate drove me and my family to Russia. Like abandoned dogs we wandered to all the corners of that great land. However at time of need or of suffering my soul was in Radzyn.

When working in the thick forests of Siberia, I saw my home. When sleeping under the free sky of Kazakhstan I saw the stars that were shining at the same time over Radzyn. In the long hungry months when I saw my children flickering and expiring I heard my mother reciting the Watchman of Israel prayer. We survived because the idea never left us that our home is waiting for us there in the Polish Shtetl together with a father and mother and a place to live and they are all waiting for the lost daughter to turn up.

The day arrived on which tired, hungry, abandoned, homeless and devastated, I fled home. The train snaked its way over the familiar Polish roads, from Stetchin to Lodz and from Lodz to Warsaw, Siedlce, Lukow and to Radzyn.

___*___

It was at five o'clock on a glorious May morning in 1946. I stood glued to the train window, my heart almost bursting from excitement. Smaller and larger familiar woods and there is the familiar bridge! There is the crooked path that leads to Bedalna ………

There was a lot of movement in the train. Some non-Jews got off and I followed them. The wagon with a horse followed along and stopped at exactly the same spot to where my father had accompanied me to six years ago.

I stood there and felt my feet collapsing under me. Where to go to? What is through the ruined Warszawa Street. People approached me who had strange non-Jewish faces and looked at me inquisitively.

I am standing in front of my father's house, in front of my longed for home, in front of the longed for magic that that kept me alive in the Siberian forests, in front of the home of my youth.

The shutters are closed. I guess they are still asleep. It is that house, that yard, that wood shed. There is the street that leads to the orchard and the apple tree that stands under the window and gives off the smell of apple blossoms. Everything is alive and growing as it was before. But what happened? Is there no one left from the big family to take in the homeless daughter? And maybe there is no one left alive from Shia Shabashiner's family?

However the shutters did open and a young Shikse (non-Jewish girl) looked at me curiously. Then an older non-Jewish woman came out and invited me into the house. I became dizzy the minute I stepped into the kitchen. In the corner, where my mother would sit every day praying, there hung a large Christian picture. I left and went immediately to my sister's (Lazar family) house. The printing machines were clattering. All the rooms were filled with boxes of type for setting. The oldest employee must have recognized me because his first words were "Payne Zishe! (Madam Zishe) You are alive?" He asked me to sit down. I looked around and saw a large mirror that had belonged to my sister and in it I could see the faces, the last despairing and suffering looks of the entire Lozer family.

A non-Jewish neighbor took me into her house and tried to calm me. After which she nonchalantly told me that my father and the whole family had been placed on a wagon on the 18th of November 1943 and sent away to Mezritsh. My father was blind and his head was tied up in a kerchief. However they returned quickly. It seems that on the way all of them were shot immediately.

This made me burst into tears that flowed unceasingly for all those years of hardship, hunger and suffering. Why father did you not take your daughter with you so that we could all be together?

Shattered, I left Radzyn and after a number of days of wandering through various ruined towns I returned to my husband and children in Shtetchin.

I resolved to leave Poland for ever.

———

[Pages 294-300]

Radzyn After the Destruction

Rachel Zaltshtein-Freter(Rishon Ltzion- Israel)

An the end of July 1944, shortly after the liberation of Radzyn by the Russian Army, I came back there from Mezritsh on a freight truck and was very happy when it stopped near Tsheplinsky's mill. I believed I would immediately meet Salke Shtarkman and Golde Fal here. Holding my breath, I knocked on the door. My heart was beating rapidly! The door will open soon and Salke will be standing in front of me! We will both be very happy because we haven't seen each other for a long time. Her grandmother, grandfather and her sisters too will be delighted to see me. They will all be anxious to hear about my experience in the Soviet Union. But I will not tell them too much, because I want to feel at home as quickly as possible. The door opens and a non-Jewish girl asks me what I want. What do I want from her? Nothing! She, seeing that I do not answer immediately, slams the door shut in front of my nose, and I remain standing for a while not knowing what to do.

Suddenly it occurs to me: Go into Golde Fal and you will certainly hear about everyone. I go to Golde and knock on the door. The door opens and Golde is not standing there, nor is it her mother, nor anyone else from the family. Again it is a non-Jewess! What has happened here? Where am I? Where are they? I look around the yard. There are some children playing there. I look for a Jewish face but to no avail. I ask myself again: Where are the Jews from here? They lived here for many years, and now all of a sudden everything has disappeared. I think: Maybe they now live in the center of the shtetl itself. I go with my heart beating into the center of the town. The road is the same, so near and familiar, and yet I am frightened. As I walk along, I pass the park of which I was so fond. I spent all my youthful years in that park, but now it stands there so lonely as if it wants to say something very sad. Instead of running back home as quickly as possible and being happy, I suddenly do not want to get there. I want to be far away from my former home.

I don't know how it happened, that while being near the market place where our house was located, I go up instead to Ostroweicka Street. I walk along and see that almost all of the shops are open. The street is very quiet, and there is very little traffic, and I don't see one Jew. What has happened? Where are our Radzyner Jews? I go into one shop and into a second and third one. The shops are still shops, but there is not a Jew in them, only Pollocks. In the end I come into the market place and I think surely there is a Pollock in our shop too. To my joy I did not meet a non-Jew there. A bomb had destroyed our whole building.

I walk on further. Near Yitzchak Gellerman's business too, there stands a non-Jew. Beryl Rubinstein's tavern is the same tavern but Berl Rubinstein does not stand there, now a Christian stands there. The same thing happens at Yossel Sziteh's place. What shall I do? Where can I go? I remain standing and think: where can I find a Jew in the Jewish shtetl of Radzyn? At that moment, suddenly, a thought occurs to me, that I should go up to Kalushinski's and from them I will find out if there is at least one Jew left in the shtetl. I head for Kalushinski's business which is not too far away. I come in and meet Mrs. Kalushinski behind the counter. She, on seeing me, pretends to be very happy.

"I am happy that at least you have remained alive", she says. Those words struck like an axe on my head. That means that I am the only one who has remained alive? Yes! That is what it means. I felt that the earth on which I was standing had suddenly started burning under me, and my feet begin to wobble.

I asked, "Are there any other Jews in the town?" "Only a few" she answered. She does not know who they are. She knows only one of them, Meir Turkeltaub. I thanked her and left the shop. To this day I do not know how I managed to continue walking. I started in the direction of Meir Turkeltaub when suddenly I saw a Jew but I did not recognize him. He, seeing a Jewish woman, stopped me with the question: "Where are you going?" I remained frozen to the spot. Is this really a Jew? I ask myself after so much roaming around in the streets of Radzyn. He asks me again: "Are you from Radzyn?" I reply: "Berl Fretter is my father." "Then come with me," he answers.

I gladly go with him even though I don't know who he is. I think about what is happening to me. I thought that I knew all the Jews in Radzyn, and it turns out that the first Jew that I meet I do not recognize. As it turns out later, this Jew was the Radzyner Rabbi's son-in-law. I follow him but am afraid to ask him whether my father is still alive. Somehow my mouth refuses to function, and a terrible fear overcomes me. I am afraid to ask the question: Where are all the Jews from Radzyn, all those who lived here for such a long time and have suddenly disappeared? Silently he leads me to Sarah Fass. The door opens and I see a few Jews, Sarah Fass, her sister and a few others. Seeing me, they all run over and start questioning me. But I do not answer them. What happened to me? I do not know.

When I opened my eyes, Sarah Fass was standing near me. She asked me if I wanted anything. I did not understand her question. What has happened to me? Where am I? Am I lying in bed? Little by little I begin to understand that the few Jews that are here are all the survivors from our beloved shtetl Radzyn. All the others have perished including my father and mother, brothers and sisters, grandfather, uncles, aunts and their children. I realize that I am the only one left alive. There was only one thing I could not understand. Why did I survive?

Two, three days passed. I heard many stories about the Majdanek, Treblinka and Auschwitz extermination camps where the Hitler beasts burned six million Jews whose only sin was that they were Jews. I learned later that my father Beryl Fretter also died in the 'infamous' Auschwitz extermination camp.

While walking in the street one day, I met the wife of the deceased Chomatshevky who was also "very happy that I had survived." From her I learned that Vientkovsky, a non-Jewish lawyer, had recently returned from the Auschwitz extermination camp where he was together with my father. Before that I new that my father had been arrested in Radzyn together with seventeen Poles among whom was the above mentioned Vientskovsky the lawyer, the former head of the Radzyner Municipal Council, an infamous Jew hater. The Poles remained alive and came back, but without my father.

I come into his house. He greets me very politely. He too is very happy that I have remained alive. Yes, I know what he is so happy about. He reached his anti-Semitic goal: Radzyn is 'Yudenrein' (clean of Jews).

In answer to my question about how my father spent his last days in the camp, he answered me in a very quiet voice as if it was a very normal matter. "It was on Sunday that they gathered us into a big hall. We all sat around on benches. In the middle of the hall there was a large table. A number of German officers entered leading your father and a big dog from a wolf like breed. Then the entertainment began for them. Your father must fight with this big dog. The "play" did not last very long, and your father lay dead with torn off pieces of flesh." I did not hear anything further that he told me. I remained seated and saw before my eyes my dear father in a pool of blood with torn out pieces of flesh and with the blood still dripping. His soul expires with the last drops of blood and I hear his final words: "Rachel! Take revenge for my blood."

For a long time after that, I wandered around the harvested fields and thought about what to do and to whom to turn. Suddenly and idea came to me: You have nothing more to do in Radzyn! Go to the front line and take revenge for your father's spilled blood and for the blood of all the Jews!

Without even going into my house, I decided to join the Red Army. It wasn't so easy for me to be accepted in the Red Army. But because the Colonel with whom I spoke was Jewish and understood my desire for revenge, he made it easier for me to join the Red Army and I became a nurse.

We were always some 120 kilometers from the front line and pushing forward toward Germany. Our medical unit pushed forward together behind the rest of the army and after a short while we crossed the German border.

On one lovely February morning (1945) we entered the first German village. The streets were deadly quiet. There was not a soul to be seen. The streets were white with loose feathers, devastated houses, and tattered furniture. My heart burst with joy. I thought: this is exactly how our town Radzyn looked after the German beasts carried out their pogrom there. At least let them, too, know in the end, how it feels. Some time later when I saw a park in another German town with children playing, I stopped, amazed, and could not continue moving on. I thought that if I had a revolver I would shoot a number of them right on the spot even though I know that these children were not guilty. I would want the German mothers to feel the pain that our mothers felt when their children were torn away from them and murdered in front of them.

I knew that I would be arrested for that, but at least I would have a chance to reveal at the trial before the Russian judges, the whole terrible history of our holocaust. How my heart bleeds for our children. Why did our children not have the right to live and to play? With my head lowered I left the park and the children continued playing.

Berel Freter

___*___

On May the ninth 1945, about four o'clock in the morning, the army doctor wakes me up, despite his knowing that I am miserable because I have lost everything. He tells me that the war has ended and that there is no more bloodshed. I stand in front of him with my head lowered: "Yes doctor," I tell him "for me the war ended a long time ago and our blood is not shed any longer, our town of Radzyn ended its life a long time ago."

A day later we arrived in Berlin. The Russian flag flutters over the Reichstag. Everyone is dancing and kissing, and the orchestra is playing. Everyone is happy.

But all that does not concern me. I am sad. I see before my eyes the murdered shtetl of Radzyn. I see my father's body torn up by the wolfish dogs. His blood cries out to me: "You have no right to be happy. This is not your celebration." I am choked by tears. My heart is torn to shreds. I want to scream from pain, but who cares that my people have been murdered.

I decide to go back to Radzyn. That is still my real home. There are only a few Jews there, but they are Jews. With them I have a common language, shared feelings, one heart. I go in to the Jewish colonel and tell him that I want to go home immediately, and that I have nothing further to do here. He looks at me, and we have a long conversation like father and daughter. He understands me and my feelings very well. He provides me with a troop transport that goes all the way to Lukow. I am overcome by his fatherly concern for me. We part, and he wishes me good luck in the future, but can people like me ever be happy in life?

—— * ——

I find myself for the second time in our Radzyn. I meet more Jews than I did the last time but for them there is no normal life in the town. Everyone knows that, sooner or later, they will leave Radzyn. There are a number of anti-Semitic attacks. One of them ended with the murder of Mrs. Greenblatt, the widow of Yechezkiel Greenblatt (who was already missing both legs). This opened our eyes. We Jews have no reason to stay here, and we must take our walking sticks in hand again. We hire a wagon to carry Mrs. Greenblatt to her place of eternal rest in the Radzyn cemetery accompanied by a number of Russian soldiers with automatic weapons in their hands. We almost did not recognize the cemetery. Half the place was plowed up and had corn growing. Cows are grazing on the other half, and there is not a sign of a tombstone. In answer to our question as to why he is pasturing his cows there the shepherd answers: "There's good grass here."

With great sadness, we leave the Jewish cemetery for the last time. What once was does not exist anymore. Our return has made it clear to us that we have nothing more to do here. The air is stifling. For years I dreamt about the shtetl, but now everything is strange to us, and we must escape from here.

I wait impatiently at the Bedlano station for the train which will take me, away from Radzyn, my birth place, as fast as possible and forever.

———————

[Pages 301-304]

On the Ruins of My Shtetl

Tzvi Leiberson (Hadera, Israel)

In August of 1944 the battleground came close to Warsaw. We are lying in a bunker some eighteen kilometers from Warsaw. After violent slaughter on both sides of our bunker that lasted for weeks, we manage, despite the great danger, to run away from there and go over to the Russian troops on the eastern side. Many dead soldiers and slaughtered horses lie along the way. We run between fire, smoke, and dust. We see no one. Apparently the troops are dug into shelters.

Approximately a kilometer from the front line we are overtaken by the Soviets, and after interrogation, they send us to Minsk Mazowieke. There we meet the first few Jews who have also just come out of the different bunkers.

Two days later we, my wife and our son and I, as well as my wife's two sisters decide to go to Radzyn. The road back is difficult and all the roads are filled with soldiers on both sides. When we reach Lukow, we decide to get off. At the edge of the town we are greeted by Poles shouting "Yastshe szion" (They are still alive!). In the town itself we are greeted by Christians yelling: "They are coming out of the woods like mushrooms after the rain".

Fatigued and starving from the trip, we found a few Jews who had survived and were wandering around like shadows on the ruins of the town. The first questions we asked was do they know anything about Radzyn? Has anyone remained alive and are any of them in Radzyn? We find out that there are a few, but they do not know their names. Our curiosity grows. We are prepared to go to Radzyn immediately, but the Jews from Lukow do not let us go at night because it is too dangerous.

I slept very little that night. I was burning with desire to get home as soon as possible. In the morning an army truck took us speedily in the direction of Radzyn. The villages between Lukow and Radzyn stood untouched. In the village of Stach where many Jews, including both merchants and farmers had lived, and where Jewish coachmen used to stop to give their horses something to eat and down a glass of whiskey themselves, there was not one Jew left. A little further on we passed through the village of Ulan, where a mill, operated by Jews, had clattered rhythmically. Now it did so without any Jews. We approach the pine forest of Biala from which anxiety echoes. On the left side, opposite the forest, dogs belonging to the peasants can be heard barking from the Polish cabins. Suddenly a thought comes to me. How many Jews tried to hide deep in the forest? How much Jewish groaning and crying was swallowed up by the forest.

The truck takes us further. The smell of freshly cut grain tied up in sheaves shows us that it is harvest time. From a distance we can already see the Radzyn sawmill. Suddenly fear overcomes me. I am afraid that in a few minutes I will see that in my home town there are empty streets with the burnt ruins of empty houses.

The truck stops abruptly by the old theatre. Slowly we climb down from the vehicle, and with the last of our strength drag our feet. Our bodies are exhausted and thin like reeds, we are shadows of human beings. We start moving but where to? Where will the first door open to us?

Along the way I see familiar non-Jewish faces that look at us curiously. I see that their houses stand untouched as if nothing had ever happened: the verandas are green up to the edge of the roof with potted plants standing in the windows. Non-Jewish children run around playing in the streets. A mother calls to one of them 'sinku' (my little son) and it is hard to imagine that not far from here lay the ruins of Jewish Radzyn where many generations of life have been torn up by the roots. We ask a non-Jew if there are any Jews and we get the answer: "There are still more than enough". We walk through the length of Warszawa St. Only non-Jewish faces look out at us from the Jewish houses. We have seen many non-Jews but not one Jew.

A few minutes later we open the door of the first Jewish house, the one belonging to Blumenkoff's. I can only hear the shrieking of names and see the shadows of people kissing and hugging each other. For many minutes no one spoke a word only sobbed mournfully. So I found myself in the first Jewish home in the shtetl, that belonging to the two sisters Zloteh and Sarah Fass, the wives of the Blumenkoff's brothers. The men had perished but the women managed to survive along with their children.

Altogether we were twenty one people there. The darkness moved in and gloom descended on all of us. The street became silent. There is no movement. From time to time gunfire is heard and the echoes of artillery from the Demblin   front   sector. There, we, the remnants of the four thousand Jews from our shtetl, sit and tell stories about our experiences. Although the clock shows that it is past midnight, and we are all tired from our trip, we cannot fall asleep. We want to know everything. Under what circumstances had our friends perished? How did every one of them struggle until his final moments?

The loud movement wakes us up after we have just gone asleep. In the blue of the morning, we go out into the street. Masses of soldiers march back from the Demblin front. We become depressed. The non-Jews spread a rumor saying that the Germans have broken through on the Demblin front. We question some Russian soldiers but they remain silent. We begin to think that maybe we will again fall into German hands. However the tension subsides when fresh troops arrive, heading in the opposite direction toward Demblin.

On that same day I go out to look at the ruins. The Jewish streets, Szkolna, Kashiwa, Kotlarska, Kalen, the First and Second Market and almost all of Kozia Street are burnt. Only the outside walls are left from the houses built of bricks, and nothing is left of the wooden cottages. Many places are still smoldering from the firebombs that the Germans dropped as they retreated. I walk along Szkolna Street and remain standing by the house in which I was born; a complete ruin. I continue on and stop as if glued to the earth, by the ruins of the Yiddish School. The memory of all the Jewish children heading here from all directions together with the teachers Freedman and Blechovitz, flashes before my eyes. A bit further on I see the ruins of the house of Benjamin Yoresh Rubinstein a great tailor of second hand clothing, who was a member of the biggest family in town. There were fourteen children, twelve of them married daughters who had so many grandchildren. But now no one is left.

A few minutes later I find myself standing among the burnt walls of the synagogue and the study house. Where are all the people who used to study here? I wander around some more but the emptiness drives me back to the two Jews who are sitting and waiting for me. The night has brought us together again in the empty hut.

—— * ——

We stayed in Radzyn some time longer and felt more and more uncomfortable. We were waiting for the war to end quickly so that we could leave the cursed Polish soil saturated with so much Jewish blood.

[Pages 304-305]

Radzyn in 1946 - After the Destruction

Zevel Zaltstein (Rishon Le'tzion)

Right after my return from the Soviet Union to Lodi (Poland) on Passover 1946, I decided to go to Radzyn. I knew that this involved mortal danger because the Lublin district was the most dangerous of all and General Anders' gangs ruled the province after the war and murdered the remaining Jewish survivors.

On a nice spring evening, at the end of April, I went by train to Warsaw and from there to Radzyn. On the train, I huddled into a corner so that I would not be not be too noticeable, because, after all I am a Jew. When we finally got close to Radzyn, it had dawned. I remembered how on such spring mornings we used to get up from bed when everything around us was still sleeping and unseen by anyone in the house, slip out and go to the Visnitz Highway. We carried with us books and newspapers. We became intoxicated by the odors that surrounded us and we would sit reading this way in the fields for a few hours.

Now my heart starts beating more rapidly. Will I meet anyone in the town of those who are connected with these memories?

The train suddenly begins to slow down and it stops at... Bedlano! Yes that's it. It was only six and a half years ago that I had arrived in Radzyn on foot and tired from Warsaw, where I had escaped from the oncoming enemy. This was the first bloody Sabbath in the town when the German planes sowed death and destruction. I then took my wanderers' stick in hand, parted from my parents and went to the eastern border. Now I am coming back. Will I meet at least someone? The Radzyn station gives little reason for optimism. Where are all the Jewish horse cab drivers? Of course I did not dare ask anyone such a question

The cab that took me from the station stops suddenly in the middle of the town. The streets are silent, and there is no one to be seen. I walk silently as if not wanting to wake up any of my dear Radzyner Jews. I go into Warszawska St. and turn to Sarah Fass' house. Even in Lodz we Radzyners said that there is only one house in Radzyn to which everyone can come to, that of Sarah Fass. There we called it the Fass Collective. I knock on the door and soon find myself shaking the hand of Sarah Fass and a few other surviving Jews. Sarah is like a mother to us all.

Two hours later I am again outside. I walk along my heart beating loudly. Here is that street where my Melamed (teacher) Dovid Chana's, lived. Here is the bakery that belonged to Kovelblum. I am afraid of going any further. It is hard for me to get closer to the house in which I was born and spent my early years. I am afraid of going too close. But maybe someone has remained alive there. I go closer. There is the entrance and there are the two windows through which I looked out at the people strolling by. A bit further on is Yisroelke Saltzer's alley. There too lived his sisters and parents, also Mateh Bashes with her sons and daughters. Everything was so near and familiar. Where did that luscious life disappear to?

I knock on the door of the house where I was born. An old non-Jewish woman opens the door and asks who I am. I answer that I was born in that house. She becomes very excited but does not lose control. She tells me immediately that she has invested much money in redecorating the rooms. She does not forget to praise the Hitlerites who were such fine people. They knew how to maintain order unlike the new Polish government. I could not take it for long and left quickly passing through the store that had belonged to Neche Koppelman (in our building). There I saw a Christian store keeper wrapping his merchandise in the pages of a Gomorra. That is what the reality looks like.

I stayed in the Shtetl only a short time longer, because I could not find any rest. I left there forever.

[Pages 306-308]

Radzyner Jews in the Partisan Groups

Tzvi Leiberson (Hadera, Israel)

With the first news about the liquidation of the Warsaw Ghetto, the center of Polish Jewry, the Jews of Radzyn began to understand that what was involved was the liquidation of all of Polish Jewry. At first many Jews believed the German promises that those Jews being taken out of their towns were being taken only to work. The later information confirmed that they were being taken out to be gassed and cremated.

Many Jews in Radzyn began to think about resistance. The forests that surrounded the town and stretched for many kilometers in all directions were suitable terrain for partisan groups. As a result, there was a demand for weapons among the Jewish youth. Weapons became the dream of all the Jewish youth that did not want to go like sheep to slaughter.

In the winter of 1942, the first partisan groups were formed and many Jewish young people went out to the forests. The most important group was organized by Yitzchak Kleinman. They left the town in January of 1943 and dug into two bunkers in the woods between Radzyn and Kotzk not far from the village of Stara Wiesz. Fifteen people were housed in each bunker.

A short time later one of these two groups, with Kleinman in command, went far away to obtain arms in return for money. The plan was that if they succeeded the second group would follow the same course. The mediator for this transaction was a Polish peasant who would receive a lot of money in return for his services. The group obtained fifteen guns for a large sum of money,

The way back was very difficult. During the day they had to lie in previously prepared hiding places, and at night they continued on their way back to the bunker. But when they finally got back they did not find their comrades from the first bunker. It had been blown up by grenades. A little later they found out that the Germans had discovered the footprints that led to the bunker. Thirteen Jews were killed by German grenades that were thrown into it. The two surviving Jews, one Moishe Shtestshinaz and second a fellow from Warsaw were tortured to death by the German beasts.

The Partisan group, led by Kleinman, began operating in that area at the end of February. In their first bold attack, they killed two Gestapo members. In March they attacked a small milk processing plant located on the landowners estate near Stara Wiesz. The director of the factory, a Polish born German ,was shot and barrels of cheese and butter were taken away transported by horse and wagon from the landowners' estate to the forest. The horse and wagon were set free on other roundabout roads so as to cover its tracks.

The Jewish hospital in Meseritz

In that same forest there was another bunker with sixteen Jews from Kotzk. A peasant discovered this and reported it to the Germans. The German gendarmes captured them alive and shot them on the spot. Kleinman's partisan group decided to take revenge on the peasant. One night all the partisans went armed to that peasant's house, locked everything from the outside and set it on fire from all sides. The peasant and his whole family perished in the flames.

At almost the same time they also carried out a very bold attack on the Radzyn- Kotzk highway. A taxi carrying three high military officials was stopped by blocking of the road. They were shot by the partisans and their arms and uniforms confiscated.

Fate had it that Kleinman came down with typhus. He had to go back to Mezritsh ghetto and enter the Jewish Hospital. As part of a campaign to liquidate the Jews in Mezritsh the patients were taken out of the hospital and the Radzyner partisan hero was killed.

— * —

Another group of partisans operated in the woods between Radzyn and Wisnitz headed by Liebl Lev and Laizer Pantshak. Many Radzyners were killed in a battle with a group of Germans that took place in the winter of 1943 including Laizer Pantshak. Liebl Lev and some other Radzyners managed to get organized in another bunker. This group operated in that area until the summer of 1944, the summer before the liberation, but this group was liquidated by a group of Polish anti-Semitic partisans from the "Armia Krayowa"(A.K.).

Many Radzyner Jews fought in various Polish and Ukrainian areas to which fate and circumstances had carried them. In that way Dina Rosenwald took an active part in the Vilna Circle. Unfortunately, I do no have any details about her activities.

Yaakov Puntshak, who was later killed in a traffic accident in Tel-Aviv, participated in many partisan activities that took place in different areas. After the liberation he was decorated by the Polish government for his outstanding acts of heroism. He also played an admirable role in the Polish Army.

The Radzyner Moshe Agman played a leading role among the Ukrainian partisans. The Germans offered a heavy reward for him. He was captured and his body was left hanging for three days.

Thus the Radzyner young Jewish heroes shed their blood in the Polish forests, in the struggle against the German beasts. Their memories will be inscribed forever in the memory of our people.

Precis: Radzyner Jews in the Partisan Groups

When the news of the liquidation of the Warsaw Ghetto reached Radzyn, its Jews began to think about resistance. The first Partisan groups were established in the winter of 1942.

The most significant of these groups was organized by Yitzchak Kleinman. In January of 1943 they left the town and took up positions in two bunkers in the forests between Radzyn and Kotsk with 15 people in each and went away to buy fifteen rifles. The way back was very difficult and took a long time because they could advance only under the cover of darkness. When they finally returned they found that the bunker of the other group had been blown up and thirteen of its inhabitants killed by grenades. The two that survived were then tortured to death by the Germans.

The partisans led by Kleinman began operating in that area and killed two Gestapo agents and later attacked a dairy products plant, killed its director, a Polish born German, and stole some merchandise which they transferred to their comrades in forest.

In that same forest there was another bunker with 16 Jews from Kotzk who were discovered by a peasant and shot by the German gendarmes. Klineman's group decided to take revenge on the peasant and set his house on fire killing him and his whole family. They also carried out a daring attack on the Radzyn-Kotzk highway, blocked the road of a taxi carrying three high ranking military personnel, shot and killed them. About this time Yitzchak Kleinman came down with typhus fever and had to go back to the Jewish Hospital in Mezritsh. He was killed later in an attack on the Jewish community.

——*——

In the winter of 1943 another partisan group led by Liebl Lev and Laizer Pontshak battled a group of Germans in the forests between Radzyn and Visnitz. Many Radzyner were killed including Pontshak. Lev and some others fled and took refuge in another bunker. This group operated in this area until the liberation in summer of 1944 when they were liquidated by a group of Polish anti-Semitic Partisans from the "Armyia Krayowa" (A.K).

Many Jews from Radzyn fought in various other Polish and Ukrainian areas including Dinah Rosenwald of the Vilna who fought in and around Vilna.

One of the persons most active in the Partisan movement was Yaakov Puntshak who died later in a traffic accident in Tel-Aviv. After the liberation he was rewarded by the Polish government for his bravery. Moshe Agman took a leading role in the Partisan movement in the Ukraine but was captured and hanged.

This is how the Radzyner heroes contributed their blood in the struggle with the German beast. Their memory will be inscribed forever in the memory of our nation for eternity.

————

[Pages 309-311]

Liebl Lev Leader of the Radzyn Partisan Group

Shifra Lev (Tel Aviv)

Liebl Lev, my brother, was born in Radzyn in 1912. His childhood was spent in the Polish village of Pashki near Radzyn. He went from there to Warsaw where he became active in the labor movement especially in ranks of the leather workers. He was prominent and greatly admired in the Worker's Movement.

All my life I observed my brother Leibl Lev from up close and he appeared like a figure sculpted from bronze. He was honest and courageous in thought and in deed. I would think how come that this modest fellow, raised in a small Polish village, has such a rich inner world, such dignity, such pride? Later, especially in those last months of long dark nights at the end of 1939, those terrible nights of self reckoning, I got to know him even better and deeper and was impressed by his belief, his revolutionary zeal, also by his enormous sorrow for his tortured people.

Therefore, added to the sorrow of losing such a brother, there came the thought: Is it possible that he too allowed himself to be led like a sheep to slaughter? It became a consolation and an encouragement for me when I learned that my wonderful brother maintained his brave and human appearance until the very end; that he was active as a partisan in the Radzyn forest until 1943 and that heroic acts can be attributed to his doing.

This is what Feigele Pantshick, then fourteen years old, told us:

"In November of 1942 they gathered together all the Jews in Radzyn in the synagogue and shipped them off to Mezritsh. Two hundred Jews remained behind who worked on German worksites. I, too, remained behind and for a month was together with my uncles Gershon Henich Pantshik, and Herzl Pantshik and their families. At that time, our cousin Leible Lev came to us from the forest carrying a rifle on his shoulder. He had been with the partisans for a long time and he called on all of us to come to the forest. He was courageous and sure that we would survive. He told us that they were a large armed group and they carried out important actions. We decided together with him that he should come to get us before the last selection. At the appointed time, Gershon Henich Pantshik, Laizer Pantshik, Avremele and Beryl Pantshik from Fashke, the two Tunkleswartz brothers and a number of other boys from Radzyn joined him in the forest.

They got a bunker for me from a Pole in village of Branich. There I met Gedaliah Goldwasser's wife. After a short time the Pole moved her to another bunker and some days later he was supposed to move me there. Once, on a Sunday morning, when the Pole went to church, his mother came in to me with tears in her eyes and said: "Run away as fast as you can because they want to drown you in the river today in the same way that they drowned that other woman: I cannot go to the other world with such a sin on my soul."

I did not have any money because the Pole had taken all that I had, but I ran away without knowing the way. I ran away to the shtetl of Vahin and from there to the ghetto in Mezritsh. There I met Gershon Pantshik's wife, Chava Katz. She too had been hidden out in a bunker and was driven out by a Pole. Six or seven months later Gershon came back from the partisans and stayed in the ghetto tying his fate to that of his wife and children. He told us a lot about the heroic deeds of our Leible Lev.

From Mezritsh we were deported to Majdanek. There Chava Katz and her younger child were killed. Her older daughter Chanaleh and I were sent to Auschwitz. There she came down with typhus. I did not see her after that. Once when going to work there I met Gershon Henoch by chance. He was in a terrible state, looked like a skeleton and could hardly walk. He asked me for a piece of bread but unfortunately I did not have any. His last words to me were: "Hold On!"

Zviah Pantshek, Hershel Pantshek's wife, tells: "In 1942 our cousin Leible Lev was hidden by a Polish school friend in the village of Pashke. We sent him some food and clothes but he got tired of hiding out so he got in touch with some partisans in the forest and went to join them. A few times after that he came to Radzyn and called on the young people to go into the forest, and many went with him. Before the last call I hid in a bunker belonging to a settler in the town of Brasaveh near the forest.

Leible Lev's group carried out different campaigns at that time. I know a lot about one of them: The group 'led out' two horses belonging to a certain rich peasant called Pashkovski. The peasants informed the S.S. as to where they were and the S.S. caught them near the village of Bialka near Radzyn. A fierce battle ensued in which a number of Germans were killed. Among the Partisans only Laizer Pantshek fell, the others escaped.

Many Polish partisans from the anti-Semitic A.K. Division gathered in my landlord's house. Lying in the cellar under the house I would listen with tense nerves to everything that they said. On a certain day in November of 1943, I heard how the gentiles from the A.K. were drinking and telling happily that they had already succeeded in liquidating all the Jewish Partisans from Pashke (this is what they called the Radzyn partisans after the name of the village in which they had hidden out at the beginning). Our hero Liebl Lev was among those killed. They went on to tell that when they discovered their hiding place in the forest they ordered the Jews to surrender which they absolutely refused to do. A violent battle ensued and all the Jewish partisans were killed by exploding grenades.

This is how my only brother Leible Lev lived and died.

The Holocaust Survivors from Radzyn

On the road to their homeland in Israel and to other countries
(According to material provided by Tzvi Liberzon)

Spring 1945. The battle lines move deeper and deeper into German territory and the Polish territories have fewer and fewer Russian troops: The Soviets are preparing for their grand offensive against Berlin that will be the final blow to Hitlerism.

The Russian Air Force unit, which was stationed in Radzyn at the aerodrome in the Marianka suburb, was sent westward, and only a few Russian military personnel remained. The reactionary Polish Underground Organization, as well as the partisan "Armye Kryova", utilized this situation and stepped up the war against the few Jewish survivors of the tempest who were scattered about in cities and towns.

Great fear fell upon the few Jews who were left in Radzyn. They could still see before them the sad picture of the seven Jews from the Shtetl of Wohyn who were killed recently by the above-mentioned Polish murderers. The district was shocked again by another murder of Jews this time in Czemierniki among whose victims was Hershel Pontshak from Radzyn.

The life of the Jews in the whole of the Lublin region became more and more difficult and unsafe. The Polish underground organization turned the area into a partisan murder zone, especially so among the scattered Jewish towns. Parczew, Wohyn and Czemierniki again became 'yudenrein'. Jews began fleeing from Lukow too. Traveling from one city to another became perilous. The Polish bandits took people off the trains and automobiles and shot them. Along the way could be seen graffiti 'bi jzida' (beat the Jews) as if the millions of Polish Jewish victims had not been enough. It suddenly became clear to the Jewish survivors that there was no possibility of remaining in Poland and that they must again take the wanderers staff in hand.

From the entire Lublin region the Jews began to move in the direction of Silesia, which had just recently been taken from the Germans. The Russian Army was in control, and life was safe. Many Jews settled in Warsaw. Many others set out on an illegal journey to Italy, from there to sail to Eretz Yisroel.

Many Jews who had survived the war in Russia began arriving in the previously mentioned German evacuated areas. Thus most of the Polish Jewish survivors (including those from Radzyn) were gathered in this Polish-German area, and especially in Lodz, Szczecin, and Dzierzoniow.

"Hit the Jews"

Mail from all over the world, from Russia, America and from Eretz Yisroel began arriving with questions about the surviving relatives, as well as with help for the survivors. From here were heard the first of the survivors cries for help.

In Lodz a committee of Radzyner Jews was founded which established a Self-Help Fund and then made contact with the Radzyner Relief in New York. The Radzyn Jews in America (whose leader was the Yaakov Greenblatt succeeded by Mendel Lichtenshtein) responded warmly by giving all possible aid. Committees similar to the one in Lublin were established in Szczecin and Dzierzoniow.

Lodz and its surroundings served only as a temporary oasis. The main stream of survivors of Polish Jewry, including those from Radzyn, went on to Germany, which was already in the hands of the Americans and the British. The Jews gathered in the camps with hope of finding a way from there to Israel. The Jews from Radzyn (approximately 100 souls) were located mostly in Bad-Reichenhall and Ulm.

On the sixth of May 1947 almost all the Radzyn Jews in Germany gathered in Ulm for a memorial service for the departed. This first gathering was both moving and heart-rending. This was the first meeting for many of the survivors since the end of the fearsome war and slaughter. The eulogy was made by Hershel Liberson and the cantor sang the 'El Molle Rachamim' (God The

Merciful) prayer. When the gathering heard that four thousand Radzyners had perished, they broke out into weeping that no one could or wanted to calm.

לאנדסלייט פון. ראדזין־פאדלאסקי אין פוילן
און אין אנדערע לענדער, גענומט פון ראדזין־
פאדלאסקי רעליעֿ אין ניו־יארק. ווענדן זיך:

J. Greenblatt
1357 Boynton Ave.
Bronx, 59, N.Y.

Information in America.

A year later a second memorial took place in Bad-Reichenhall. Fewer Radzyners came to this service because many had left Germany on their way to their new homes.

In 1949 the last Radzyners left Germany (two of them Menachem Appleboim and Menachem Niskern 'of blessed memory' died in Germany). With a curse on their lips, they left for Israel by different direct and indirect routes. Many of them were first sent to the island of Cyprus but most of them found their way to Israel.

With a blessing in their hearts the remnants of Radzyn Jewry reached home.
'One of the first letters received from Poland'
Lodz, 13. vi-46

13. VI-46

Żydowskie ~~Zrzeszenie~~ Zrzeszenie Religijne w Łodzi.

H. Bursztyn   UL. ZACHODNIA 66

dla Radzyńskiego komitetu żydowskiego.

Letter 13 June 1946

Best and Dearest Radzyn Jewish brothers in New York!

After more than six and a half nightmarish and difficult years, brought on by the war, after six and a half years being torn away from our homes and families, we a small group of Radzyners , returned from Russia. We found none of our near ones and could not even recognize the town in which we once lived .The houses are gone, and the streets of our Radzyn are unrecognizable. We met only a few Radzyn Jews who were saved from the hands of the German murderers. Just a shadow of the four thousand Radzyner Jews. There are now left in Poland up to 220 Radzyners, spread out among a few towns. We are in a terrible and disastrous state, with no means of making a living, uprooted, hungry and sick. Where we spend the day we do not spend the night, we are literally homeless. The help given by the committee is minimal. Therefore we appeal to you our closest brothers in America to help us materially, the sooner the better. In Lodz we have set up a committee with five members, which quickly organized a campaign among Radzyner Jews to which they contributed their last coins for those who were needier. We collected fifteen thousand zlotes, which we immediately distributed among the most destitute. There are already some seventy Radzyn Jews in Lodz and others will are still coming. If you could send money with an emissary it would be appreciated.

This is the composition of the committee.

Honorary President H. Burstein (The secretary of the Jewish Community in Lodz)

Itsche Meir Reb Eizish
H. Liberzon – president (is already in Austria)
Yisrael Appeloig (has left for Germany)
Moshe Goldfarb – Treasurer
Zavel Fine – Member
Ethel Tshervian – Member

The commemoration in the city of Ulam

Near the presidential table- El Male Rachamim

Eulogy

The commemoration at the city of Bed Reichenhal

An encouraging letter from Mendel Lichtenstein in New York

Translation of "An Encouraging Letter"

To my dear Radzyn friends,

I read the letter from H. Liberson, Nussboim, Pontshak and others. My heart cries over that which has happened to our Radzyn, and to all the people in Poland. In a short while, the last person will be leaving Radzyn. The same is happening in other cities, and the last chapter is coming to a close of what was once home, nostalgia, and longing. It is gone, and it will never be again. It is hard to believe, but it seems that the unfortunate reality is that none of my close family and friends survived, for if they would have been alive, they would have reached out to me. I did hear that Boruch Hersh Appelboim's son Henich survived. Is that true? My Radzyn friends, do not despair. Group up in bigger cities and safer areas. Let us know where you are and we will come to your aid. If we are able, we will send affidavits, and we won't stop at anything to help you.

So writes to you Mendel - from [illegible] - Lichtenstein. With greetings to all Radzyn fellows and hope for better days,

Mendel Lichtenstein

We ask to send all correspondence and aid to the following address:

THE JEWISH RELIGIOUS COMMUNITY ORGANIZATION OF LODZ
66 Zachodnia St.
c/o H. Burystyn for the Committee of Radzyn Jews.
President: Liberson.

PS The only active member of the committee is Yisroel Goldreich, Sheiveh Tzinies' Aron the bookeeper.

A List of Holocaust Survivors who gathered in Germany

1. Abman, Wolf
2. Abman, Freda
3. Eagelnick, Golde
4. Appleboim, Yankel
5. Appleboim, Henech
6. Appleboim, Menachem
7. Appeloig, Yosef
8. Appeloig, Blume (Fishboim)
9. Appeloig, Zelig

10. Appeloig, Yisroel
11. Ackereisen, Yitzchak
12. Ackereisen, Feivel
13. Ackereisen, Avraham
14. Barger, Mottel
15. Butman, Yoel
16. Blumenkop, Zlote
17. Blumenkop, Sarah
18. Blumenkop, Manya
19. Berman, Regina
20. Goldbord, Leibl
21. Gottesdiner, Yisroel
22. Gottesdiner, Chaya
23. Gottesdiner, Sarah
24. Goldwasser, Yosef
25. Gradovtchick, Leah
26. Greenberg, Dora
27. Greenberg, Tetsche (Zilberberg)
28. Grindland, Chana
29. Gritzmacher, Sheime
30. Horowitz, Bashe (Vorember)
31. Himmelboim, Binyomin
32. Hirshbein, Yitzchak
33. Hirshbein, Yossel
34. Hirshbein, Miriam
35. Hirshbein, Rachel
36. Hirshbein, Pola
37. Herbst, Mendel
38. Vagonski, Isaac
39. Volovski, Malka (Burak)
40. Vassershtrom,Yisroel
41. Vassershtrom, Menuchah (Fleisik)
42. Weissgroz, Nechemia
43. Weissgroz, Rachel
44. Weissgroz, Malkeh
45. Weisman, Fradel,
46. Weitzman, Itke (Goldwasser)
47. Visoka, Binye (Shulman)
48. Vrubel, Shiye
49. Vrubel, Liebe (Fleisik)
50. Vrubel, Tzviah (Shulman)
51. Zaltzstein, Zanvel
52. Zaltzstein, Mordecai
53. Zilbermintz, Yankel
54. Zilberberstein, Chaim
55. Szelonickviat, Berish

56. Turkeltoib, Yossel
57. Tannenboim, Tzviah (Appleboim)
58. Tentzer, Gusta (Finkelstein)
59. Last, Bracha (Feigenboim)
60. Liberzson, Hershel
61. Liberzson, Rachel (Artstein)
62. Liberzson, Tzviah
63. Liberzson, Zelig
64. Leichter, Yoseph
65. Levin, Tobe(Branitzka)
66. Moravietz, Rachel (Zysman)
67. Migdal, Feivel
68. Mittlebach, Leah (Appleloig)
69. Mintzmacher, Shalom
70. Nussboim, Moishe-Hersh
71. Sudberg, Frania
72. Sudberg, Chana
73. Sudberg, Yente
74. Pasternak, Azshe
75. Farbiasz, Lieber
76. Fine, Sara
77. Finebuch, Bracha (Artstein)
78. Fleisik, Devora (Lerner)
79. Fleisik, Michael
80. Fleisik, Lipe
81. Friedman, Tzvia (Zysman)
82. Friedman, Moishe
83. Freter, Rachel
84. Kagan, Shoshe (Goldstein)
85. Korman, Sender
86. Kupervasser, Devora
87. Kuperschmid, Moishe
88. Rovniak, Leibl
89. Rovniak, Hertzke
90. Rosenboim, Levi
91. Rosenboim, ???
92. Rosenblum, Peretz
93. Rotshtein, Chaim
94. Rubinshtein,Yossel
95. Rubinshtein, Simeh (Weissgrosz)
96. Shulman,Yisroel
97. Schtzupak,Yosef
98. Schmietankah, Nechemia
99. Schmietankah, Dovid
100.   Schmietankah, Chana (Rosenboim)
101.   Shenker, Shprintze

———

[Pages 321]

About Moishelach and Shloimelach and a Life that Vanished (Poem)

Aryeh Lozer (Tel Aviv)

There under the little green trees
Little Moshes and little Shlomos play no more
It's been long since Moshe has gone to the forest
And Shlomo has reached a new shore
Let me tell you now, their story again
About Little Moshes and little Shlomos, and the life that was then.

This shtetl was like all the shtetls around
Surrounded by forests, with a river flowing through
With fields along the length and breadth
Sown and farmed by the peasants
With gardeners, bathers and Sadovnike Jews
And Market-day each Wednesday and pompous fairs
Many peasants with their heavily loaded wagons
With merchandise of all sorts for all that wanted
Wheat merchants, swift and strong like burning fire
And wagon drivers ready. A bustling town!
A shtetl with Jews, many workers and very few rich men
A Rabbinical court. A Rabbi and chassids
And a youth who felt that their shtetl was small
And wishes to go out into the big wide world
Radzyn was a town with varied dwellers
Like all the shtetls around it
But now we'll leave the shtatl aside
And tell of just two who lived there in stormy times

The country didn't hear much of Moshe
There were no legends about him, and no songs written of him
Until today, no one has built a memorial for him
But still, Moshe was a hero of heroes
His childhood years flew by,
Hot summers, cool autumns, and snow falls
Behold he sits in *Cheder* and ponders a *Rashi.*

The hours pass by, night is already falling
And can Mendel Hersh, Lipa's son, the teacher, understand
That besides for *Chumash* and *Rashi*, the street is so beautiful
And that swimming in Midlartzik is so refreshing
Or the fun of racing on the open meadows
To play [illegible] on the empty field
And even the balls made of rags, (fathers don't give money for balls).

You find him later with the rich children
In shul by "Dovid Fishel's", that's where he is learning now
He is learning Tanach and Hebrew and other studies
(Blavowitz is the teacher there, ever so devoted
And he and Shua Friedman help raise the generation)
He left the Jewish school in Pawshechna
Fought with the gentiles, and learnt there with fear
That's how his childhood and school years disappeared
A Jewish teen, in the cycle of life.

A Jewish teen in the cycle of life
What can he demand, to what can he aspire
If the shtetl is small, and around him, it is shining
The country is like a stepmother, an obvious enemy
From early on, he searches for the point of the journey
Is it possible to escape the horrible threatening days
The streets of the shtetl crisscross, they run on far
Those who seek their fortunes, search on the other side of the ocean
On far off seashores, although foreign and alone
He sets out on the long journey
Another one gets fascinated by the tidings from Israel
What the Jews are building there for their Jewish brethren
A third one says "fight!" against the bad world
And will fight with power for his rights
Moshe, a boy no more, left the shtetl then
He learnt a trade and works very hard
In his workplace, Moshe took up

His place with the fighters, gearing up for the times to come
He threw himself then into Life's fervor
He's not afraid of hunger and laughs at danger-
-That surrounds him, but follows his path
Moshe found his path for life
So day follows day, and years go by
He joined the leagues in the front lines.

From times gone by, from the distance of paths
The figure of R' Shlomo comes towards me
Behold he walks steadily, his head held high
He generates power, and he radiates belief
He is the Rabbi, and his students-
- Are the young fathers, Radzyn *chassids*
This generation, full of Torah and Heavenly awe
And with true belief in the Almighty Creator
In the heavens, which are full of His holy name
And on earth, He will redeem us when the Messiah will come
And until the time of redemption comes
He is the Rabbi, A loyal shepherd, a consoler
Their leader, their doer, and their supplicator before God
For health and wealth, for his herd, his city
So what if hatred and fury overwhelm

Hanging like a sword over the Jewish streets
The Rabbi believes, his faith is strong,
That God will guard every Jewish home
And protect the Jews, His nation, from stormy times
Like a father to his child, like a loyal shepherd
For him, everything around him is meaningless
Save for his prayers, his learning the holy books
The Rabbi is tranquil, he knows of no fear
He is protected by the heavens and the holy Torah.

In September 1939, the shtetl was awoken
By the explosion of bombs, by death and fear

From then, like a shadow that never passes
Death followed all, until the last Jewish soul yet
The cross and wings, (swastika) emblem on the uniform of the angel of death
He knows of no mercy, no boundary, no limit
The old, and the young, the big, and chick-like small
There is no more Radzyn, nobody is left
But -it's not silent in the shtetl, of ruins and graves,
Of lives cut short and holy books burned
Of rivers full of tears, of wounds of pain
The last cry is carried over the country
Of boiling bloods, they know of no comfort
And until the last Jew, they cry out for revenge!

The Polish forests stand, clothed in night
From there, Moshe leads the partisans to battle
He gathered them, those who escaped the ghettos
Those who jumped from the cattle trains, and hid in bunkers
He armed them with guns, with bullets and dynamite
Now they carried fire and burning hatred
It grew in their hearts like branches on trees
And cannot endure, promised no longer to remain silent
So they carried along under the wings of night
For Germans on the roads, for soldiers on guard
For trains cutting through land, like knives slicing through bread
For all, they now carried revenge and death
Moshe Partisan, his name rang out with terror
He reigned like a ghost on the Polish routes
The enemies' footsteps burned him, robbed him of sleep,
Demanded and judged, sentenced them and punished
For homes, fathers and mothers, for ruined cities
For snuffed out lives, for jeering and shame.

In a house in Wladova, in those trial-filled days
R' Shlomo searched for a path to the heavens

The heavens that hung silent and grim
In the face of slaughter and destruction below
He fasted many a day, and many times

Cried over his Tehillim [psalms] together with the congregation
With broken hearts, begged for mercy
But his prayers did not reach all the way
And but a small handful of people remained alive
So what should he do, what advice can he give them
What should he tell his flock
The Rabbi, R' Shlomo, the last of the readers
In the days of struggle with himself and with God
Finally, Rabbi Shlomo came up with the answer to the secret
If the fate is death, and destruction the end
Let it be an eye for an eye and a tooth for a tooth
And so from the shtetls, the young and the old
Upon instruction of the Radzyn Rabbi, set out toward the forests
To the forest they went and with ammunition in their hands
Had the enemy pay with their lives for the murder and mockery
May be the hand of revenge be praised and exalted
As long as there is breath, and until the last licks of spirit

Many years have passed since then
Poland fell, then was freed and built up again
Once again the streets were full of life and joy
And the wounds of yesterday are healed with time
Just one wound remained, she's bloody and dripping still
The wound of the slaughtered Polish Jew.

And there under the little green trees
Little Moshes and Little Shlomos play no more
The earth covered Moshe in the forests with love
And R' Shlomo also passed on to the eternal world

Shimon Kleinbaum:

From the most noted activists of Radzyn Jewry. He was smart, educated
and noble, and despite that, a man of the people. He was alert to the goings-
on, lent a listening ear to every needy requester. He was beloved by the entire
city. He was murdered along with his wife and their daughter towards the end
of the war, shortly before liberation.

Yisroel Moshe Rubinstein:

Externally, he was tall and handsome, but this was accompanied by broad
knowledge. He was blessed with rare talent. He was the livewire of many
activities and organizations in Radzyn. On top of all that, he had a gentle
heart.

Out in the wild, the Nazi beast cut his life short at the young age of 32
years.

Y. Lust

[Pages 326-327]

Yisrael Lichtenstein: His Last Will and Testament

Idah Zigelman

I met Yisrael Lichtenstein for the first time in 1935 in Warsaw where I had gone after living for many years in Palestine. I saw him then full of youthful energy and ready to take on different functions but most of all he wanted to go to Palestine. His brother in Tel-Aviv and my husband, who was a childhood friend, could not arrange this. The obstacles to his doing so were not overcome and the war of annihilation befell him in Warsaw where he had already developed and became known as an excellent educator and talented editor.

It was a decree from the god of history and memory that he should remain among his people in Warsaw and be the right hand man to Dr. Emmanuel Ringleblum the founder of the secret archive of the Warsaw ghetto.

Already in the winter of 1939-40 when the first group of collectors was established, Israel Lichtenstein became the secretary of the archives and the collector and the preserver of the materials. Because of his training as a metal worker, which he had acquired before beginning his pedagogic work, he succeeded in preserving all the material that was collected during the whole ghetto period and to hide them in metal boxes which he made with his own two hands. He gathered all this material in the kitchen of his former school ("Borochov"). There it was sorted, packed and hidden in a special pit dug in the cellar of the house. He was helped by his wife, the artist Gila Sakstein.

Yisrael Lichtenstein (left) and Yitchak Zigelman

His tremendous eagerness to leave behind some remembrance and documentation of the terrible suffering that the magnificent Jewish community of Warsaw had experienced, gave him and his friends the strength to resist the persecution and the destruction. Until the last moment, they were hiding in the depths of the earth doing their holy work. However, with the ghetto revolt and the third German 'Aktzia', he and his family were destroyed by the Nazi fire.

In one of those boxes, Yisrael Lichtenstein's personal will was found in which we are commanded to remember Amalek forever and to record his foul deeds in eternal disgrace. This part of his will, especially the part about the suffering of our town of Radzyn, was edited with great love and perseverance by my husband who was a close friend of Lichtenstein's and collected and carefully edited this material thus creating The Radzyn Book.

Yes, "those who were lovely and pleasant during their lives, and in their death not divided."

On the right: Shimon Kleinbaum
One of the most noted activists of Radzyn Jewry. He was smart, educated and noble, and a man of the people. He was aware of the situation around him, and lent an ear to everyone in need. He was loved by the entire city. Towards the end of the war, he was murdered along with his wife and their daughter, shortly before liberation.

On the left: Yisroel Moshe Rubinstein
He was tall and handsome, but also possessed a broad knowledge of various subjects. He was blessed with rare oratory talent. He was the life of many activities in Radzyn. On top of all that, he had a kind heart. Out in the wilderness, the Nazis cut his life short at the young age of 32 years.

Y. Lust

[Page 328]

Among the Fallen

Yisroel'ke Saltzer

Was in recent years a leader and mentor of the Zionist-Pioneer Youth. He was the nerve center of all Zionist activities.

Gershon Hanoch Puntshak

Was among the first members of "Zeire Zion." He was an educated and refined leader of the Po'alei Zion Zionist Socialists. Fell at Oesweincem.

Shlomo Muscat

One of the spiritual leaders of the Left Po'alei Zion in Radzyn. Murdered by those Poles who gave him refuge.

Yaakov Levi

A leader of the Left Po'alei Zion Youth. Devoted and faithful to both its ideals and to his friends. Fell in the town of Starie-Dorogi in the Minsk district.

Yitzchak Butman

A noble activist of the Bund in Radzyn. He was an intellectual, who lived his whole life in poverty supporting himself by manual labor. Died in exile in Russia.

Leah'tze Gelibter

An activist of the Bund and its representative to the Radzyn City Council. There she was a brave and stubborn opponent of every manifestation of anti-Semitism or reaction.

Moshe- Shua Rotshtein

One of the veteran Bund organizers in Radzyn. He was an intellectual well versed in Yiddish literature. Supported himself by working as a carpenter his whole life.

Chaim-Yitzchak Gelerma

Representative of the Jewish National Fund for some twenty five years. His house served as a meeting place for Zionists of all persuasions.

Matityahu Goldwasser

Served as Gelerman's right hand man in work for the Jewish National Fund and other Zionist funds.Was active and activated others for various Zionist projects.

Simcha Goldwasser

Active in various Jewish national affairs. Director of the Jewish People's Bank after the death of Yaakov Kantor.

Yaakov Blechovitz

Principal of the Jewish National School (later Tarbut School) from the date of its founding in 1916 He educated toward Hebrew and Zionism He played a very important part in the development of the Zionist Pioneer Youth Movements in the city.

New Roots

Radzyners in Israel

Yitzchak Avi-Arah

Building Erezt Yisrael (The land of Israel)

The beginning of aliya (immigration) from our town to Eretz Yisroel was at the beginning of the 20th century. Reb Elimelech Lichtenstein, who was the head of a large family, was among those whose great desire was to find his eternal rest in the soil of the Holy Land. While deeply absorbed, together with others, in study at the ancient Hebron Yeshiva, he was murdered in the light of day and in cold blood by Arab rioters in the riots of 1929.

After the events of 1921, two idealistic young people from our town arrived, filled with desire to settle. The first one, Zalman Tzvi Lichtenstein dried the swamps of the Sharon. Later he went over to the surveying department of the Barron's project in Zichron (Yaakov). The second one, Ephraim Eidelman, the grandson of Reb Liebl Nachtingal was the first to be employed by the railroad at the time of the Mandate. Later he joined those who laid the foundations for the electricity generating station in Naharayim. From there he moved to the Reading Station in Tel Aviv where he is one of the labor leaders to this day.

When the Fourth Wave of immigration began, it brought with it the graduates of the pioneering youth organizations, first and foremost those from Hashomer Hastzair and some from Poele Zion and others who were unaffiliated. Some of them did not have the strength to overcome suffering and the terrible conditions of that time and returned to Poland.

Where did our people go to in Palestine at that time? Being graduates of Hashomer Hatzair (The Young Guards) and with unbounded love for the land and pioneering movement, most of them joined the Ein Harod company of the G'dud Haavodah (Worker's Battalion) and participated in the establishment of Kibbutz Tel Yosef and Ein Harod in the Jezreel Valley and Ayelet Hashachar in the Galilee. The rest joined settlements in Judea and Sharon areas where they participated in the struggle for Hebrew labor and in securing the rights of hired laborers in the orchards, vineyards, building trade and workshops during the unemployment and suffering of that period.

-----*-----

A meeting of Radzyners in Tel-Aviv

The reverberations of the 1929 riots in Palestine raised the desire for immigration to Palestine among the youth in Radzyn as well as in the other cities and towns of Poland. Groups of youths abandoned their parental homes to go to the pioneer training farms, and carried by the waves of immigration both legal and illegal, reached Palestine.

The period between 1930 and 1940 marks the expansion of immigration from our town. This was based on an astute view of the uncertain future of the Jews in the towns of Poland on the one hand, and the pioneering spirit that influencing the best of the youth, on the other. Except for a few middle class and small artisan families who immigrated at that time, the rest of the immigration was all the result of the Socialist-Zionist educational activities carried out ably and persistently for some twenty years. When they became acclimated to the new conditions and were absorbed into the society and into work, we see them spreading out into the following agricultural communities; Ayelet Hashachar, Merchavia, Ein Hachoresh, Degania, Negba, Tzofit, Gan Chaim, Nes Tziona, Hadera, Petach Tikva, Even Yehuda, Kadimah, Zichron Yaakov, and others. The rest, a small number, went to the cities of Tel Aviv, Haifa, and Jerusalem.

----*-----

And guarding at night...

What were the accomplishments of the Radzyners in Israel from then to now? They were never absent from the various struggles that took place in the community in all periods starting with the beginning of settlement in the Jezreel Valley and continuing on through the Haganah (Defense Forces) and the War for Independence and contributed to many social and cultural projects.

Now Radzyners can be found in Merchavia, Negba, Shuval, Degania, Tzofit and Gan Chaim following in the path of Jewish revolution as farmers rooted in their homeland and its new society.

We have seen Radzyners in the upper ranks of the Zionist movement and as leaders in the Labor parties. We have seen one who founded and managed a very important worker's publishing house and another who directed his energy to enhancing our language and publishing it in important publications. We also have seen our people involved in the planning of significant housing projects and other important projects for housing and employment. In the municipalities they were elected or appointed officials and as well as in the two universities. One even became the vice-president of the world wide Joint Distribution Committee and was active in the capitals of the world. On his private initiative he started many industrial projects such as flour mills, gas stations, floor tiles glass, and metal manufacturing, and also intensive agriculture. Others were found in citrus cultivation in the south and in the management of the Labor Office there, in the Sick Fund offices and in the editorial offices of the Davar newspaper.

After the Holocaust and a long and tiring journey, many survivors arrived filled with anguish and grief but filled with the Jewish spirit and the belief that they had finally arrived at a safe haven.

The local Radzyners welcomed the survivors from their home town with love and open arms. Their committee did its utmost to helping them both spiritually and materially to become absorbed as quickly as possible in their new homeland.

The new Radzyner immigrants trod in the footsteps of veterans, spread out through the whole country, went through a period of acclimatization and today they look forward to the future with confidence.

Yes the Radzyners have rebuilt their home in Israel.

----*-----

However there were those who were not so fortunate and fell along the way and were buried in Israel. Some died a natural death while others died while fulfilling their duties as guards or workers.

Friendly get together of friends from Radzyn

Let us remember:

Mendel the bookbinder and his wife- who died of old age in Holy Jerusalem.

The couple, **Chuneh and Malkah Idelman,** who worked hard to support their family and who were fortunate enough to live for many years together with their children here in Israel. They passed away in Tel-Aviv.

The young and brave **Asher Rosenfeld** who was killed in the riots of 1936 while guarding the citrus orchards in Ness Tziona. He is buried in Ness Tziona.

Avraham-Meir Reichenberg was a pioneer who was one of the founders of Kfar Azar and was killed by a jackal while loading local produce on a truck at night. He is buried in Kfar Azar.

Hanoch Berman was a modest, dear and lonely soul. He fell while working at hard physical labor in Haifa

Moshe Goldfarb, who went through all seven stations of hell in the progroms. He finally reached his homeland but did not survive. He is buried in Tel-Aviv.

Amalia Rosenboim-Greenberg, a good hearted and pioneering woman. She was the director of a private children's institution and died in Tel-Aviv.

Pnina Appleoig-Hochman was a graduate of Hashomer Hatzair. She immigrated to Palestine after World War II. She took sick and died while setting up her home in Ramat Yitzchak.

Yaakov Punchak arrived in Palestine after World War II. He was a partisan in the forests of Poland and an outstanding soldier in the Red Army. Was killed in a work accident in Tel- Aviv.

May their souls be bound up in the bond of the new life that is being renewed in the homeland.

And every year mentioning the fallen in the holocaust

[Page 335]

Asher Rosenfeld
Died in the Line of Duty

Simcha Reichenberg

Asher Rosenfeld, fell while guarding the country. A good looking, tall and courageous young man. Helpful to any opressed and torchured- that was Asher. Started working as a young boy, offenly suffered from distress and lack of work, as he wandered from Radzyn to the capital Warsaw. Following hardships and suffering he was brought to Nes Tziona Israel by his brother Yaakov, which immigrated to Israel a long time before. Here he worked as a guard in the citrus orchards and in the 1936 fell while on duty- young of age and only 2 years in Israel.

His appearance was young, lively, and brave looking. He was a good friend who responded to the afflicted and the depressed. He started working at a young age and was often unemployed and suffered from hunger and hardship. He wandered back and forth between Radzyn and Warsaw the capitol.

After much suffering and hunger, he was brought to the settlement Ness-Ziona by his older brother Yaakov who had come to Palestine long before him. Here he began working as a watchman in the orchards during the riots of 1936 and was killed while on duty as he was in springtime of his life and after only two years in the country.

A visit to Israel of the Goldberg couple from America (At the center of the first row)

Radzyners in America

A. From The Late Yaakov Greenblatt (New York)

As is well known, in the beginning of the 20th Century immigration to America was looked upon almost like conversion in the Polish shtetl. Therefore, very few immigrated. Many also did not have the where-with-all to do so. However a few did manage to get there. Among those that did were: Mendel Turkeltoib a brother of Emmanuel and Pesach Turkeltoib, Yossel Shainman and A. Weingarten, a son of Butshe. Later a few dozen 'ordinary' people arrived. Because they suffered as 'greenhorns', they did not have in mind or understand the necessity of organizing a landsman shaft.

[Page 336]

The editorial staff
Top, from right: Aba Danilak (Toronto), Yizchak Zigelman-Editor, Mendel
Lichtenstein (New York). Center, from right: A. Lazar, Y. Avi-Eira, Y. Lust.
Bottom, from right: L. Winderboim, B. Burstein, M. Gatasdiner

The Editorial Board for the Book

Radzyn imigrants in America
From the right, first row: Kastan, Krein, Greenblat, Shreiber; second row:
Yonshtein, Levin, Goldberg, Rubin

Then they heard that the people who had come from the larger cities Warsaw, Siedlce and even from Mezritsh already had 'societies' and some even had their own synagogues. In 1910 a small group got together including Mordecai, Yonah Tshechanovski's brother, Chaim-Shiya Tanenbaum, Dobreh's son, and Yisroel Yitzchak Berenson the grandson of Beryl Avraham Shlomo's grandson, as well as the writer of theses lines. They founded the Radzyn Young Men's Society with fifteen members. However it lasted only one year. People just did not come to the meetings and there was no one to talk to. In 1917 another attempt was made to organize, but without success. This was the situation until 1923 when I personally visited our shtetl and saw the tremendous havoc that W.W.1 had wrought on Radzyn and that those who had suffered did not even have anyone to help them. When I got home, I raised a cry among the landsleit and this time it worked.

Radzy emigrants in Canada
From the right, sitting: Y. Freeman, H. On, M. Alexen, A. Danilak; standing: S. Day, P. Nachtigal, A. Lanhef, A. Zalavitz, H. Tanzer, M. Frieman, A. Kuchberg, S. Schtzupak

We got together in the home of Tama-Yenta Youngshtein (from the Kupietz family), and there, on the 23rd of February 1924, the Radzyn Progressive Society was founded which still exists in New York. The first 'voluntary' secretary was Zishe Goldwasser the cantor. On the following Passover, we sent 200 dollars for Maoth Chitim (a fund for buying Passover food for the poor). After that we sent another 400 dollars for a mutual loan fund. Later the Joint 'lent' another 600 dollars and the fund was set up. When we would get the annual financial statement from the secretary, the late Yehoshua Keitelgisser, we would send them a few hundred dollars. When the big fire took place in Radzyn in 1929, we sent 500 dollars to help those who were affected.

Thus we continued on until the German murderers destroyed our hometown Radzyn.

Radzyn imigrants in Canada
From the right, sitting: H. Smith, A. Danilak, C. Eisen. Standing: M. Nirenberg,
Y. Goldwasser, Y. Handelsman, P. Rosenblum, A. Nirenberg

B. From: Mendel Lichtenstein (New York)

Even though we can go back seventy years, it is hard to determine who was the Radzyn's Columbus, the first one from that town to set his foot on American soil. Only a very few left the shtetl then to go wandering. True, the place could not support all of its children and people left, first to the nearby big cities and then further out into the wide world. Having torn themselves away from home, they allowed themselves to be carried along with the current which flowed in the direction of Switzerland, Paris, London and then to America. This last leap was hard to make, and even though the above mentioned cities served as good jumping off places, for many of them the suffering that they experienced there became etched in their memories and they could not go any further.

We can divide those wanderers into five categories: 1. Those who fled from Russia and did not want to serve the Czar. 2. The strong, powerful, healthy Jews such as many of the coachmen who were confident of their strength and were sure that they would be able to make a living anywhere. 3. Craftsmen such as tailors, shoemakers, etc. who hoped to benefit from their crafts in the new country. 4. A few enlightened, curious and plain idealists with a desire to see themselves walking with their heads down and their feet in the air under them on the other side of the world. 5. And the last, that I almost forgot to our shame, ten times tfue, tfue, --- criminals. Just as there cannot be day without night so there could not be only good and refined Jews in Radzyn.

Things did not go too well for anyone in the beginning. Gold was not found in the streets. A "greenhorn" had to look for a job. But here, unlike in Europe, you got paid for it even though at that time you had to work long hours. A family man could not manage without taking in a few borders. This was the time before there were trade unions.

With the passage of time things changed, the "greenhorns" became less green, those without a trade learned one, and the craftsmen became manufacturers.

However it did not happen too quickly. The Radzyner did some of the hardest work. Some of them became pressers in the new factories, some became house painters and some of them just worked very hard. From the early years of my arrival here I still remember very well the Radzyners; Liebl Glassberg, Hefner (Yossel Glatz's son), Chaim-Shiya Tennenbaum and Yaltshe the daughter of Boruch-Hirsh. All of them were very sick as a result of working too hard.

Mendel Goldwasser

See page 57 for his contribution to the Yizkor Book

[Page 341]

Meir Segal

Born in Radzyn in 1911, he was the son of Yitzchak Segal. In 1927 he came to Canada with a group of orphans. (The Mezritch Radzyner group was accompanied by Yosef Donilak z"l).

From then, he made himself known as a poet. In later years he settled in Brooklyn, New York, where he came out with Y. [illegible] and H. Leiwachs Collections, larger series of songs. In 1940, his song book, "Nonte Erd" (Close Earth) was warmly received by the Jewish Literature Association in America.

The son of Yitzchak Asher Segal, who was born in Radzyn in 1911.He came to Canada with a group of orphans in 1927 (This Mezritsh-Radzyn group was accompanied by the late Yosef Danilak) from where he began to make a name for himself as a poet. Years later he settled in Brooklyn, New York where he published in Y. Apotoshu's and H.Leivik's "Collection Books" larger collections of his poems. In 1940 his book of poems "Near Earth" was warmly received by the Yiddish literary public in America.

Meir Segal

[Page 342]

Yosef Danilak Zichrono Le'Bracha (of blessed memory)
Up and above all, served as an unofficial youth leader in the town during and after WWI. Unofficial, because he did not belong to any party and belonged to everyone and all. He was active mainly in the fields of literature and culture, and that is why he was loved by youth and adults. His short stories and writings published in the Polish Jewish press at that time granted him a special charm. When he "disappeared" from the city and moved to neighboring Mezeritz to run the local orphans home, he left a vacume that was not filled in for a long period... After several years he left Mezeritz and moved to Canada. In his new country he worked with enthusiasm and loyaly in his beloved field of culture, and here also he became cherised by all. First in Toronto as a teacher, and from 1947 as the head of the Jewish public library in Montreal. During this period the library imroved, branched out and became a main hub of the Jewish institutions of the city. His sudden death in Shavuot 1951 abruptly stopped his life events.

At the memorial evening in New York, in memory of Greenblatt, his friend Mendel Lichtenstein said: "Many will mourn and cry, in all corners of the world, because through his noble heart and good deeds they have become his children. To those that were liberated after Hitler's destruction, he became a father. He was devoted to them and sent letters to console them, encourage and help them. These unfortunates didn't have to search for him; he came to look for them and took them under his wing. Without him, we would never have known about many survivors. His humanitarian deeds have earned him eternal gratitude.

The late Yosef Danielak

Yosef Danielak was the most important uncrowned youth leader in Radzyn in the years of W.W.1 and for many years after that. "Uncrowned" because he did not belong to any party but belonged to everyone, to the entire public. His main fields of activity were books and culture, and so he was loved by both young and old. The short pieces he published in the various Jewish periodicals in all of Poland had a special charm. When he 'disappeared' from the town and showed up in Mezritsh to run the orphan home there, he left a vacuum that was not filled for a long time. After some time he also left Mezritsh and the orphanage and immigrated to Canada.

In this new country too, he worked faithfully and enthusiastically in the field of culture that he loved so much. Here too he was loved by all, first in Toronto as a teacher and later, from the year 1947 director of the Jewish Public Library in Montreal.

His active life was suddenly terminated in 1950.

Compiled by Idah Z-N

The Late Yaakov Greenblatt

At the memorial evening in New York dedicated to Greenblatt, his friend Mendel Lichtenstein said: "Many dozens and hundreds of people from all the corners of the earth became his children as a result of his good heart and good deeds. He was a father to all those who were saved after Hitler's ravages. He tried to console, help and strength them by his letters. The unfortunate did not have to search for him, he went to look for them and usually found them. If it wasn't for him we would not have inkling about many of them. For his humanitarian deeds he deserves an eternal memorial."

Yad VaShem –Yizkor

"זכרון עולם לקדושי"

קהלת ר דזין פולין

שהוגלו, נשרפו והושמדו

ע"י הצוררים הנאצים הגרמ'

בשנת תש – תש"ג

זכרם הטהור

לא ימוש מקרבנו לנצח

ומלב כל עם ישראל

עד סוף כל הדורות

ת נ צ ב "ה

הונצחה ע"י ארגון יוצאי
דדזין פודלסקי בישראל

Zikarom Olam (Eternity memorial) for the Radzyn community in Poland who were exiled, burnt, and destroyed by the hateful German Nazis in the years 1940-1943. Their memory will be with us and all of the Israeli people forever until the end of time. Tanzeba. Memorial plaque by the Radzyn Podlaski imigrants organization in Israel.

List of the Missing

Compiled by:
Avraham Ziegelman (Tel-Aviv) and Yisrael Lust (Ramat-Gan)

List Presented by Street Name

Warshava Street

family	Given Name	family Members	Remarks
Zilbermintz	David	With wife	From the town of Gradawitz
Herman	Boruch	With wife	Cereal Grinder
Herman	Matityahu	With wife	
Vinderboim	Shmuel	With wife and child	
Fest	Reeva		
Tenenboim	Eliyahu	With wife	Brick Layer
Kashemacher	Yisachar	With wife & children	
Turkeltoib	Pinchas	With wife & children	
Shapiro-Turkeltoib	Miriam		School Teacher
Vinderboim	Itzil	With wife	
Lozer	Yaakov	With wife & children	
Kupietz	Chana-Bracha	With children	
Lublinerman	Leibel	With wife & children	
Appeloig	Berl-Leib	With wife & children	
Turkeltoib	Nathan	With wife & son	
Shuchmacher	Avraham	With wife & son	
Feigenboim	Reshe	With children	
Kupietz	Yaakov-Moshe	With wife & child	
Kopelman	Hershel	With wife	
Kratzshtein	Meir-Laizer	With wife & children	
Kavelblume	Yisrael Hersch	With children	Baker
Damb	Yaakov	With wife & children	
Agman	Yaakov-Leib	With children	
Kupietz	Yantshe	With wife	
Feigenboim	Eliyahu	With wife & children	
Kligsberg	Nechama	With children	
Berman	Yaakov	With wife & children	
Vebman	Velvel	With wife & children	
Samiatizki	Moshe	With wife	
Levy	Levi	With wife & child	
Pomerantz			
Keiytelgisser	Yehoshua	With wife & children	
Zavidowitz	Berl	With wife & children	
Rubinshtein	Tabeh		
Appeloig	Shlomo	With wife	

Blumenknop	Velvel	With wife	
Vohiner	Avraham	With wife & children	Miller
Hardshtein	Yitzchak	With wife & children	Quilt maker
Adelman	Meir	With wife & children	
Nissenboim	Henik	With son & grandson	From the town of Yoellasvinsk
Helfenboim	Shmuel	With wife & children	
Frident	Chaim	With wife & children	
Pomeranietz	Bayleh	With children	Woolen scarves maker

[Page 346]

Goldwasser	Ephraim	With wife & children	
Reichenberg	Leibel	With wife & son	
Kupietz	Mendel	With wife & children	
Kimmel	Shmuel	With wife & children	
Fass	Yechezkel	With wife & children	
Fass	Yehoshua	With wife & children	
Vishkovski	Yehoshua	With wife	Brick Layer
Verubel	Laizer	With wife	
Slavic	Yaakov-Shmuel	With wife & children	Tailor
Fenig		With wife & children	Butcher
Bandeh	Shaul	With wife & children	Tailor
Blachovitsh	Yisrael	With wife	Tinsmith
Greenberg	Avraham	With wife & children	
Blachovitsh	Shammai		Tinsmith
Shaimes' daughter	Chaya-Yehudith	With son	
Zeidel	Yisrael	With wife & children	Carpenter
Appelboim	Laizer	With wife	
Libfreind	Simcha		
Heiblum	Motil	With wife & children	Fisherman
Kuperschmit	Zalman	With wife & children	Shoemaker
Adelman	Meir	With wife & children	Tailor
Danilak	Mendel	With wife & children	Book Binder
Blachovitsh	Leah	With children	Alter's wife
Blachovitsh	Yisrael	With wife & children	Alter's son
Blachovitsh	Yisrael	With wife & children	The son of Blonde Yaakov
Berman	Mosheh	With wife	
Lichtenstein	Gotteleh	With wife & children	
Leiner (The Great Scholar)	Shlomo	With wife & children mother & sister	The Radzyner Rabbi
The Blind Asher	With family		
Tubman	Yehoshua	With wife & children	
Blumenkop	Moshe	With son	
Appeloig	Yankel	With wife & child	

family	Given Name	family Members	Remarks
Schneider	Yoel	With wife & child	
Vebman	Velvel	With wife & child	
Hochboim	Toltzeh	With children	

Ostroweitzka Street

family	Given Name	family Members	Remarks
Lichtenstein	Sender	With wife & child	
Fantshak	Gershon-Henich	With wife & children	
Fantshak	Hershel		
Fenig	Velvel	With wife & child	
Hochboim	Yankel	With wife & child	
Shlimak	Yitzchak	With wife	

[Page 347]

family	Given Name	family Members	Remarks
Schtzupak	Mishel	With wife & child	
Schtzupak	Yoseph		
Schtzupak	Mordecai	With wife & child	
Kapshtack	Alter	With wife & children	
Finkelstein	Avraham-Leib	With wife & children	
Goldfarb	Nochum-Yankel	With wife & children	Brezers?
Kronenberg	Dovid		Wagoner
Blumenkop	Mattityahu		
Butman	Yitzchak (Bieh)	With wife & children	Tailor
Lichtenstein	Dovid	With wife & children	
Kleinman	Mendil	With wife	
Kleinman	Aaron-Hersh	With wife & children	
Kleinman	Tzviah	With husband & child	
Kleinman	Leah		
Kleinman	Yosef	With wife & children	
Hirshbein	Chaim-Zishe	With wife & children	
Zaltzshtein	Eliyahu	With wife & children	Sticher of upper shoe leather
Kopelman	Neche		Kaplak?
Spector	Yosef		Painter, Art
Herbst	Elimelech	With wife & children	
Herbst	Moishe	With wife & children	
Freter	Yosef	With wife & children	
Vishnieh	Dan	With wife & children	Saloonkeeper
Rubinshtein	Yehoshua	With wife & children	Yoresh = heir (Nickname?)
Lichtenstein	Shimon	With wife	
Kavelblume	Yosef-Ahron	With wife	Baker
Lichtenstein	Beril	With wife & child	The son of Yoel Midlarnick
The Yellow	Itshe	With wife & children	Butcher
Vineappel	Rochele		Midwife
Blumen	Yosef	With wife & children	Barber
Rosenberg	Dovid	With wife & children	From the town of Sochavol
Goldwasser	Frede		

Berman	Teme-Yente	With husband	
Shteper	Chaim	With wife & children	
Domininer	Moishe	With wife & children	Shoemaker
Tratsch	Yehoshua	With wife & children	
Engelman	Shmulke	With wife & children	Sexton of the synagogue
Meicher	Chaim	With wife & children	Tailor
Shuster	Shmuel-Leib	With wife	
Vineappel	Mottel	With wife & children	Barber
Rubinshtein	Hershel	With wife & children	
Tukeltoib	Kraindel	With children	
Nusssboim	Henich	With wife & children	
Nusssboim	Yankel	With wife & children	
Turkeltoib	Natan(Pinchas)	With wife & child	

[Page 348]

Handelsman	Zalman Mechal		
Rubinstein	Yankel	With wife & children	
Zilberberg	Yeshiah	With wife	
Eisen	Avraham-Velvel	With wife & children	Brushmaker
Turkeltoib	Fishel	With wife & children	
Nussblat	Yisroel	With wife & Daughters	
Rosenboim	Elchanan	With wife & children	
Shampam	Chaim- Leib	With wife & children	Shoemaker
Feigenboim	Adel	With children	
Neiman	Mordechai	With wife & children	Barber
Kupietz	Shimon	With wife & children	
Blumenkop	Yankel	With wife & children	
Ratushnik	Doctor	With wife & child	
Adelman	Tuviah		
Tannenboim	Moshe	With wife & children	Nickname Kugeleh = Pudding
Adelman	Batyah		
Hochman	Yankel	With wife & children	
Rotshtein	Rochele	With children	
Rotshtein	Moishe-Shayeh	With wife & children	
Rotshtein		With children	Yisroel-Shimons wife
Lichtenstein	Yisroel	With family	Teacher
Lichtenstein	Berl		Yankel Lichtenstein's son
Kamienyetzka	Sara	With children	
Pinkus	Sholom	With wife & children	
Chavaleh Die Kleine			(Little Chava)
Pontshak	Yitzchak	With wife & children	Shoemaker
Pontshak	Yechezkel	With wife & children	Shoemaker
Pontshak	Lieber	With wife & children	Shoemaker

Bober	Yankel	With wife & children	
Zambakofsky	Yankel	With wife	Feldsher = Barber surgeon
Rosenboim	Reuven	With wife & child	Barber
Himmelboim	Sime-Pese	With husband & child	Hatmaker
Viazcszher	Yudel	With wife & children	Tailor
Gottesdiner	Hindeh	With children	Chaya-Bayle's daughter
Zuker	Mosheh	With child	Knop = knot (Nickname)
Adamovski	Itsche-Meir	With wife	
Greenberg	Avraham	With wife & children	Baker
Levenstein	Itsche	With wife & children	
Rotberg	Abatsche	With wife & children	Tailor
Berman	Avraham	With wife & child	
Vohiner	Yasha	With wife & child	Miller
Shulshtein	Aharon	With wife & children	Baker

[Page 349]

		Cosze Street	
family	**Given Name**	**family Members**	**Remarks**
Fine	Reb Chaim	With children	The Rabbi of Radzyn
Shineman	Eliyahu	With wife & son	
Kuperschmidt	Yosef	With wife & children	
Zuker	Hershel ("Knop")	With wife & children	
Voves	Yisrael	With children	
Shumlak	Leybel	With children	Wagoner
Goldwasser	Yechiel	With wife & children	
Biderman	Shlomo ("Nega")	With family	
Veidenboim	Roise	With children	Dzabak(family nickname)
Veidenboim	Shmuel	With wife & children	Dyer
Vinderboim	Yisrael	With wife & children	Dzabak(family nickname)
Eisenberg	Moishe	With wife & children	Grain Merchant From the town of Stok
Reichnadel	Berl	With wife & children	Barrel Maker
Vetshtein	Chava	With children	
Becker	Yekutiel	With children	
Becker	Yosef	With children	(Yekutiel's son)
Shuchmacher	Yankel	With children	Pepper Grinder
Bershtenmacher	Yosef-Eli	With children	
Schuster	Yankele	With children	
Goldapple	Yitzchak	With children	Painter (Artist)
Shtshetshshinaz	Chayah Esther	With children	
Chaim	Eishe	With family	Levi's son in-Law
Goldshtein	Ovadia	With wife & children	Ritual Slaughterer
Goldbord	Fayge		
Berman	Elisheva	With children	
Wolf	Chantshe	With daughter	

Wolf	Yitzchakl	With family	
Weisman	Uziel	With family	
Blachovitsh	Yaakov	With family	
Sudberg	Chanina	With family	
Kaveh	Gershon	With family	Haapidona?- (Nickname?)
Eisen	Shlomo-Zalman	With family	Butcher (Borshtash = Brushmaker?)
Adelman	Moshe	With wife & children	Quilter
Adelman	Menachem	With wife & children	Quilter
Yazger		With family	
Steinberg	Meir	With family	
Arye's	Hershel	With family	Tailor
Bronitzki	Shmuel-Leib	With family	
Saltzer	Dinah	With family	
Saltzer	Yisroelke	With family	
Levi	Rishe	With family	
Lust	Yossel	With family	Mezzuzah scribe
Katzenelboigen	Motiye	Bashe's son	

[Page 350]

Isaacs	Meir Yoel	With wife & children	Wagoner
Szonche	Moishe	With wife & children	The sexton of the synagogue
Tikatchinsky	Finkel	With wife & children	
Tikatchinsky	Motke	With wife & children	Humorist-"tik-tak"
Tikatchinsky	Yisroelke	With wife & children	Artist-painter
Ackerman	Shaulke	With wife & children	
Tikatchinsky	Avraham Moishe	With wife & children	
Tikatchinsky	Hershel		Newspaper Vendor
Tikatchinsky	Mnachem-Yehoshua		
Maneshes	Hinde	With family	Yoel Isaac's wife
Kroinenberg	Mechel	With family	Wagoner
Vrubal	Chanina	With family	Glazier
Katz	Avraham-Mordecai	With family	Dispatch clerk
Fenick	Sarah-Perel	With family	Butcher
Chudaver	Gittel (Tshipes)	With family	
Eisen	Yitzchak	With family	Butcher ("Borshtash") = Brush Maker? family Nickname
Vinderboim	Gittel	With children	Dshabak? family nickname?
Ackereisen	Sheindel	With children	
Warshever	Leibush	With children	Shoemaker

		The First Market	
family	Given Name	family Members	Remarks
Lichtenstein Midlarnick (The Soapmaker)?	Yosef	With wife & children	Lozer, Henia
Appeloig	Moishe	With wife & children	
Lichtenstein	Yocheved	With children	
Lichtenstein	Leibel	With wife & children	
Sapir	Chava	With husband & children	Watchmaker
Mushkat	Shlomo	With wife & children	
Mushkat	Esther		
Shulshtein	Yaakov-Zelig	With wife & children	
Rosenkrantz	Yankel	With wife & children	
Rosenwald	Shaul-Henich	With wife & children	
Rosenwald	Itche	With wife & children	
Gottesdiner	Henich	With wife & children	
Meicher	Esther	With children	
Himmelboim	Hershel	With wife & children	Hatmaker
Rosenboim	Yeshiah	With wife & children	
Rosenboim	Kalman	With wife & children	
Sudberg	Nachman -Yudel	With wife & children	Tailor
Blumen	Avraham	With wife & children	
Diamant	Chaim	With wife & children	Hat maker
Shlep	Yonaleh	With wife & children	Storekeeper
Himmelboim	Rivka	With husband & children	
Borchovsky	Leah	With children	

[Page 351]

		The Second Market	
family	Given Name	Members of the family	Remarks
Pshenizeh	Yosef-Eli	With wife & children	
Mantshaz	Yosel	With wife & children	
Zigelman	Eliezer		
Kavelblume	Chaim-Shimon	With wife & child	
Fruchtman	Yehudith (ne:Zigelman)	With husband & children	
Zilbermintz	Lippe	With wife & children	
Zysman	Zyshe	With children	
Zysman	Shimon-Velvel	With wife & children	
Zysman	Pesach	With wife & children	
Zysman	Yisroel-Hersh	With wife & children	

Rosenfeld	Shlomo		
Rosenfeld	Laibel	With wife & children	
Zaidel	Sarah Dintshe	With family	
Levi	Gittele	Avraham Moishe's little girl	
Freedman.	Motke	With wife & child	Scribe
Rosenboim	Meir	With wife & children	Quilter
Weisman	Mordechai	With children	
Weisman	Leibel	With wife	Hatter
Tunkelroit	Chaim Shieh	With wife & children	
Zysman	Dobe	With children	
Zysman	Dovidtshe	With wife & children	
Zysman	Yossele	With wife & children	
Zysman	Beinem	With wife	
Levi	Yankel	With wife & children	
Goldstein	Yankel	With wife & children	Lumber merchant
Zshita	Yossel	With wife & children	
Vinderboim	Yankel	With wife	Bookeeper
Goldberg	Nachke	With wife & child	
Zuckerman	Yitzchak-Eli	With wife & children	Watchmaker
Goldwasser	Matityahu	With wife & child	Bookeeper
Rubinstein	Berl	With wife & children	Saloon keeper
Lust	Charne	With child	
Ehkaeizer	Boruch	With wife	
Rosenboim	Yankel	With wife & child	The Blind one
Gelerman	Chaim Yitzchak	With wife & children	Paint merchant
Finkelstein	Yehoshua	With wife & son	
Finkelstein	Yehoshua's son	With wife	
Nirenberg	Yossel	With wife & children	
Kaptchak	Moshe	With wife & children	
Nirenberg-Hochmans	Sarah	3 children	
Kupietz	Avraham- Chaim	With wife & children	Dry Goods Merchant
Freter	Berl	With wife & children	Shtrik = Rope Nickname or - Rope maker
Weidenboim	David	With wife & children	Dry Goods Merchant

[Page 352]

Lamke	David	With wife & children	
Fartik	Mordechai	With wife & children	Tailor
Nissboim	Fishel	With wife & children	Dealer in secondhand goods
Nissboim	Moishele	With wife & children	
Lichtenstein	Yantshe	With wife & daughter	Painter Artist
Dann	Hershel	With wife	
Pshenitza	Yankel	With wife & children	Tailor

family	Given Name	family Members	Remarks
Pshenitza	Mottel	With wife & children	Tailor
Zhlaza	Leah		
Kotlarska	Menuchle		

Kashive Street

family	Given Name	family Members	Remarks
Smetanka	Mordechai	With wife & children	Pantsmaker
Smetanka	Moishe	With wife & children	Pantsmaker
Smetanka	Meir	With wife & children	Pantsmaker
Moishe-Hershel	Aryeh's son	With wife & children	
Rimasz	Shalom	With wife & children	
Rimasz	Chaim	With wife & children	
Zegman	Leibishel	With wife & children	Baker
Patchkes	Dovid		
Kochman	Dovid	With wife & children	Baker
Berman	Sheindel	With children	
Moshe-Binem's wife		With children	Shoemaker
Tshervien	Shlomo	With wife & children	Porter
Krein	Yankel	With wife & children	Tailor
Berman	Sarah-Feige	With children	Bar tender
Stollar	Shmuel	With wife & children	
Roitman	Broche	With children	
Lieberzon	Lieber	With wife & children	Shoemaker
Ackerman	Nochuniah	With wife & children	Dyer
Leichter	Yitzchak	With wife & children	
Goldreich	Yossel	With wife & children	
Finkelstein	Chaim	With wife & children	

Third Of May Street

family	Given Name	family Members	Remarks
Greenblatt	Yechezkel	With wife & children	
Kleinboim	Shimon	With wife & child	
Kleinman	Shmuel	With wife & child	From the town of Kotzk
Gottesdiner	Yankel	With wife & children	
Lemberg	Yisroel	With wife & children	Shoemaker
Lifshitz	Shaul		
Lifshitz	Moshe	With wife & children	
Label der Lomer	(from Lom)	With wife & children	Teacher

[Page 353]

family	Given Name	family Members	Remarks
Zilberberg	Avremele	With wife & children	Money Changer
Zilberberg	Shlomo	With wife & children	

Mezerich Street

family	Given Name	family Members	Remarks
Nussboim	Moshe	With wife & children	
Nussboim	Hershel	With wife & children	

family	Given Name	family Members	Remarks
Tshepelinski	Avraham	With wife & children	
Aronyack	Chava		
Blumenfeld	Shaul	With wife & children	
Morgenshtern	Sarah'tshe	With child	
Rosenboim	Shammai	With wife	
Faal	Feivel	With wife & children	
Goldwasser	Gedalia	With wife & children	Grain merchant
Gradovtshik	Moshe		
Herman	Avraham	With wife	
Kalenko	Moshe	With wife & children	The Blonde One
Goldwasser	Simcha	With wife & children	Bank director
Freedman	Yehoshua	With wife & children	Teacher
Freedman	Yisroel-Isser	With wife & children	
Levenda	Shlomo	With wife & children	Smith
Kashtenboim	Chana	With children	
Roitman			
Blumen	Leah	With children	
Fishboim		With wife & children	
Adelman	Velvel	With wife & children	Katshuba = The brush used for cleaning chimneys. Nickname or occupation.
Meria	Shia	With wife & children	Glazier
Freter	Hershel	With wife & children	Shtrik = Rope maker or Nickname.
Shlafshtein	Avraham	With wife & children	Porter

The Train Station

family	Given Name	family Members	Remarks
Finkelstien	Leibel	With family	Shipping clerk
Finkelstien	Nachum-Tzadok	With family	
Finkelstien	Shamai	With family	
Nissenkorn	Yossel	With family	
Nissenkorn	Menachem	WithFamily	
Nissenkorn	Moshe	With family	
Nissenkorn	Tziril	With husband & children	

Shkalneh Street

family	Given Name	family Members	Remarks
Kotzker	Yankel	With wife & children	Shoemaker
Heibloom	Mendel	With wife & children	

[Page 354]

Shteinberg	Smuel -Gottel	With wife & children	Butcher
Shteinberg	Pinieh	With wife & children	
Apploig	Moshe- -Bunims	With wife & children	Shoemaker
Ravniak	Yekutiel	With wife & children	Paver

Koptshak	Shaye	With wife & children	Wagoner
Kotzker	Hershel	With wife & children	Shoemaker
Bernzon	Shaye	With wife & children	
Rotberg	Dovid (Feivush's)	With wife & children	Tailor
Gelibter	Yaakov Leib	With wife & children	
Gelibter	Leahtshe	With husband & children	
Levi.	Shammai	With wife & children	Scribe
Levi	Feige Rivke	With husband & child	
Luft	Shlome Dovid	With wife & children	
Luft	Mottele	With wife & child	Scribe
Rotberg	Feige	With children	
Rotberg	Yonale	With wife & children	
Rotberg	Tove Gritzmacher	With child	
Berchat	Hertzke	With wife & children	Shoemaker
Rotstein	Berl	With wife & children	Shoemaker
Hersh-	Yidel	With wife & children	Shoemaker
Kashenmacher	Eli	With wife & children	Tailor
Kashenmacher	Shmuelke	With wife & children	Tailor
Vaiazshor	Aiver	With wife & children	Tailor
Trackternick	Orele	With wife & children	Oldclothes dealer
Trackternick	Yankel	With wife & children	
Wasserman	Berele	With wife & children	Gravedigger
Montshaz	Elimelech	With wife & children	HarnessMaker
Monish		With wife & children	Shoemaker
Melinasz	Mordechai	With wife & children	Pamp = navel. (Nickname)
Melinasz	Chaim-Zelig	With wife & children	Scribe
Lynn	Mendil		
Mletshak	Nissan	With wife & children	Tailor
Kirshner	Chanina	With wife & children	Butter Merchant
Krein	Yaakov-Leib	With wife & children	Tailor
Sarahke-Fanes	Reuven	With wife & children	Miller
Berman	Chaim-Reuven	With wife & child	Quilt Maker
Rotberg	Pessach	With wife & child	
Rotberg family		With all the children	Cossacks. (Nickname)
Farbiash	Shmuel	With wife & child	Butcher
Vasserman (Hershel Lipe's)	Mendel	With wife & children	Teacher
Rosenberg	Itsche	With children	Baker
Pesachovitz	Moishe-Laizer	With wife & children	Tailor
Tszerwin	Moishe	With wife & children	Patsch = slap.(Nickname)
Kavelblume	Heitze	With children	

[Page 355]

Tzimmerman-	Tziporah	With child	Tailor

Kavelblume			
Klein	Meir	With wife & children	Ritual Slaughterer
Berman	Moshe	With wife & children	Tailor
Berman	Yudel	With wife & child	Tailor
Szelonikviat	Shalom	With wife & child	Butcher
Eizens	Yisroel Mendel	family	Butcher Barshtash Family nickname = The Brush Maker
Gritzmacher	Ben-Zion	With family	Shoemaker
Zabikover	Moshe	With wife	Harness Maker

Kotlarska Street

family Name	Given Name	family Members	Remarks
Burshtin	Itshe Meir	With family	Merchant
Burshtin	Menachem	With family	
Burshtin	Avraham	With family	
Burshtin	Yechiel		
Tshervien	Velvel	With wife	
	Yonah	With wife	
Burak	Gershon	With wife & children	Tailor Kugel = pudding family nickname
Burak	Chaim	With wife & children	Fisherman Kugel = pudding family nickname
Burak	Moishe	With wife & children	Fisherman Kugel = pudding family nickname
Vrubal	Leibele	With family	Glazier
Moishele	The Rabinical Judge's	With family	
Fruchtnberg	Mordechai	With family	Wagoner
Fruchtnberg	Yantel	With family	Wagoner
Eisen	Nechemia	With family	Butcher (Borshtash = Brushmaker?) family nickname?
Eisen	Hershel	With family	Butcher Barshtash = brush maker family nickname?
Klezmer	Velvel	With family	Bartek = family name
Schneider	Hershel	With family	Bartek = family name
Bartek	Scheindele		Laundress
Koptshak	Shimon-Hersh	With the whole family	Wagoner
Koptshak	Simcha-Geler	With the whole family	Wagoner
Koptshak	Itzele	With the whole family	Wagoner
Koptshak	Pinchas	With the whole family	Wagoner
Koptshak	Mordechai	With the whole family	Wagoner
Koptshak	Tileh	With the whole family	

Scniezsac	Tzalkeh	With the whole family	Shoemaker

family	Given Name	Kalen Street family Members	Remarks
Smetanka	Motel	With wife & children	Shoemaker
Fleisick	Shlomoh-Lozer	With wife & children	Butcher
Fleisick	Feivel	With wife & children	Grain Merchant
Ravniak	Moshe	With wife & children	Paver
Saltzer	Sarah		

[Page 356]

Saltzer	Shimon	With wife & child	Tailor
Herman	Yechiel	With wife & children	Miller
Herman	Isaac	With wife	Miller
Feigenblat	Noach	With wife & children	
Herman	Berl	With wife	
Vassershtrom	Eiszesche	With wife	
Vassershtrom	Mashe	With husband	
Pomerantz	Avishi -Melech	With family	Merchant
Kaptchak	Moishe (Veves)	With family	Wagoner
Goldshtein	Yudale	With wife & children	Shoemaker
Ganski	Shimon	With wife & children	(Split lip)
Nissboim	Efraim	With wife & children	Porter
Berchat	Simchale	With wife & children	Shoemaker
Pasternak	Pesach (Pietsh)	With wife & children	Water Carrier
Shlafshtein	Yoel	With wife & children	Merchant
Pomerantz	Reuven	With wife & children	Porter
	Sarah Bashe Reuven's daughter	With children	

And Many Many More...

May Their Memory Be Bound Up In The Eternal Life Of The Nation

R A D Z Y N

Jews walked your streets, lived, labored, dreamed, and struggled in your houses for many years. There were three Jews in the city in the middle of the 16th century. More than three thousand men, women, children, infants and old people were tortured, burned and led to cold-blooded slaughter by the German Fascists in the middle of the 20th century. The first Jews of Radzyn were killed in the German bombings of 1939. In 1943 the last remnants of this community were murdered. May Their Memory Be Preserved For Eternity!

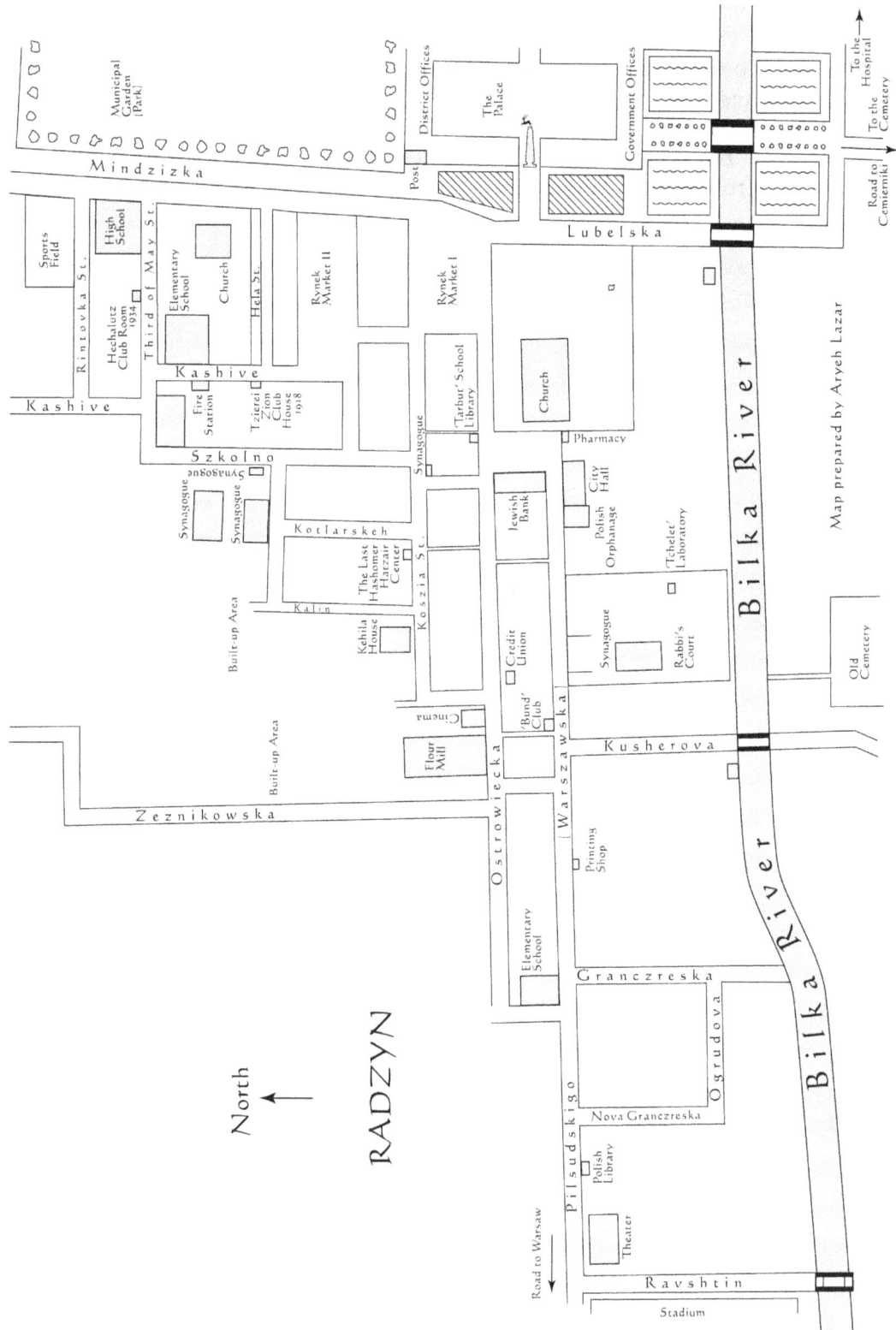

RADZYN

North

Map prepared by Aryeh Lazar

Municipal Garden (Park)

District Offices

The Palace

Government Offices

Post

Mindzizka

Lubelska

To the Hospital

To the Cemetery

Road to Cemierniki

Sports Field

Rintovka St.

High School

Third of May St.

Hechalutz Club Room 1934

Elementary School

Church

Hela St.

Rynek Market II

Rynek Market I

Kashive

Fire Station

Tzierei Zion Club House 1918

Kashive

Tarbut' School Library

Church

Synagogue

Pharmacy

Szkolno

Synagogue

Synagogue

Synagogue

City Hall

Polish Orphanage

'Tchelet' Laboratory

Kotlarskeh

Jewish Bank

Built-up Area

The Last Hashomer Hatzair Center

Koszia St.

Kalin

Synagogue

Rabbi's Court

Bilka River

Kehila House

Credit Union

Old Cemetery

Built-up Area

Cinema

'Bund' Club

Kusherova

Flour Mill

Zeznikowska

Ostrowiecka

Warszawska

Printing Shop

Elementary School

Granczreska

Ogrudova

Nova Granczreska

Bilka River

Pilsudskigo

Polish Library

Road to Warsaw

Theater

Ravshtin

Stadium

Places marked on the map.

Stadium. Built in the years just before the war. Its sports fields and modern swimming pool were for the use of the whole population.

Palace. A very old magnificent building with many statues and ornaments. At one time it was the residence of the local rulers and in later years housed the municipal and district offices.

"Bund". One of the first Jewish political parties in the town, active in many areas of public life. Maintained a club room, library and sports club and for a short time, a school.

Jewish Bank. Founded in 1906. After years of growth, moved into its own building and stayed there until the outbreak of W.W.II.

"Tarbut" (Culture) School. Founded in 1916 under the name "David Fishel's School". For a long time it maintained only a few elementary school classes with a very comprehensive educational curriculum. Many of the finest youth studied there. In 1933 it was incorporated into the "Tarbut" network with seven different classes.

Elementary School. A government school that provided free education for all the children of the town.

Synagogues. Were scattered throughout the town and filled with Jews praying and studying the Torah, the most outstanding of them was the "Great Synagogue".

Gmilat Chesed. (Free Loan Association) Founded in 1912. Helped the needy.

Gymnasia. The Municipal High School that had very few Jewish students because of high tuition and because Saturday classes were mandatory.

Hashomer Hatzair. (The Young Guards) Founded in 1915. Included most of the Zionist youth in the town. In 1935 the first members emigrated to Eretz Yisrael. The majority of the Radzyn immigrants to Israel were from among the members. When the war broke out many of its young members joined the Anti-Nazi Underground.

Hechalutz. Educated toward preparation for and immigration to Palestine. Its' members were scattered on training farms throughout Poland.

The Rabbi's Courtyard. It began with the arrival in Radzyn of "Beth Yaakov" (The House of Jacob) and the discovery of the snail used in manufacturing of the "tchelet" (the blue color used to color the fringes of their prayer shawls) by his son Reb Gershon Chanoch. During the World War II, the last Radzyn Rabbi Reb Shlomoh, who had called for resistance to the Germans and the "Yudenrat", was killed by the Nazis on the eve of Shavuoth 1942.

Library. Founded in 1923 and served all Radzyn readers. When the Communists took over, the local authorities closed it down and its books confiscated and dispersed.

Tziere Tzion Poele Tzion (Young Zionists, Labor Zionists) Among the first Zionist groups in the town. Founded in 1918. Maintained clubhouses and carried on organizational political activities.

INDEX

A

Abman, 192, 193, 280
Achicam-Fine, 245
Ackereisen, 280, 281, 315
Ackerman, 22, 143, 315, 318
Adamovitz, 243
Adamovski, 314
Adelman, 22, 118, 136, 311, 313, 315, 319
Adelman (Katshuveh), 136
Agman, 267, 268, 310
Akusht, 237
Alexen, 302
Ansky, 106
Apellboim, 160
Apotoshu, 306
Appelboim, 78, 88, 89, 105, 111, 280, 311
Appeloig, 23, 107, 112, 114, 145, 203, 208, 275, 280, 310, 311, 316
Applebaum, 56, 160
Appleboim, 97, 106, 108, 121, 138, 273, 280, 281
Appleloig, 282
Appleoig, 296
Appleoig-Hochman, 296
Apploig, 319
Areshtant, 42
Aronyack, 319
Artshe, 24
Artstein, 282
Arye's, 315
Asher, 311
Ashman, 217
Ashman Zaltzstein, 217
Avi-Arah, 291
Avi-Eira, 299, 300
Avman, 148
Azshes, 115, 123

B

Babel, 20
Balshatziac, 108
Bandeh, 311
Bar Yoel, 205

Barger, 281
Barishover, 71, 75, 76
Bartek, 213, 321
Barver, 20
Bashes, 16, 264
Bear, 135
Becker, 314
Beinish, 43
Ben Shmuel, 98, 167
Ben-Shmuel, 96
Berchat, 216, 320, 322
Berenson, 301
Berman, 23, 111, 144, 150, 152, 212, 213, 281, 295, 310, 311, 312, 314, 318, 320, 321
Bernzon, 320
Bershtenmacher, 314
Beryl Avraham Shlomo, 301
Biderman, 314
Blachavits, 23
Blachawitz, 114
Blachovitch, 29, 31
Blachovitsh, 311, 315
Blachovitz, 117, 130
Blachowitz, 30
Blavowitz, 284
Blechovitz, 22, 209, 210, 211, 262, 290
Blechowitz, 203, 211
Blichovitz, 111
Blumen, 185, 195, 203, 204, 312, 316, 319
Blumenfeld, 9, 213, 319
Blumenknop, 310
Blumenkoff, 261
Blumenkop, 121, 281, 311, 312, 313
Bober, 313
Bonk, 120
Borchovsky, 316
Borochov, 153, 287
Borochovski, 141
Borochovsky, 140
Borochvski, 141
Boruch, 23, 40
Borver, 136
Branitzka, 282
Brezers, 120
Bronitzki, 315

Bruder, 140
Buber, 120
Bunim, 79
Burak, 281, 321
Burker, 115
Burshtein, 118
Burshtin, 300, 321
Burstein, 14, 243, 275, 299
Butesman, 145
Butman, 9, 120, 137, 138, 281, 289, 312

C

Cantor, 122
Chaim, 314
Chaim the Sexton, 77
Chana Pesseh, 49
Chana's, 45, 263
Chava, 150
Chavaleh Die Kleine, 313
Chetvarshinski, 186
Chlenov, 132
Chomatshevky, 257
Chudaver, 315
Cnaanii, 104
Cnaanii (Kopeck), 104
Crazy Sarah'le, 43

D

Daitsch, 52, 72
Damb, 310
Danielak, 5, 23, 300, 308
Daniely, 62
Danilack, 66
Danilak, 24, 32, 57, 58, 70, 78, 109, 132,
    137, 138, 144, 154, 299, 302, 303, 306,
    307, 311
Danilak (Einvinder), 78
Danilek, 137
Daniliak, 56
Dann, 317
Day, 302
Dematshever, 96
Diamant, 121, 316
Die Shtumeh (The Mute), 120
Domininer, 313
Donilak, 306
Dshabak, 315
Dzabak, 123, 314

E

Eagelnick, 280
Edelman, 202, 229
Ehkaeizer, 317

Eidel, 123
Eidelman, 229, 291
Eiger, 81
Einbinder, 22
Einvinder, 78
Eisen, 303, 313, 315, 321
Eisenberg, 314
Eizens, 321
Elazar, 7
Eliorke, 44
Eliyahu-Aaron, 44
Eliyorke, 44
Elyorke, 44, 45
Engelman, 313

F

Faal, 319
Fal, 255
Falshspan, 23, 150
Fantshak, 312
Farbiash, 229, 320
Farbiasz, 282
Fartik, 317
Fass, 235, 256, 261, 263, 311
Fast, 105
Feigenblat, 322
Feigenboim, 281, 310, 313
Feigles, 42
Feival Yisroel Moishe, 43
Felinda the manicurist, 120
Fenick, 315
Fenig, 311, 312
Fest, 144, 310
Fine, 9, 16, 35, 42, 106, 133, 143, 199,
    245, 249, 275, 282, 314
Finebuch, 282
Finkelshtein, 9, 150
Finkelstein, 54, 155, 281, 312, 317, 318
Finkelstein (Lichtenstein), 155
Finkelstien, 319
Firshtenberg, 161
Firstenberg, 54
Fishboim, 280, 319
Fishel, 127, 154, 156, 208, 236, 283, 325
Fishel (Lichtenshtein), 154
Fishel (Lichtenstein), 208
Fisher, 49, 208, 233, 236
Fishl's, 202
Fishl's (Lichtenstein), 202
Flatzman, 202
Fleisick, 322
Fleisik, 281, 282
Fleiss, 230, 231
Fletzman, 209
Freedman, 117, 130, 262, 317, 319

Freedman-On, 31
Freeman, 302
Freidel the Midwife, 120
Freidman, 30
Freter, 190, 192, 258, 282, 312, 317, 319
Freter (Shtein), 192
Fretter, 256
Frident, 311
Friedman, 282, 284
Frieman, 302
Fruchtman, 316
Fruchtnberg, 321
Fullman, 121

G

Ganski, 322
Gansky, 141
Gatasdiner, 299
Gedalia-Yudel the Sexton's son, 19
Gelerma, 290
Gelerman, 9, 115, 124, 290, 317
Gelibter, 110, 139, 289, 320
Gellerman, 150, 203, 255
Gershon the Feldsher, 18
Gershun, 120
Glantz, 42
Glassberg, 304
Glatz, 304
Glazer, 161, 202
Gliksberg, 23
Glutz, 117
Godel's, 77
Godl, 20
Godl's, 20, 77
Goldapple, 314
Goldberg, 124, 298, 301, 317
Goldbord, 281, 314
Golde, 19
Goldes, 110
Goldfarb, 152, 275, 296, 312
Goldreich, 280, 318
Goldshtein, 314, 322
Goldstein, 282, 317
Goldwasser, 44, 121, 150, 152, 161, 203,
    209, 269, 281, 290, 302, 303, 305, 311,
    312, 314, 317, 319
Gottel, 154, 161
Gottesdiner, 120, 132, 144, 145, 153, 281,
    300, 314, 316, 318
Gottlakes, 154
Gotttel, 160
Gradovtchick, 281
Gradovtshik, 319
Gradwitzer, 41
Green, 40

Greenbaum, 56, 161
Greenberg, 22, 120, 281, 296, 311, 314
Greenblat, 301
Greenblatt, 23, 43, 112, 137, 138, 139,
    259, 272, 273, 298, 307, 308, 318
Greenboim, 54, 137
Grindland, 281
Gritzmacher, 281, 320, 321
Gshuri, 79
Guta, 30

H

Haltz, 28, 29
Handelsman, 145, 303, 313
Hanegbi, 132
Hardshtein, 311
Hartglass, 31
Hauptman, 23
Hehen, 208
Heibloom, 319
Heiblum, 311
Heiblume, 216
Heiblumzil, 216
Helfenboim, 311
Henya'le Bracha, 121
Herbst, 120, 281, 312
Herman, 310, 319, 322
Hersh, 23, 320
Hershe'le the Angel, 108
Hershel Avram the son of Moshe the Ritual
    Slaughterer, 20
Hertzel, 156
Himmelboim, 281, 314, 316
Hirsch, 73, 78
Hirsh, 77, 304
Hirshbein, 106, 188, 193, 213, 281, 312
Hochbein, 143
Hochboim, 312
Hochman, 205, 296, 313
Hochmans, 317
Hoftman, 121
Horowitz, 281

I

Idelman, 115, 215, 295
Isaacs, 315
Itshe The Yellow, 312
Itshele Chaneh, 17
Itshe-Meir from Sladowitz, 40
Itshke the Pig, 46, 47, 48

J

Jabak, 193

K

Kagan, 282
Kalber, 197
Kalbers, 197
Kalenko, 319
Kalinka, 23
Kalushinski, 256
Kamienyetzka, 313
Kaminsky, 161
Kantor, 22, 90, 120, 121, 290
Kapshtack, 312
Kaptchak, 317, 322
Kaptshock, 216
Karman, 193
Karman (Shlep), 193
Kashemacher, 213, 310
Kashenmacher, 320
Kashmacher, 202
Kashtenbaum, 139
Kashtenboim, 319
Kastan, 301
Katshuveh, 136
Katz, 270, 315
Katzenelbogen, 146
Katzenelboigen, 315
Katzenelenbogen, 23
Katzenelson, 11
Katznelbogen, 119
Kautzky, 20
Kavebloom, 108
Kaveh, 315
Kavelblume, 310, 312, 316, 320
Keitelgisser, 126, 253, 302
Keiytelgisser, 310
Kelba, 42
Kevelboim, 121
Kiettelgisser, 109
Kimmel, 138, 139, 184, 195, 311
Kirshner, 320
Kisles, 20
Klayman, 119
Klein, 321
Kleinbaum, 30, 286, 288
Kleinboim, 21, 22, 112, 115, 120, 124, 156,
    203, 205, 210, 318
Kleinman, 116, 119, 139, 153, 265, 266,
    267, 312, 318
Klezmer, 321
Kligsberg, 310
Klinkeh, 213
Knop, 120
Kobrin, 167
Kochman, 318
Kokosh the Barber, 200
Kolenko, 40

Koones, 42
Kopeck, 104
Kopelman, 310, 312
Kopietz, 107
Koppelman, 23, 108, 264
Koptchak, 25, 41, 42
Koptshak, 25, 150, 216, 320, 321
Korman, 282
Koshitzki, 196
Kotlarska, 318
Kotzker, 90, 91, 319, 320
Kovelblum, 263
Kratzshtein, 310
Krein, 215, 301, 318, 320
Kroinenberg, 315
Kronenberg, 59, 312
Kuchberg, 302
Kune, 117
Kuperschmid, 282
Kuperschmidt, 314
Kuperschmit, 311
Kupershmit, 137
Kupervasser, 282
Kupietz, 20, 22, 23, 29, 302, 310, 311, 313,
    317
Kupitz, 121, 213
Kupliak, 120
Kutner, 95

L

Label der Lomer, 318
Lainer, 99, 101, 102
Laizer, 123, 160, 202
Laizer the Sexton, 69
Laizers, 115
Lamke, 317
Landau, 26
Lanhef, 302
Last, 281
Lazar, 112, 167, 206, 254, 299, 300
Lazer, 107
Leibel Moishe Mates, 54
Leiberson, 260, 265
Leichter, 282, 318
Leiner, 311
Leivik, 306
Leiwachs, 306
Lemberg, 318
Lerner, 282
Leskovsky, 114
Letz, 121
Lev, 266, 267, 269, 270
Levenda, 319
Levenstein, 120, 189, 314
Levi, 20, 30, 289, 315, 317, 320

Levi Yudel the Sexton, 20
Levin, 282, 301
Levy, 310
Leyner, 79, 84
Liberson, 136, 272, 280
Liberzan, 144
Liberzon, 271, 275
Liberzson, 282
Libfreind, 311
Lichtenberg, 119, 145
Lichtenshtein, 9, 154, 180, 272, 300
Lichtenstein, 8, 10, 21, 22, 28, 30, 31, 34,
    46, 51, 52, 55, 111, 112, 114, 115, 117,
    118, 119, 130, 131, 134, 136, 137, 155,
    156, 167, 198, 202, 203, 204, 208, 211,
    214, 215, 225, 226, 236, 279, 280, 287,
    288, 291, 299, 303, 307, 308, 311, 312,
    313, 316, 317
Lichtenstein Zakalik, 31
Lieberfreint, 144
Lieberzon, 318
Liechtenstein, 119, 141
Lifshitz, 139, 318
Lipe, 117, 126, 127, 320
List, 49
Lomka, 115
Loser the teacher, 134
Lozer, 117, 143, 254, 283, 310
Lublinerman, 242, 310
Luft, 320
Luria, 20, 247
Lurkis, 114
Lust, 286, 288, 299, 300, 310, 315, 317
Lynn, 320

M

Machlis, 153
Maizil, 158
Malichava, 138
Mandleboim, 118
Maneshes, 315
Mantshaz, 316
Marcus, 249
Mattiyahu the Hashmonae, 47
Mechel, 121
Mecheles, 123
Mechlis, 221
Meicher, 136, 138, 313, 316
Meicheren, 137
Meirwasser, 136
Mekeh, 42
Melamed, 42, 117, 134, 135
Melinasz, 139, 320
Meltzer, 204
Mendel the bookbinder, 295

Mendel the Moreh Halacha, 53
Meria, 319
Michel, 43
Michelovsky, 107
Midlarnick, 43, 312, 316
Midlarnik, 42
Migdael, 145
Migdal, 230, 231, 282
Miller, 136, 322
Milson, 120
Mintz, 21
Mintzmacher, 282
Mittlebach, 282
Mlamed, 43
Mletshak, 320
Moishe-Hershel, 318
Moishele, 321
Monish, 320
Montshaz, 320
Moravietz, 282
Mordechai the Sexton, 73
Mordkhe Yosef Elazar, 87
Morgenshtern, 319
Moshe The Provider, 62
Moshe-Binem, 318
Muscat, 289
Mushkat, 114, 152, 153, 316

N

Nachtigal, 97, 302
Nachtingal, 291
Nachtingel, 120
Naiman, 200, 205
Naiman (Kokosh the Barber), 200
Neiman, 121, 214, 236, 313
Nicoliawitz, 26
Nievieski, 136
Nirenberg, 303, 317
Nirenberg-Hochmans, 317
Niskern, 273
Nissboim, 317, 322
Nissenbaum, 144
Nissenboim, 138, 311
Nissenkorn, 319
Nussbaum, 235
Nussblat, 313
Nussboim, 121, 280, 282, 318
Nusssboim, 313

O

On, 302
Orlich-Rickman, 187

P

Pantshak, 266
Pantshek, 270
Pantshick, 269
Pantshik, 269, 270
Parsky, 113
Partisan, 285
Pashkovski, 270
Pasternak, 282, 322
Patchkes, 318
Patshek, 108
Peretsovitch, 136
Peretz, 23, 106, 161
Pesachovitz, 320
Pessach Yehoshua, 110
Pessachovitz, 138
Petrolivich, 106
Pig Family, 48
Pinchasl the Teacher, 135
Pincus, 120
Pinkas, 148
Pinkus, 135, 196, 313
Pomeranietz, 311
Pomerantz, 310, 322
Pontshak, 132, 267, 271, 280, 313
Pototzki, 207
Prizant, 136
Pruchnitzky, 108
Pshenitza, 110, 317, 318
Pshenitze, 142
Pshenitzeh, 142, 192
Pshenizeh, 316
Punchak, 296
Punchiak, 119
Puntshak, 267, 289
Putzig, 117

R

Rabbi Avraham Yehoshua Heshil, 84
Rabbi Gershon, 84
Rabbi Gershon Chanoch, 7, 84, 87
Rabbi Gershon Henoch, 17
Rabbi Gershon-Henich, 45
Rabbi Mendely, 80
Rabbi Mordchai Yosef Elazar, 87
Rabbi Mordecai Yosef, 17, 54
Rabbi Shlomo'le, 13
Rabbi Shmuel Dov Asher, 81
Rabbi Shmuel Shlomo, 87
Rabbi Yaakov, 81, 82, 84
Rabbi Yaakov Ben Shlomo, 58
Rabbi Yaakov Wolf, 100
Rabbi Yakov of Izbitsa, 81
Rabbi Yitchak, 146

Rabbi Yitzchak Meir, 80
Rabbi, R' Shlomo, 286
Rabinovitch, 138
Rabinowitz, 81
Rachlis, 117, 138, 151, 152
Raisin, 159
Ratshtein, 138
Ratushnik, 313
Ravniak, 140, 233, 319, 322
Ravniak (Bruder), 140
Reb Chaim Asher, 57, 58, 60
Reb Eishes, 16
Reb Eliezer The Great, 76
Reb Gershon Chanoch, 94, 95, 124, 325
Reb Gershon Hanoch, 73, 74, 90
Reb Gershon Henach, 42
Reb Gershon Henich, 102
Reb Gershon Henoch, 17, 54
Reb Gershon-Chanoch, 92, 94, 95
Reb Gershon-Hanoch, 42
Reb Henoch, 52
Reb Itsche Meir, 118, 275
Reb Itshe Meir, 16, 123
Reb Laizer the Watchmaker, 123
Reb Mordecai Yosef, 42
Reb Mordecai-Yosef, 42, 160
Reb Mordechai Yosef, 93, 96, 98
Reb Mordechai Yosef Eliezer, 76
Reb Mordechai-Yosef, 92, 93, 94
Reb Shlomo Yitzchaki, 68
Reb Shmuel Shlomo, 102
Reb Yaakov, 93
Reb Yaakov Moshe, 108
Reb Yaakov Wolf, 100
Reb Yisroel, 91
Reb Yitzchak, 146, 147, 148, 149
Reb Yoel Yosef, 46
Reb Yoel-Yosef, 45
Reb Yosef, 148
Reb Yoske Shiyah Dovid, 43
Reb Zavel, 35
Rebbe Gershon Hanoch, 91
Reichenberg, 110, 121, 126, 150, 295, 297, 311
Reichnadel, 314
Reshke, 106, 120, 121
Richter, 121, 150
Rimasz, 318
Ringelblumen, 30
Rochles, 31, 130
Rochman, 99
Roisenboim, 23
Roitman, 318, 319
Rosenbaum, 132
Rosenbaum (now: Hanegbi), 132
Rosenberg, 312, 320

Rosenblum, 282, 303
Rosenboim, 216, 282, 296, 313, 314, 316, 317, 319
Rosenboim-Greenberg, 296
Rosencrantz, 195
Rosenfeld, 105, 132, 139, 150, 295, 297, 317
Rosenkrantz, 316
Rosenwald, 22, 29, 124, 267, 268, 316
Rotberg, 314, 320
Rotenberg, 205
Rothstein, 202
Rotshtein, 130, 137, 282, 289, 313
Rotstein, 320
Rovniak, 282
Royal Highness Franz Yosef, 27
Rubenstein, 22
Rubin, 301
Rubinshtein, 119, 282, 310, 312, 313
Rubinstein, 21, 22, 130, 145, 160, 222, 255, 262, 286, 288, 313, 317
Rutberg, 216

S

Sakstein, 287
Salasheh, 160
Saltzer, 264, 289, 315, 322
Saltzman, 185
Samiatizki, 310
Sapir, 316
Sarahke-Fanes, 320
Schmietankah, 282
Schneider, 311, 321
Schneor, 75
Schtzupak, 222, 282, 302, 312
Schupak, 213
Schuster, 314
Scniezsac, 322
Segal, 4, 64, 306
Segalovitch, 159
Seltzer, 209
Sforim, 199
Shabashiner, 254
Shachar, 41
Shaimes, 311
Shainman, 298
Shamesh, 23
Shampam, 313
Shapiro, 310
Shapiro-Turkeltoib, 310
Shaul Henich, 115
Shenker, 282
Shiffer, 152
Shimon, 41, 322
Shineman, 203, 314

Shitkovski, 27
Shiyeh the Teacher, 42
Shlafshtein, 319, 322
Shlep, 193, 316
Shlibovsky, 113
Shlimak, 118, 119, 132, 172, 312
Shlimek, 127
Shlobovski, 182
Shlubovski, 15, 185
Shlubowski, 58
Shochet, 49
Shoshanah the milkmaid, 108
Shpigel, 150, 152
Shpivak, 214
Shpizeisen, 103
Shragai, 103
Shreiber, 301
Shtarkman, 255
Shtein, 192
Shteinberg, 319
Shteper, 120, 313
Shtestshinaz, 265
Shtrik, 115
Shtshetshshinaz, 314
Shuchmacher, 108, 130, 137, 140, 142, 145, 213, 310, 314
Shulman, 281, 282
Shulshtein, 314, 316
Shumlak, 314
Shurek, 152
Shuster, 313
Shvalbeh, 112
Shwalbe, 55, 56, 158, 159
Shwalbeh, 158, 159
Sikorsky, 249
Slavic, 311
Smetanka, 318, 322
Smetankeh, 145
Smith, 303
Smolarz, 63
Smolasz, 62
Sneh, 120
Sneh (Kleinbaum), 30
Sodberg, 185
Spector, 312
Steinberg, 216, 315
Stollar, 318
Sudberg, 195, 196, 198, 210, 213, 282, 315, 316
Szalasheh, 160
Szelonickviat, 281
Szelonikviat, 321
Sziteh, 256
Szonche, 315

T

Tabatchnik, 152
Tanenbaum, 301
Tannenbaum, 102, 130
Tannenboim, 281, 313
Tanzer, 302
Tenenbaum, 9
Tenenboim, 310
Tennenbaum, 304
Tennenboim, 22, 106, 110, 136, 137, 138, 140
Tentzer, 281
Tikatchinsky, 121, 315
Tikochinsky, 54, 56
Tiles, 16, 41
Toibman, 23
Toker, 41
Tor, 162
Trackternick, 320
Tratsch, 313
Trunk, 92
Tshechanovski, 301
Tshepelinski, 319
Tsheplinsky, 255
Tshervian, 275
Tshervien, 318, 321
Tszerwin, 320
Tubman, 311
Tukeltoib, 313
Tunkelroit, 317
Tunkleswartz, 269
Turkeltaub, 30, 213, 256
Turkeltoib, 121, 206, 281, 298, 310, 313
Turkltoib, 27
Tzalkeh, 117
Tzelke the shoemaker, 202
Tzimmerman, 320
Tzimmerman-Kavelblume, 320
Tzucker, 24, 137, 140, 152
Tzuker, 185, 186
Tzukerblatt, 152

V

Vagonski, 281
Vaiazshor, 320
Varskin, 141
Vashner, 42
Vasserman, 320
Vassershtrom, 281, 322
Vayazsher, 242
Vebman, 310, 312
Veidenboim, 314
Verubel, 311
Vetshtein, 137, 314

Viazcszher, 314
Vientkovsky, 257
Vinapple, 209
Vinderbaum, 123, 179
Vinderboim, 118, 124, 246, 247, 310, 314, 315, 317
Vineappel, 312, 313
Vineapple, 106
Vishkovski, 216, 311
Vishkovsky, 145
Vishnieh, 312
Visoka, 281
Vohiner, 311, 314
Volovski,, 281
von Pinkerfeld, 198
Vorember, 281
Voves, 314
Voyazsher, 214
Vrubal, 315, 321
Vrubel, 281

W

Walpes, 28
Warshever, 315
Wasserman, 320
Wassermann, 137, 139, 140
Weidenboim, 300, 317
Weingarten, 56, 150, 298
Weisman, 23, 211, 281, 315, 317
Weissgrosz, 282
Weissgroz, 281
Weitzman, 103, 281
Wienderbaum, 97
Wiesman, 108
Windenbaum, 193
Windenbaum (Jabak), 193
Winderbaum, 9
Winderboim, 299
Wineapple, 121
Wiseman, 138
Wolf, 22, 115, 118, 204, 211, 314

Y

Yaakov Moshe, 20
Yaakov the carpenter, 146
Yankel the Coppersmith, 46, 47
Yantel the wagoner, 141
Yazger, 315
Yehoshua Meir from Piotrokov, 126
Yehoshua the builder, 110
Yiskar, 121
Yonshtein, 301
Yosef Dovid Wolf, 115, 118
Yoske Shaya Dovid, 41

Yoske Shyeh-Dovids, 42
Yoske Yehoshua, 18
Yoske Yehoshua Dovid, 18
Youngshtein, 302
Yudel the Sexton, 35, 44
Yudel The Shamash, 50

Z

Z'alaza, 167
Z'elekover, 74
Z'laza, 112
Zabidovitz, 121
Zabikover, 321
Zaidel, 317
Zakalik, 31, 131
Zalasheh, 161
Zalavitz, 302
Zalman'ke the Coachman, 67, 68
Zaltshtein-Freter, 255
Zaltstein, 223, 263
Zaltzman-Freter, 190
Zaltzshtefenikein, 141
Zaltzshtein, 141, 312

Zaltzstein, 134, 217, 223, 281
Zambakofsky, 314
Zavidowitz, 310
Zegman, 318
Zeidel, 311
Zelig, 41
Zeligman, 132, 169
Zelikovs, 43
Zhlaza, 318
Ziegelman, 310
Zigelman, 2, 23, 30, 112, 115, 130, 137, 287, 299, 300, 316
Zilberberg, 9, 23, 121, 124, 281, 313, 318
Zilberberstein, 281
Zilbermintz, 281, 310, 316
Zishele the painter and cantor, 77
Zita, 115, 197
Zoiberman, 216
Zshita, 223, 317
Zuckerman, 198, 317
Zuker, 56, 314
Zussman, 150
Zysman, 233, 282, 316, 317